America's First Black Town

America's First Black Town

Brooklyn, Illinois, 1830–1915

SUNDIATA KEITA CHA-JUA

University of Illinois Press

URBANA AND CHICAGO

Publication of this work has been supported by a grant from the
Oliver M. Dickerson Fund. The fund was established by Mr. Dickerson
(Ph.D., Illinois, 1906) to enable the University of Illinois Press to pub-
lish selected works in American history, designated by the executive
committee of the Department of History.

Library of Congress Cataloging-in-Publication Data
Cha-Jua, Sundiata Keita, 1953–
America's first Black town : Brooklyn, Illinois, 1830–1915 /
Sundiata Keita Cha-Jua.
p.   cm.
Includes bibliographical references (p.) and index.
ISBN 0-252-02537-7 (alk. paper)
1. Lovejoy (Ill.)—History.
2. Afro-Americans—Illinois—Lovejoy—History.
I. Title.
F549.L87C48   2000
977.3'89—dc21   99-6776
CIP

C 5 4 3 2 1

To the memory of Clady Smith,
my maternal grandmother

Contents

Preface

GROWING UP DURING the early 1960s, I, like many of my generation, was captivated and transformed by the rise of Black nationalism. I spent much of my high school years involved in militant local activism and radical study groups. During my undergraduate years, I came to believe fervently in the dream of an independent African American nation-state and joined the Republic of New Africa. By the time I became a doctoral student, I had transcended the narrow nationalism that inspired my initial intellectual and political development; however, as a Marxist-influenced revolutionary nationalist, I remained interested in Black nationalism as a subject of scholarship and committed to the right of Afro-American national self-determination. I first became aware of Brooklyn, Illinois, as a doctoral student at the University of Illinois at Urbana-Champaign in a course taught by Dr. Juliet Walker called "African American Land Formations." In an article entitled "The All-Negro Town: Its Evolution and Function," Harold Rose identified Brooklyn as the first all-Black town. According to Rose, Brooklyn, like the other pre–Civil War all-Black communities, resulted from the curious combination of abolitionist activity and white hostility to Blacks in northern communities. Brooklyn was originally established by a group of free Blacks and escaped slaves from St. Louis, Missouri, as a freedom village in 1830. Freedom villages, "organized Black communities," and maroon colonies were the earliest expressions of territorial Black nationalism. That the town is popularly known as "Lovejoy" in honor of Elijah P. Lovejoy, the region's martyred abolitionist, reflects its historic origins in the antislavery movement. Brooklyn offered an opportunity to examine a concrete example of independent Black community building. Excited by the possibility of combining my interests in Black nationalism and community studies, I decided to write a seminar paper on Brooklyn, Illinois, in spring of 1985.

Besides my interest in African American nationalism, I was attracted to Brooklyn for two other reasons. First, it was only a couple of hours' drive from the Urbana-Champaign campus. Its proximity meant that I could complete my research with minimal reliance on grants. Second, it was in an urban industrial area. People's experiences in Brooklyn, unlike most of the western and southern Black towns, more closely resembled the experiences of contemporary African American people.

Afro-Brooklynites acquired political power as a consequence of three factors. First, in 1870, after decades of African American activity, the Illinois legislature repealed the state's so-called Black Laws, thereby granting Afro-Americans civil rights, including the right of men to vote. Second, Brooklyn was incorporated as a village under the municipal charter laws of Illinois. Third, Brooklyn's Black population swelled because of the post–Civil War migration. After 1890, African American migration to Brooklyn was tied to the industrial development of the area. Pushed from the South by racial oppression and pulled to the North for myriad reasons, although primarily drawn by the prospect of industrial jobs, Afro-Brooklynites struggled to build a prosperous community against the powerful forces of capitalism and white supremacy. These courageous Black men and women achieved much, but ultimately capitalism and racial oppression stunted their efforts to develop a viable local economy. In many ways, their story presages the post-1960s Black urban experience. Brooklyn's fate was determined by the dialectical interaction between migration, racial oppression, proletarianization, the rise of Black political power, white flight, and eventual deindustrialization.

This work is divided into an introduction and four parts. The introduction situates Brooklyn's development within the historical and theoretical contexts of Black-town studies, Black nationalism, and the industrialization of what is now known as the St. Louis metro-east region. Race, class, proletarianization, and dependency, the study's central concepts, are introduced and their usages are discussed here. In trying to make sense of Brooklyn's history, I divided its development into four historical periods: (1) 1830–70; (2) 1870–85; (3) 1886–97; and (4) 1898–1915. I conceive of these periods not as Chinese walls but as permeable structures through which continuities flow from older periods into newer ones, thus helping shape the new period. This periodization scheme is a social construct, although it is not arbitrary. Each period is characterized by a different moment in Brooklyn's racial demography, degree and type of incorporation into the region's dominant political economy, character of internal social and political relations, and relationship to external governmental entities.

Part 1 traces Brooklyn's early history from its founding in 1830 to the abolition of the Black Laws in 1870. Brooklyn's first period consists of two stages. During the first stage, 1830 to 1837, Brooklyn was a separate settlement of fugitive and free Blacks. Chapter 1 chronicles Brooklyn's transformation from a freedom village into an unincorporated biracial town. It also examines the process of community formation, antislavery activity, and the effect of early economic decisions on the majority-Black town. Chapter 2 provides an intensive analysis of Brooklyn's social structure. Using the 1850 federal manuscript census, I examine Brooklyn's racial housing patterns and the Black community's social, occupational, and family structures.

Part 2 examines Brooklyn's second and third historical periods, 1870–85 and 1886–97. Moreover, it follows John Evans's political career until his death in 1910. These years were characterized by Brooklyn's political incorporation as a village and the rise of Black political power. Brooklyn's development was shaped by transformations in the region's political economy as much as by these political developments. This period also had two phases. The first stage was very brief. It included the years from the abolition of the Black Codes and passage of the Fifteenth Amendment to the town's incorporation in 1873. The second stage began in 1873, when the white minority began dominating town politics, and concluded in 1886, when African Americans captured control of the local government.

Chapter 3 surveys the transformation of African Americans from "outlaws" to lawmakers. It examines how the migration and proletarianization of African Americans laid the basis for the development of new social institutions from which a new leadership class sprang. Activated by a struggle to desegregate the town's school district, this new Black leadership ultimately overthrew minority rule and seized political power. I contend that the process of gaining majority rule was analogous to decolonization. Chapter 4 focuses on the struggles and successes of John Evans, Brooklyn's first Black mayor. It chronicles Evans's career as a politician and as a political activist in the Illinois Afro-American League. It also explores his clashes with the town's white minority, his efforts at infrastructural development, and his contributions to constructing an African American political culture.

Part 3 examines how economic factors and white racism undermined Blacks' political power and limited Brooklyn's economic development. Two contradictory processes—Black political empowerment and economic underdevelopment—defined Brooklyn during the third and fourth periods, 1886–97 and 1898–1915, respectively. The fourth period was especially chaotic, characterized by economic underdevelopment and political instability. These periods of Brooklyn's history coincided with the metro-east's "golden age" of industrialization. In chapter 5, I explore the metro-east's transformation into a booming industrial economy and a site for cheap Black commuter labor and what effects this had on Brooklyn's social structure.

Here I look at how mass migration and proletarianization reconstructed Brooklyn's occupational, family, and social structures. To accomplish this, I rely on the 1900 and 1910 federal manuscript censuses and the 1906 census of Brooklyn businesses. Chapter 6 explores how the transformations of Brooklyn's *racial class* structure and social relations affected its political culture and relations with the white county government. It focuses on Frederick Vanderberg, leader of the Peoples party, a local political party. It chronicles Vanderberg's numerous indictments and convictions and examines the use of violence to settle political disputes. The chapter concludes with the St. Clair County sheriff's imposing martial law after police forces appointed by rival mayoral candidates attempted to conduct a new election with bullets.

In telling this story, I use the terms *Afro-American, African American,* and *Black* interchangeably. Because I am using *Black* as a national or ethnic designation, it is capitalized throughout the text. I have used the lowercase *black* in sections where it was necessary to distinguish among African Americans, to differentiate between people classified as "mulattoes" and the majority African American nationality. When *black* is capitalized (unless at the beginning of a sentence), it is being used as an exclusive synonym for Afro-American or African American, whether black or mulatto, and refers to nationality.

Acknowledgments

During the course of researching and writing this book, I was aided immensely by friends, family, libraries and librarians, archives and archivists, and the staffs at the following St. Clair County offices: the Recorder of Deeds, the Circuit Clerk, and Probate Records. Special thanks to Regina Agnew, the librarian at the East St. Louis Library who provided me with an initial list of articles on Brooklyn that appeared in turn-of-the-century metro-east newspapers. She also made available the library's rapidly deteriorating copies of late nineteenth– and early twentieth–century East St. Louis city directories. Special thanks must also go to Rosemary Stevenson and Vera Mitchell of the Afro-Americana Library at the University of Illinois and the staffs at the Illinois State Library, the Illinois State Archives, and the Missouri State Historical Library on the University of Missouri at Columbia campus. The late Louisa Bowen, the archivist at Southern University at Edwardsville, was especially helpful.

A semester leave by the Pennsylvania State University provided time for me to work on this project.

Several friends and colleagues read drafts of all or part of the manuscript and offered many helpful ideas for revision as well as copyediting. My dear friend and former colleague Susan Porter Benson graciously gave of her time and energy. She read the entire manuscript. Not only did her ideas improve the work, but her mentorship and encouragement helped me stay focused and upbeat. Dave Roediger and Ted Koditchek, two other friends and former colleagues, provided important insights that helped me rethink the manuscript. Throughout this process, I have benefited from discussions with John H. McClendon III about a range of ideas and issues that greatly influenced the present work. Several other friends, colleagues, and students provided critical readings, important insights, and encouragement, including Marvin Lewis, Jeff Williams, Jean Allman, James Stewart, Wilson Moses, Shirley Portwood, Jennifer Hamer, Clarence Lang, and Minkah Makalani. Juliet Walker and Vernon Burton deserve special thanks. Juliet Walker introduced me to the study of Black towns, chaired my dissertation committee, and provided friendship, mentorship, and support over the years. Vernon Burton, too, has continued to provide direction, encouragement, and opportunities for career advancement.

I would like to thank the anonymous reviewers, whose recommendations significantly improved the intellectual and stylistic quality of the final work; Jane Mohraz, whose dedicated copyediting tremendously improved the manuscript; and Martin L. White, who created an outstanding index. I am grateful to the Office of the Vice Provost for Diversity, the Graduate School, and the dean of Arts and Science at Southern Illinois University at Edwardsville for their support.

Finally, I want to thank my mother, Floradine Hall; my daughters, Jamila and Montenia; and my partner, Helen Neville. Without their support and sacrifices, none of this would have been possible. Specifically, Helen's support has been total: she provided intellectual and stylistic criticism, understanding, and love.

America's First Black Town

Introduction: Brooklyn in Historical and Theoretical Context

"FOUNDED BY CHANCE, Sustained by Courage" is the motto of the nation's oldest Black town, Brooklyn, Illinois.[1] Brooklyn's slogan alludes to its people's struggle to build their community into a monument of autonomous African American achievement. Brooklyn has had a curious history. The town originated as a historic African American enclave in the American Bottoms. According to oral tradition, during the 1820s a band of eleven families, consisting of free persons of color and fugitive slaves, led by "Mother" Priscilla Baltimore, fled the slave state of Missouri, crossed the Mississippi River, and settled in the wilderness in St. Clair County, Illinois. The settlement that became Brooklyn was founded just as reformers were establishing several Euro-American utopian communes. Freedom villages and "organized black communities" constituted African American complements to the utopian communities, albeit usually without the communal social relations. Most were located in the states of the old Northwest Territory. Organized Black communities often represented philanthropic efforts by slave masters to divest themselves of their slaves. The establishment of a Black community of farmers outside Edwardsville, Illinois, in 1819 by Edward Coles is a prime example. Thomas and Jemmima Woodson's farming community at Berlin Crossroads in Milton Township, Jackson County, Ohio, is an example of a freedom village. The Woodsons started Berlin Crossroads about the same time Mother Baltimore began Brooklyn. Unlike Berlin Crossroads, Brooklyn was transformed into a biracial town in 1837 when five white men platted the land and named it Brooklyn. The town remained unincorporated until July 1873, when Brooklyn's citizens voted to incorporate it as a village. Thirteen years later, Blacks led by John Evans seized control of the local governmental apparatuses from the white minority and brought majority rule to Brooklyn. Blacks' acquisition of political power initially met with resistance from the white minority but eventually activated a process of white flight that transformed Brooklyn back into an all-Black community.[2]

Brooklyn, Illinois, is one of a hundred or so Black towns built in the United States between the early 1800s and the mid-1900s.[3] In many ways, Brooklyn was an anomaly; in others, it was a harbinger. It is one of the few freedom villages and organized Black communities that survived from the antebellum era into modern times. Lawnside, New Jersey; Menifee, Arkansas; and Lyles Station, Indiana, are others. Most Black towns were founded between 1890 and 1910, as part of what the African American sociologist Mozell C. Hill called the "Great Black March West." To a great extent, it represented the aspirations of African American sharecroppers and peasants for freedom from racial oppression and land. This migration occurred as the United States was concluding its transformation from an agrarian-based, commercial capitalist political economy to an industrial capitalist political economy. Most of the sixty or so Black towns built during this era were farming villages in the South or the West. Whereas such towns as Kendleton and Broad House, Texas; Nicodemus, Kansas; Mound Bayou, Mississippi; and Boley, Oklahoma, were isolated, rural communities, Brooklyn built in what is now known as the metro-east region, in the heart of an expanding urban-industrial complex. The metro-east region is the Illinois, or the eastern, side of the St. Louis metropolitan area and encompasses Madison and St. Clair counties. By 1854, Brooklyn was connected by river, road, and rail to East St. Louis, Alton, Belleville, Granite City, and approximately twenty-five smaller towns in the metro-east region. Brooklyn was also part of the American Bottoms, an area noted for its rich topsoil. Initially, the bottoms emerged as a prime farming area, but by the last quarter of the nineteenth century it was being transformed into a major urban industrial area. By 1890, St. Clair County was the state's leader in coal production, and coal was mined at virtually every entrance to Brooklyn. In November of 1873, the St. Louis National Stock Yards began operation. Located between Brooklyn and East St. Louis, the National Stock Yards encompassed 650 acres and was one of the largest stockyards in the world. Brooklyn's Black male population, employed mainly as common laborers on the docks, at the stockyards, in the rolling mills, and on the railroads, entered industrial wage labor more than a generation before proletarianization became a common experience among African American males. Whereas nationally 57 percent of African American men worked in agriculture in 1910, no Black men in Brooklyn did. Although initially an anomaly among Black towns, Brooklyn would become the model for the new type of Black communities that developed in the wake of the "great migration." Between 1910 and 1929, Afro-Americans built several Black towns in urban industrial areas throughout the Midwest. Such communities as Urban Crest, Ohio; Kinloch, Missouri; Robbins, Illinois; Lincoln Heights, Ohio; and Fairmount and Glengarden, Maryland, would come to resemble Brooklyn more than the southern and western Black towns. Because they began as outposts for Afro-Americans employed in nearby industrial metropolises, these towns developed occupational structures similar to Brooklyn's. These communities joined Brooklyn as Black commuter "suburbs," housing tens of thousands African American laborers who worked in predominantly white communities.[4]

According to Hill, "the underlying philosophy" of the Black-town movement was the "ideology of separation from the dominant white caste." The work of several scholars since Hill's pioneering studies claims the construction of Black towns was both a response to racial oppression and a product of protonationalism. By *protonationalism,* I mean an ensemble of political attitudes that represent racial solidarity or a commitment to Black empowerment by organizing Blacks into autonomous organizations, institutions, and communities. The interaction between racial oppression and protonationalism generated the impulse to build Black towns. Although Brooklyn differed from the southern and western Black towns in several respects, it also shared many features with them. First, Brooklyn's formation flowed from the same nationalistic aspirations Hill articulated. That is, Brooklyn's creation was also a manifestation of African Americans' desire to free themselves from racial oppression and to determine their own development. Second, like most Black towns, Brooklyn remained underdeveloped, its economic development circumscribed by racial capitalism (racism's permeation of capitalism) and white supremacist politics. Third, just like Blacks in the southern and western Black towns, Afro-Brooklynites were enveloped in a web of racially motivated violence and suffered threats of invasion. Fourth, like most incorporated African American towns, Brooklyn had a mayor-council form of government. However, the most important social factors uniting Black towns were the dialectically connected processes of political autonomy and economic dependence.[5]

Five sets of questions frame the major issues examined in this study. The first set concerns community formation and agency. How did racial oppression affect the lives of Afro-Brooklynites? Why did African Americans migrate to Brooklyn, Illinois, between 1830 and 1915? What were race relations like before and after Blacks gained political control? Was Brooklyn segregated? How did Afro-Brooklynites build a cohesive well-organized community during the antebellum era? What factors facilitated or militate against building a tight-knit community? What type of social institutions and organizations did Afro-Brooklynites create and maintain? How did Afro-Brooklynites' household structure change over time? How did their institutional structures change over time? What were the core values, especially political values, permeating Afro-Brooklyn? How and why did these beliefs and practices change over time?

The second series of questions revolves around political power. Who were the founders and leaders of the freedom settlement and Brooklyn's Black community before enfranchisement and incorporation? Around what issues did Blacks agitate before 1886? What strategies and tactics did African American leaders use to mobilize Blacks to take political power in 1886? How did Brooklyn's white citizens react to Blacks' acquisition of political control? How did the acquisition of political rights and Black political power affect community cohesion? To what extent were Black leaders able to use political power to improve the quality of life for the town's residents? From which classes did Afro-Brooklyn's political leadership come?

The third group of questions concerns gender. What role did Black women play in the community's formation and development? How did the way Brooklyn was incorporated into the metro-east region's political economy affect gender roles and relations? Where did Black women work, and what types of occupations did they have? How did gender constructions affect Black self-activity?

A fourth group of queries focuses on the relationship between race and class, specifically the *racial class,* or the intersection between race and class. What were relations like between Brooklyn's majority Black population and its white minority? Were Blacks and white equally affected by proletarianization? What effect did proletarianization have on Brooklyn's social and institutional structures? Were Afro-Brooklynites stratified by class, or were they separated only by minor differences of "lifestyle" and values? Did race determine class in Brooklyn? How did the complex interaction between race and class affect Brooklyn's development? Who owned the businesses and housing in Brooklyn?

The fifth set of inquiries asks whether, how, and to what extent Brooklyn's political autonomy and economic development were conditioned by racism and capitalism. What role did racism play in the locational decisions of industrialist capitalists? Was Brooklyn's population growth a result of racism, or did African Americans move there for protonationalist reasons? To what extent was racism a significant factor affecting Brooklyn's external relations with neighboring white towns and the St. Clair County government?

This project reconstructs and analyzes the residues of the social and political history of African Americans in Brooklyn, Illinois, from 1830 to 1915. A significant aspect of this study is that it situates Brooklyn within the broader stream of Black-town development and reconnects Black-town building to African American nationalism. It also explores how the metro-east's political economy and racial oppression facilitated Brooklyn's underdevelopment. This project also examines how Afro-Brooklynites responded to racism and economic dependency. I characterize Brooklyn's underdevelopment as dependency because the racial and capital accumulation policies of private and other public actors in the region severely compromised the town's capacity to shape its own economic and social development. My central contention in this book is that Brooklyn was systematically underdeveloped by the nature of its incorporation into the metro-east region's political economy. It was incorporated into the region's political economy as an unindustrialized residential satellite. Brooklyn supplied cheap Black commuter labor to the region's industries in nearby predominantly white towns. The mode of incorporation undermined attempts at self-development by Brooklyn's political leadership.

The historical significance of Brooklyn, Illinois, lies mainly in its being the oldest Black town in the United States. Nonetheless, outside the St. Louis metropolitan area, Brooklyn is largely unknown. Very few Americans, Black or white, have heard of it. To some extent this is because of the confusion over its name. Many more African Americans know the town by its popular name, Lovejoy, than by its official designation; yet the town remains anonymous even under this nomenclature. Few Black towns have become part of the nation's consciousness. Mound Bayou, Mississippi, and Nicodemus, Kansas, are better known in Black America, but even they are more likely to be answers to "Black facts" trivia questions than to be regarded as important sites of African American historical development. This is amazing considering that African Americans have built Black towns in every period of their existence in the United States. The last major attempt to build an all-Black town occurred during the late 1960s when Floyd McKissick, the former chairperson of the Congress on Racial Equality, secured support from President Richard M. Nixon to build Soul City in North Carolina.

The Historical Neglect in Studying Black Towns

Black-town construction was a component of a more comprehensive nationalist element in African American ideology and praxis.[6] The creation of maroon societies and the establishment of freedom villages and organized Black communities on free soil were the initial expressions of the territorial nationalist undercurrent.[7] This wave of Black nationalism crested during what the historian Rayford Logan termed "the nadir," 1890–1915, a time of extraordinary physical and political repression. During this era, African Americans built more than sixty Black towns.[8] In *Black Nationalism in America,* John Bracey, August Meier, and Elliott Rudwick contend that "during the late nineteenth and early twentieth centuries, emigration was a less prominent form of territorial separatist ideology than were proposals to create Black communities within the United States."[9] Strangely, however, scholars, including Bracey, Meier, and Rudwick, have chosen to stress the emigration movement rather than the Black-town movement.

Although the building of Black towns is the most concrete example of African American nationalist theory and praxis, few scholars have studied these towns. Hill's comment concerning the scholarly neglect of Black towns still resonates a half century after he made it. Explaining the significance of his dissertation in 1946, Hill stated, "The signal importance of this investigation lies in the fact that little attention has been devoted to the Negro's experiences in the United States in developing a separate society of his own." In 1957, William Bittle and Gilbert Geis echoed Hill's observation. Thirty-six years later, Andrew Wiese could make a similar statement about the metropolitan area Black towns. Wiese claimed "little attention or historical analysis" had been paid to these communities. Autonomous African American communities, whether maroon societies, freedom villages, organized Black communities, rural farming villages, or urban commuter towns, have generally escaped scholarly interest. Why have scholars, especially historians, paid so little attention to Black towns?[10]

Three reasons may explain this gap in the study of African American life and culture. First, historically both Black and white mainstream scholars have been guided by a paradigm that led them to concentrate on interracial relations. Scholars working from the race relations paradigm emphasized integration into white America and ignored or deprecated the nationalist heritage. Black nationalism was an invisible and voiceless social movement to academics until the late 1960s.[11] It emerged as a topic worthy of scholarly treatment only after it was "rediscovered" during the 1960s nationalist renaissance. The title of Theodore Draper's antinationalist treatise, *The Rediscovery of Black Nationalism,* underscores this proposition. Draper's monograph contains only one reference to Black towns. Shocked by the sudden rise of the new nationalism, white scholars searched for antecedents to explain what most believed was a problematic occurrence. Motivated mainly by presentist concerns, Euro-American scholars began to investigate Black nationalism in the late 1960s. Young African American scholars also pursued precursors, but unlike most of their Euro-American colleagues, they sought to delineate the genealogy of Black nationalist traditions.[12]

As scholars peeled away the veils obscuring large sections of the African American nationalist legacy, they uncovered Marcus Garvey and the Universal Negro Improvement Association. The towering figure of Garvey and his back-to-Africa movement during the 1920s overshadowed expressions of territorial nationalism, especially the Black-town movement. Garvey studies have become a major area of scholarly inquiry. The prominence of Garvey constitutes a second reason that Black towns have been underemphasized even in studies of Black nationalism. However, because Garvey was an emigrationist, emphasizing him and his movement neatly dovetails into the third reason for the scholarly neglect of Black towns.[13]

Scholars' tendency to focus on emigrationism is the third reason there are not more studies of Black towns. Because major contemporary Pan-African nationalists, such as Kwame Toure (Stokely Carmichael) and the All African Peoples party during the 1970s, rearticulated Garvey's emphasis on Africa, it encouraged the emigrationist bias. It is not surprising that Pan-Africanism and emigrationism consumed the attention of scholars, given the often implicit presentist presuppositions underlining much of the research on Black nationalism. Another cause for this misplaced emphasis was the particular historical era examined by academicians interested in the African American experience. The study of Black nationalism was tied to the dominant eras then under investigation in African American history. The study of African American nationalism has therefore been skewed toward the antebellum period, the 1920s, and the 1960s. Only recently has the period from 1879 to 1920 become a major focus in African American history. Bracey, Meier, and Rudwick claim this era was one of four historical periods in which African American nationalism was ascendant. Nevertheless, as their work evidences, even when scholars of Black nationalism have examined this period, they have generally ignored the Black-town movement. As mentioned earlier, Draper's *Rediscovery of Black Nationalism* contains only one reference to Black towns. Edwin Redkey's *Black Exodus: Black Nationalist and Back-to-Africa Movements, 1890–1910* and Wilson Jeremiah Moses's *Golden Age of Black Nationalism, 1850–1925* are other cases in point. The study of antebellum Black nationalism profited from the upsurge in slavery studies, but the dominance of slave studies has been a double-edged sword for students of African American nationalism. During the 1970s, historians discovered a rich vein in African American slavery. Their diggings were so profitable that scholarship on slavery emerged as a boom area in American history and became the primary area of research in African American studies. Yet caught in the whirlpool of slave studies, scholars of Black nationalism were pulled inexorably toward emigrationism, the dominant expression of African American nationalism during the antebellum period. Maroon societies and organized Black communities, the main manifestations of territorial nationalism during the antebellum era, have proven almost impossible to reconstruct using traditional historical sources and methods. Consequently, few scholars, with the notable exception of Herbert Aptheker, have examined maroon societies in the United States. Furthermore, until Sterling Stucky wrote *Slave Culture: Nationalist Theory and the Foundations of Black America,* few scholars had interrogated the cultural or other dimensions of slave-era Black nationalism. Although emigrationism is a variant of Black nationalism, focusing on it diverted academic attention away from studying freedom villages and organized Black communities.[14]

Scholars have generally treated Black towns as oddities, as tributaries of a

minor political tendency. Consequently, Black-town studies barely benefited from the post-1960 rediscovery of Black nationalism. The most salient
point about Black-town studies is the scarcity of monographs. Sociologists
and social scientists have dominated the field. Because they write articles,
their dominance has meant that few monographs have been produced on
Black towns. For instance, Hill published six articles but never wrote a monograph on Black towns. Elizabeth Rauh Bethel's *Promiseland: A Century of Life
in a Negro Community* is the only book-length study of a Black town published by a sociologist. Bethel's work is important in other ways as well. She
breaks with the social scientists' tradition of ignoring or diminishing the
temporal dimension and studying Black towns mostly as static phenomena.
Promiseland is also one of the few works that examine a single community.
This is extremely important because Hill's work had established a tradition
of Black-town scholars' doing multicommunity studies, for instance, Thomas Knight's *Sunset on Utopian Dreams: An Experiment of Black Separatism on
the American Frontier* (1977), Norman Crockett's *Black Towns* (1979), and
Kenneth Hamilton's *Black Towns and Profit: Promotion and Development in
the Trans-Appalachian West, 1877–1915* (1991). Even Janet Sharp Hermann's
Pursuit of a Dream examines two communities. Often a comparative approach is a refreshing break from tradition and sheds light on aspects that
would otherwise remain hidden, but not in this field.[15] The most recent work
in the field, Hamilton's *Black Towns and Profit,* reflects the dilemmas associated with multitown studies. The book provides brief overviews of five all-
Black towns: Nicodemus, Kansas; Mound Bayou, Mississippi; Langston City,
Oklahoma; Boley, Oklahoma; and Allensworth, California. Like Hill and
Crockett, Hamilton uses a lens that is so wide that the lived experiences of
town residents are obscured. Most studies of Black towns have been narrative sketches that eschewed analysis of governmental records, such as census
data, city directories, and city council minutes. Nor have scholars mined local newspapers and organizational records. They therefore cannot reproduce
occupational, family, or class structures for any of the communities studied.
Lurking just under the surface of the multitown studies is the implication
that none of these towns is worthy of a monograph.

Even when historians have traversed this terrain, they have utilized athe-
oretical approaches. They have failed to profit from the various theories used
by sociologists, geographers, and political scientists to explain either the internal or external relations of Black towns. For instance, Hill and Thelma
Ackiss contended nearly fifty years ago that class was the best framework for
studying relations among Black-town residents, yet no contemporary study
has made class a central analytical category. Joseph Taylor and Ramla Bandele attempted to establish different approaches. In a brief article, Taylor
attempted to examine historical development, dependency, social structure,

and leadership in Black towns. Unfortunately, he conceived of dependency in psychological terms rather than as an economic relationship. Bandele, an urban planner focusing on economic development, entitled her work "The Underdevelopment of Black Towns." She evaluated Black towns by general factors necessary for town development, such as an export (processing/manufacturing) sector, support industries (e.g., financial institutions, retail merchandisers, and entertainment), accessibility, and infrastructure. Her study detailed the processes of underdevelopment, but her discussion suffered because she failed to situate it theoretically. Bandele's evidence described the underdevelopment of Black towns, but she did not explain it. She would have aided her project immensely if she had grounded it in dependency theory or internal colonialism.[16]

The late Guyanese historian and Marxist activist-intellectual Walter Rodney once wrote, "At the level of social groups development therefore implies an increasing capacity to regulate both internal and external relationships." Rodney's logic suggests that underdevelopment implies an increasing inability to control internal and external relationships. The dialectical relationship between internal colonialism or dependency and proletarianization is foundational for this study. Michael Hechter defined internal colonialism as the structure of oppression that develops when peripheral (read: ethnic and racial) groups are incorporated into a core or a dominant group's political economy. Exploitation and discrimination are the bases on which the subordinate group is absorbed into the dominant group's social formation. To emphasize uneven development within a nation-state, Hechter adopted the language of world capitalist systems theory. According to Hechter, the state institutionalizes and maintains a relationship of domination through discriminatory policies. Paul Kantor also used this mode of discourse to explain the historical development of the U.S. urban system. Discussing the industrializing era, Kantor claimed, "Uneven patterns of urban economic development emerged, creating a 'core and periphery' system of cities; small numbers of major urban centers quickly established a dominant market position in relation to much larger numbers of other cities, which assumed a subordinate place in the industrial order." Racism exacerbated the normal capitalist tendency toward uneven development. The tendency of capitalists to favor investment in established urban centers adversely affected all small towns, but Black towns were more likely to remain peripheral, even in eras and regions in which capitalists broke with this tradition. Dependency theory or internal colonialism allows me to explore the external relations between Brooklyn and the industrial capitalists who owned factories in the metro-east, the city of East St. Louis, the St. Clair County government, and other predominately white industrial suburbs.[17]

The concept of proletarianization is also essential to this study because

Afro-Brooklynites were incorporated into the metro-east political economy as primarily wage laborers. Between 1865 and 1910, many Afro-Brooklynites who had been sharecroppers, nonindustrial workers, and small farmers were drawn to the metro-east from the border states of Missouri, Kentucky, and Tennessee. The proletarianization process involves mechanisms by which peasants, sharecroppers, and artisans were incorporated into capitalist relations. Karl Marx described and analyzed the classic process by which proletarianization occurred:

> Self-earned private property, that is based, so to say, on the fusing together of the isolated, independent labouring-individual with the conditions of his labour, is supplanted by capitalistic private property, which rests on exploitation of the nominally free labour of others, i.e., on wage labour. . . . as soon as the labourers are turned into proletarians, their means of labour into capital. . . . then the further socialisation of labour and further transformation of the land and other means of production into socially exploited and, therefore, common proprietors, takes a new form. That which is now to be expropriated is no longer the labourer working for himself, but the capitalist exploiting many labourers. This expropriation is accomplished by the action of the immanent laws of capitalistic production itself, by the centralisation of capital. . . . Hand in hand with this centralisation, or this expropriation of many capitalists by few, develop, on an ever-extending scale, the co-operative form of the labour-process, the conscious technical application of science, the methodical cultivation of the soil, the transformation of the instruments of labour into instruments of labour only usable in common, the encompassing of the means of production by their use as the means of production of combined, socialised labour, the entanglement of all peoples in the net of the world market, and with this, the international character of the capitalistic regime.[18]

Marx's discussion explains the process by which European and Euro-American workers were proletarianized, but according to Joe W. Trotter Jr., the leading advocate of the proletarianization thesis in African American urban history, the proletarianization of African Americans was different. In the United States, whites experienced proletarianization mainly as a downward process in which they often lost their land, were frequently deskilled, and saw their wages plummet. For most African Americans trapped in the plantation economy and domestic and personal service, however, proletarianization generally represented upward mobility. Blacks often gained industrial skills and were usually paid wages for the first time. Nevertheless, Marx's description of capitalist production and accumulation illuminates the new economic relations in which Afro-Brooklynites entered, especially after 1870. With the abolition of slavery and the industrialization of the metro-east region, Afro-Brooklynites increasingly found themselves enmeshed in the lower rungs of the proletariat, even if they did initially benefit from being incorporated into the processes of industrial capitalism.[19]

The Industrial Development of the Metro-East Region, 1830–1919

Brooklyn's evolution into a dependent town was rooted in its incorporation into the political economy of the metro-east region, and its historical development must be situated in that context. Before Brooklyn's history can be adequately discussed, it is therefore necessary to trace the industrialization of the metro-east region. Six periods of industrialization can be identified in the development of the metro-east region. The first period, 1830–50, covers initial manufacturing in the region. The second, 1850–75, consisted of the construction of an industrial infrastructure, including docks, railroads, and bridges, and the creation of East St. Louis and National City as industrial suburbs by national capitalists. During the third period, 1875–90, East St. Louis emerged as a major industrial suburb. The fourth period, 1890–1919, was characterized by extensive national capital investment as the region became a preferred site for industrial suburbanization. This was the metro-east region's "golden era" of manufacturing and its nadir in race relations. Racial and class violence culminating in the 1903 lynching of the Brooklyn schoolteacher David Wyatt, numerous strikes, and the 1917 East St. Louis race riot were the obverse side of industrialization. During the fifth period, 1919–55, the region gradually began to decline. New Deal programs and war production temporarily boosted the economy, but new plant construction came to a halt. Deindustrialization became the dominant structural process after 1955. Industrial flight and failure characterized the region, and in East St. Louis, it was followed by white flight and Black political empowerment. My comments focus on the first four periods, from 1830 to 1919, because they correspond to the period of this study.[20]

Industrial capitalism was the dominant force shaping the region's development. This is, of course, true for the United States as a whole between 1870 and 1920; however, the difference is that the metro-east consisted mainly of industrial suburbs created primarily to protect industrial interests. Three major differences flow from this. First, as Andrew Theising, a historically grounded political scientist, noted, "industrial suburbs are not founded on the social contract, but rather business principles which place industrial profitability before residential needs for city services." Seeking to evade taxes and regulation, businesses accelerated the establishment of industrial suburbs beyond the reach of restrictive governmental entities. According to Theising, "every major city needs a workbench, a trash heap, a washbasin; some kind of repository for the unattractive yet essential elements of urban life—slaughterhouses, smokestacks, rail yards, and those who make them work." Industrial suburbs fulfill these functions, and the metro-east developed as a huge complex of contiguous industrial suburbs. Theising identifies two types of industrial suburbs: complex and simple. East St. Louis, National City, Granite City, and Monsanto (Sauget) are prime examples of the complex suburb. Complex industrial suburbs include several firms doing different functions in the production-distribution process. These are companies in related industries whose production-distribution costs can be cut significantly by locating in the vicinity. The relationship between the St. Louis National Stock Yards and the meat-packers in National City is a model of how proximity facilitates vertical coordination and decreases costs. Alcoa (Alorton), Wood River, Roxana, and Hartford represent the simple suburb. Industrial suburbs of the simple type are created by a single firm for cost reduction and social control. For example, in 1902 the Aluminum Ore Company, the largest employer in East St. Louis, decided to build a new plant along the southeastern edge of East St. Louis, outside of municipal boundaries. The workers/residents at the new production site were subjected to paternalism. After four decades of undisputed corporate control, the town was incorporated as Alcoa but changed to Alorton, an acronym for Aluminum Ore Town, in 1944. Another example of the simple industrial suburb is Wood River, created by Standard Oil Company in 1906 as a site for a new refinery. Both simple and complex industrial suburbs existed to fulfill the needs of business instead of the needs of citizens. Whether capitalists established unincorporated industrial sites (e.g., St. Louis National [City] Stock Yards) or incorporated towns (e.g., Granite City), their goal was to ensure that business avoided or got special consideration concerning taxes, assessments, zoning, regulation, and labor disputes.[21]

Second, the industrialization of the metro-east contradicted the national pattern. *Centralization* was the most prominent feature of the first wave of industrialization, 1850–90. During this phase, industrial capitalists placed factories in major cities, such as New York, Philadelphia, Boston, and St. Louis. The rise of factories as production sites both facilitated and was a product of centralization. During this period, industrialization and urbanization occurred in a pattern in which residential suburbs grew up around an industrial center. In the period 1898–1920, however, capitalists reversed this pattern and emphasized *decentralization*. The metro-east region's "golden age" of industrial development, 1890–1919, coincides with the period in which U.S. capitalists were pursuing a policy of industrial decentralization and were locating factories in new suburban manufacturing towns. National City, Granite City, Monsanto (Sauget), Alcoa (Alorton), Wood River, Roxana, and Hartford were all incorporated during this period. National City and Monsanto most grotesquely reflect this policy. Neither has ever had a large residential population because they were established by capitalists as industrial rather than residential suburbs. Other industrial suburbs of East St. Louis are not nearly as extreme as National City and Monsanto, though only Washington Park's population preceded the construction of a major plant, and it abuts Fairmount City's industrial district. Although the metro-east's greatest period of industrial development coincided with the corporate policy of industrial decentralization, several industrial suburbs were created in the metro-east *prior* to the advent of this policy. During the era of industrial centralization, 1850–90, cartels of national capitalists constructed East St. Louis, National City, Madison, and Venice as sites where profits could be maximized and taxes and adverse policies minimized. The establishment of this infrastructure significantly influenced locational decisions during the 1890–1920 period. The metro-east's "golden age" was thus predicated on a pattern of industrial suburbanization that contradicted rather than conformed to the national pattern of industrial centralization.[22]

Third, the metro-east's industrial suburbs were created by national capital to take advantage of the region's strategic location on the Mississippi River across from St. Louis, to avoid or minimize municipal taxes, and to circumvent policies unfavorable to corporate interests. Major national capitalists, such as J. P. Morgan, Jay Gould, Andrew Mellon, John Rockefeller, and Nelson Morris, utilized three strategies in creating the metro-east's industrial suburbs. Seeking to maximize profits and evade municipal restrictions, industrial capitalists either located in an existing small town they could dominate (Venice), constructed their own unincorporated town (National City), or incorporated a town they created (Granite City). The last two options predominated in the metro-east because capitalists there preferred to build a town rather than convert older communities into industrial suburbs. In a speech during Granite City's fiftieth anniversary celebration, Heyward Niedringhaus, a grandson of William Niedringhaus, who along with his brother Frederick founded Granite City, described his grandfather as "something of a social philosopher and idealist, who chose to build a new town, one laid out by industry for industry but eventually to be owned by the inhabitants themselves." The other capitalists, such as Rockefeller, who built new towns in the metro-east to protect their profits may not have been "social philosophers" like William Niedringhaus, but they shared his probusiness beliefs.[23]

The central questions of this study are how and why Brooklyn was underdeveloped. The failure of a major factory to locate in Brooklyn during the first four periods of metro-east industrialization condemned it to exist as a commuter suburb. The industrial capitalists' decision not to build a plant in Brooklyn was a result of the complex interplay of several factors, including strategic, economic, political, and arbitrary. Harry Dixon, Robert A. Harper, Doris Rose Henle Beuttenmuller, A. Doyne Horsely, Andrew Theising, and other scholars have commented on the *strategic advantages* of the metro-east

region. Among the metro-east's strategic advantages was its location along
the Mississippi River across from St. Louis, an industrial center billed as the
"Gateway to the West." Development of the region was seen as part of the
push for integrating the national market, connecting the eastern manufacturers and customers to raw materials, animals, minerals, and consumers
from the West. The region was near an abundant supply of raw materials,
especially bituminous coal, and had a very productive agricultural industry.
These strategic factors largely explain why industrial suburbanization occurred so early in the metro-east. Doris Rose Henle Beuttenmuller identified
several *economic* factors, such as cheap land, access to water and railroad facilities, proximity to a labor force, low taxes, inexpensive building materials,
and cheap fuel and electric power, that also made the east side extremely
attractive to industrial capitalists. Andrew Theising has elaborated on a set
of *political economic* factors Beuttenmuller overlooked. Theising emphasized
the capitalist imperative to reduce production costs. As he noted, local taxes, property assessments, zoning, and antinoise and pollution regulations are
production costs that capitalists constantly strive to reduce. For example,
beginning in 1914, the health officer in St. Louis was granted the regulatory
power to restrict or shut down businesses deemed nuisances. Industrialists
also preferred building new towns and creating governments subservient to
corporate interests. I refer to this tendency as a *political factor.*[24]

Obviously, corporations evaluated strategic, economic, political economic,
and political factors, but most sites in the metro-east shared the region's strategic, economic, and political economic advantages. For example, Brooklyn
essentially occupied the same land area as National City and Venice and economically was not very different from the towns that became industrial suburbs. The political economic factors essentially explain why firms were looking to settle outside the corporate limits of industrial centers, in this case St.
Louis. The decision not to remake Brooklyn into an industrial suburb was
partly based on the corporations' tendency at this historical moment to build
company towns. They preferred this to locating in existing towns, even unincorporated ones. There is no reason to believe that industrialists would have
been unable to reach acceptable arrangements with Brooklyn town officials,
though. Because capitalists built new towns in the metro-east throughout
industrialization, I conclude that political factors in the metro-east were
decisive in the corporate locational decisions. However, by itself, the capitalist
predilection to build new industrial suburbs does not explain why Brooklyn did not become an industrial suburb. This corporate tendency was applied not uniformly but *arbitrarily.* For instance, Venice became the site of
railroad industries, while Brooklyn became one of only two metro-east towns
(Cahokia was the other) that developed as residential rather than industrial
suburbs. Also, in other areas, capitalists turned small towns into simple in-

dustrial suburbs. Because the strategic, economic, and political economic differences between Brooklyn and those communities that became industrial suburbs were negligible and because the political factors were applied contradictorily, race/racism must be considered a possible factor.

The two primary factors shaping Brooklyn's history have been *race* and *capitalism*. Brooklyn's development has been influenced by the interface between the region's evolving capitalist political economy and the changing structure of its racial control system. Brooklyn was founded as a safe haven for fugitive slaves and free Blacks in St. Clair County, Illinois, a place in which racialized servitude substituted for slavery. Race was therefore deeply inscribed in its origin. For Brooklyn's Blacks, race was most appropriately understood as a protonationalist perspective that bound them together in a quest for freedom from racial oppression. For the region's whites, race served both to structure and to rationalize the discriminatory distribution of social goods and services, thereby mitigating intraracial class conflict because the profits derived from racism were partly used to "buy off" the white working class. Race thus served different purposes for Blacks and whites. Black "race men and women" (individuals committed to racial uplift) celebrated Brooklyn as "a place of their own," while white racists, who excluded Blacks from such towns as Granite City, saw Brooklyn as a "place for them." Since African Americans' and Euro-Americans' constructions and reconstructions of race are essential to understanding Brooklyn's historical development, clarifying my conceptualization of race is important.

The race concept has both biological and social dimensions. There are real differences in appearance among social groups classified into different racial categories, but these differences are not essential, and like gender differences, they have no inherent meaning. The meanings attached to "race" are socially determined. Although physical differences among social groups are natural—that is, biologically based—the essential elements constituting the race concept are predominately sociohistorical. Since the essence of race is social, what really is important is not race per se but racism. Racism is usually conceptualized as an ensemble of beliefs and attitudes that posit that people's intelligence and morality can be inferred from their physical features. This definition treats racism as an ideology, but it only partially represents reality because it ignores the material basis for racial oppression. A more complete definition would account for both the material and ideological elements embedded in racial oppression. From this perspective, racism is a relationship of domination that includes both institutional and ideological aspects. That is, racism is more than just the belief that another group of people is inherently inferior; more important, it is the organization of a society's institutional infrastructure so that the rules, policies, and social relations give preference to the privileged "race" and discriminate against the oppressed "race." This materialist understanding of racism enables us to explain the myriad and intimate connections between race, racism, and capitalist development in the St. Louis metro-east region.[25]

Brooklyn was bypassed during the metro-east's first two periods of industrialization, 1830–50 and 1850–75, and the decisions made during these eras significantly shaped Brooklyn's future. Nevertheless, the process could have been reversed between 1875–90 and 1890–1919, the third and fourth periods of metro-east industrial development. It was during these years that nine of the region's thirteen industrial suburbs were developed. These were the most crucial years in Brooklyn's underdevelopment. Interestingly, between 1875 and 1886, no new industrial suburbs were created in the metro-east, but ten were developed between 1887 and 1926. The greatest period of industrialization in the metro-east thus occurred after Afro-Brooklynites acquired political power. Significantly, a year after Blacks gained control of Brooklyn's political apparatus, Madison was created as a site for the Merchants Bridge. Was race/racism a factor in the locational decisions of industrial capitalists in the metro-east?

The main periods of metro-east industrialization, especially 1890–1919, coincided with national industrialization and the formation of a new racial control system. The transition to this new racial formation entailed disfranchisement of southern Blacks, the institutionalization of segregation, the resurgence of racist violence, especially lynching, and the rise of scientific racism to rationalize the new racial order. Lynching was not confined to the South. At least twenty-two lynchings occurred in Illinois between 1891 and 1914. A lynching and perhaps the worst race riot in U.S. history occurred in the region during this period. The prevalence of racism in the area is manifested in the lynching of David Wyatt, racial segregation throughout the region, and the 1917 East St. Louis race riot. Furthermore, racial ideology structured industrial capitalists' decision making in a variety of ways. Race and ethnicity/nationality were factors in hiring decisions, departmental assignments, and labor-management relations. At the turn of the century, metro-east industrialists were open about their racially biased hiring and deployment decisions. In *Race Riot at East St. Louis, July 2, 1917,* Elliott Rudwick summarized the meat-packers' reasons for employing African Americans: "Negroes did not object to performing low-paying, dirty, unpleasant tasks involved in fertilizer manufacturing and hog-killing." A Granite City superintendent made a less blunt but similar comment when he claimed he would take two African American laborers over three Macedonians. In a similar vein, the Monsanto Chemical Company claimed that "colored workers are available here in large numbers, and, according to reports, are more intelligent and of a better class than those farther south, being especially useful for different kinds of *rough or disagreeable work.*" Swift, Granite City, Monsanto, and Alcoa confined or disproportionately assigned African Americans to the hottest, hardest, most dangerous, and lowest-paying jobs. The racial lens through which they depicted African Americans saw them as pliant, easily exploitable brutes. The contradictions of this racist and ethnocentrist world-view would be comical if the consequences were not so tragic. This preference for African American workers apparently did not transcend labor usage, because Macedonians could live in Granite City, but Blacks could not. Furthermore, although at least one industrial manager preferred Blacks to a Hungarian ethnic group, most workers at the East St. Louis National Stock Yards and Granite City's steel mills were East Europeans. European immigrants also had more desirable and better paying jobs than their fellow African American laborers had. The point, of course, is that metro-east industrialists figured race into their hiring and work assignment calculations. Because race/racism was part of industrialists' employment, deployment, and residential policies, it is reasonable to assume that race was also part of their locational calculus. Race was one of the two major components determining how Brooklyn was incorporated into the St. Louis metro-east's capitalist political economy. Race determined that Brooklyn would become primarily a site of commuter labor for the factories in the region's predominately white industrial suburbs.[26]

A Periodization of Brooklyn's History, 1830–1915

In its 170 years of existence, the African American enclave of Brooklyn, Illinois, has evolved from a freedom village through a biracial "pseudo" town into a "dependent" Black town. Between 1830 and 1915, Brooklyn went through this process in four historical periods: (1) 1830–70, (2) 1870–85, (3) 1886–97, and (4) 1898–1915. I periodize Brooklyn's history in terms of its racial demography, its incorporation into the St. Louis metro-east region's dominant political economy, its citizens' social and political relations within the community, and its relationship with external governmental entities. Racial beliefs and practices structured Brooklyn's role in the metro-east's political economy and its relations to other governmental entities. Brooklyn's economic role, as a site for commuter labor, was defined by the locational and personnel decisions of the region's industrial capitalists.

During the first period, 1830–70, African Americans were governed by the notorious "Black Laws," the Illinois version of the slave codes. The historian Elmer Gertz, when referring to the slave codes (which he termed Black Codes, because they governed every aspect of slave and free African Americans' lives), stated, "These southern Black Codes were taken over almost completely in Illinois and other northern states, including the self-righteous New England region." Denied citizenship and the franchise by law and circumscribed in business ownership by practice, Blacks found Illinois and other midwestern states only slightly more tolerable than the southern slave states.[27]

This period included two stages: from 1830 to 1837, Brooklyn was a freedom village on the Illinois frontier; and from 1837 to 1870, it was an unincorporated majority-Black, biracial pseudo town. During the initial stage, when the community consisted of freedpeople and fugitives, Afro-Brooklynites built two of their core social institutions, the family and church. These institutions socialized young and new migrants into the community's core values, including the founders' raison d'être: to aid fugitive slaves and to offer free Blacks a safe haven. Though freed from slavery, African Americans still found themselves bound by racial restrictions in employment and enterprise.

The second stage began in 1837, when five white men, who were abolitionist capitalists, purchased land near the African American colony and laid out the town of Brooklyn. Ironically, the men who platted Brooklyn chose the site because they wished to exploit its locational advantages. Racism ultimately thwarted their entrepreneurial aspirations, however. The future of this majority–African American town was shaped early in this phase when a group of Euro-American mining magnates selected Illinoistown rather than Brooklyn as the terminus for a railroad line connecting the coal mines in the bluffs to the Mississippi River. In 1859, Illinoistown became the first town to incorporate in the American Bottoms. Several other towns were platted in the area, but none was incorporated. Between 1861 and 1863, the city of East St. Louis was created by the merging of East St. Louis town, St. Clair, and Illinois City and by the annexing of Bloody Island, the town of Washington, and the Wiggins Ferry landing. East St. Louis was created by national railroad barons as a "safe haven for investment." According to Andrew Theising, "It was clear that Bloody Island and the ferry landing was going to be the locus of economic power, and the city which controlled it would command the regional destiny." Formation of the city of East St. Louis secured control of the metro-east region for such industrial capitalists as Jay P. Gould, J. P. Morgan, Nelson Morris, Gustavus Swift, and Philip Armour.[28]

The incorporation of East St. Louis would affect Brooklyn in three important ways. First, it ensured that initial industrialization would continue to bypass Brooklyn. Second, the highly developed transportation infrastructure (especially after the streetcar system was developed) made it possible for Blacks to live in Brooklyn and commute to East St. Louis and the industrial suburbs that developed between 1872 and 1915. This arrangement was most obvious in Granite City, a company town created by William and Frederick Niedringhaus to house the employees of their Granite Iron Rolling Mills. Although "employees" were required the live in Granite City, Black workers were subject to a "sunset law." A significant number of black steelworkers therefore commuted to work from Brooklyn. The white industrial suburbs thus deflected social reproduction costs for their African American labor force onto the unindustrialized Black town. Third, since Brooklyn was only about a mile from East St. Louis, its retail business sector was dominated by its rapidly growing neighbor. Donald William Clements used the theories of metropolitan dominance and gradient to explain the relationship between East St. Louis and the small towns in the metro-east. According to Clements, "metropolitan dominance maintains that socioeconomic influence of an urban place diminishes with increasing distance from that center. . . . Certainly those towns adjacent or close to the East St. Louis–Belleville axis may be considered to be within a metropolitan or urban area of influence." Clements determined on the basis of retail sales, number of establishments and function, total sales tax, and sale tax by categories that Brooklyn was the metro-east community most economically dominated by East St. Louis. Brooklyn's development of an independent internal business sector was undermined by its proximity to East St. Louis and its incorporation into the metro-east's political economy as a cheap commuter labor force.[29]

During this historical period, Afro-Brooklynites were excluded from or severely restricted in agriculture and mining, the major industries in the metro-east. Although residential areas in antebellum Brooklyn were stratified by class and occupation as much as race, the proximity of Blacks and whites did not dissipate social segregation. Blacks were the majority population and shared residential space but not social space with the dominant white minority. Moreover, economic exclusion, limitation, and concentration created conditions in which none of Brooklyn's Black males were employed as miners and less than 13 percent were farmers in 1850. Meanwhile, more than 47 percent were employed as common laborers or boatmen.[30]

After decades of African American struggle, the Illinois state legislature abolished the Black Laws and ratified the Fifteenth Amendment in 1870, thereby enfranchising Black men. These social and political changes established the conditions for Brooklyn's second historical period, 1870–85. These sociopolitical processes were supplemented by more decisive economic forces as the region's political economy changed from commercial to industrial capitalism. Expanding industrial development led to the creation of three new industrial suburbs, National City (1872/1907), Venice (1873), and Madison (1887), and eventually spurred the migration of tens of thousands of African American laborers into the metro-east region. Once in St. Clair and Madison counties, the post–Civil War migrants cooperated with the forces of industrial capitalism in transforming themselves into urban industrial proletarians. Many new migrants chose to live in the predominately Black village rather than in one of the majority-white industrial suburbs.[31]

This period also had two stages. The first was extremely brief. From 1870 until Brooklyn was incorporated in July of 1873, African American men could exercise their newly acquired political rights only in county, state, and national elections. African American women, like Euro-American women, remained disfranchised. The second stage of this period began when the town was incorporated as a village and ended in 1886 after Afro-Americans captured control of the local government. The timing of Brooklyn's incorporation suggests that its residents were reacting to the changing political and economic environment around them. National City, which borders Brooklyn on the south, and Venice, which borders it on the north, were created and incorporated in 1872 and 1873, respectively. The National Stock Yards was a corporately owned unincorporated village. It became the site of one of the world's largest stock yards, and the meat-packers operating there (e.g., Morris, Armour, and Swift) became major employers of male Afro-Brooklynites. Soon after incorporation, Venice developed a diversified economy anchored by the railroad industry. During this stage, Brooklyn failed to attract an industrial enterprise.[32]

Throughout this stage, 1873–85, Brooklyn was ruled by a biracial government in which the white minority held most of the political offices. The mixed government merely camouflaged white political supremacy. Thwarted politically, Afro-Brooklynites made tremendous gains in social organization and cultural development. This period was also characterized by the diversification and strengthening of Black institutions and organizations and the rumblings of Black resistance to white privilege. Local branches of national fraternal and religious organizations took root in Brooklyn throughout the 1870s. Buoyed by antidiscriminatory legislation, a growing population, increasing organization, and a new sense of efficacy, Afro-Brooklynites were ready to challenge white power. Education was the first site of contestation. The Black community's victory on "mixed schools" in 1875 presaged its seizure of the reins of local government in 1886.

During the third period, from 1886 to 1897, Brooklyn was distinguished by two contradictory processes—Black political empowerment and economic underdevelopment. This period and the next one encompassed the "golden age of manufacturing" in the metro-east region, yet for Black Brooklynites, these two periods mark the "best of times and the worst of times." Politically, Brooklyn was dominated by racial warfare as African Americans and European Americans fought for control of local government. Economically, the community was being transformed by the dramatic rise in industrialization and urbanization in the metro-east region. Collectively, these processes established the social context for what was perhaps the most important political period in Brooklyn's history, the era of Black power. In late nineteenth-century Brooklyn, Black power meant uniting the African American community around the concept of Black control of municipal government, activities that affirmed their heritage, and a commitment to advance Black people.

John Evans, Brooklyn's first African American mayor, led the movement for Black power. Once in office, Evans and his political allies used their hard-won power to improve the town's infrastructure and municipal services. Equally important, they extended the freedom-conscious political culture by continuing to celebrate freedom holidays, inaugurating commemorations and naming buildings after antiracist activists, and involving the community in the activities of the National Afro-American League.

This was also a time of rapid change. The region was industrializing and incorporating at a brisk pace. Huge manufacturing plants were locating in East St. Louis and other predominately white communities surrounding Black Brooklyn. By the turn of the century, many major companies had established production facilities in East St. Louis. Among them were Obear (Nester) Glass Works, Missouri Mallable Iron, Memphan Paint, American Steel, Aluminum Ore, and Key Boiler. In 1894, construction began on several new plants in the new industrial suburb of Granite City. By 1896, the following plants were operating in Granite City: Markel Lead Works, American Steel Foundry, St. Louis Stamping Works, and the Granite City Steel Works. The Granite City steel factories became the main employers of Afro-Brooklynites. Madison was incorporated in 1887 by the Madison Land Syndicate, a corporation composed of the St. Louis–based Merchant's Exchange and metro-east coal dealers. These industrialists wanted to build a bridge to break the pool formed by Wiggins Ferry Company and the Terminal Railroad Association. Control over Eads Bridge and the ferry gave the Terminal Railroad Association and Wiggins Ferry Company a monopoly over all commercial river crossings. A year after Merchants Bridge opened in 1890, Madison officials convinced an ancillary railroad industry, the American Car and Foundry Company, to set up shop. In East Alton, founded in 1893, the Western Cartridge Company, a munitions plant, began operation.[33]

Initially, Afro-Brooklynites thrived as African American males nearly reached full employment, but the failure of viable industries to locate in Brooklyn portended ill for the future. The white minority lost political power, and most migrated elsewhere, but whether they chose to leave or remain, whites retained economic dominance. They owned most of the businesses and a substantial amount of real estate in town. Only a meager local Black entrepreneurial class developed. Brooklyn's Black petty bourgeoisie consisted mainly of ministers, educators, public officials, and civil service employees. The small group of Black businesspeople was still confined to personal service enterprises. Under the weight of commuter proletarianization, Brooklyn's social and institutional structures began to buckle. Ultimately, the lack of internal economic development facilitated a weakening of the community's core institutions, the family and the church.

The fourth period, 1898–1915, was dominated by economic decay and political instability. By 1910, Brooklyn had begun to deteriorate economically as it felt the effects of underdevelopment. Between 1900 and 1910, the Black town was flooded by a steady stream of young southern males seeking work in the nearby industries. The African American male population jumped from 384 to 734, an increase of more than 52 percent. The African American female population increased from 353 to 649, or more than 54 percent during the same period. By 1910, adult Black men numbered 533 and constituted more than 54 percent of the African American adult population, while adult Afro-American women numbered 462 and composed only 46 percent of the adult Black population. This was a drastic change from the mid-nineteenth century when the ratio of Black men to Black women was balanced. This imbalance exacerbated the community's social problems. Changes in the work process transformed Brooklyn's occupational structure. Between 1900 and 1910, Black unskilled laborers jumped from 50 percent to more than 82 percent, and skilled workers and "foremen" plunged from 25.8 percent of the work force to only 9.4 percent. The rapidly expanding population taxed the town's supply of older houses, and by 1910, Brooklyn was beginning to resemble an urban ghetto.[34]

Brooklyn's political turmoil mirrored its economic troubles. Around the turn of the century, rival political factions consolidated into political parties. The interracial Peoples party, headed by Frederick F. Vanderberg, created a corrupt and violent political culture. Vanderberg initiated an era of kleptocracy, in which he and other members of the Peoples party looted the treasuries of the town council and the school board. During his reign, conflict between Brooklyn's Black leadership and the St. Clair County State's Attorney's Office escalated. Under Vanderberg, politics began to degenerate into armed clashes as contestants for public office resorted to extralegal means. This process culminated in 1915, when armed clashes between rival political factions provided the pretext for the St. Clair County sheriff to suspend local government and declare martial law.

In sum, the definitive era in Brooklyn's history spanned its third and fourth periods. Capitalism and race, the most important social processes shaping Brooklyn, had their greatest impact during the metro-east's "golden age" of industrial development, from 1890 to 1919. During this time, twenty large manufacturing plants were established in the region. The metro-east's manufacturing district developed while capitalists were pursuing a policy of industrial *decentralization*, locating its industries in a series of new suburban manufacturing towns scattered throughout the region. The communities of National City and Monsanto (Sauget) most grotesquely reflect this; neither has ever had a large residential population because they were established by manufacturers as production sites. Race was a primary factor influencing the locational decisions of major industries. Brooklyn and Cahokia were the only suburbs in the metro-east that developed as nonmanufacturing centers. Brooklyn, like many small towns, suffered from capitalism's tendency toward uneven economic development, and like the Black towns in the South and West, it was further victimized by racial discrimination in the distribution of political goods and services. By 1910, Brooklyn's Black leadership could no longer hold back the forces of underdevelopment, and these processes of *racial capitalism* transformed Brooklyn into a dependent town.[35]

Dependency Theory and Black Towns

During the late 1960s, Jack O'Dell, the editor of *Freedomways*, published several influential essays articulating the theory of internal colonialism. By the 1970s, groups of sociologists and political economists had postulated the internal colonial thesis as the analytical construct that best explained the processes of racial oppression. For a brief period, the colonial analogy gained wide currency. Robert Allen, influenced by O'Dell's thesis, extended it in *Black Awakening in Capitalist America: An Analytic History.* Allen and two Euro-American sociologists, William Tabb and Robert Blauner, emerged as the foremost advocates of this position. According to Robert Staples, during the 1970s, the internal colonial thesis "gained ascendancy as the explanatory model for the contemporary Black condition," yet no scholar elaborated its insights to Black towns.[36]

Two researchers did explore the question of economic dependence and Black towns. In two controversial case studies of Kinloch, Missouri, the political scientists Ingo Walter and John E. Kramer examined the relationship between political independence and economic dependence. Walter and Kramer called their research the Black City Research Project, which was funded by the Department of Health, Education, and Welfare during the late 1960s. Walter and Kramer's research had two objectives. First, they sought to learn whether the political behavior of Blacks in an all-Black town was a predictor of African American political behavior in the U.S. cities. Second, they wanted to know whether Black-governed cities would be economically viable. The Department of Health, Education, and Welfare feared the demand for federal social redistributive programs (e.g., welfare or subsidized low-income housing) would rapidly expand in cities governed by Blacks. The most useful insight derived from their studies was that by the mid-1960s, Kinloch and its residents had become extremely dependent on federal assistance. Walter and Kramer attributed part of Kinloch's underdevelopment to "patterns of implicit or explicit racial discrimination." However, they were referring only to employment opportunities. Subsequently, they undermined this observation by contending Kinloch residents' low levels of "human capital" accounted for much of their unemployment. Walter and Kramer claimed two industries employing five hundred people failed to locate in Kinloch because of "poor local planning," though they provided no evidence to support this claim. On the basis of their analysis of Kinloch, Walter and Kramer concluded that political autonomy would dramatically increase the economic dependence of majority Black municipalities on white-dominated units of government.[37]

History has demonstrated that they were right about a relationship between African American political control and municipal economic dependence. Nevertheless, the relationship is more complex than they presented. First, according to Thomas Sugrue, the urban crisis is not a consequence of Black political empowerment; instead, its origins lie in the immediate post–World War II period. He chronicles the loss of hundreds of thousands of urban industrial jobs beginning in the 1950s. In the metro-east, stagnation had already begun by the 1920s. No new plants were constructed in East St. Louis after 1919. Industrial decline was evident by the depression, but war production temporarily buoyed employment, thus shielding the region's decline in manufacturing jobs until the early 1950s, according to Theising. The connection between Black political control and urban economic dependence is thus the result of the convergence of several sociohistorical factors. The growing dependency of municipalities on transnational capitalist corporations explains much of the connection between Black political empowerment and economic dependence. African Americans achieved political control when capitalists were *concluding* the reorganization of the capital accumulation process. Major components of this reorganization included interstate highway construction, suburbanization, relocation of retail businesses, "urban renewal," deindustrialization, and the transfer of labor-intensive jobs to low-wage areas in the U.S. South and the third world. These economic factors combined with the changing balance of race-based political power and federal neglect of the urban infrastructure to construct the material conditions in which whites and eventually the Black middle class fled the cities. This flight to the suburbs produced a decreased tax-base in most of the cities in which African Americans acquired political control. The combination of these changes created a new social structure of accumulation, a new stage of capitalist development, and a new racial formation. These transformations explain the relationship between Black political power and economic dependence.[38]

Walter and Kramer emphasized such individual factors as personal values and educational level. This approach to poverty led them to underemphasize the role external structural factors played in Kinloch's underdevelopment. They never considered whether Kinloch had been systematically underdeveloped by its relations with outside economic and political structures. They did not examine the role racism may have played in the locational decisions of industries. Nor did they investigate if Kinloch had received its pro-portional share of county projects and jobs. They failed to pursue these lines of inquiry because they focused on individual factors rather than commu-nity socioeconomic factors and Kinloch's role in the region's political econ-omy. Their work was marred by the theoretical framework in which they chose to conduct it. Their use of conservative human capital theory rather than political economy led them to blame the poor. Concepts contributed by Harold Rose could have helped them conceptualize dependency in socio-economic rather than psychological terms.[39]

In 1965, Rose had developed two concepts, "pseudo towns" and "depen-dent towns," to explain the external relations of many Black towns. "Pseudo towns" were politically disfranchised economic appendages of larger munic-ipalities, while "dependent towns" were unincorporated communities that for spatial reasons were not economic appendages of central cities. Pseudo towns, Rose discovered, were usually rural villages near agricultural process-ing plants. He maintained that three historical processes created these com-munities. First, they developed as Black enclaves on the periphery of a city. Second, the larger community rapidly expanded, encompassing most of the space that previously separated the two communities. Third, the white city turned its Black community into a bantustan by disfranchising the African American community through exclusion. On close examination, the three experiences Rose identified turn out to be only two. His first two situations are actually two different moments of the same process. He did not discuss the historical processes by which dependent towns were created or the the-oretical relationship between them and pseudo towns. Rose did, however, identify their essential characteristics. According to him, dependent towns exist as distinct separate communities, but, like pseudo towns, they lack po-litical representation and suffer from economic dependence. He did not the-orize about the situation in which an incorporated Black town was spatially close enough to fall within a central city's sphere of socioeconomic influence. Rose's conceptions of "pseudo" and "dependent" towns are derived from central place theory, a popular conception of regional relationships during the 1950s and 1960s. According to this theory, urban systems were structured such that a dominant metropolis's economic-political-social-cultural in-fluence increased the closer a smaller town was to its borders. Rose's ideas elaborate central place theory by adding race as an analytical factor and emphasizing political autonomy. Race undergirds the centrality of political autonomy in his concepts. This cuts both ways, however. His conceptualiza-tions contain only a weak formulation of economic dependency because they are more political than economic. Nevertheless, Rose's ideas are extremely useful in understanding how Brooklyn was underdeveloped.[40]

A complex relationship between Brooklyn and East St. Louis that com-

bined characteristics of Harold Rose's pseudo and dependent towns developed early. The small Black town was not a political subdivision of East St.
Louis, but it was an economic appendage of the larger town because of its
proximity. It was also unincorporated and in an urban industrial rather than
a rural agricultural region. Nor did Brooklyn initially conform to one of the
three historical processes by which pseudo towns developed according to
Rose. When Brooklyn was platted in 1837, it was one of only two communities in the American Bottoms (Illinoistown was the other). After the merger
of several small villages and their subsequent incorporation as East St. Louis in 1861, Brooklyn began to reflect the characteristics of the second pattern
Rose identified. The spatial gap separating Brooklyn from East St. Louis gradually gave way. After East St. Louis emerged as the major industrial suburb
in the metro-east region, a dominant-subordinate relationship developed
between it and Brooklyn. Brooklyn's residents were employed by industries
in East St. Louis and the other industrial suburbs. The development of East
St. Louis's retail business sector also circumscribed Brooklyn's internal economic development, because goods and most services were always cheaper
in the larger industrial suburb. Though Black entrepreneurs expanded their
operations beyond racial service (businesses that have a "captured market"
because of physical differences, cultural taste, and racism), in the main they
were limited to operating enterprises that catered to or coexisted comfort-
ably with vice. Consequently, Brooklyn came to supplement "Black Valley,"
the vice district in East St. Louis. Cheap taverns, gambling dens, dance halls,
and brothels proliferated. Brooklyn also derived a significant portion of its
revenue from liquor licenses. Several members of Brooklyn's new Black political leadership, like their East St. Louis counterparts, owned and operated
many of these dives. According to the historian Irving Dillard, on the cusp
of the 1917 race riot Brooklyn's "dens of iniquity" were frequented by many
white people from East St. Louis and other predominately white industrial
suburbs in the metro-east. Brooklyn also fulfilled another essential function
for East St. Louis. The small, financially strapped Black community provided some education, housing, and entertainment for Blacks that East St. Louis
would otherwise have had to provide. That Brooklyn had the largest African
American population in St. Clair County until the second decade of the twentieth century is important. The dominant-subordinate relationship between
East St. Louis and Brooklyn ultimately undermined the possibility of Brooklyn's creating a viable internal economy. By 1910, this relationship of underdevelopment had transformed Brooklyn from a freedom village, to a biracial
"pseudo" town, and finally into an all-Black "dependent" town.[41]

    A major goal of this project is to explain this transformation. Rose's ideas,
though underarticulated, are essential to this explanation. To recast Rose's
concepts of pseudo and dependent towns into a fully articulated concept of

dependency or internal colonialism requires two reconstructions. First, his notion of a dependent town must be reformulated to account for situations in which a historic African American community develops in an urban industrial setting. These situations characterize Black-town formation in the Midwest between 1890 and 1920. Robbins, Illinois; Lincoln Heights, Ohio; and Kinloch, Missouri, followed development processes similar to Brooklyn's.[42] Second, Rose's notions of pseudo and dependent towns are static and should be turned into dynamic concepts that can express historical development from one into the other. Consequently, I modify his conceptualization of a dependent town. His notion was conceptually flawed because it failed to identify the object(s) on which the dependent town relied or how the dependent relationship functioned. Essentially, Rose's dependent towns were too small to incorporate and were on the extreme periphery of a dominant city. However, I preserve his terminology because it suggests the type of relationship that I seek to describe, that is, it fits well with dependency theory. I recast the concept to account for situations of municipal incorporation, spatial proximity, and socioeconomic dominance. In his work, Rose described two historical situations from which pseudo towns were produced. According to him, pseudo towns began as historic enclaves on the periphery of a city whose rapid growth made them contiguous or the white community attempted to disfranchise its Black community by separating from it. My reconceptualization of these concepts emphasizes the dialectical relationship between Rose's theory of a pseudo town and the reformulated concept of dependent town. This allows for historical processes and agency to transform a pseudo town into a dependent town, or for the reverse to happen.

I define a dependent town as a "local state" (municipality) whose powers of semi-autonomous governance are curtailed by the role imposed on it by more powerful structures within the regional political economy. Structural dependence intertwined with racial domination fostered underdevelopment and undermined Brooklyn's exercise of its semi-autonomous powers of governance. I posit that Brooklyn, Illinois, and other Black towns, such as Robbins, Illinois; Lincoln Heights, Ohio; Fairmount Heights, Maryland; Glengarden, Maryland; Urbancrest, Ohio; and Kinloch, Missouri, which developed as commuter towns on the fringes of major industrial cities, represent concrete cases of internal (neo) colonialism. The interaction between capitalism and racism structured the situation of Black urban residents, especially in towns and cities with majority Black populations. Although these experiences were similar, they were not the same. Brooklyn is not East St. Louis, and East St. Louis is not Detroit. Differences in population size, extent of infrastructural development, and industrial and financial mix make each community very different. The racialized process of capitalist locational and employment decision making affected Blacks in Brooklyn, Detroit, Gary,

and Washington, D.C., differently. Decisions made during the industrializing era, 1870–1919, conditioned the underdevelopment of Brooklyn, while
decisions made during the mid-century capitalist restructuring determined
the subsequent deterioration of the larger metropolises. Nevertheless, the
essential processes at work were the same. The significance of Brooklyn, Illinois, is that its experiences of racialized, capitalist locational decisions, seizure of Black political power, subsequent white flight, and economic dependence presages much of the historical experiences of such African American
majority cities as Gary, Indiana; Newark, New Jersey; Detroit, Michigan;
Washington, D.C.; and East St. Louis, Illinois.[43]

PART 1

Founding to the Abolition of the Black Laws, 1830–60

1. From Separate Settlement to Biracial Town: Blacks in Brooklyn, 1830–60

CONTROVERSY SURROUNDS the history of the oldest Black town in the United States. Both the town's origin and its original name are the subjects of myth and error. The Illinois guide done by the Federal Writers' Project claimed the community was initially incorporated as Lovejoy, in honor of the murdered abolitionist Elijah P. Lovejoy. During the 1930s, Anthony Speed, Brooklyn's treasurer during 1902–3, told Arthur Moore, a field-worker for the Works Progress Administration, that when residents were seeking a name for the town, Frederick Archer "suggested Brooklyn in honor of Brookport, Illinois," the town from which he and several other prominent African American politicians had migrated to Brooklyn. In the 1970s, Denver Moore told Elin Schoen the town was named after two of his ancestors, Brooke and Lynn Moore. These explanations are all false. It is unlikely that Speed and Moore were suffering from memory failure, though. Rather, their stories are examples of convenient narratives invented by Black interviewees for white interviewers. Though untrue, Speed and Moore's narratives consciously or unconsciously represent efforts to situate African Americans at the center of the town's history through the naming process. The truth is that the five white men who laid out its 617 lots in a standard American gridiron pattern on 17 March 1837 named Brooklyn. Why did they name the town Brooklyn? Again the facts elude us. The historical record is also unclear about when the community became known as Lovejoy. In 1891, Brooklyn's new post office was designated Lovejoy to distinguish it from a town in Schulyer County that also was named Brooklyn. The town subsequently became known by its mailing address. Whatever the origin of its name, the story of the original settlement and its African American founders preceded the legal organization of the town by European Americans.[1]

Incomplete records obscure the early history of Afro-Brooklyn. But, according to oral tradition, around 1829 a group of eleven families, including fugitives and free persons, fled the slave state of Missouri, crossed the Mississippi River, and settled in St. Clair County, Illinois. Led by Priscilla and John Baltimore, Brooklyn's Black founders included John and Matilda Anderson, Philip and Josephine Sullivan, James and Elizabeth Singleton, Daniel and Sarah Wilson, Russell Cox, Mrs. Wyatt, and Nicholas Carper. Oral tradition described them as "far above the average of their race in intelligence and manhood." By "establishing a home on free soil," some sought to free themselves from slavery's exploitative and oppressive grip, while others sought the opportunity to capitalize on their intelligence and hard work.[2] In Illinois, the maroons gained the chance to determine their own destiny.[3] They squatted near the river, in the American Bottoms, the most fertile section of the county. This area had an abundance of natural wealth: fertile soil, timber, wildlife, and fish. Part of America's racial paradox is the contrast between a beautiful and inviting landscape and an ugly and hostile social geography.

By coming to Illinois, the courageous fugitives escaped the shackles of slavery, although not the stranglehold of racism. African Americans in Illinois were subject to a set of special anti-Black legal codes known as the Black Laws.[4] Essentially, African Americans were outlaws, that is, they were outside the law, beyond the realm of citizenship and democratic rights. Since Blacks were ultimately subject to American law, perhaps this notion was more metaphorical than accurate, but during the era of slavery, both slaves and free Blacks were ruled by a set of separate, repressive legal statutes that denied them the "natural rights of men." Writing about lynching during the late 1940s, Oliver C. Cox posited that African Americans were abused with impunity because it was understood they did not have recourse to legal protection. Sarcastically echoing Supreme Court Chief Justice Roger B. Taney's comments in the 1857 Dred Scott decision, Cox alleged Euro-Americans "conceive of Negroes as extralegal, extra-democratic objects, without rights which white men are bound to respect." Similarly, twenty years later Robert Chrisman declared, "In the literal sense of the word we are out-laws. . . . Being outside of the law, black Americans are either victims or else prisoners of a law which is neither enforced or designed for us—except with repressive intent." John Hope Franklin used a politer concept to explain African Americans' exclusion from the polity and subjection to rules and regulations outside of common law. He termed the nonslave African American population "quasi-free."[5]

Once on the site, the small community of Black pioneers began the arduous tasks of clearing the land, erecting shelters, providing for their subsistence, and constructing social institutions. The focus of this discussion is the establishment of a separate settlement of self-liberated slaves and free Blacks in antebellum St. Clair County, Illinois. During this historical moment, two oppositional forces shaped the development of Black Brooklyn. On the one hand, the racial restrictions of the state of Illinois and the initial developmental decisions of capitalists limited Brooklyn's development. On the other hand, African Americans' efforts at self-development also shaped Brooklyn's development. The main story line concerns the construction of a community out of eleven families and their determination to build a refuge for others fleeing slavery.

Brooklyn's Black founders were not the first African Americans to live in separate settlements in Illinois during the epoch of slavery. Edward Coles, a white migrant from Virginia, purchased land in Pin Oak Township near Edwardsville in Madison County, where he freed nearly a score of captives in 1819. The Black settlement that became Brooklyn, however, was a beacon of hope for those still trapped in thralldom on the other side of the river. Influenced by the teachings of Bishop William Paul Quinn of the African Methodist Episcopal Church, the people of Brooklyn made their town a refuge for those fleeing the shackles of slavery. In struggling against slavery and building Brooklyn into a bastion of Black pride, Priscilla Baltimore, the "mother of Brooklyn," left an outstanding legacy. Family and religion were the pillars on which the African Americans constructed their community.

Nominally Free: Life under the Black Laws

After the ratification of its constitution, Illinois was nominally a free state, but the legislature quickly enshrined the spirit of the repressive slave codes into a set of anti-Black statutes. On 30 March 1819, it adopted the first of the state's Black Laws. These statutes denied basic civil and political rights to Blacks and deterred African American migration into the state. Section 1 declared that before settling in Illinois, all Blacks had to present a certificate of freedom from the county clerk of their former residence to the circuit clerk of the Illinois county to which they were moving. Section 2 empowered county officials to expel any African American who was unable to maintain an independent income, thereby not complying with the state's poor laws. Section 6 made it a felony for anyone knowingly to aid runaways or impede their recapture; offenders would be punished accordingly. Section 7 defined Blacks without a freedom certificate as escaped slaves and provided for their arrested. The sheriff would then advertise for six weeks. During their incarceration, the alleged runaways were rented out and enslaved for up to a year while waiting to be claimed. Other sections prescribed racially discriminatory criminal punishment. If whites and Blacks committed the same offenses, whites would be fined, but slaves and free Blacks would be whipped. Whites in Illinois, like their counterparts in the other states carved out of the old Northwest Territory, restricted the immigration of Blacks into the state. Once in Illinois, Afro-Americans were confined to a position of social and political inferiority.[6]

Free Black Communities on the Illinois Frontier

Illinois was a haven for African Americans by default. Blacks viewed the state favorably only because it bordered two slave states and was the nearest free state for Blacks fleeing servitude from most of the Deep South. More significant than the myriad Black individuals who entered Illinois pursuing the elusive American dream were the three groups of freedom seekers who established free Black enclaves in the southwestern counties of Illinois. The Edwardsville settlement, New Philadelphia, and Brooklyn developed independently of and quite differently from one another. Edwardsville was a product of white philanthropy. New Philadelphia, a biracial town, was founded in 1836 by Free Frank McWorter, a former slave who had purchased his and his family's freedom. Meanwhile, Brooklyn evolved from a freedom settlement into a biracial "pseudo" town and finally into a "dependent" African American town. Each community's story further illuminates a shadowy section of African American history and is unique and fascinating in its own right.[7]

The first organized Black community was established in 1819 when Edward Coles, a former secretary to President James Madison and the future governor of Illinois, freed his seventeen slaves. Coles compensated his former bondsmen by giving each male family head a quarter section, or 160 acres of land. The farmland was located near Edwardsville, Illinois, "in Sections 14, 15, and 16 of the Pin Oak Township."[8] Coles, reflecting on the "advice" he gave his slaves upon freeing them, wrote the following in his diary: "My anxious wish was that they should so conduct themselves as to show by their example that the descendants of Africa were competent to take care of and to govern themselves, and enjoy all the blessing of liberty, and all the other birthrights of man, and thus promote the universal emancipation of that unfortunate and outraged part of humanity."[9] Coles's action was the first recorded instance of a master's manumitting and resettling former slaves in free territory on their own land. Edwardsville's historians call him "Illinois' first Great Emancipator." However, Coles's altruism was limited to manumission. African American oral tradition alleges Coles freed his former slaves but did not give them tools or the financial resources with which to farm the land he gave them. Tragically, Ralph Crawford, who led the contingent of African Americans in Coles's absence, and Thomas Cobb lost their land to white men after they went into debt to borrow money for farm tools and provisions. Still, Coles was far ahead of Abraham Lincoln and most whites, who during Reconstruction rejected the principle of compensation or reparations for slave labor exploitation and oppression. According to William Pease and Mary Pease, this was the primary way white philanthropists contributed to the formation of organized Black communities. The Edwardsville settlement represented the simplest form of European American philanthropic support for organized Black communities. Although Ellen Nore and other scholars are beginning to reconstruct the history of the Edwardsville colony, what happened to the first organized Black community and its members still represents a gap in the African American historical record.[10]

About ten years after Edward Coles freed Crawford and company, Free Frank and his family established a Black presence in Pike County, Illinois. A few years later, in 1836, when he created the biracial town of New Philadelphia, Free Frank became the first American of African descent to found a town. Free Frank intended to attract other Blacks to the area and envisioned New Philadelphia as a place where Afro-Americans could prosper free from the hindrances of racism. Unfortunately, his dreams were only partially fulfilled. Few African Americans migrated to New Philadelphia. Although Free Frank used the community to aid fugitives and encouraged Blacks to take up residence, European Americans remained the majority in New Philadelphia. This is not surprising since only about five thousand Afro-Americans resided in the more than twenty organized Black communities. Perhaps Brooklyn, during the antebellum period, more closely resembled what Free Frank had envisioned.

The community of Brooklyn differed from the community near Edwardsville in two important ways: (1) Brooklyn was the product of Black self-activity rather than white philanthropy; and (2) Brooklyn evolved from a freedom settlement into an all-Black municipality, while the Edwardsville settlement was assimilated into larger white communities. The communities initiated by Free Frank and "Mother" Baltimore had much in common; both emerged from African American self-activity, and both became spaces hospitable to Blacks fleeing the fetters of slavery. During this period, Brooklyn differed from New Philadelphia mainly because it was a majority-Black town and offered the opportunities to join organizations and participate in Black-controlled institutions. Brooklyn thus has a more potent legacy of Black initiative than either the Edwardsville settlement or New Philadelphia.[11]

The Baltimores, African Methodism, and Support for Fugitives

The first social institution organized in the free Black settlement of Brooklyn was the African Methodist Episcopal (AME) Church. According to legend, the Reverend William Paul Quinn (1788–1873), a circuit-riding missionary for the

AME Church, molded a small group of individuals who met at John and Priscilla Baltimore's home into an AME congregation in 1825. Eventually, the congregation built a small log church, the Brooklyn African Methodist Episcopal Church, reputedly the first AME Church "west of the Allegheny Mountains." Many questions surround the accuracy of this account, however. The Baltimores, Shadrack Steward, and Thomas Allsworth, who, according to oral tradition, formed Brooklyn's first church, were not listed in the federal or state census of 1830. John and Priscilla Baltimore's names appear in the 1840 federal census for St. Clair County but not Steward's or Allsworth's. The census recorded Shadrack Steward and Thomas Ellsworth as members of a cluster of seven African Americans living in Alton, who under the leadership of Elder William Paul Quinn organized the Lower Alton African Methodist Episcopal Church in the winter of 1839. The religious historian Miles Fisher claimed the Alton AME Church was the first AME Church founded in Illinois. However, in a history of the church, the Reverend M. W. Beckly, who was a pastor at the Alton church during the 1880s, wrote the "Alton Church was the first AME Church in Madison County and the second in Illinois." Moreover, he claimed William Paul Quinn had been an elder in the church for some years before he started the Alton church. Fisher based his interpretation on a letter from Louise Ahrens of the Madison County Historical Museum and his examination of W. T. Norton's *Centennial History of Madison County and Its People, 1812–1912*. This work does not include Beckly's 1882 essay though. Fisher also claimed Chicago's Quinn Chapel, formed on July 22, 1847, was the second AME Church in Illinois. According to the historian Don Harrison Doyle, an AME congregation was formed in 1846 in "Africa," the Black enclave in Jacksonville. The Jacksonville AME congregation met at Mt. Emory Baptist Church, the local Black Baptist church, until 1850, when it got its own building. Beckly does not reveal where the first AME Church in Illinois was founded, but logic suggests it was in an area where the Reverend William Paul Quinn was active, since he was the only AME missionary operating west of the Alleghenies. The relationship between the Reverend Quinn and Priscilla Baltimore provides a strong prima facie case for Brooklyn. This historigraphical problem is partly a product of the difficulty in establishing when the maroons squatted in the area.[12]

The 1850 federal census directs us toward an answer to this question. Scholars consider it the first modern census because it was the first to use a standardized form and greatly increased the information collected about each respondent and the members of their household. The 1850 census is also the first to contain relevant information about Brooklyn's founding families. For example, it described John Baltimore as a fifty-two-year-old butcher who was born in the slave state of Virginia. According to this information, Baltimore was born in 1798. The census recorded that Priscilla Baltimore was the daughter of a slave mother and her Bourbon County, Kentucky, master and was forty-five years of age. She was therefore born in 1805. These dates should be viewed as approximates because other information contradicts them. For instance, the AME Church historian George A. Singleton cites 13 May 1801 as Priscilla Baltimore's date of birth. The key to the mystery lies in the birth dates of two Baltimore children, Lewis and Hester. Twenty-three-year-old Lewis was born in Missouri in 1829, while eighteen-year-old Hester was born in St. Clair County in 1832. Lewis was the only Baltimore child born in Missouri, and Hester was the oldest one born in Illinois. Since members of the freedom village that became Brooklyn were not included in the 1830 federal census, it is reasonable to think they did not arrive in St. Clair County until after the census was completed. Bad weather offers another possible explanation. The winter of 1830–31 was extremely bitter, and the census taker may have missed the Baltimores, but it is unlikely that he would have missed the rest of the Black enclave. The Baltimores therefore probably settled in St. Clair County between 1830 and 1832, though this contradicts oral history.[13]

At first glance the evidence suggests the Reverend William Paul Quinn began his missionary work in Illinois between 1836 and 1840. In 1836, Bishop Morris Brown authorized his assistant, Elder Quinn, to go west and "build up the Church." The General Conference, however, did not commission Elder Quinn to do missionary work west of Ohio until 1840. Nevertheless, in his eulogy for Bishop Quinn at memorial services held during the General Conference of 1876, Bishop Jabez Pitt Campbell claimed Bishop Quinn went west in 1832. Elder Quinn did not report his activities to the General Conference until 1844. The story of the Reverend Jordan Winston Early supports Bishop Campbell's statement. The Reverend Jordan Winston Early converted to Methodism in 1826, and in 1836, he joined a small AME society in St. Louis, Missouri. The AME Church credits the Reverend William Paul Quinn with planting African Methodism in the slave territory of St. Louis, Missouri. Although the historical record is murky, it appears the Reverend Quinn initiated his ministry in the area after 1829 but before 1832, and sometime between then and 1837 he helped organize the AME Church in Brooklyn.[14]

The early 1830s was a bad time for African Americans to enter Illinois. Anti-immigration and pro-emigration attitudes were spreading throughout the state like a virus. The Illinois state legislature toughened its Black Code in 1829. The new anti-Black legislation included the following provision: "No colored person who was not a citizen of another state could gain a residence in Illinois without first filing a certificate of freedom in the county commissioner's court and giving $1000 bond that he would be self-supporting." Furthermore, the new law stipulated that anyone who harbored or hired a Black person who had not complied with the provisions of the law be fined $500. The 1819 Black Law stipulated that African Americans be regarded as

fugitives until proven otherwise. It required that they be arrested and forced
to labor for the state for one year or until a slaveholder claimed them. Another section of the new law made it unconstitutional for Blacks and whites
to marry and imposed a fine of $200 on officials who sanctioned such unions.
Between 1831 and 1833, the legislature twice amended the Black Laws, and each
time it made the provisions more stringent.[15]

Illinois denied African Americans basic human rights and through law and
custom supported the maintenance of slavery in the southern states, but
despite its inhospitality, a Black person was better off in Illinois than in most
of its bordering states. Aiding or inducing a slave to escape was illegal, but
the resourceful and relentless Reverend Quinn found numerous ways to get
behind the cotton curtain. When he could not smuggle himself into the belly of the beast, he shouted his message across the river. At Alton, Illinois, he
often preached to slaves gathered on the Missouri side. According to Brooklyn legend, after the river had frozen over in the winter, the Reverend Quinn
would walk out on the frozen water and preach the gospel of freedom to those
still shackled in Missouri. His message inspired and emboldened the captives,
but it also put their enemies on notice. The "paddyrollers," the slavocracy's
armed guard, heavily patrolled the area directly across from "Bloody Island."
The slave masters must have feared the effect of the Reverend Quinn's sermons on their property. Responding to the interaction between free Blacks
and slaves in the river transport industry in 1841, a St. Louis newspaper complained, "This communication renders the slaves restless and induces them
to run away, and furnishes them a means of escape." Bishop Quinn had his
network in place. The Reverend Jordan Winston Early was one of many Black
boat workers. He worked on a ship that plied between St. Louis and New
Orleans. His employment as a boat hand facilitated his establishment of the
AME Church in New Orleans. To accomplish this mission, the Reverend Early
employed several methods of stealth taught him by his mentor, Bishop William Paul Quinn. The Reverend Early left a legacy that rivaled his mentor's.
He succeeded in spreading African Methodism into areas of southwestern
Illinois, Missouri, and Iowa not reached by Bishop Quinn.[16]

Priscilla Baltimore, a tireless worker for the AME Church and the cause
of freedom, played a significant role in this drama. A Methodist missionary
purchased Priscilla Baltimore from her slave-master father, the father-in-law
of the former governor of Missouri, for $1,100. She had previously been con-
verted to Methodism. Like Nat Turner, she was permitted to preach to the
slaves in the area. It is said that her spiritual power was so great that once the
masters in the area allowed her to take three hundred slaves into Illinois to
participate in religious services. Liberty of this sort was rare but not unknown.
Edward Coles had permitted Ralph Crawford to travel across the country by
himself. Baltimore was apparently very enterprising because within seven

years she managed to purchase her freedom from her Christian owner for the same price he had paid for her. The record does not show how she earned the money to buy her freedom, but many Black women were hired out as cooks, nurses, or dressmakers. Priscilla Baltimore's purchase price compares favorably with that of Elizabeth Keckley, another St. Louis, Missouri, Black woman who bought herself for $1,200. She earned the money by working as a dressmaker. Perhaps Baltimore did so as well. Once free, she led the group of free and fugitive Blacks to the site that became Brooklyn, Illinois. Baltimore may have used her trip to a camp meeting in Illinois to scout for land on which to start a freedom settlement.[17]

This extraordinary woman was often called on to risk her life by ferrying the Reverend Quinn and Ezekiel Pines across the river at night, so that they could sneak into St. Louis and spread the word of salvation and liberation. Crossing the Mississippi River under the cloak of darkness on a ferry was no easy task because of the river's renowned treacherous snags and bars. Once on shore, they had to contend with the slave patrollers' network. Their lives depended on their cunning. When Quinn was captured outside St. Louis, he reportedly informed the court that as a native of India and a British citizen, he was not subject to U.S. jurisdiction. The authorities apparently shared this interpretation because they ordered him to stay out of Missouri and released him. For the most part, the Reverend Quinn and Pines managed to elude the hounds of slavery and their masters. Once in St. Louis, they met in the homes of the members of the small society that the Reverend Quinn had organized, which Jordan Winston Early now led. The small congregation that gathered to hear the gospel of liberation eventually grew to become St. Paul's African Methodist Episcopal Church, the oldest Black church in St. Louis, Missouri. Perhaps they took a couple of absconding slaves with them back to Illinois. Although most white abolitionists opposed entering the belly of the beast, the less publicized Black antislavery fighters apparently had no such compunction.[18]

Slaveholders accused abolitionists every time a slave attempted to flee to freedom. Most often, besides antislavery rhetoric in such abolitionist newspapers as the *Western Citizen,* the slaveholders had little supporting evidence for their claims and were blaming abolitionists to maintain the fiction that their slaves were content. However, the activities of the Reverend William Paul Quinn and his unheralded network of AME activists were helping fugitives escape bondage. Despite the sentinels, many fugitives, perhaps encouraged by the Reverend Quinn's stinging condemnation of the "peculiar institution," chose to risk death in the hope of obtaining freedom. Unfortunately, flight was only mildly successful for obtaining freedom. Only an estimated six thousand slaves escaped along tracks of the underground railroad that ran through Illinois. Regardless of whether they were successful, flight was an effective means through which slaves could assert their humanity. If the human chattel got away, the master suffered a complete loss of property. If the fugitive was captured, the resale value diminished. Rarely were absconding slaves aided by abolitionists while still on the slavocracy's terrain. For the most part, they had to get themselves to free territory. Many escaped to freedom by stealing a skiff and rowing across the river. Probably many more were captured or lost their lives trying to make it to Illinois. William Wells Brown was one such fugitive who successfully fled St. Louis without aid from abolitionists until he reached the east bank of the river. From Bloody Island, fugitives traversed the swampy "bottoms" until they made their way to Brooklyn, the first station on the underground railroad. In Brooklyn, fugitives were hidden in the Brooklyn AME Church, Antioch Baptist Church, or private homes until they could be smuggled through the woods to Alton, one of the best-known underground lines. Shielded by the night and following the North Star, the runaways were secreted from Alton and traveled past Jacksonville along the Illinois River to La Salle and Ottawa, through Chicago, and finally to Canada. The role of the Reverend William Paul Quinn and the settlers of Brooklyn in the underground railroad, like the contribution of free Blacks overall, has been diminished in the official histories. For her efforts, Priscilla Baltimore was revered as "Mother Baltimore" throughout the settlement of Brooklyn and deserves a place in the pantheon of courageous African Americans, such as Harriet Tubman and Josiah Henson, who led their people out of bondage.[19]

The Early Development of Brooklyn as a Town

The year 1837 was not a good year to start a town. The panic of 1837 ended speculative town platting in other sections of Illinois, and Caseyville and St. Clair were the only other towns begun in St. Clair County that year. Why build a new town during a major national depression? Two reasons have been cited for why Thomas Osburn and others invested in town building during such a financially inopportune time. Some sources maintain that Osburn and company were speculators who intended Brooklyn to be a "paper town"; others claim they were abolitionists who platted the town so that Blacks would have a safe haven from slavery in Missouri and racial violence in Illinois. The American Bottoms was an excellent site to build another town. Thomas Osburn and company apparently hoped to capitalize on the village's locational advantages: a prime agricultural area, productive coal-mining operations, the expectation of industrial development in the region, and an emerging transportation and industrial center just across the river. Situated directly across from St. Louis, the rapidly developing "Gateway to the West," Brooklyn lay near the center of a growing transportation network. The multitude of settlers heading west, accelerating agricultural trade along the Mississippi River, and the development of manufacturing in St. Louis suggested that a town in the American Bottoms would be quite profitable.[20]

The metro-east was part of the eastern interior bituminous coal region, and its grade C bituminous coal was an ideal industrial fuel. Belleville, the county seat, developed early into a mining center. Coal was being mined as early as 1823, and by 1833, six thousand tons a year were being shipped to St. Louis. John Reynolds, a U.S. representative and a former governor of Illinois, headed a group of Belleville entrepreneurs who recognized the growing needs of St. Louis–based industries for coal. In 1837, the Reynolds group financed the construction of a railway from the mines south of Belleville through the American Bottoms to the riverfront opposite St. Louis. Illinoistown was the only town in the bottoms when Brooklyn was platted. It reputedly was the preserve of a nomadic criminal element. According to the *Belleville Advocate,* during this period, "Illinoistown was known only for its reputation as a rough town of gamblers and vice with its disreputable floating population and its sink holes of iniquity where the moral filth of St. Louis could take refuge to plan its deeds of crime." Brooklyn's town platters thought a more reputable community would thrive in the bottoms. As businesspeople, they understood the potential economic advantages of building an industrial center and railroad near a profitable mining operation. By 1844, "two-thirds of all cattle, vegetables and fruit used in St. Louis came from the American Bottoms," most of which, along with coal, was transported by the Reynolds group's railroad. Brooklyn did not become the terminus for the railroad, however. The Reynolds group chose a route through Illinoistown, despite its "disreputable floating population." How did race figure into the group's locational decision? Why would the Reynolds group choose a site populated by a notorious group of criminals when they could have dictated the development of a newly platted town? We may never discover the role race played in this decision, but the failure to attract this rail line had dire consequences for Brooklyn's economic development. Decisions of this nature are cumulative; within a decade, ten railroads had established terminals at Illinoistown, while none had in Brooklyn. Fourteen years after the Reynolds group made Illinoistown the terminus of its railroad, the Illinois Coal Company built a railway that took coal from Caseyville to Brooklyn, where it was shipped daily to northern St. Louis. This, however, occurred too late to stimulate Brooklyn's early economic development. By then, the railroads in Illinoistown had already begun to attract other industries, such as iron works and warehouses, and initially these industries stimulated the ferry business. Ironically, at its incorporation in 1859, Illinoistown was smaller than Brooklyn; however, acquisition of the railroad and mergers enabled Illinoistown to evolve into East St. Louis, the major industrial suburb in the metro-east. The failure to secure a railway was disastrous for a community's future. New Philadelphia's dissolution in 1885 resulted from its inability to attract a rail line in 1869. After that, New Philadelphia withered, while the surrounding towns through which the railroad passed blossomed into market centers. According to Kenneth M. Hamilton, "Regardless of the racial factor, if a town did not gain a rail line, it either specialized its boosting or, like Nicodemus, it stopped growing." He concluded, "Relatively few of the total number of towns founded . . . obtained rail lines." While Hamilton's conclusion is correct, it does not account for the fact that almost none of the all-Black towns obtained a railroad.[21]

Initially, Brooklyn developed very slowly. The sale of town lots was sluggish because of the depression, and the lack of a transportation infrastructure did not help matters. What occurred after the state legislature authorized the building of a road connecting Brooklyn to Columbus in the spring of 1841 is an indication of what might have happened had the Reynolds railroad conglomerate selected Brooklyn instead of Illinoistown. After the road was built, lots immediately began to sell.[22] The following winter, on 5 December 1841, John Baltimore, husband of "Mother" Baltimore and a fairly wealthy free Black artisan, became the first African American property owner in Brooklyn when he purchased several lots from Thomas and Ann M. Osburn. The deed read in part:

> This indenture made this fifth day of December in the year of our Lord One Thousand Eight Hundred and forty-one, between Thomas Osburn and Ann M. Osburn of the County of St. Clair and the State of Illinois of the one part and John Baltimore of the county and state aforesaid of the other part, [?], Sell, that the same Thomas Osburn and Ann M. Osburn and in consideration of the sum *Eight hundred dollars* to them in hand, said the receipt whereof is hereby acknowledged, do hereby grant, bargain, Sue, convey and confirm onto the said John Baltimore . . . *twenty lots in the town of Brooklyn and a fraction of land laying North and East of said lots, and three lots in the town of upper Brooklyn,* together with and [?] the [?] belonging in any use [?] "is to have and to hold" the above described, named lands [?] John Baltimore his heirs and assigns forever and the Said Thomas Osburn the said Ann M. his wife the aforesaid [?] John Baltimore his heirs and assigns . . . signed.
>
> Thomas Osburn (seal)
Ann M. Osburn (seal)[23]

Why had Blacks not purchased the land, surveyed it, and platted the town? The Black Laws of Illinois circumscribed the rights of African Americans in many areas, such as the right to sue, testify in court, or vote, but the Illinois Town Plat Act contained no racial restrictions. Town founders were required to own the land and provide for it "to be surveyed, and a plat or map thereof made by the county surveyor." Although African Americans lived there before its platting, they did not purchase land in the new town until four years after its formation. Baltimore's delay of four years before he purchased property in the new town suggests that they lacked the financial resources to buy land before the 1840s. The Baltimores had recently paid $1,100 for the freedom of Priscilla and may have posted two $1,000 bonds as part of the 1829 Illinois Black Law. A thousand dollars represented more than three years' wages for an unskilled worker. Because the African American majority lacked financial resources, was disfranchised, and was denied legal rights, real power in Brooklyn resided in the hands of whites from its legal formation.[24]

John Baltimore purchased twenty-three lots and a fraction of land from the Osburns for eight hundred dollars. This was a considerable sum, both as a total amount and as the price per lot. The price suggested the property was valuable because it was located near the river. Brooklyn's proprietors retained the right to assign ferry privileges because of the commercial value of its land base. This arrangement established the relationship between Brooklyn and the Wiggins Ferry Company for the rest of the nineteenth century. What did the Baltimores do with all of this land? This was definitely more land than the Baltimores could live on. Furthermore, the land was in town, and John Baltimore was never listed in the census as a farmer, so it is doubtful that it was for farming. Twenty of the lots Baltimore bought were "in the town of Brooklyn" and the other three were "in the town of upper Brooklyn." Baltimore used at least one lot in "upper Brooklyn" as a site for the African Methodist Episcopal Church. The St. Clair County deed books contain no land transactions by the Baltimores, either selling or renting property, until after John died in the spring of 1866. What did the Baltimores do with the other lots? Mother Baltimore and her husband had led the initial group of families out of Missouri into St. Clair County. Priscilla Baltimore had been a slave, many other founding pioneers were fugitives, and the community developed as a haven for escaped slaves until emancipation. Given the Baltimores' support for runaways, it is likely that large parts of their property holdings were used to provide for fugitives. Perhaps Priscilla was unburdening herself of her large holdings after her husband's death, or perhaps after emancipation ex-fugitives were now free to engage in legal transactions.[25]

Brooklyn: An Antislavery Community

Built as an expression of its founders' desire for freedom and inspired by the examples of Bishop William Paul Quinn and Mother Baltimore, Brooklyn committed itself to the antislavery movement. Afro-Brooklynites readily converted their small village into a place of refuge for their fellow Blacks. Nicholas Carper, a key activist in the early days of the community, was a leading conductor of the Brooklyn section of the underground railroad. He played a central role in organizing the town into one big vigilance committee.[26]

Through its involvement in the underground railroad and its participation in the AME and Black Baptist churches, the community of Brooklyn was connected to the broader national Black community. It is likely that through the Reverend Quinn's contacts in the AME Church, they were aware of the resolution passed at the National Black Convention of 1835, held in Philadelphia, the home of African Methodism. The delegates passed the following resolution: "That our duty to God, and to the principles of human rights, so far exceeds our allegiance to those laws that return the slave again to his master . . . that we recommend our people to peaceably bear the punishment of those [laws] inflicted, rather than aid in returning their brethren again to slavery."[27] Regardless of whether they knew about the resolution, the people of Brooklyn resolved to provide aid and comfort to those fleeing the horrors of slavery. Supporting runaways was a dangerous endeavor for any group, but it was an extraordinarily courageous act for a predominately Black town. Slaveholders stood to lose between $700 and $2,000 for each enslaved person who escaped in the first half of the nineteenth century. As capitalists, they dealt harshly with anyone who interfered with their profit from "their" human property. The slavocracy extended its violent arm into Brooklyn. Looking for a runaway, a group of slave catchers rode into Brooklyn, and upon finding the fugitive at William Carper's home, they murdered Carper and recaptured the escaped slave. Despite the martyrdom of William Carper, his father and the people of Brooklyn continued their acts of civil disobedience.[28]

During the Civil War, Afro-Brooklynites continued to work with antislavery networks in St. Louis to ferry fugitives to freedom. In a 1911 interview with the *St. Louis Post-Dispatch*, James Milton Turner, Missouri's foremost African American leader in the nineteenth century, related his role in helping slaves escape to Brooklyn during the Civil War: "Often, at night . . . [I] tied a skiff containing a fugitive slave to the stern of a steamboat and was towed to the Illinois shore. There the slave would be entrusted to the Rev. John Anderson of Brooklyn, Ill." Turner was part of a Black Baptist network led by the Reverend John Berry Meachum, pastor of the African Baptist Church. This network operated through Black Baptist circles, just as the Quinn-Baltimore-Early network worked through African Methodist circles. Collectively, these men and women were imbued with a religiously based opposition to slavery.[29]

Although Brooklyn was founded largely by free Blacks, in many ways its growth was tied to its ability to attract runaways. The town was a city of refuge. In this, it was no different from other Black enclaves that developed along the underground railroad routes throughout Illinois, in Alton, Chicago, Jacksonville, and Springfield. What distinguished Brooklyn from other Illinois communities where free Blacks gathered, or more precisely huddled, was that it offered not only quasi-freedom but also the fellowship of a majority-Black population. Though it was a small community, it was a place where Black artisans, farmers, and merchants could strive for their dreams.

The European American developers did not intend to promote an "all-Black" town, though they were willing to see it established as a safe haven for African Americans. During the 1840s, Brooklyn became an unincorporated biracial town with a Black majority. Describing Brooklyn during this period, the historian John Hinchcliffe stated, "Its population is chiefly colored, and numbered 300." Of course, the Black majority was disfranchised, but since the town was unincorporated, local electoral politics were nonexistent. As a predominately Black community, Brooklyn offered its Afro-American residents social institutions and a sense of community. In 1850, the Black population in Chicago numbered 378, while in St. Clair County it totaled 518, of which approximately 200 lived in Brooklyn. The origin of the community inspired a sense of efficacy and pride, but Brooklyn was no idyll. The town's small size meant it lacked the anonymity of such cities as Cincinnati or Philadelphia, and although it possessed a Black majority, its small population lacked the critical mass and the capital to support "complexional" institutions and the social life comparable with that in St. Louis, Cincinnati, or other large urban centers. Its proximity to the slavocracy also made fugitives especially vulnerable to recapture. Like Blacks throughout the state, they were not considered part of the polity and were therefore denied their "inalienable rights."[30]

Conclusion

The beginnings of Brooklyn represented something new in the African American experience. The colony of fugitive and free Blacks who escaped slavery on the Missouri side of the Mississippi River transcended the contemporary expression of territorial nationalism—maroon settlements, freedom villages, and organized Black communities—by starting the first Black town. Though unincorporated from 1837 to 1873, Brooklyn became a municipality four years before Nicodemus, Kansas, was founded. Priscilla Baltimore and Brooklyn's founding families through their self-activity initiated an innovation in African American nationalist theory and practice. Although many of the founders were literate, surviving records do not reveal their rationales for establishing a separate settlement. They were not theoreticians but men and women who acted to acquire liberty for themselves and others. Their actions left a legacy for others to explicate the embryonic nationalist ideology that guided their behavior. In this sense, Priscilla Baltimore and the other original founders were practicing an inherent ideology of Black self-determination. We do not know what role African cultural survivals played in formulating their values and behavior, but the importance of religion,

especially African Methodism, is clear. Their god was a "god of the oppressed." Their religious leaders—Bishops William Paul Quinn and Jordan
Winston Early, Priscilla Baltimore, and the Reverend John Richard Anderson—preached a "gospel of liberation." Religion was the main source of their
ideology.

What began as a separate Afro-American settlement was transformed in
1837 into a biracial town. Through their actions, we can discern their nationalist inclinations. After losing their separate community, Afro-Brooklynites
continued to maintain their own institutions instead of attempting to assim-
ilate. The white population increased the need for stealth, but despite the
greater possibility of being exposed, Afro-Brooklynites refused to curtail their
antislavery activities and continued to support runaways. Their actions were
made more difficult and more extraordinary because Brooklyn was in the
heart of an emerging industrial district. Brooklyn was connected by rail and
by road to other towns and cities in the metro-east region. This was a double-edged sword. On the one hand, it made it more difficult to assist fugitives without whites' knowledge; on the other, it facilitated the incorporation of African Americans into the regional political economy, and their jobs
on the river in the transport industry aided their antislavery work.

2. Uncovering Brooklyn's African American Population, 1850

BEFORE THOMAS OSBURN and company platted the town of Brooklyn in 1837, the African American pioneers had already created many aspects of community. Between 1830 and 1840, they had carved out a common space, formed key social networks, and built core institutions. Community formation among Afro-Brooklynites accelerated after John Baltimore purchased twenty-three town lots in 1841. Between then and 1850, a small but steady stream of fugitives and free persons joined Brooklyn's founders. By 1850, Afro-Brooklynites composed 60 percent of the approximately three hundred residents in Brooklyn. Although they were united by the reality of racism and the desire to determine their own destiny, Afro-Brooklynites were also divided by different experiences, colors, classes, and genders. The new arrivals came mainly from the border slave states of Missouri, Kentucky, and Tennessee, but some came from as far away as Virginia and Alabama or from as close as St. Clair and Madison counties in Illinois. Some came from such cities as St. Louis; others came from rural areas, such as the cotton plantations of eastern Tennessee. Apart from coming from diverse regional backgrounds, Afro-Brooklynites had had different statuses. Many members of the original settlers had been free before coming to Brooklyn, and this previous status provided an advantage that persisted over time. The five richest African Americans in Brooklyn were all members of the founding families. Furthermore, most founding males, whether skilled or unskilled, became property owners. Occupation was another source of division. Generally, it indicated class and influenced housing location and property ownership. Occupations also reflected previous statuses and often skin color. The overwhelming majority had been categorized as "African" or "black" and had experienced both slavery and "quasi-freedom" differently than did those who had been designated "mulattoes" by the racialization process, the process by which Euro-Americans made and remade races. Slave narratives and works by such scholars as James O. Horton, Leonard P. Curry, Theodore Hershberg, and Henry Williams have demonstrated that the division of African Americans into "blacks" and "mulattoes" was a source of conflict. Occupation, property ownership, and color often coalesced to make mulattoes an elite among Afro-Americans. Despite this diversity and the tensions and conflicts embedded in it, by 1850 Black Brooklynites had acquired the numbers, concentration, and proximity to generate the social interaction necessary to build institutions, create a consciousness of kind, and produce a set of shared values to mold themselves into a community.[1]

A major question addressed here is how did Afro-Brooklynites overcome these divisions and forge themselves into a community? What social and structural factors facilitated or impeded Afro-Brooklynites in constructing the community? Before the process by which Black Brooklynites built community is discussed, it should first be defined. Community is a slippery concept that has generated multiple meanings, but these definitions can be divided into two categories: those that stress locality and those that emphasize social relations. In his study of community, Thomas Bender explained how the concept in urban areas changed after 1890 from emphasizing locality to stressing social interaction. Most contemporary definitions of community therefore conceive of it as a site of interaction, as both a locus and a process, which incorporates propinquity into a predominately relational construct. For instance, the British sociologist Craig Calhoun defined community "as a pattern of social organization and as a culturally defined way of life, depending on a fairly high degree of stability. The bonds of community are indeed bonds: they tie social actors to each other and their own pasts." For Calhoun, the essences of community—social relationships, social bonds, and political mechanisms—are characterized by the properties of "density, multiplicity, and systematicity." The first, *density*, refers to the abundance of direct face-to-face relations. This social property is best approximated in small towns, such as Brooklyn, in which many residents are related and the limited space and modest size make it possible for everyone to know everyone else. The second concept, *multiplicity*, refers to the extent to which individuals share interlocking relationships. Calhoun contends that when individuals are involved in a matrix of such mutually reinforcing relationships as kinship, neighborhood, employment, occupation, and church and organizational membership, they are more likely to develop the close bonds necessary for cooperation. Because of racial oppression, on the one hand, and Black self-organization, on the other, Afro-Brooklynites developed a web of relationships that augmented each other. This brings us to *systematicity*, Calhoun's last concept. Systematicity points to the incorporation of individuals into social collectives and to the ordering of the groups within a social formation. What is important here is that it addresses the sociality of the individual, that is, how in class- and race-ordered societies the actions of an exploited or oppressed individual, especially those deemed negative, reflect on the entire social group to which the individual belongs. Race/racism and Black nationalism provided the substance for systematicity among Afro-Brooklynites. Since all African Americans, even "mulattoes," were subject to the racial control system, including its structures of domination and ideologies of racial inferiority, all African Americans were forced to unite for protection, companionship, mutual aid, and development. In Brooklyn, mulattoes did not form an upper class that segregated itself from blacks, nor did they function as an elite leadership that dominated the African American community. Collectively, the concepts of density, multiplicity, and systematicity describe the processes of social organization and identity formation by which Afro-Brooklynites constructed a common identity and transformed themselves into a community.[2]

The central thesis of this chapter is that the concentration of more than 61 percent of Afro-Brooklynites in one large residential cluster by 1850 facilitated the face-to-face relationships necessary for African Americans to stitch their diverse strands of experiences and social positions into a single quilt for survival and development. This cluster encompassed the twenty-three lots purchased by John Baltimore and was the locale of the community's most important institutions, the Brooklyn AME Church (Quinn Chapel) and the Antioch Missionary Baptist Church. The de facto segregation of most Blacks into "lower" Brooklyn in this small "walking" town meant that most Blacks came into direct contact with one another on a daily basis. Nearly 43 percent of Afro-Brooklynites lived in extended family households in 1850, and another 7 percent resided in augmented homes in which an apparently unrelated person (or persons) lived with a nuclear or extended family. Approximately 50 percent of Afro-Brooklynites thus lived in households encompassing more than the nuclear family unit. Furthermore, 47 percent of Black males in Brooklyn were common laborers working at menial jobs on the river or in the surrounding predominately white towns for meager wages. During most of this period, Brooklyn had only two churches, Antioch Missionary Baptist and Brooklyn AME (Quinn Chapel). The small number of churches reinforced unity because the existence of several churches in a small community is often the result of doctrinal disputes that produce church splintering. Many churches are therefore generally a sign of community fragmentation. The combination of natural, social, and institutional relationships tied Afro-Brooklynites together in multiplex relationships that encouraged individual responsibility for collective interests. The magnitude of social interactions, the functioning of central socializing institutions, the existence of racism, the need to cooperate for mutual protection, and the presence of an experienced and skilled leadership generated strong bonds of unity. Afro-Brooklynites' identity was rooted in their collective identity, the result of their common experiences of racial oppression and a common culture based on nationality.

Since Brooklyn was not incorporated during this period, the disfranchisement of the African American majority was not a crucial factor in local affairs. Social rather than political factors governed Black-white relations in Brooklyn before the passage of the Fifteenth Amendment, abolition of the state's Black Laws, and incorporation of the town in 1873. By today's standards, residential segregation was minimal, though by mid-nineteenth-century standards it was quite high. African Americans resided in three racial clusters, two small ones and a large one. Henry L. Taylor Jr. and Vicky Dula defined a racial cluster "as two or more families that live in the same dwelling unit with another African American family, next door to an African American, or a few doors away from other African American households." According to Taylor and Dula, the cluster was the antebellum equivalent of the neighborhood, and in Cincinnati, it was the primary spatial organizational unit among African Americans. This was also true for Afro-Brooklynites. Although fluid, segregation was rigid enough in Brooklyn that by Taylor's definition the Black community could be considered a single cluster. This spatial configuration facilitated direct personal relations among most African Americans and generated high degrees of density among them. Within their respective clusters, each racial group maintained its own set of social institutions, which apparently helped mitigate friction. Beyond conflict precipitated by acts of personal humiliation, schooling was the major source of racial tension because Blacks were excluded from the Brooklyn public schools. In this, Brooklyn was merely a microcosm of a broader statewide pattern regarding African American access to education. This chapter investigates structural relations in Brooklyn, including the residential housing patterns, employment opportunities for African American men, family structure, efforts to obtain education, relations between blacks and mulattoes, and the development of African American leadership.[3]

Reconstructing the Social Structure of Black Brooklyn

Historians of African American urban history have long used federal census data as an essential source from which to piece together the quilt of African American social history in urban enclaves. Historians of Black towns, however, are just beginning to tap this rich wellspring. Traditionally, Black-town scholars have eschewed or sparingly used public records, such as manuscript censuses, city directories, probate records, or other government documents.

This is because historians and other scholars studying Black societies have not been interested in reconstructing the family, occupational, and social structures of these communities. According to Mozell C. Hill, the premier scholar of Black-town studies, class position was a critical factor shaping social relations and influencing the personality development of Black-town residents. Hill believed class should be *the* prism for studying Black societies. In 1943, he and his coauthor, Thelma Ackiss, claimed, "As regards social organization and stratification . . . it should be pointed out first that the determinants are largely economic in character. There are, for instance, four rough economic divisions, the members of which recognize each other and are in turn recognized by others to have certain economic and social interests in common."[4] To their credit Hill and Ackiss conceptualized class in primarily economic rather than status terms as was prevalent in the race relations literature of the 1940s. Class was Hill and Ackiss's central analytical concept, although they arrived at it through a questionable methodology. Hill and Ackiss reconstructed the class structures of Black towns using the then popular observation-participation and reputational methodologies rather than empirical information contained in census records. Although their advocacy of class as the framework for analyzing Black towns was a theoretical breakthrough, their subjective methodology severely hampered their model. Since 1943, scholars have not seen class as an important analytical tool for investigating social interaction in Black towns. The class structure of Black communities has therefore rarely been studied and because ferreting out the actual class composition of these communities has not been a central concern, very little has been learned about the interaction of various social strata within these towns.[5]

What is class? *Class* has been defined in many different ways, but most definitions can be categorized by whether they are based on subjective or objective criteria. Subjective approaches, of which Weberianism is the dominant type, view class as income groups and focus on social status, lifestyle, life opportunities, consciousness, and values. Whereas subjective definitions of class are ultimately dependent on one's personal interpretation, objective definitions are determined independent of one's personal opinions. Objective, or Marxist, approaches examine class as a structurally determined position in a society's power structure. I have chosen to use a Marxist definition because Marxism offers the most objective criteria for determining class. Marxism conceives of class in relational rather than gradational terms and provides a way of understanding the role of subjective factors (e.g., class consciousness) in both class and social development. In Marxist terms, class is a relationship between different social groups based on their location in the economic structure and function in the production process and whether they own the means of production.[6] According to V. I. Lenin, classes are large groups of people differing from each other by the place they occupy in a historically determined system of social production, by their relation (in most cases fixed and formulated by law) to the means of production, by their role in the social organization of labour, and consequently, by the dimensions of the share of social wealth of which they dispose and the mode of acquiring it. Classes are groups of people one of which can appropriate the labour of another owing to the different places they occupy in a definite system of social economy.[7]

Lenin's definition emphasizes the relational character of class and locates the production process as the primary site for class formation. This framework thus focuses attention on the structure of capitalist economic development, the resulting class structure, and social relations.

According to the historian Matthew Sobek, census data allow researchers to "assess the class location of most persons" in the United States across time. Occupation and income are two of the variables in the census from which the class structure of a community, city, or society can be reconstructed. The occupational hierarchy is the main mechanism reproducing the class structure in the United States, according to the economist Nancy Bertaux. Sobek considers it "indispensable" and "the closest we can come to ascertaining a person's position in the social relations of production." Income is another important variable for identifying the class of individuals and for re-creating a community's class structure. Because income did not become available until 1940, I have substituted the categories "wealth," which consists of "value of real property," and "value of personal property," which is available for the censuses between 1850 and 1910. Although not perfect, these variables permit a reasonable reconstruction of Brooklyn's class structure and the location of individuals within it.[8]

Apart from brief newspaper accounts, snapshots occasionally found in county histories, and historical background reported in the East St. Louis city directories of 1903 and 1905, no records of life in predominately Black Brooklyn during this era remain. The 1850 census provides the best antebellum source of information on Brooklyn's Black community during this period. For a number of reasons, this census is more reliable than its predecessors. First, the census takers were instructed to visit every dwelling by going up one side of the street and then down the other. Second, the information collected is much more detailed. For instance, unlike the 1840 census, the 1850 census contains the name, age, and sex of all persons living in a home. Third, unlike previous censuses, it specifies the occupation, value of real estate owned, birthplace, school attendance, and whether the individual was married during the past year. Fourth, for the first time, census takers were instructed to identify African Americans as either "black" or "mulatto." The new reporting procedures provided the type of extensive data necessary for intensive racial and class analysis. These innovations facilitate reproduction of Brooklyn's patterns of racial and subethnic residential clustering, segregation, and kinship networks. They also enable reconstruction of each household and identification of the relationships among individuals. Furthermore, the new data help in approximating, if not ascertaining, an individual's class position.[9]

In pre–Civil War Brooklyn, as in most antebellum towns and cities, housing was not legally segregated. However, Brooklyn departed from the national antebellum housing pattern. Although Blacks lived in all parts of town, de facto racial segregation existed. Housing patterns were preconditioned by race, but they were also influenced by occupation and class. Though residence was not strictly determined by race, school attendance and church membership were. Each racial group tended to live in clusters. African Americans were clustered together into three enclaves in an area of town known as "lower Brooklyn." At this time, few African Americans lived in the area known as "upper Brooklyn." The term *upper Brooklyn* initially referred to the part of town that was on the highest ground near the river. Because of periodic flooding, the wealthier residents built their homes in upper Brooklyn. Upper Brooklyn developed as the site that embodied the community's racial and class stratification. African Americans could buy and rent in upper Brooklyn, but only the wealthiest could afford to do so. Two examples support this. John Baltimore, the wealthiest African American in Brooklyn, owned twenty-three lots, of which only three were in upper Brooklyn. John Anderson, one of the five richest Blacks in Brooklyn, purchased lot 44 on Jefferson Street and near First Street in upper Brooklyn in 1849. Government documents from the 1840s give the impression that two separate towns existed. The Recorder of Deeds Office listed land transactions in Brooklyn under three different characterizations: "Upper Brooklyn," "Town of Brooklyn," and "Brooklyn." A 1874 plat map identifies "Upper Brooklyn" between First and Seventh streets and west of Madison Street. It included blocks 1, 2, 3, 4, 13, 14, 27, 28, 40, 41. "Brooklyn" and "Town of Brooklyn" connote the same meaning, but "Upper Brooklyn" inspires an image of a different place, of somewhere better than "Brooklyn" or the "Town of Brooklyn." Few African Americans lived in upper Brooklyn during the 1840s and 1850s, but by the 1860s, the wealthiest African Americans resided there.[10]

Analysis of Brooklyn's Black Residential Clusters

The seventh federal census of St. Clair County includes Brooklyn as part of District Six, the American Bottoms. This district also includes Illinoistown. In Brooklyn, there were 180 Blacks. They lived mainly in one large enclave, bracketed by whites but with a few whites in the African American enclave. Two smaller African American clusters also existed. The first cluster of African Americans recorded in the census consisted of five households and included twenty-three people: seven men, five women, six boys, and five girls. Their ages ranged from four months to forty-five years, with a mean age of sixteen years and six months. Fifteen of the cluster's residents were classified as black, while five were listed as "mulatto." This cluster contained three married couples; one female head of household; one mother who, with her two children, resided with another family; two men who lived with a married couple and their children; and two brothers who lived together. Five of the employed African American men worked as boatmen, one was a cooper, and the other was a common laborer. None of the women listed an occupation. William Hill, a thirty-five-year-old boatman, was the only African American in the first cluster who owned real estate. Hill's property was valued at a hundred dollars.[11]

Bracketing this Black cluster was a thirty-two-year-old white laborer from England and the family of a fifty-year-old white laborer from Indiana. Fourteen white households separated the first cluster of African Americans from the next African American household. Sixteen employed white males lived in this area; among them were a police officer, a carpenter, a pine maker, three steamboat captains, one boat pilot, five boatmen, two fishers, one laborer, and a hunter. Five of the African Americans and eleven Euro-Americans worked on the river; the large number of river workers in this area indicates that this section of town was closest to the river. Most of the river workers were probably employed by Wiggins Ferry Company. Founded by Samuel Wiggins, the company was incorporated in 1852 for one million dollars. Wiggins Ferry Company owned one hundred acres of land along the river where its wharves and docks were. The company had a monopoly on transporting goods between Illinois and St. Louis until 1865, when the Brooklyn Ferry Company was incorporated.[12]

Worksite rather than race or wealth appears to have influenced residence in this part of town. For instance, only three property owners lived in this area. William Hill was the only African American that owned real estate, and William Conn and H. L. Bennett were the only white property owners. Conn and Bennett, however, were part of the wealthiest strata in Brooklyn. A steamboat captain, Conn owned real estate valued at $1,500. Bennett, a fisher, owned property worth $2,200. Steamer pilots often made $1,000 for a trip down the Mississippi River to New Orleans and back. Apparently, this section of the community was not stratified by race or class. Nevertheless, five of the thirteen white families were immigrants: four from Germany and one from France. Two of the three white boat captains plus three of four river workers were immigrants. This suggests that immigrants were more likely than native whites to work on the river. They were therefore more likely to live near African Americans. It is worth noting the racially stratified division of labor: four of the eleven whites were captains or pilots, while all five of the Blacks were boat hands. Boatmen, or "roustabouts," constituted the bottom of the river transportation industry and did menial jobs that free African Americans were restricted to in antebellum America.[13]

Charles Pensanau, a peace officer, and his wife resided in this cluster along with a Black male and a white female servant, ages fifteen and twelve, respectively. They lived next to the Rects, the last Black household. The Rect family was unique. It was headed by Peter Rect, a sixty-year-old laborer who was born in Africa. Rect was one of three Black men in Brooklyn who were married to women classified as mulattoes. His forty-eight-year-old wife, Ellen, was the oldest Black person living in Brooklyn who had been born in St. Clair County. If her age was correct in the census data, she was born in 1802 and probably was a former slave. Their six children ranged in age from three to twenty-four. Levi Sharp, the census taker, classified all of the Rect children as black except the oldest child, twenty-four-year-old Antivini, and twelve-year-old John. The different racial classifications assigned the Rect children serves to remind us that race and ethnicity are *predominately* socially constructed categories that were often determined by the subjective interpretations of government bureaucrats. Since Sharp, like most census takers, probably determined race by sight, we should be cautious when using these data to decide subethnicity among African Americans.[14]

Twenty white households separated the Rect family from the Strowders, the next Black household. John Strowder was a forty-year-old farmer from Virginia. Celia Strowder, his twenty-seven-year-old wife, was also from Virginia. She was one of the few women, Black or white, whose occupation was listed in the census. She stated her occupation as "farming." The Strowders did not claim any real or personal wealth. Five Euro-American households separated the Strowders from the second Black cluster. The second cluster of African Americans consisted of fifteen people divided among four households. The cluster included five men, four boys, four women, and three girls, all classified as black. Lewis Chatman, a fifty-year-old laborer, and his wife, Agnes, were part of this small group. Their family included Lewis's forty-year-old sister and five children, who ranged in age from one to ten. Agnes Chatman and all five of her children were born in St. Clair County. Agnes Chatman was born in 1820 and thus was one of the earliest Black residents in the county. Another home contained a father and his teenaged son. A third home, headed by a sixty-five-year-old woman, included three apparently unrelated adult males. The fourth and final house in this cluster was occupied by a sixteen-year-old woman. Only two of the residents were employed. Lewis Chatman was a laborer, and Dick Menard, a widower, listed his occupation as farming. Since Menard listed no real estate, he was probably a farm laborer or sharecropper rather than a farm owner.[15]

Four white families resided between the second and third clusters of African Americans. Among them were a farmer, a laborer, a tavern operator, and a farm worker. The farmer, a German immigrant, owned real estate valued at $2,000. One African American, James H. Good, lived with the family of his white employer, George H. Lewis, a tavern owner who was the wealthiest person in Brooklyn. Lewis's wealth was valued at $4,000. African Americans in the third cluster numbered 110, resided in twenty-three different households, and constituted nearly 61 percent of all Afro-Brooklynites.[16]

The third cluster apparently lived on the site of the original African American settlement, because the community's two oldest institutions were there and Brooklyn's Black pioneering families—the Baltimores, Sullivans, and Wilsons—resided there. Taylor and Dula consider the location of social institutions as the determinate of a location's importance to a community. Quinn Chapel, the African Methodist Episcopal Church, was originally on Short Street, but in 1832 it was moved to 108 Fifth Street, precisely the area in which John Baltimore purchased twenty lots. Antioch Missionary Baptist Church was four blocks away, on Jefferson Street near First. On 3 September 1866, Pastor John Anderson and his wife, Matilda, transferred lot 40, located across from the church's original site, to the congregation. A new church was built there in 1879 at a cost of $2,500. All of the ministers listed in the census resided in the third cluster. Nineteen of the twenty African American owners of real estate and six of the nine African American artisans lived in the third cluster.[17]

The third cluster consisted of thirty men, twenty-seven women, twenty-seven girls, and twenty-six boys. Of the 110 African Americans residing in this cluster, 62 were "blacks" (29 males and 33 females), and 48 were "mulattoes" (27 males and 21 females). The percentages of blacks and mulattoes in the cluster were 56.4 percent and 43.6 percent, respectively. In the mulatto population, males outnumbered females 56 percent to 44 percent. The opposite was true among blacks, where women made up 53 percent of the population and men only 47 percent. Nineteen couples were married: eleven "blacks," seven "mulattoes," and two "mixed" couples. According to the census, Peter and Ellen Rect and James and Louisa Boyd were the only mulattoes and blacks who intermarried. James Boyd was a thirty-five-year-old mulatto barber, and his wife, Louisa, was a thirty-one-year-old black homemaker. Since Priscilla Baltimore was also listed as a mulatto and her husband was classified as black, there were clearly at least three "mixed" couples, not two, as the census taker reported.[18]

African Americans in the third and largest cluster, for the obvious reasons, had the most diverse occupational structure. Twenty-eight of the twenty-nine adult males were employed. Lewis Baltimore, the twenty-three-year-old son of John and Priscilla, was the only African American male over the age of twenty-one who did not list an occupation. Of the employed African American men in this cluster, eleven were laborers (ten blacks and one mulatto); four were farmers (three blacks and one mulatto); two were barbers (both mulattoes); two were carpenters (a black and a mulatto); two were boatmen (both mulattoes); one was brickmason (a mulatto); two were butchers (both black); and four were ministers (three blacks and one mulatto).[19]

Work and Wealth

Brooklyn was in an area that was rapidly industrializing and was connected to the developing industrial sites through a well-developed railway and road system. By the middle 1820s, coal was a major export. As the area was settled, commercial agriculture also developed into an important industry. Thousands of ships and barges came to St. Louis because of its place as a key nodal point on the Mississippi River's north-south trading route. After St. Louis emerged as the "Gateway to the West," ferrying agricultural produce and coal across the river became one of the most profitable industries on the Illinois side. The town's location along the east side of the Mississippi River offered its residents employment in the river transportation industry dominated by the Wiggins Ferry Company. Despite Brooklyn's location in a thriving economic area, Afro-Brooklynites were not occupationally diverse when compared with white Brooklynites. Black men worked in only nine occupational categories (see table 1), whereas Euro-Brooklynites were employed in twelve. This disparity was compounded by the type of occupations in which Blacks and whites were employed. Whites were more likely to hold positions

Table 1. Occupations of African American Males in Brooklyn, Illinois, 1850

Occupation	Mulatto	Total	Percentage of Total
Barber	2	2	4.26
Boatman	4	8	17.02
Brickmason	1	1	2.13
Butcher	0	2	4.26
Carpenter	2	3	6.38
Cooper	0	1	2.13
Farmer	1	6	12.77
Laborer	2	16	34.04
Minister	1	4	8.51
Unemployed	2	4	8.51
	15	47	100.01

Source: Population Schedules of the Seventh Census of the United States, 1850, Illinois, St. Clair County, Roll 94, 110–27.

of authority and stature that paid higher wages, such as proprietor, steamboat captain, and police officer; Blacks were more likely to occupy positions with no authority, low prestige, and meager compensation, such as roustabout and common labor. Nevertheless, Black Brooklynites' occupational distribution compared favorably with that of Cincinnati Blacks, who worked in only ten different fields in 1850. Only six Afro-Brooklynites (less than 13 percent) were farmers, and none were employed as farm laborers according to the 1850 manuscript census. Few made their living as farmers, probably because they could not afford the cost of land. Not one Black Brooklynite worked in the mining industry, although coal was shipped daily from Brooklyn to St. Louis. Most male Afro-Brooklynites were menial laborers: 47 percent worked as common laborers and boat hands. The wealthier Afro-Brooklynites possessed a skilled trade, such as carpentry, butchery, or barbering. Collectively, the nine artisans, including a brickmason and a cooper, accounted for nearly 20 percent of Brooklyn's employed Black men. More important, all of Brooklyn's Black proprietors came from this stratum. Four male Afro-Brooklynites (8.5 percent) listed minister as their occupation. Since Pastor John Anderson, one the community's five richest Black men, listed his occupation as carpenter, it is highly unlikely that four other African Americans could have made their living solely from the ministry. They were probably employed in another field, such as laborer. Forty-three Black men (91.5 percent) worked, while four (8.5 percent) were unemployed. The region was still largely a frontier area, and agricultural workers were in demand. Johann Kohler, a twenty-four-year-old German immigrant who spent eight weeks working on a St. Clair County farm in 1851, claimed, "Help is hard to find and costly." According to Kohler, day laborers earned $1.00 a day, and he speculated that soon they would demand a $1.50 a day. Since no Afro-Brooklynite worked as a farm laborer, it seems that white farmers preferred to hire European immigrants like Kohler rather than pay Blacks $1.00 a day and work in close contact with them.[20]

Wealth was extremely contradictory for Afro-Brooklynites: compared with other free Blacks, they were doing very well, but compared with their white peers, they lagged far behind. Twenty out of thirty-six African American households (55 percent) in Brooklyn owned real estate. This figure is remarkable considering only sixteen African Americans owned real property in St. Louis. Yet the total value of African American real property was only $7,700. Property owned by African American families had a mean value of $208.10. These figures clearly indicate economic marginality, but even this dismal level of assessed property value masks the true impoverished status of the African American community. Five African American families held a disproportionate share of the total dollar value of African American–owned property (see table 2). John Baltimore owned real estate worth $2,000; Philip Sullivan

Table 2. African American Property Owners in Brooklyn, 1850

Name	Color	Occupation	Value of Property
William Hill[a]	black	boatman	$ 100
Daniel Wilson	black	farmer	550
Baker Brown	mulatto	minister (AME)	100
Lefrey Boss	mulatto	boatman	300
John Baltimore	black	butcher	2,000
Benjamin West	black	minister (AME)	150
Henry McAllister	black	labor	150
Philip Sullivan	mulatto	boatman	1,000
Jeremiah Thompson	black	laborer	150
John Anderson	black	carpenter	700
Amanda King	black	—	150
Theo Boyd	mulatto	brickmason	250
Isaac Stephanson	black	farmer	150
Hiram Boyd	mulatto	barber	150
Israel Cole	black	minister (AME)	150
William Jackson	mulatto	farmer	100
James Boyd	mulatto	barber	1,000
Alphas Bass	black	butcher	150
James Singleton	black	laborer	200
Charlotte Retts	mulatto	—	200

Source: Population Schedules of the Seventh Census of the United States, 1850, Illinois, St. Clair County, Roll 94, 110–27.

a. William Hill who resided in the first cluster was the only African American landowner who lived outside the third cluster.

and James Boyd owned property valued at $1,000; John Anderson's real property was assessed at $700; and Daniel Wilson owned property valued at $550. John Baltimore's wealth represented nearly 26 percent of African American real estate holdings. Collectively Baltimore, Boyd, Sullivan, Anderson, and Wilson owned $5,250, or more than 68 percent of the $7,700 of property owned by African Americans. The other fifteen African American property owners owned only $2,450 worth of property. Eight of the nineteen African American property owners owned property worth $150. The modal value of property owned by people of African descent was $150. The frequency with which this figure appeared suggests that it was the estimated value of a small home and a lot in Brooklyn, Illinois, in 1850.[21]

The poverty of the African American community is furthered underscored when the value of real estate holdings owned by the five wealthiest African Americans is compared with that of the five wealthiest European property owners (of seven) who resided in clusters adjacent to African Americans. H. L. Bennett, a fisher, owned property valued at $2,200; J. Plappirt, a German immigrant, held farm property valued at $2,000; William Conn, a steamboat captain, owned $1,500 worth of real estate; an immigrant steamboat captain, whose name was illegible, had $2,000 worth of property; and George Lewis, a tavern keeper, had real property valued at $4,000. The real property of the five richest whites who resided next to the clusters of African Americans in Brooklyn totaled $11,700. The five wealthiest African Americans' real property holdings totaled $5,520, or 47.18 percent of that held by Brooklyn's five wealthiest whites. Besides the seven, no other whites in the twenty-nine European American households bordering the African American community owned real property. The actual gap in wealth therefore narrows when all property owners are considered. Collectively, twenty African Americans owned $7,700 of real property, or 57.46 percent of the $13,400 owned by seven Euro-Americans. Like John Baltimore's holdings, George Lewis's real estate skewed these figures tremendously. Lewis owned nearly 30 percent of the value of white property holdings. Racism may explain the racial disparity in wealth, but it must be contextualized by the proletarian character of Brooklyn. The reality was that in 1850 Brooklyn was a community composed mainly of poor propertyless African American and European immigrant workers. Although their actual wealth was minimal, this reality was complicated by the high percentage of Blacks who owned real property. Afro-Brooklynites had more property and wealth than most "quasi-free" Blacks. Afro-Brooklynites had achieved a high degree of success; they had climbed far above their enslaved and destitute free Black brothers and sisters. Yet they had obtained only about 58 percent of the wealth of whites.[22]

Wealth was also gendered in favor of men. Only two of the twenty property holders (10 percent) were women (see table 2). Charlotte Retts's and Amanda King's properties were valued at $200 and $150, respectively. Together, they owned 4.54 percent of African American wealth. This was unusual. In his study of free Black communities between 1800 and 1850, Leonard P. Curry found that African American women in many cities, especially in the South, constituted "surprisingly large percentages" of African American real property holders. Orville Vernon Burton's study of Edgefield, South Carolina, revealed that in 1850 women "owned three-fourths of the land owned by African Americans." In nearby St. Louis, Missouri, only two of the sixteen African American real estate owners were women, but they constituted 12.5 percent of African American property owners. Brooklyn differed from the norm because of the large percentage of families and minute percentage of female-headed households. Furthermore, unlike the wealth of their male counterparts, Afro-Brooklynite women's wealth was also "colored." Retts and King, the only African American women who owned real estate, were both mulattoes. This was a result of the greater propensity of slaveholders to manumit women with whom they had a sexual relationship and the progeny of those encounters.[23]

Brooklyn was a small village composed largely of African American migrants and European immigrants whose wealth was negligible. But it is quite possible that the census enumerator inconsistently recorded property hold-ings or that residents, fearing that census data would be used for tax purposes, consciously devalued their wealth. Land was relatively cheap; federal land sold for $1.25 an acre, and land already under cultivation sold for between $6.00 and $14.00 an acre. In 1855, Christian Schweig purchased 75.46 acres from John Nicholas Daab in section (T1SR9W), which was next to Brooklyn (T2N R10W), for $600, or approximately $8.00 an acre. In 1841, John Baltimore purchased twenty-three town lots for $800, or $34.78 a lot. Given the num-ber of lots he purchased, Baltimore probably got a deal. Presumably, then, if lots were bought in quantity during Brooklyn's early days, a lot could be purchased for approximately $35. For building costs plus another $40, house-hold furnishings and equipment for the kitchen could be purchased. Prices had risen, but in the late 1840s, one could still buy a lot and build a small house for about $150. Yet most Brooklynites, Black or white, could not afford to purchase a lot and build a home.[24]

Family Structure and Relationships

Largely because of employment opportunities during the mid-1800s, the family structure of African Americans in Brooklyn was unusual for a Black urban population. Most Black enclaves, especially in the North, had a pre-dominantly female adult population, but in Brooklyn in 1850, adult Black men outnumbered women nearly two to one. More than 61 percent of all families were nuclear family units, while only 11 percent were female-head-ed. In Brooklyn, African American life and culture revolved around family relationships. The initial pioneers fled Missouri's slave society in family units, founded churches in the homes of leading families, and ultimately built churches based on family units. Structured on these institutions, the com-munity was remarkably stable during this era and remained so until the end of the century. Brooklyn's African American population lived overwhelm-ingly in male-headed households: a plurality resided in extended families, a significant percentage lived in two-parent nuclear families, and several Afro-Brooklynites augmented households with friends or boarders. It is necessary here to distinguish between a household and a family. Before 1947, the Cen-sus Bureau categorized living arrangements solely as households; since then, they have added family as a category. According to Paul Lammermeier, dur-ing the nineteenth century, the Census Bureau defined *household* as one per-son or more living in a separate dwelling. Both single-person homes and boardinghouses were considered households then. The term *augmented* is used here to differentiate a household of unrelated persons from one com-posed of family members, whether nuclear or extended. A *family* is defined by the Census Bureau as two or more people related by blood, marriage, or adoption who occupy the same house. Families may be nuclear, that is, composed only of immediate family members, such as fathers, mothers, and children; or they may be extended to include more distant relatives, such as in-laws, uncles, aunts, and cousins who live together.[25]

In Brooklyn, twenty-two of the thirty-six African American homes were nuclear family units (see table 3). Nuclear families represented more than 61 percent of African American family units but contained less than 48 percent of the African American population. Nuclear family homes included seventeen two-parent and child households; three single-parent homes, of which two were female-headed; and two households in which married couples resided without children. Single individuals lived alone in two homes, and two African Americans lived with their employers. Ten family units were extended. These households accounted for only 28 percent of African American families, but they contained nearly 43 percent of the African American population. In addition, two households were augmented; this household form represented only about 5.5 percent of Black families but more than 7.0 percent of the African American population. Nuclear two-parent and extended two-parent families accounted for nearly 89.0 percent of African American households and 83.9 percent of the African American population.[26]

Table 3. Household Structure of Brooklyn's African American Population, 1850

	No. of Households (%)		No. of People (%)	
Nuclear				
Two parents, children	17	(47.20)	74	(41.10)
One parent, children	3	(8.30)	8	(4.40)
Married couple, no children	2	(5.60)	4	(2.20)
	22	(61.10)	86	(47.80)
Single-person residences				
Individuals living in				
non-Black homes	2	(5.60)	2	(1.10)
Extended				
Two parents, children, and				
others	10	(27.70)	77	(42.80)
One parent, children, and				
others	0		0	
	10	(27.70)	77	(42.80)
Augmented				
Unrelated individuals	2	(5.60)	13	(7.20)
Grand totals	36	(100.00)	180	(100.00)

Source: *Population Schedules of the Seventh Census of the United States, 1850, Illinois, St. Clair County,* Roll 94, 110–27.

Because many members of this community took in extended family members, friends, or lodgers, the median size of nuclear families is not an accurate reflection of Afro-American household size. The median family size of Afro-Brooklynites in 1850 was 3.90, but the average household size was 4.94, a difference of 1.04. The tradition of adoptive kinship among African Americans was an Africanism, a survival of African cultures; yet the reasons this practice survived are rooted in the material conditions of slavery and subsequent racial oppression. In Brooklyn, the conditions favoring the tradition of adoptive kinship were the community's support for runaways and a large percentage of married couples. Taking in fugitives and offering a safe haven for African American development were the basic reasons for the community's founding. Married couples were better situated financially to house relatives and others. These conditions established the foundation on which the African American tradition of adaptive extended kinship networks flourished.[27]

Adoptive kinship was just one Africanism that survived among Afro-Brooklynites. The family, as the central social institution, was the repository of other African cultural traditions, such as naming practices. The centrality of family, especially the father's role, was underscored by the naming practices of Afro-Brooklyn families. Thirty-three Afro-Brooklyn families had children in residence. In six instances, children were named after one of their parents, and at least four children were named after other relatives. According to the 1850 census, ten of thirty-three families with children (30.3 percent) named at least one child after a relative, usually the father. Five were given their father's names, three were named after uncles, one was named after a mother, and one was given an aunt's name. According to Herbert Gutman, slave naming practices (and Brooklyn was a community composed of many self-liberated slaves) represented both a continuation of African patterns and an oppositional tactic in a society determined to destroy African American familial ties. For Gutman, the frequency with which slave children were named after uncles and aunts implied the continuity of African kinship obligations. Gutman contended that the frequent naming of sons after their fathers, together with the infrequent naming of daughters after their mothers, reflected (1) the patriarchal structure of the slave family; and (2) an attempt to solidify familial ties since fathers were "more likely to be separated from their children than [were] mothers." The first represented a carry-over from African societies, and the second related to the material conditions of enslavement.[28]

The percentage of female-headed households was significantly lower in Brooklyn than in most other communities. Of thirty-six family units, only four (11.1 percent) were headed by women in Brooklyn. Paul J. Lammermeier compared the family structure of African American families in seven Ohio Valley towns and cities between 1850 and 1880. Lammermeier's study is particularly valuable for this work because the four smaller communities of Steubenville, Wheeling, Marietta, and Portsmouth in 1850 had Black populations similar in size to Brooklyn's. Collectively, female-headed households made up 18.8 percent of African American families in the towns Lammermeier studied. The percentage of female-headed Black families generally grew as the Black population increased. The larger cities of Pittsburgh, Pennsylvania; Louisville, Kentucky; and Cincinnati, Ohio, had female-headed African American households of 17.0, 28.0, and 37.7 percent, respectively. Orville Vernon Burton's study of Edgefield, South Carolina, found that in 1850, women headed nearly 66.0 percent of the sixty-two free African American households. In a study of African American clusters in Cincinnati in 1850, Taylor and Dula found that 30.0 percent of households were headed by women.[29]

Interestingly, all of the women who headed households except one were mulattoes. The four women were Sarah Woodruff, Amanda King, Tina Fitts, and Charlotte Retts. Woodruff was a thirty-year-old mother of two small children. The thirty-four-year-old King was also a mother of two sons. Fitts, a sixteen-year-old lived alone. Retts's household consisted of her son, who was a boat worker, and his family. Surprisingly, the tendency of urban free Black families to be female-headed did not manifest itself in a disproportionately larger female population in Brooklyn, though it did among the mulattoes. Brooklyn was unusual in that most Afro-Brooklynites were blacks and males. In the smaller towns in Lammermeier's study, the ratio of African American men to women was 1:1.24. Brooklyn, however, had an unusual male to female ratio of 1.22:1. This situation was even more skewed among the adult population. The male to female ratio for adult Afro-Brooklynites was 1.64:1.[30]

Why was Brooklyn so radically different from most other urban Black communities? Curry posited that the peculiar gender structure of urban free African Americans resulted from (1) manumission practices that favored women, (2) better employment opportunities for African American women, and (3) a higher mortality rate for African American males. A racist social system that was particularly discriminatory against African American men, however, was the critical factor that skewed the structure of African American urban populations toward a preponderance of women. Lack of employment opportunities for Afro-American men and the corresponding availability of opportunities, albeit as domestics in white homes, for African American women in cities converged to produce a gendered population with a high percentage of female-headed households. This was the national trend, but Brooklyn was different. In the oldest Black town, 91.5 percent of African American men were employed (see table 1). Black men worked on the river as boat hands and on the docks and railroads as laborers. Furthermore, because Brooklyn was a predominately Black town, African Americans had better opportunities to become independent artisans, farmers, and merchants than did Blacks in many other communities.[31]

Education

During the late 1840s, at least one child of African ancestry attended the Brooklyn district school for a short time. The experience of James Henry Magee offers a rare glimpse into a Black child's struggle to obtain an education in the metro-east region during the antebellum era. Magee became perhaps the first African American to teach in an Illinois public school, he was ordained a Baptist minister by the Wood River Colored Baptist Association in August of 1863, and he was a notable leader in postbellum Illinois. He described his educational experiences in his autobiography, *Night of Affliction and Morning of Recovery*. As a child, Magee resided on a farm in the southern part of Madison County near the St. Clair County line. He began his education in the Merryweather district school, and after it closed he attended a school for "Blacks," run by Mrs. Daniel Barton. This school was on his parent's farm and was attended by his whole family. Later, he was inexplicably sent to the Brooklyn district school. Reflecting on his experiences there, he wrote, "I was next sent to the Brooklyn district school, to which I went for some considerable time. At length prejudice began to show itself by the parents of some children, which was communicated to the trustees. Many of the parents of the children were perfectly willing that I should go to school with their children, but there were others who thought that their children were too good to go to the same school with a colored person. The trustees thought it best, for peace sake, to have my parents withdraw me from the school." Continuing with his story, Magee explained how another opportunity for education arose: "A school was opened immediately after this by a white lady exclusively for the benefit of colored children. I went to this school for six months after which I was detained at home to attend to duties connected with the farm."[32]

Magee's account provides a number of insights into the schooling experiences of Afro-Illinoisans. One, school districts were inconsistent in enforcing the exclusionary laws. It seems that at least sometimes public officials implemented school segregation laws only when white citizens objected to the inclusion of Blacks. Magee's experience in the Merryweather and Brooklyn school districts demonstrates how school districts separated by only a few miles could respond differently to the Black presence. Second, African Americans despite their age sought to transcend the limits imposed on them by illiteracy. Third, some whites aided African Americans in obtaining an education. Fourth, educated Blacks, such as Mrs. Daniel Barton, were indispensable in obtaining an education. I suspect that Mrs. Barton was an African American because Magee identifies the race of the woman who taught him after he was excluded from the school in Brooklyn, but he saw no need to provide a racial designation for Mrs. Barton. Perhaps this was part of the effort by the Wood River Baptist Association to provide schooling for Blacks in the Madison County area. It may have been the failure of efforts like this that drove them to press the 1853 Illinois Black Convention for a statewide solution to the problem of taxation without participation. (The Black state conventions were statewide meetings of African American leaders who framed an agenda for their betterment. They were part of the national Black convention movement.) Finally, since Magee does not mention that any other Black children attended the Brooklyn district school, it is reasonable to assume that he was the only one.

During the 1849 school year, only four (8.51 percent) of forty-seven school-age (5–17) Afro-Brooklyn children attended school. They were Olive Sullivan, the eleven-year-old daughter of Philip and Josephine Sullivan; Nancy Cole, the eleven-year-old daughter of the Reverend Israel Cole; and Elizabeth and Julia Boyd, the seven and five-year-old daughters of James and Louisa Boyd. It is not clear whether gender was a determining factor, but all of the Afro-Brooklynites who attended school were girls. Olive Sullivan had an eight-year-old sister, Julia, who was not sent to school. John, Nancy Cole's six-year-old brother, also was not enrolled in school. It appears that they schooled the oldest child. The Boyds, however, also enrolled Julia, their second-oldest child in school. School attendance was definitely connected to property ownership. All of the families whose children attended school were propertied. The Boyds and Sullivans held property worth $1,000, and the Coles had $150 worth of property. Nevertheless, property ownership alone does not explain who went to school and who did not. The Baltimores and Andersons had school-age children, yet none of them attended school in the year before the census. Perhaps color was a factor. Olive Sullivan was listed as a "mulatto," but Nancy Cole was not. The two Boyd girls were listed as black, following the categorization of their mother, Louisa, although James, their father, was a mulatto. Color, however, does not appear to have been a factor. Like James Henry Magee, these children must have attended a predominately white school, if not in Brooklyn then in another district.[33]

In 1855, the Illinois General Assembly passed an act that on the surface aided African Americans' quest for an education. Section 84 of the act mandated local school boards to return to African Americans the amount of taxes they paid into the public education fund: "*Schools of Persons of Color.* In townships in which there shall be persons of color, the board of education shall allow such persons a portion of the school fund, equal to the amount of taxes collected for school purposes from such persons of color in their respective townships."[34] This act was designed to supplement the voluntarism advocated by the Wood River Baptist Association and the Illinois Black Convention. The monies returned were, of course, meager and even when added to the funds raised by Blacks were inadequate to fund African Americans' education. It appears that in only two instances were the available funds even collected by Blacks.[35]

Blacks, Mulattoes, and Leadership in Brooklyn's African American Population

Scholars long ago pointed out the disproportionate percentage of mulattoes among the nation's free African American population and have recently begun to trace the uneven pattern of mulattoes' status over time and across space. John Blassingame claimed that "90 percent of all blacks were slaves and 70 percent of all mulattoes were freemen." The preliminary data confirm the traditional view that mulattoes fared, in the main, better than darker African Americans did. Evidence also proves that mulattoes' socioeconomic status slid gradually but persistently during the nineteenth century. Mulattoes also experienced "quasi-freedom" differently by region. However, their situations cannot be reduced to the simple notion that their status worsened the further south they lived. The different form of partial liberty experienced in each region was far more complex than that. Overall, scholars agree that the further north, the more political and social rights free African Americans, especially mulattoes, could exercise. In the South, especially the lower South, business opportunities were greater. Among the push and pull factors that individuals consider in deciding whether to migrate are economic opportunities, and many southern free Blacks valued economic prosperity over the limited political and social rights afforded them in the North.[36]

Color conveyed real occupational, material, social, and psychological advantages in a racist society. The "mulatto question" is the gray area that best exposes the ideological character of racial designations. Perhaps even more than the categories "black" and "white," the "mulatto" category shows that "race" is predominantly a social construction. Race, as Michael Omi and Howard Winant revealed, is a highly unstable category. Census takers' shifting designations of individuals as "mulattoes" vividly underscore the fluidity of color classifications. For instance, Theodore Hershberg and Henry Williams found that a third of African Americans changed color from census to census. More important, this change was connected with occupation. Mulattoes who experienced occupational downgrading were also "downgraded" in terms of color; they were "reduced" to black in later censuses. Conversely, some blacks who improved their occupations, and thus their social status, lightened over time. The prevalence of this practice suggests that economic position signified "race" and "color." Despite the arbitrariness of these categories, they represent real social relations and can therefore help explain much about Black Brooklyn's internal dynamics and external relations.[37]

Mulattoes composed more than 41.0 percent of Brooklyn's African American population. This percentage is greater than the national figure of 36.7 percent for free Black people, the northern percentage of 28.9 percent, the upper South figure of 38.5 percent, and the Missouri percentage of 35.6 percent. The really noticeable difference was the more than 10 percent difference between the percentage of mulattoes in Brooklyn's African American population and the percentage of mulattoes among free Blacks in the North. The high percentage of mulattoes in Brooklyn is partially explained by the town's proximity to the slave state of Missouri, especially to the sizable slave and free Black populations in St. Louis.[38]

Priscilla Baltimore was one of several settlers who had been enslaved in St. Louis, and like many urban slaves and a disproportionate percentage of free Blacks, she was a mulatto. Her life is a lens through which we can observe the advantages that urban slaves and mulattoes enjoyed over their fellow bondspeople. She was permitted extraordinary freedom of movement, even for an urban slave. She was either hired out or allowed to hire her own time. As noted previously, she routinely gathered slaves in the area together for religious services and once, with authorization, took a group of slaves into Illinois for a camp meeting. Of course, these actions cannot be explained simply by whites' tendency to favor mulattoes. Leaving the plantation was a privilege reserved for a minuscule number of slaves.[39]

By 1850, the emerging economy of the metro-east region was tied to the transport of goods across the river to St. Louis. Brooklyn, like the other towns in the region, was economically bound to the border port city. This is accented by the large percentage of Black and white men who worked on the river. Further, the region was populated by southern migrants and in most respects was southern in social values. Brooklyn, unlike Cincinnati and other border river cities, was too small to develop extensive color segregation among African Americans, but there is no evidence of even clustering among mulattoes in Brooklyn. According to the 1850 census, mulattoes never dwelt in three consecutive houses. In fact, mulatto families lived next to each other in only two instances. While they did not practice residential segregation, in other facets of social life, such as marriage, Brooklyn mulattoes conformed to national patterns of intracolor preference. Intercolor marriages generally involved darker men and lighter women. In Brooklyn, only three marriages occurred between mulattoes and blacks, of which only one was between a mulatto man and a black woman. Race prejudice between whites and Blacks became color prejudice among Afro-Americans and manifested itself in a predilection for lighter women. It is therefore not surprising that the community's wealthiest African American, John Baltimore, a black man, married a mulatto, the revered Mother Baltimore. It also appears that mulattoes preferred intracolor unions and associations. John Blassingame posited that whites' attitudes toward color had a "profound effect on the way Negroes viewed themselves." He argued that acceptance of white beliefs about race led many mulattoes to draw the color line in relationships with blacks and prompted some to seek to pass into the white world. The other side of this was the black person who applied the same criteria toward light-skinned African Americans and believed that they enhanced their position by marrying light.[40]

Occupationally, the story was complex. Seven of the fifteen mulatto men (46.66 percent) held jobs above the unskilled labor category in 1850, compared with thirteen of the thirty-two black men (40.62 percent). But mulattoes held five out of nine (55 percent) of the skilled positions occupied by African American men, while they composed only 20 percent of the farmers and ministers in 1850. Put more graphically, both barbers, two of the three carpenters, and the only brickmason in Brooklyn were mulattoes (see table 1). As James O. Horton claimed, this reflected the tendency of mulattoes to have been skilled slaves and thus more likely to have been hired out. They were therefore better able to purchase their freedom and better equipped to make a living once they were free. Furthermore, though the ministry, dominated by blacks in Brooklyn, was a prestigious profession, it did not translate into higher income. Mulatto males consequently did fare slightly better than black men economically.[41]

The four Boyd brothers, three mulattoes and one black, illustrate this proposition. The three mulattoes, James, Theo, and Hiram Boyd, were all artisans; Bird, the lone black was an African Methodist Episcopal minister. He was also the only brother who was propertyless. Bird and his wife resided with his brother James. Thirty-five-year-old James was a barber who owned real estate valued at $1,000. James was also a small businessperson who owned other properties besides his barber shop. Twenty-nine-year-old Theo was a brickmason who owned $250 worth of real property. Hiram, the youngest brother at twenty-three, was a barber and was probably employed by his older brother James. Hiram's property was valued as $150. What factors accounted for the discrepancy between Bird Boyd's life fortunes and those of his three younger brothers? It is possible that Bird Boyd was a recent migrant to Brooklyn. This could account for his lack of property ownership. Yet how do we explain the differences in the occupational and economic situations among the four Boyd brothers? Possibly, Bird Boyd lacked initiative and intelligence and was less frugal than his three brothers. Nevertheless, it is instructive that he was the only Boyd brother without a skilled trade. It seems more logical that his economic status resulted from his not receiving training in a skill

while his brothers had. It is quite likely that this crucial life decision was determined by parentage and color. While the example of the Boyd brothers is
not conclusive, it does conform to the national pattern of mulatto dominance
of the skilled trades among African Americans.[42]

In general, Afro-American males desirous of prestige and wealth found the
ministry the one profession open to them; it is therefore not surprising that
lacking a trade, Bird Boyd selected the ministry as his vocation. It is amazing, however, that in Brooklyn only one minister was a mulatto. Baker Brown,
a forty-four-year-old from Kentucky, was the only mulatto among five men
who reported their occupations as ministers. This is startling since all four
cited their denominational affiliation as Methodist. The only Methodist
church in Brooklyn was the African Methodist Episcopal Church, later called
Quinn Chapel. The AME Church, created by free African Americans in 1787,
had a disproportionate percentage of mulattoes, especially among its ministry, during the antebellum period. The prevalence and prominence of
mulattoes in Quinn Chapel's history indicate that it remained the church of
choice among Brooklyn's mulattoes until the late nineteenth century.[43]

The church was the primary institution from which antebellum African
American leaders emerged, but it was not the only one. The basis of the
church's power in the African American community may have been as much
a reflection of its autonomy from white control as its religiosity. Like ministers, independent businesspeople often led local African American enclaves.
John Jones is one of the best examples of secular African American leadership. A Chicago mulatto tailor, Jones had been tricked into slavery as a youth
and consequently dedicated his life to the abolition of slavery and the repeal
of the Black Laws in Illinois. In Brooklyn, John Baltimore represented this
type of secular leadership. Baltimore was the wealthiest and largest African
American property owner. The oldest community institution, Quinn Chapel,
of which he was a steward, was founded in his home. James Boyd, one of
Brooklyn's wealthiest and most influential mulattoes, exercised a similar
secular-based leadership.[44]

Boyd operated the only barber shop in town, and because of his success
as an artisan and entrepreneur, he played an important role in community
affairs. Boyd is the only mulatto besides Mother Baltimore who figured prom-
inently in the community's antebellum folklore. His shop, like old and modern African American barber shops, was probably a place where African
American men held informal discussions on the burning issues of the day.
Community folklore speaks positively of him. By 1860, James Boyd had become a farmer. The written record reveals that he was part of the campaign
for school desegregation in 1875. His participation in the struggle for mixed
schools culminated in his election to the school board. In 1875, Boyd was the
only mulatto among three African Americans elected to the three-person
board of education.

Mulattoes did not dominate Afro-Brooklyn as they did most African American urban enclaves. Black dominance of such middle-class occupations as the ministry and farming served to offset mulatto preeminence in the skilled trades. For instance, in 1850, four out of five ministers and five out of six African American farmers were classified as black (see table 1). Twelve out of twenty African American property holders were designated as black. The twelve blacks (eleven men and one woman) constituted 60 percent of the African American owners of real property, while the eight mulattoes (seven men and one woman) constituted only 40 percent (see table 2). Mulattoes composed 41 percent of Afro-Brooklynites but owned only $3,100 of $7,700 (40.26 percent) of the African American community's wealth. Mulattoes' share of home ownership and wealth was slightly less than their proportion in the African American community. The occupational advantage enjoyed by mulattoes was therefore not translated into a financial edge or social privilege.[45]

It is possible that lightness of color was a desirable asset among African Americans in Brooklyn, as it was nationally in the nineteenth century, but it appears that in Brooklyn leadership derived from one's community activism—primarily from participation in the church and the antislavery crusade—and from one's personal wealth more than from such ascribed traits as skin color. Mulattoes had an edge in occupational status but not in wealth or in social leadership positions. During Afro-Brooklyn's formative years, the community was led by one woman and five men: Priscilla Baltimore, John Baltimore, the Reverend John Richard Anderson, the Reverend Jordan Winston Early, James Boyd, and the martyred abolitionist Nicholas Carper. Priscilla Baltimore and James Boyd were the only mulattoes who were significant actors in the development of Afro-Brooklyn during this period.

Conclusion

Between 1837 and 1865, Brooklyn was transformed from an unplatted all-black freedom village into an unincorporated biracial town. Although Afro-Brooklynites were the numerical majority from the community's inception, they were not part of the polity; denied political and legal rights, they were governed by an extralegal set of repressive exclusionary codes known as the Illinois Black Laws. Outside the protection of the law, they were, in a word, outlaws. Education was the main sphere of racial conflict. Here whites enforced a color bar that Blacks resented and later resisted. A few African Americans went to school for a brief time, but for the most part African Americans were refused entrance in the halls of education. Nevertheless, even when the color line was drawn in schooling, it was an uneven and porous barrier rather than a solid, impenetrable one. African Americans reorganized their churches to provide the education denied them by the public schools.

Black males worked mainly as roustabouts on the river and as common laborers in the surrounding predominately white towns, yet unlike many free Blacks in other towns, they were employed. Only two of the forty-seven men older than twenty-one were unemployed. Twenty African Americans owned property, although only two women were included in this number. Afro-Brooklynites, like their European immigrant counterparts, were impoverished. Though 55 percent of families owned real estate collectively, they owned on average only $213 worth of real property. Furthermore, wealth was disproportionately held by the founding families, many of whom were artisans. A few Afro-Brooklynite artisans started businesses, but they were limited mainly to small enterprises catering to their race, such as barbershops.

During this stage, Afro-Brooklynites fortified their central institutions, the family and the Brooklyn AME and Antioch Baptist churches. The male to female ratio was the reverse of the national norm for free Black populations. Men greatly outnumbered women in Brooklyn. This drastically skewed gender ratio served to create conditions in which almost all adult African American women were married, and more than 90 percent of Blacks lived in either nuclear or extended families. Few Afro-Brooklynites resided alone, and very few female-headed households existed. The family structure contributed to social harmony. The extended family was functional in a variety of ways: it helped cement familial and community bonds; it eased financial burdens for many families; and it bred a sense of security, which was particularly important given their proximity to slave territory and the hostility of many whites in St. Clair County. Building on family, by 1850, Afro-Brooklynites had established their core social institutions, had developed a social value system that stressed freedom and mutual assistance, had purchased property, and were prepared to meet the challenge of citizenship. However, it would be another twenty years before they acquired the franchise and another thirty-six years before they would gain majority rule in Brooklyn.

Separation was maintained in social institutions. Blacks worshiped together, as did whites, and both groups probably preferred it that way. Brooklyn had a high degree of racial segregation for a mid-nineteenth-century town. Racial segregation combined with the town's small population and limited spatial boundaries to create an environment in which most Afro-Brooklynites knew each other. These structural factors were reinforced by Black Brooklynites' efforts at self-development. Afro-Brooklynites expressed their own agency by constructing an extended and augmented family structure built on African cultural survivals and by making the *political decision* to create their community as a haven for fugitives fleeing enslavement. The regularity of face-to-face interactions among Afro-Brooklynites was reinforced by structural factors and Afro-Brooklynites' effort to generate *dense* social relations among themselves. Racial clusters, occupational discrimination, culture, family structure, and institutional networks bound Afro-Brooklynites in a web of multiple relationships that fortified their objective common interests. This sense of mutuality was also conditioned by systematic racial oppression. Racism mitigated class, color, and even gender differences among Afro-Brooklynites. Moreover, a freedom ethos expressed the desirability of African Americans' uniting across these fault lines.

PART 2

The Transition to Black Power: Anticolonialism and the Development of Black Political Power, 1870–1906

3. From Outlaws to Lawmakers, 1870–80

THE END OF THE Civil War and the passage of the Thirteenth, Fourteenth, and Fifteenth amendments established the legal foundation for African Americans to participate as full-fledged American citizens. In Illinois, repealing the infamous Black Laws was also necessary before African Americans could join the polity. As citizens, Blacks probably initiated the drive to incorporate Brooklyn as a village under the state's incorporation act. The transition from "outlaws" to lawmakers facilitated the social and the political transformation of the African American community.

During the antebellum era, Brooklyn had been a haven for fugitives and free Blacks fleeing the bordering slave states of Missouri, Tennessee, and Kentucky. During the postwar years, newly freed persons who wished to leave the South streamed into Brooklyn, bolstering its Black population. In 1870, nearly 45 percent of the 119 Black adults living in Brooklyn came from these three former slave states (see table 4). Nearly 27 percent came from Missouri alone. Only sixteen African American adults (13 percent) were born in Illinois, including only six heads of households, while fifteen heads of households were born in Virginia, nine in Missouri, and six each in Kentucky and North Carolina. By 1880, 93 Afro-Brooklynites (43 percent) had been born in the three contiguous former slave states and 48 (22 percent) in the states of the Deep South, compared with only 29 (less than 14 percent) in Illinois (see table 5). Twenty-one Black heads of households had been born in Tennessee, ten in Kentucky, nine in Virginia, eight in Missouri, and seven in Mississippi. Initially these southern migrants pursued their dreams of land ownership, and some flourished briefly as independent farmers. By 1880, however, they were being forced from the farms into the factories of the emerging industrial economy. Afro-Brooklynites were pulled into industri-

Table 4. Place of Birth of Adult Afro-Brooklynites, 1870

	Men	Women	Total
Deep South			
Alabama	5	2	7
Arkansas	2	0	2
Louisiana	3	5	8
	10	7	17
Upper South			
North Carolina	6	5	11
Virginia	10	9	19
	16	14	30
Contiguous slave states			
Kentucky	4	8	12
Missouri	14	18	32
Tennessee	4	5	9
	22	31	53
Old Northeast			
Pennsylvania	0	2	2
Illinois	8	8	16
Unknown	0	1	1
Grand totals	56	63	119

Source: Population Schedules of the Ninth Census of the United States, 1870, Illinois, St. Clair County, Roll 280, 620–25.

al jobs, partly because they were the most marginal members of society and partly because few were landowners, a legacy of their impoverished and former slave status. In many ways, at least during this period, their transformation from peasants to proletarians was an advance and represented, if not a liberating experience, at least a less repressive one.[1]

Their growing population and changing production relations, along with their new political status, established the groundwork for a reconstruction of their basic social structure. Lured by the dream of land ownership or the hope of industrial employment, Blacks flowed into Brooklyn. As the town became darker, it witnessed a corresponding increase in residential racial segregation. Proletarianization incrementally reversed male to female ratios during this period, thus transforming established patterns of family organization. Industrial occupations, freedom, and citizenship created a social environment that encouraged African Americans to expand and develop their institutions and cultural life. Blacks readily took advantage of these opportunities by organizing formal fraternal and community organizations and expanding existing churches and building new ones.[2]

Table 5. Place of Birth of Adult Afro-Brooklynites, 1880

	Men	Women	Total
Outside United States			
Africa	1	0	1
Deep South			
Georgia	2	1	3
Louisiana	2	7	9
Mississippi	11	17	28
South Carolina	1	1	2
Alabama	3	3	6
	19	29	48
Upper South			
Maryland	0	1	1
North Carolina	5	2	7
Virginia	9	9	18
Arkansas	3	1	4
	17	13	30
Contiguous southern states			
Kentucky	16	3	19
Missouri	14	18	32
Tennessee	21	21	42
	51	42	93
Northern and northwestern states			
Indiana	0	2	2
Iowa	0	1	1
Ohio	2	1	3
	2	4	6
Illinois	15	14	29
Unknown	6	5	11
Grand totals	111	107	218

Source: Population Schedules of the Tenth Census of the United States, 1880, Illinois, St. Clair County, Roll 246, 19–24.

A new and different type of leadership emerged from these rapidly changing social conditions. As electoral politics became possible, politicians replaced ministers as the leaders of the Black community. The men who led Black Brooklynites inspired them to participate in national and statewide efforts for Afro-American advancement and in ceremonies honoring significant personages and events in African American history. These new leaders also initiated a struggle against segregated schools. The 1876 campaign for "mixed" schools unveiled white racism and correspondingly revealed the political possibilities for mobilizing the Afro-American population to oppose white supremacy.

Becoming Citizens, 1865–70

Between 1865 and 1870, African Americans in Illinois were transformed from "outlaws" into lawmakers. In the main, Blacks became citizens and officeholders through the efforts of African Americans and radical Republicans on the national level, but their resistance to the Illinois Black Laws contributed enormously to this process. Black agency, expressed mainly through the Black convention movement, led to their repeal in 1865. This was a tremendous accomplishment and evidence of growing Black political strength. The Black convention movement began as local meetings around 1817 and became a national movement in 1830. The first national meeting was held in Philadelphia, in large part a response to the Cincinnati race riot of 1829. The convention movement developed an agenda for common action by quasi-free Blacks.

The political leaders in Lincoln's home state had continued to support southern slavery and the denial of civil rights to African Americans during the war. Illinois was the first state to ratify a proposed constitutional amendment that would have preserved slavery. The amendment failed, but, as the historian Roger D. Bridges commented, Illinois legislators' support for it revealed their racial antipathy. Also, in the midst of the sectional conflict, a constitutional convention approved a proposal that would have incorporated the essential aspects of the state's Black Laws in the new Illinois constitution. The new constitution was rejected, but not because of its anti-Black provisions.[3]

During the last three years of the war, the attitudes of Illinois General Assembly members changed significantly. With Black refugees seeking better opportunities, Illinois legislators prepared to repeal the state's Black code. After much tribulation, on 24 January and 4 February 1865, the Illinois Senate and House of Representatives voted to repeal the Black Laws. On 7 February the governor signed the bill, thus allowing Blacks unqualified entrance into the state and access to the courts. Nevertheless, the legislators did not grant Blacks the franchise, the right to sit on juries, or the right to attend public schools. Those struggles would continue into the 1870s.

Governor John Palmer committed himself to support suffrage, and on virtually a straight party vote, the General Assembly ratified the Fifteenth Amendment on 27 March 1869. At the upcoming state constitutional convention, the delegates would have the task of converting a negative federal proscription into positive state law. The delegates produced a document without reference to race, but this "color-blind" approach would prove controversial. Regarding the franchise, the new state constitution read:

> Every person having resided in this State one year, in the county ninety days, and in the election district thirty days next preceding any election therein, who

was an elector in this state on the first day of April, in the year of our Lord one thousand eight hundred and forty-eight, or obtained a certificate of naturalization before any court of record in this state prior to the first day of January, in the year of our Lord one thousand eight hundred and seventy, or who shall be a male citizen of the United States, above the age of twenty-one years, shall be entitled to vote at such election.[4]

Ratification of the Fifteenth Amendment granted African Americans the right to vote. The Illinois legislature now accorded African Americans full civil rights; Blacks could finally serve on juries, join the militia, or attend schools. African Americans exercised their newly obtained franchise rights for the first time in the 1870 Illinois general election. St. Clair County African Americans, like their counterparts nationally, naturally voted Republican.

The provision on education, section 1, article 8, read, "The General Assembly shall provide a through and efficient system of free schools, whereby all children of this State may receive a good common school education." This clause must be considered ambiguous at best and a subtle continuation of African American exclusion at worst. Robert McCaul posits that the ambiguity of the expression "all children" opened the door for a struggle over interpretation. Since historically the adjective "white" had modified the phrase "all children," for this article to affirm African Americans' access to the public school system, it would have had to state "all children regardless of race, creed, or color" were to "receive a good common school education." The 1870s saw pitched battles around this question. In Brooklyn, public school integration would continue to represent a terrain of struggle through the middle 1890s.[5]

The Incorporation of Brooklyn into the Metro-East's Political Economy

The General Assembly passed the Cities and Villages Act of 1872 that provided for the establishment of municipalities in Illinois. This statute allowed an unincorporated community with at least one hundred people who lived in an area of two square miles or less and at least one mile from any other municipality to hold an incorporation election. On 30 July 1873, a year after the Cities and Villages Act was passed and three years after Afro-Americans obtained the franchise, the village of Brooklyn voted to incorporate.[6] The incorporation record reads:

In the matter of the incorporation　}　August 2, 1873.
of the village of Brooklyn　}　Returns of election
On the eighth day of July 1873, a petition was filed to the County Judge signed by forty legal voters for the incorporation of the platted town of Brooklyn a

village, under the laws of the state of Illinois and an election was ordered by the County Judge to be held in the said town of Brooklyn as a village, for or against the incorporation of said Brooklyn as a village on the 30th of July 1873 as appears in the county record. And now the returns of said election having been made to the County Judge, he called to his assistance two Justices of the Peace, signs Martin Medert and Henry R. Challenor, to canvass said returns, the result of which was "For village organization" Sixty-six votes, "Against Village organization" none.

Which is by the court, ordered to be entered of record.

State of Illinois   }
St. Clair County   }   I, Geo. K. Thomas Clerk of the County Court, do hereby certify that the forgoing is a true and correct copy of the original as appears in my office, in Probate Record "I," page 204. In witness thereof, I have here unto set my hand and official seal, this 23rd day of September, 1901.

Geo. K. Thomas Clerk
By L. Rhers Dpy

Filed for Record Sept. 23, 1901 at 1 O'clock P.M.[7]

It is unclear whether there was a racial dimension to the move to gain self-government, but it is interesting that the movement for self-government occurred less than three years after African Americans gained the right to vote. According to the 1870 census, of the ninety-two male citizens age twenty-one or older, fifty-four were African Americans, and only thirty-eight were Euro-Americans. The Black majority, historically excluded from the political process, no doubt craved the opportunity for majority rule. Roughly 44 percent of the eligible electorate signed the petition for a village charter. Sixty-six (72 percent) of the ninety-two eligible voters voted unanimously to incorporate as a village. Twenty-six men (28 percent of the electorate) were either opposed or apathetic since they did not vote.[8]

The community was probably not fragmented by race on the incorporation issue. First, the newspapers eagerly reported racial discord, and none mentioned racial conflict in Brooklyn. Second, Brooklyn's incorporation was probably designed to gain jurisdiction over the St. Louis National Stock Yards. Acquisition of the stockyards was, of course, unrealistic. After the St. Louis Union Stock Yards relocated to St. Louis, Missouri, in the 1860s, John Bowman, the entrepreneurial mayor of East St. Louis began a campaign to attract a new meat-packing operation to the east side. In 1871, when it was clear that the Eads Bridge would be erected, Bowman convinced a consortium of primarily eastern railroad capitalists, led by the meat-packer magnate Nelson Morris, to invest more than $1.6 million to build the St. Louis National Stock Yards. The Morris group built pens and sheds for 55,000 cattle and hogs on a 656-acre site. In exchange for the stockyards' locating "in" East St. Louis,

Bowman agreed the city of East St. Louis would "make no claim in the stock-yard area" and would supply the yards with municipal services, such as fire protection. For their part, the packers were required "to build in the city a hotel, office building and other business facilities." The investors complied by building a two-story operations center with telegraph communications and the Allerton House, a first-class five-story hotel, and they granted Mayor Bowman a seat on the board of directors of the St. Louis National Stock Yards Company. Obviously, Brooklyn was unable to acquire tax rights to so powerful an entity that did not want to pay municipal taxes. Consequently, the St. Louis National Stock Yards, one of the world's largest stockyards and Brooklyn's major employer, was in neither East St. Louis nor Brooklyn, but between them and beyond either's jurisdiction. National City was incorporated in 1907, but it never developed much of a residential base and remained essentially a site on which the St. Louis National Stock Yards and its corporations operated.[9]

For the most part, Brooklyn's efforts at economic development, like its attempt to obtain the stockyards, ended in failure. Initially Brooklyn's future appeared promising. From its platting, Brooklyn shared the metro-east region's *strategic* advantage of being located along the Mississippi River and across from St. Louis. Brooklyn was situated in the heart of a thriving agricultural region and near a large deposit of bituminous coal. By 1870, St. Clair County was third among Illinois counties, producing $7 million in gross value of industrial product. Moreover, St. Clair County led the state in tons of coal produced from 1870 to 1898. "Coal was mined at virtually every entrance to the village," according to Newton Bateman and Paul Selby. Brooklyn's locational benefits, such as cheap land, access to river and railroad transportation networks, and cheap fuel and electric power, were transformed into *economic* advantages. When combined with a growing cheap labor force, these factors should have made Brooklyn very attractive to industrialists. For instance, although not incorporated until 1873, the town's economic infrastructure developed much earlier. During the 1850s, Brooklyn obtained railway service. Though this did not offset the loss of the Reynold's group line in 1837, it did mitigate it. Railroad and coal companies owned large sections of land in the town. During the 1850s, the Illinois Coal Company was a major real estate holder in Brooklyn. In 1851, the Illinois Coal Company built a railroad that connected Caseyville to Brooklyn, from which coal was shipped daily to St. Louis. In 1854, the St. Louis, Alton, and Terre Haute Railroad Company opened a line from Illinoistown, which would soon become East St. Louis, to Belleville that ran through Brooklyn. In 1857 and 1858, the Belleville and Illinois Railroad obtained thirty-nine lots running through Brooklyn. The Brooklyn Ferry Company began its attempt to break Wiggins Ferry Company's monopoly of cargo transport across the river in 1865. In 1867, the General Assembly approved the building of another road to Brooklyn, this time from East St. Louis. In 1873, in anticipation of an increased market because of the opening of the National Stock Yards, the St. Louis, Alton, and Terre Haute Railroad Company extended its rail line to Duquoin, Illinois, where it merged with the Illinois Central and ran onto Cairo, Illinois. Much of the railroad activity was designed to facilitate shipments of coal and agricultural products to St. Louis.[10]

Despite its strategic and economic advantages, Brooklyn did not attract a major industrial plant. The town's attributes were offset by factors of political economy and politics. The creation of the St. Louis National Stock Yards is a prime example of how capitalists used politics to their benefit. The agreement between the Nelson Morris–led investors and Mayor Bowman placed the stockyards beyond the jurisdiction of the city of East St. Louis but made the city responsible for providing services to them. Brooklyn was also negatively affected by the capitalists' preference for building their own corporate-controlled industrial suburbs instead of locating in existing towns. Because this preference was arbitrarily applied in the metro-east, it masked racial factors. Race and racism largely explain Brooklyn's failure to attract major industries, and the lack of an industrial base circumscribed the town's development.

Nevertheless, at its incorporation Brooklyn was better situated than the Black towns in the West and the South. Unlike such Black towns as Nicodemus, Kansas; Boley, Oklahoma; and Mound Bayou, Mississippi, Brooklyn was tied into its region's infrastructure and was readily accessible by road, rail, and waterway. Brooklyn thus grew during the 1870s, while other Black towns, such as Nicodemus, Kansas, began to decline. Most African American towns, like Nicodemus, were isolated agricultural outlets servicing small Black farmers. In contrast, Brooklyn developed in an industrializing zone and therefore not only was accessible but also was in a prime developing area. This, of course, could cut both ways. Isolation could lead to underdevelopment or stagnation and eventual decay, as it did with most of the sixty Black towns in the West. But incorporation into a wider industrial economy as simply a supplier of cheap labor could lead to dependency and eventual ruination. The prospects of success for any Black town were quite dismal, yet of the two options—isolation or incorporation—the latter at least offered some opportunity for circumscribed development.

During the period from 1875 to 1890, the metro-east emerged as a major industrial area, mirroring the growth of St. Louis's economy. The meat-packing industry was the dominant industry on the Illinois side, employing 1,200 by 1907, and the meat-packers quickly became Brooklyn's major employer, especially for skilled labor. By 1880, the slaughtering of animals accounted for 46 percent of industrial employment and total value of manufacturing products in St. Clair County. Race was the variable that tipped the town's future away from development and toward underdevelopment. Despite the advantages of site, few Brooklynites were employed in the mines surrounding it. A year after its incorporation, the major forces shaping Brooklyn's destiny—industrial capitalism and racism—were already operative. In 1873, the future looked bright as the African American majority, fortified with the right to vote, prepared to share power with the white minority. Between 1872 and 1890, however, the politics and demographics of Brooklyn were more similar to those in predominately Black southern counties, like Halifax County, North Carolina, than to such Black settlements as Promiseland, South Carolina, or the Black towns that developed after 1890.[11]

Social Transformation and Black Community Development, 1870–80

In Brooklyn, as elsewhere during the era of slavery, free African Americans made themselves into a viable community by creating a racially conscious culture constructed on a system of independent institutions. Through their churches, schools, and voluntary associations, African Americans sought to enhance their independence from white control. Started by families and individuals fleeing either the brutalities of slavery or the racial restrictions of a social system based on the assumption of Black inferiority, Afro-Brooklynites developed a political culture in which the desire for freedom became its most distinguishing feature. Before emancipation and the elimination of the Black Laws, Afro-Brooklynites displayed their desire for freedom by aiding fugitives and supporting efforts to repeal the state's anti-Black ordinances. After emancipation, they ritualized celebrations of Emancipation Day and their accomplishments as a community. Central to their vision of freedom were the concepts of community, autonomy, self-government, and Black power. Emancipation, citizenship, and incorporation of their town generated favorable conditions for African Americans to expand the number and type of their social institutions. By strengthening their indigenous institutions, African Americans established an organizational nexus through which they could gain political power.[12]

According to the ninth census, Brooklyn had a population of 435 people, 208 Afro-Americans and 227 Euro-Americans. The census taker obviously missed many African American households, since all observers at this time reported that Brooklyn was a majority-Black town. Several significant Afro-Brooklynites, such as Tazwell Bird, Philip Sullivan, and Henry McAllister, did not appear in the ninth federal manuscript census. The tenth federal census recorded the reality of a predominately African American population in Brooklyn. The manuscript census for that year listed a total population of 574, of which 371 were African Americans and 203 were European Americans.

Less than a year after Brooklyn's incorporation, the *St. Louis Republican* claimed Brooklyn had "taken a start," despite its "natural disadvantages." The reporter did not identify or elaborate on the town's "natural disadvantages." Perhaps, he was referring to Brooklyn's location in the American Bottoms and its lack of elevation above the floodplain. According to the reporter, St. Louis and other towns suffered from the same disadvantages, but the *Republican*'s reporter did not specify what those were. It was clear that they were something other than Brooklyn's racial composition. Be that as it may, the reporter, estimating the village's population at 550, stated "a large number of cottages had been erected within the past year." Segregation continued to crystallize in postwar Brooklyn. In 1870, whites resided mainly in two clusters on the town's fringe, but they were also interspersed between African American clusters in the town's core. For example, five of the first eight households and thirty-one of the last thirty-four households listed by Charles During, the census taker, were white. Furthermore, two of the three Afro-Americans households on both ends of town lived next to each other. In the town's center, several clusters of six to eleven Black households were often separated by only a single Euro-American home. For example, beginning with Sophia Carroll's residence and ending with Alex and Carolina Broady's home, seven Afro-American households were separated from another cluster of eleven African American residences only by Thomas and Catherine Campbell's home. The first cluster contained thirty-six people; the second included forty-one members. The white merchant Henry Roundtree, his wife, and his child were surrounded by a cluster of eleven African American homes on one side and four more on the other. Enranud Brummer, a German immigrant merchant, separated a cluster of four Afro-American homes, beginning with Hubert and Destiny Carper's household and ending with John and Amanda Lee's home, from another cluster of six African American households. The second cluster began with Susan Henry's home and ended with Nelson and America Nicholas's household.[13]

Between 1870 and 1880, as southern Black migrants flooded into Brooklyn, the towns' Morse Code–style configuration gave way to a more rigid form of residential segregation. By 1880, segregation was so extensive that the African American and European American communities almost constituted two distinct towns. Brooklyn was designated "Township 2-N, R 10" in the tenth census, but the census enumerator listed the first 45 households separately from the remaining 88. The first group of residences contained 45 households and 182 individuals, including 42 white households with 172 members. The 3 African American households had 10 members. The Afro-Brooklynites consisted of a married couple, a family of seven, and a single individual. I call this area "white Brooklyn." Three white households were interspersed among the 88 African American homes in "Black Brooklyn," and

3 Euro-American households were located on the fringe of the town. Essentially, Brooklyn was taking on the residential architecture of a late twentieth-century city, a Black center with a white outer shell.[14]

Race continued to structure religious and social affiliations. The schools, as part of the town's evolving public life, became the first battleground for Blacks and whites contending over racial determinations. Repeal of the Black Codes, Blacks' acquisition of citizenship and the franchise, and village incorporation combined to increase the significance of race. Politics was the crucial variable that hoisted race into dominance or, perhaps more accurate, dispersed the mists that had previously shrouded racial oppression in Brooklyn. The changing social structure was the foundation that conditioned and partly determined the success of insurgent Black power politics.

The African American Community: Work and the Family, 1870–80

Only a trickle of southern Blacks migrated into Illinois during the 1870s and 1880s compared with the tide that would flood into the state during the great migration of 1916–29. Fueled by dreams of land ownership or drawn by farm work, southern Afro-American migrants often moved to the rural North. Their dreams of land ownership or farm work would go largely unrealized, however. Most good farmland in Illinois had been acquired long before the postwar migration began. Moreover, the metro-east region was beginning its rapid transformation from an agricultural economy to an industrial one. During this early period, however, Black farmers initially gained a footing in Brooklyn, though it would prove to be fleeting, because the forces of industrialization were reshaping the region's political economy and its production and social relations.

In 1850, only six Afro-Brooklynites made their living from farming, although they represented more than 12 percent of the African American occupational structure. By 1870, farmers constituted the single largest occupational category among African American men, numbering twenty-two individuals and constituting more than 36 percent of the Black male labor force (see table 6). In 1880, the number of Afro-American farmers had decreased to twenty-one but had fallen to only 13.37 percent of the African American male occupational force (see table 7). The tremendous drop in the percentage of farmers in the labor force was because of an explosion in the number and percentage of Black men who were being incorporated into the industrial economy. Furthermore, there was a high turnover rate among Black farmers; few Blacks were listed as farmers in the 1870 and 1880 censuses. Most, like Susan Henry, Morris Williams, and John Lee, had left Brooklyn before 1880. Some, like Richard Haney and Moses Ballad, were forced to

Table 6. Occupations of Afro-American Males in Brooklyn, 1870

Occupation	Number	Percentage
Skilled workers	3	4.92
Cook	5	8.20
Farmer	22	36.07
Laborer	22	36.07
Saloonkeeper	1	1.63
Servant	1	1.63
Unemployed or occupation unlisted	7	11.48
	61	100.00

Source: Population Schedules of the Ninth Census of the United States, 1870, Illinois, St. Clair County, Roll 280, 620–25.

Table 7. Occupations of Afro-American Males in Brooklyn, 1880

Occupation	Number	Percentage
Professional persons	2	1.28
Farmers	21	13.37
Proprietors, managers, and officials	2	1.28
Clerical workers	1	0.63
Skilled workers and foremen	14	8.91
Semiskilled workers	2	1.28
Farm Laborers	21	13.37
Unskilled laborers	92	58.60
Personal and domestic servants	2	1.28
	157	100.00

Source: Population Schedules of the Tenth Census of the United States, 1880, Illinois, St. Clair County, Roll 246, 19–24.

join the proletariat. In 1870, Moses Ballad was a thirty-seven-year-old farmer whose estimated wealth was valued at $300, $150 each in real and personal property; within a decade, he described his occupation as "works on farm." He had been reduced from a farmer to a farm laborer. In 1870, the forty-three-year-old Haney was listed in the census as a farmer; in 1880, the census taker noted that Haney "works in packing house." It is possible, however, that these statistics mask complex labor participation. For example, Anthony Barnes, elected to the village board in 1886 as part of the all-Black winning slate, was listed as a farmer with minimal wealth in the 1870 census. In 1880, his occupation was listed as a laborer. He worked at the stockyards, but John Freeman, a native of Kentucky like Barnes, was listed as a servant who "works on the farm." Anthony Barnes had not left farming but had employed a farm laborer to work the farm while he took more secure employment. Marginal farmers (and most Black farmers in Brooklyn were marginal) tried to function in a mixed economy before they were completely reduced to working for wages. This contrasts sharply with the experiences of similarly situated Black farmers in all-Black towns. The example of the Simon Gaither family of Mound Bayou, Mississippi, illustrates the options open to struggling Black farmers in a typical all-Black town. To survive, Gaither's wife and children hired themselves out as agricultural laborers, while he contracted to clear land for others and entered a sharecropping arrangement with a white farmer. In Brooklyn, Blacks did not experience the semi-proletarianization of sharecropping, though many probably had before they went there. Once there, they either directly entered wage work or were reduced from farm owner to proletarian status.[15]

The historical process that produced the proletariat, according to Karl Marx, was the expropriation of peasants from their land and their reappearance as wage workers for industrial capitalists. The marginal status of Black farmers is revealed when the value of their real property is compared with that of whites. In 1870, twenty-two African American farmers owned $5,975 worth of real property compared with $40,995 of real property owned by twenty-three white farmers. The Black farmers real property wealth was about 15 percent of white farmers'. Undercapitalized and working much smaller plots of land, Black farmers were extremely vulnerable to becoming a rural or industrial proletariat. The rise in Afro-American farm laborers between 1850 and 1880 underscores this point. The census listed no Afro-American farm laborers in 1850. In 1870, there were eight farm laborers in Brooklyn, but only one Afro-American. By 1880, however, Blacks outnumbered white farm laborers twenty-one to nine. Like their farming brethren, they represented 13.37 percent of African American workers (see table 7). Collectively, these small farmers and farm laborers made-up more than 26 percent of all employed Afro-American males.[16]

There were only two Afro-Americans listed as servants in 1870. Both resided with their farmer employers. M. E. Bennett, a fifty-five-year-old Black man from Missouri, lived with Peter Labodie, a fifty-nine-year-old white farmer also from Missouri. Parthia Young, a twenty-one-year-old mulatto woman, lived in the farm home of William and Sarah Vincent, her employers. The Vincents were also mulattoes. Moreover, male domestic workers constituted only 1.3 percent of the Afro-American male labor force in Brooklyn in 1880. Furthermore, by 1880, two of the three Afro-American servants lived with their Afro-American employers. John Freeman resided with the Barneses, and twelve-year-old Ada Martin was a servant in the household of Harrison and Fanny Edwards. "Servant" was listed both as Martin's relationship to Harrison Edwards, head of the household, and as her occupation. Oliver, the eleven-year-old son of Alex and Elizabeth Lucas, worked as a servant but lived with his parents and sixteen-year-old brother, Theodore, who attended school. Since African Americans, especially recent southern migrants, were too impoverished to purchase land for self-sufficient farming or lacked artisanal skills, they were incorporated into the expanding metro-east industrial economy, mainly as wage workers. In 1880, all servants except for forty-one-year-old Andrew Palmer worked for farmers. Palmer worked as a bartender.[17]

John Freeman may have had a status analogous to that of white women household "help" during the first part of the nineteenth century. Faye Dudden argued that the "help" was a fairly egalitarian arrangement that cannot be precisely defined but is best understood by identifying "work behavior that often appeared casual and unsystematic at the time." Dudden discussed several social relations that embody the "help" concept, such as eating with the family, working alongside one's employer, and rejecting the term *servant*. This type of work relationship was a product of rural agricultural economies and most often occurred when the employer knew the employees' family or when the employer and employee had similar class backgrounds. Race had often been a similar variable among African American "owners" of slaves. In the 1880s, John Freeman may have had a similar arrangement with the Barneses. Martin's relationship most likely conformed to the traditional role of servant, though.[18]

In 1850, nine skilled workers constituted more than 15 percent of African American laborers, but by 1870, only three Afro-Americans defined themselves as "craftspeople," and they made up less than 5 percent of the Black labor force. After the opening of the stockyards in 1873 and the rapid industrialization of the metro-east region, the number and percent of Afro-American skilled workers changed dramatically. At first, these changes occurred very slowly; by 1880, the number of skilled workers had only increased to fourteen, which was less than 9 percent of the Afro-American male labor force. From 1850 to 1870, Afro-American artisans, for the most part, had occupied the traditional skilled trades—carpentry, blacksmithing, brickmasonry, coopery, and barbering. In 1850, Brooklyn had only two butchers, and both were traditional retail meat cutters. One worked in a meat market and may have been self-employed. In 1880, the traditional trades still predominated, but a small corps of Black "foremen" and butcher workers were beginning to appear. Anthony Speed, a worker from Arkansas, represented the mainstream. In 1880, he worked as a common laborer, but by 1891, Speed managed his own butcher shop and meat dealership. He was typical of Brooklyn's Afro-American artisan entrepreneurs. Speed would become town marshal and treasurer of the Stites County Highway Commission in the early twentieth century. John Henry Holliday, who bore the same name as the notorious gunfighter "Doc" Holliday, was atypical of Black artisans in Brooklyn at this time. Holliday was an "electric light man," who eventually served nearly twenty years on the village board of trustees. It was not until 1900 that the new craftspeople and "foremen" replaced the old as the overwhelming majority of Black Brooklyn's skilled labor force. This, of course, spelled the end of the independent Afro-American artisan. Skilled workers and "foremen" numbered sixty-eight and constituted about 26 percent of employed African American males in 1900. The tremendous increase in Black skilled workers had a downside, however. They were now employees in major capitalist firms rather than independent entrepreneurs. Worse still, they went into the meat-packing industry just when the "deskilling" process was underway and thus lacked the power over the production process that earlier generations of butcher workers possessed.[19]

Twenty-two Afro-Americans were listed as laborers or boat hands in 1870. Some Black river workers, such as the forty-year-old Martin Gillium, listed themselves as "roustabouts," while others, such as forty-four-year-old Tauby Bowles, stated they "worked on ferry boat." Whether they identified themselves as "roustabouts" or not, most Black river workers were classified in this lowest category of river workers in 1880, just as they had been thirty years earlier. Because roustabouts were manual workers, I have included them as common laborers. Common laborers and farmers formed the largest occupational categories among African American workers, each constituting more than 36 percent of the labor force in 1870. By 1880, with the growth in industrial employment throughout the region, Black common laborers numbered ninety-two, making up more than 58 percent of the Afro-American labor force. They worked on the docks loading and unloading freight, on the ships for the Wiggins Ferry Company, at the stockyards, at the Morris, Armour, or Swift packing companies, at the sawmills, at the rolling mills, and on the railroads.[20]

Although Brooklyn was surrounded by coal mines, the censuses of 1850 and 1870 list no Afro-Brooklynites as miners, and the 1880 census lists only one, Theodore Joiner. Joiner was a twenty-four-year-old who lived in an augmented home with his mother, Elizabeth, and Elliot Thomas, a boarder who worked at the stockyards. At first glance, the exclusion of Afro-Brooklynites from mining seems curious. Blacks were employed in Illinois mines extensively throughout this period, often to break strikes. Warren Whatley catalogued ten instances in which Blacks were used to break mining strikes in Illinois between 1874 and 1899. Included in his list was a strike in Freeberg near Brooklyn. In 1874, shortly after Brooklyn's incorporation, three hundred white miners called a strike at a mine owned by Robert W. Lemen. African Americans refused to support white miners' demand for a penny increase a bushel and continued to work for three cents. Enraged, the white miners attacked twenty-five Black miners, destroyed their shanties and personal property, and drove many of them out of the county. The violence reached such proportions that Governor John L. Beveridge sent rifles and ammunition to the sheriff to prevent further violence. Was the absence of Afro-American miners in the metro-east due to this legacy of racial violence? In his excellent study of Black workers since the Civil War, William H. Harris explained that because of the racism of white owners and white workers, a strike was often the only context in which Afro-Americans would be employed. As he lamented, "Though it did little to develop class consciousness between Black and white workers, Blacks sided with the employers—who at least gave them jobs, even if at pitiably low wages." Whatley's research refutes the traditional view of extensive strikebreaking by Blacks. He was able to document only 124 instances of Afro-American strikebreaking between 1870 and 1929. During this era, industrial capitalists sporadically used racial antagonisms to undermine worker unity. Moreover, the evidence suggests although capitalists preferred European immigrants, they discovered that Black southern migrants often produced the same results and that their employment helped undermine worker unity. Whatley did identify one profound difference between the use of Europeans and Blacks to break strikes. According to Whatley, the introduction of Black strikebreakers "increased the probability that a strike would turn violent," thus inducing the state to intervene. Intervention, especially by the state or federal government, usually meant on behalf of the capitalists, to protect their property and the lives of their strikebreakers. Given this tendency, it is surprising more Afro-Brooklynites were not employed in the region's mines.[21]

The relationship between residence, race, and worksite changed drastically in the three decades between 1850 and 1880. Residence was influenced by worksite more than by race in 1850; however, by 1870, race had increased in significance, and by 1880, it was the primary determinant of residence. In Brooklyn, race was beginning to structure employment as well. For instance, in "white Brooklyn" twenty-five out of forty-five heads of families (56 percent) were farmers, and only five (2 percent) were employed as factory workers. Moreover, all five white industrial employees worked at the bone plant. Andrew Stein, a thirty-nine-year-old born in Baden, Germany, was an engineer; forty-year-old Frenchman August Mousfield and thirty-one-year-old Russian immigrant August Kraft worked there as skinners; while thirty-two-year-old Swiss immigrant Christ Hoffman and twenty-seven-year-old native white American John Trigg simply listed the bone factory as their place of employment. Not one African American worked there. Ten (40 percent) of the white farmers were European immigrants. All except a Russian and a Canadian were of old immigrant stock. That 56 percent of Euro-Brooklynites were farmers and that 40 percent of the white farmers were immigrants suggests that ethnicity conjoined with whiteness to secure a stable position for these men. It is likely that these men brought money with them from the "old" country. That European immigrants had a privileged status is supported by the presence of Stein, the German engineer, and Christopher Young, a retired French shoemaker. Nevertheless, six (66 percent) of the nine white servants were immigrants: three came from France, two from England, and one from Canada. This partly undermines the privileged position of white immigrants. Although this complicates the issue, it does not negate the advantage European (and Canadian) immigrants had in "capital" and the skilled trades. It simply serves to remind us that class was an ever-present variable shaping race, ethnicity, and gender.[22]

For whites, occupation may have continued to influence where they lived. They were overwhelmingly a farming community; this partly explains why they resided on the town's periphery, yet that is not the whole story. Only four white families lived in Brooklyn's core. The heads of three of them, August George, William Johnson, and John Bundiff, were, respectively, a miller, an owner of a candy stand, and a carpenter. This, however, does not explain why many African American farmers lived inside the village's core. The need for racial unity, companionship, and mutual aid explains why Afro-Brooklyn farmers lived in the center of the town and why whites remained on the town's fringe.[23]

Ninety-two Black men worked in the factories in 1880, whereas only five white men did. Apparently, whites could retain their independent economic roles either as farmers or as traditional craftspeople longer than Blacks, who were forced into industrial wage labor much earlier. This sequence of proletarianization was precisely the reverse of the historic national pattern. Nationally, industrialization and Afro-American self-activity combined to transform Blacks into proletarians during the early twentieth century, decades after native and immigrant whites had undergone the proletarianization process. Whites in Brooklyn were mainly of old immigrant stock and entered the American economy primarily as independent craftspeople and farmers; they were therefore better situated to resist the initial pull of industrial capitalism.[24]

Race was not the only social category structuring residential patterns in postwar Brooklyn. Color never developed into a factor that influenced housing patterns among African Americans but the region from which they came did. In 1870, this tendency was apparent but underdeveloped. For instance, seven of the eight Afro-Americans from Louisiana resided next door to each other in houses numbered 22–24 in the census. Twenty-one-year-old Andrew Jackson and twenty-year-old Frank Sanders, who listed their occupations, respectively, as a "streamboatman" and laborer, resided with sixty-seven-year-old Sophia Carroll at number 22. Eliza Patterson, a fifty-four-year-old housekeeper, lived next door at number 23 with her three daughters, Jane, age thirty-two; Eliza, age twenty-two; and Johanna, age twenty-one, who were all born in Louisiana. Another Louisianan, twenty-nine-year-old blacksmith Henry Canoll, and his family lived at number 24. Virginians Parker Strickland, a seventy-two-year-old farmer; Matilda Anderson, a seventy-four-year-old widow; Alex Lucas, a thirty-nine-year-old laborer; William Lorell, a fifty-six-year-old farmer; and Arel and Amilia Wells, a thirty-nine-year-old cook and thirty-eight-year-old housekeeper and their ten-year-old son, Lawrence, lived at 61, 64, 65–67, and 69. They constituted seven of the nineteen Virginians.[25]

This pattern of regional clustering had intensified by 1880. The 1880 census reveals that Black southern migrants preferred to live near others from their state. For instance, thirteen Tennesseans, including twelve adults, lived in a cluster between dwelling units 43 and 61. This group resided in nine different households. This cluster included Green Harts, a twenty-seven-year-old laborer who, along with John Evans, would represent Stites Township at the 1892 St. Clair County Republican Party Convention. Henry McAllister, a fifty-year-old Baptist preacher who would win a seat on Brooklyn's initial village board, was also part of this cluster. Another cluster of twenty-four Tennesseans resided near the edge of town in units 110 to 118. This cluster contained eight adults and thirteen children, including Daniel Miller, a forty-year-old blacksmith. Thirty-seven (88 percent) of the forty-two Tennesseans living in Brooklyn resided in these two clusters. The 1870 census records not one Afro-American who was born in Mississippi, but by 1880, there were twenty-eight former Mississippians in Brooklyn, seventeen of which were women. A cluster of Mississippians resided between numbers 68 and 84. Eleven adults and a total of twenty-six people lived in this cluster. The cluster reflected the Mississippians' peculiar gender structure. Thirteen (half) of the cluster were women, but seven of the eleven adults were women. Furthermore, only two male heads of households were from Mississippi, but all seven adult Mississippi women were married to men from other states. The twenty-six Mississippians who clustered in this area constituted nearly 93 percent of Mississippi-born Afro-Brooklynites.[26]

The tendency of Afro-Brooklynites to live in clusters based on their states of origin differs greatly from what Henry Taylor and Vicky Dula found in Cincinnati in 1850. There, nativity played little or no role in cluster formation. Eighteen of the twenty clusters contained Afro-Americans from at least four different states. In contrast, in Brooklyn nativity increased as a factor in cluster formation between 1870 and 1880 and became a major basis of community formation among Afro-Brooklynites. Nativity undergirded friendship and perhaps membership in churches and fraternal organizations. For instance, the formation of the Corinthian Baptist Church may have resulted from issues associated with nativity. Corinthian was organized after the southern migration of the late 1880s and early 1890s. James Grossman found the organization of new churches and fraternal groups during the great migration in Chicago was often tied to nativity. In Chicago, new social institutions as well as social networks often consisted of rebuilding transplanted churches and organizations.[27]

Between 1850 and 1870, the percentage of married-couple nuclear African American households and the percentage of Blacks living in such arrangements changed in contradictory ways. The percentage of two-parent households declined from approximately 47 percent to 43 percent, but the percentage of persons living in two-parent households increased sightly, from more than 41 percent to more than 43 percent. In 1850, almost 43 percent of Black Brooklynites lived in extended families, whereas in 1870, less than 20 percent did (see table 8). In 1870, nearly four times as many African Americans were residing in augmented homes than they were in 1850. Often these augmented homes did not include children and appear to have been boardinghouses. The median family size for Afro-Brooklynites was 4.16, which was a slight increase over the 1850 figure of 3.90. Families were larger, but households were getting smaller. The difference between family and household size was only 0.09; while this is statistically insignificant, it does represent a closing of the gap between these two indicators since 1850. The median size of African American–headed households, however, steadily declined, from 4.94 in 1850 to 3.74 in 1880. The decline in the number and percentage of extended families accounts for the major differences between the family and household structures in 1850 and 1870. In 1850, extended families numbered only ten, but they represented nearly 28 percent of all African American households. By 1860, seventy-seven people lived in these arrangements, and they composed almost 43 percent of Black families. A decade later these figures had plummeted dramatically. In 1870, there were only four Black extended families, and they composed a meager 8.5 percent of Afro-Brooklynite households, although extended families comprised nearly 20.0 percent of the Black population there (see table 8). Nationally, the extended family arrangement was the dominant family formation among African Americans.[28]

The following statistics further illustrate Brooklyn's uniqueness. While the two-parent nuclear family was beginning to decline elsewhere, two-parent Afro-Brooklynite families were quite numerous in 1870. In the four small Ohio Valley cities Paul Lammermeier studied, only 59.2 percent of African American households were nuclear families, whereas nearly 66 percent were in Brooklyn. Nearly 41 percent of Black homes were extended or augmented in the Ohio communities, but in Brooklyn less than 30 percent were. Perhaps the most powerful testimony to Brooklyn's extraordinary family structure is that among the Black Ohio Valley families residing in comparable communities, nearly 23 percent were headed by women, while in Brooklyn only 15 percent of Black households were female-headed. Black female-headed households in Brooklyn came in an array of configurations. For instance,

Table 8. Household Structure of Brooklyn's African American Population, 1870

	No. of Households (%)	No. of People (%)
Nuclear		
Married couple, children	20 (42.56)	90 (43.27)
Married couple, no children	10 (21.27)	20 (9.61)
Female-headed	1 (2.12)	6 (2.89)
	31 (65.95)	116 (55.77)
Single-person residences		
Individuals living in		
non-Black households	1 (2.12)	1 (.48)
Blacks living alone	1 (2.12)	1 (.48)
	2 (4.24)	2 (.96)
Extended Families		
Two parents, children,		
and relatives	2 (4.26)	23 (11.06)
Female-headed	2 (4.26)	17 (8.17)
	4 (8.52)	40 (19.23)
Augmented		
Female-headed	4 (8.51)	21 (10.09)
Mixed (married couples		
and unrelated individuals)	6 (12.77)	29 (13.95)
	10 (21.28)	50 (24.04)
Grand totals	47 (99.99)	208 (100.00)

Source: *Population Schedules of the Ninth Census of the United States, 1870, Illinois, St. Clair County,* Roll 280, 620–25.

Eliza Patterson, fifty-four, and her four adolescent children, three daughters and a son, made up Brooklyn's only household composed of a single mother and children. Another consisted of a single woman. Most were augmented and consisted of an enterprising woman supplementing her income through boarders. Susan Henry offers a unique example. The forty-six-year-old Henry was Brooklyn's wealthiest African American in 1870, owning real and personal property assessed at $3,375. She employed James Smith on her farm, though the 1870 census lists the forty-year-old Smith as a farmer rather than as a farm laborer. Smith and his twenty-two-year-old wife, Chaney, resided with Henry. The census did not address Chaney Smith's role in the production or reproduction processes. Perhaps, like 40 percent of Black women in the Cotton Belt in 1870, she worked in the fields with her husband. She may have also "helped" Henry in the housekeeping tasks.[29]

The multigenerational extended family household of the Archer family was more typical of Brooklyn's Black female-headed households. Thirty-five-year-old Frederick; his thirty-year-old wife, Josephine; their six-year-old son,

Sylvester; their two-year-old daughter, Ellen; and Frederick's twenty-two-year-old brother, Joseph, lived with the men's mother, sixty-two-year-old Prudence Archer, a widow. Frederick and Joseph listed their occupations as farmers. They farmed the land owned by their mother. In 1860, the St. Clair County assessor had valued her real estate at $300 and her personal property at $100, and in 1870, the assessor appraised her real estate at the same value and her personal belongings at $400. Frederick was also a property owner, owning two lots on the periphery of town. The 1870 census does not list the worth of his property, but according to the 1860 census, he was a laborer who owned personal property valued at $300. Susan A. Mann reminds us that the spouse who contributed the greatest share to the family income generally made the family's major decisions. Though contemporary studies of family decision making does not address this issue, it seems highly likely that the major breadwinner would also make the key decisions in extended family arrangements. In all likelihood, Prudence made the decision in consultation with her oldest son.[30]

Fred Archer was a powerful figure in Brooklyn politics. He was elected to Brooklyn's first village board in 1874, and between 1874 and 1886, he was Brooklyn's and Stites Township's dominant African American politician. He was powerful enough to help his brother Joseph become town treasurer. By 1880, members of the Archer extended family had moved into separate homes. Fred and Josephine now had four children and their own home. Although still listed in the census as a farmer, Fred Archer had become the proprietor of one of Brooklyn's largest groceries. His mulatto clerk, the twenty-year-old Frederick Vanderberg, resided with the Archer family in an augmented arrangement.[31]

Widows composed the majority of female-headed households, and all but one was the major source of income for her family. Mary J. Smith, Nancy Washington, Martha Goodwin, and Eliza Hamilton, four of the seven women who headed households in 1880, were widows. The following nonwidowed Black women were also reported as family heads: Elizabeth Joiner, Amanda Thompson, and Thea Alexander. Census enumerators in St. Clair County did not report occupations for women except "keeps house" and "servant" until 1880, when "washing" and "cooking" appeared. Knowing what led some women to list "keeps house" and others to list "at home" would be interesting. Did the difference reflect a latent or an overt consciousness that reproductive labor *was labor?* Thirty-one-year-old Martha Goodwin, thirty-two-year-old Nancy Washington, and thirty-two-year-old Eliza Hamilton were all widows who lived next door to one another. Hamilton listed her occupation as "washing," but Goodwin and Washington listed theirs as "washing & cc [cleaning clothes]." Except for Mary J. Smith all of the other female heads of homes were laundresses. The thirty-three-year-old Smith maintained herself and her twelve-year-old daughter by working as a farm laborer. Elizabeth Joiner, forty-two, washed and took in a boarder, who worked at the stockyards. Her twenty-four-year-old son, Theodore, was the only African American miner residing in Brooklyn.[32]

With respect to its small number and percentage of female-headed households, Brooklyn's family structure was closer to that of rural African American families; as Herbert Gutman stated, female-headed households were "an urban phenomenon." He maintained the existence of father-absent households was the result of the "large surplus of adult Black women." This was not the case in Brooklyn, however. There, the percentages of adult Black men and women were nearly equal and remained about the same throughout this period. In 1870, African American adult women numbered sixty-six and accounted for 52 percent of the adult Black population. By the 1880 census, African American men had become a slight majority, numbering 113 and representing about 51 percent of adult Afro-Americans. The parity between African American men and women explains the small number of female-headed households.[33]

In 1880, 371 African Americans lived in 94 households, composed of 101 Black families. The percentage of African Americans living in nuclear families had dropped sharply, to 53 percent, and now constituted only about 47 percent of all households (see table 9). In the ten years since 1870, two-parent households declined from 43 percent to about 29 percent. Female-headed households remained stable at seven and contained fourteen individuals. The

Table 9. Household Structure of Brooklyn's African American Population, 1880

	No. of Households (%)	No. of People (%)
Nuclear		
Married couple, children	27 (28.72)	128 (34.50)
Male-headed	8 (8.51)	16 (4.32)
Female-headed	7 (7.45)	14 (3.77)
Married couple, no children	8 (8.51)	16 (4.31)
	50 (53.19)	174 (46.90)
Single-person residences	9 (9.57)	9 (2.42)
Extended families		
Two parents, children, and relatives	15 (15.96)	75 (20.22)
Single parent, children, and relatives	—	—
	15 (15.96)	75 (20.22)
Augmented	20 (21.28)	113 (30.46)
Grand totals	94 (100.00)	371 (100.00)

Source: *Population Schedules of the Tenth Census of the United States, 1880, Illinois, St. Clair County,* Roll 246, 19–24.

decrease in two-parent nuclear families was related to the rise of extended families and augmented households. Fifteen households, encompassing seventy-five African Americans, included relatives in 1880. An augmented household, headed by John S. Bryant, included another family, the Harrison Dorseys, with whom Dorseys's great-grandmother, Phyllis Eubanks, lived. At 104, she was the oldest resident in Brooklyn. Gutman claimed that it was more common for Black extended urban households to include mothers and mothers-in-law and brothers and sisters, while grandchildren were more likely to reside in rural households. He concluded that young relatives of the head of household, rather than elderly family members, most often lived in extended families. In contrast, Andrea Hunter found in Atlanta that extended kin generally came from the head couple's parents' generation or from the generation after theirs and rarely from their own generation. In Brooklyn, the extended family pattern did not conform to either the rural or the urban configurations that Gutman found. Eight of the individuals living with relatives fit the rural model, and seven approximated the urban formulation. Brooklyn had both urban and rural features, and its extended family pattern reflected its location at the nexus between rural and urban communities. This aspect of Brooklyn—its position at the crossroads between urban and rural, a Black town and an African American urban enclave—is further underscored by the town's small farming population and large industrial proletariat.[34]

Many Afro-Brooklynite families "took-in" relatives. The extended family, according to Hunter, represented "a family strategy," an adaptation to socioeconomic conditions. Antonio McDaniel acknowledged the practical function of extended family arrangements but emphasized it as a continuation of African cultural practices. McDaniel highlighted the family's role in promoting a communal ethos and conveying African cultural survivals from one generation to the next. Many scholars have traced the extended family to Blacks' African past. Niara Sudarkasa suggested extended family bonds were as strong as nuclear family ties in African societies. The work of W. E. B. Du Bois, Gutman, Sterling Stucky, and other historians of American slavery has discussed how racial oppression contributed to African Americans' constructing a unique culture based largely on African cultural carryovers. African survivals have had a decided influence on African American family relations and structure. Nevertheless, African Americans' motivations were based on kinship ties and economic factors.[35]

This was certainly the case in Brooklyn. Twenty-five-year-old Reuben Holifield lived with his fifty-year-old uncle and aunt, Edward and Rachel Williams. This arrangement was mutually beneficial. Twenty-six-year-old Richard Jones, who worked as a common laborer, and his wife, Nancy, took in Frank Martin, Richard's six-year-old nephew. The thirty-five-year-old Nancy's two children by a previous marriage also lived with the couple; Eighteen-year-old Henry Johnson worked as a common laborer, and fifteen-year-old Charles attended school. Most Afro-Brooklynite families, like the Jones family, were not wealthy and the addition of another person placed a financial burden on the family. Fifty-five-year-old Maria Speed lived with her twenty-three-year-old grandson, Samuel Speed, a boatman; his wife, Rita; and their two-year-old daughter, Birdetta. The census enumerator listed Rita's employment as "house keeping." Grandma Speed recorded her occupation in the census as "nothing." On the surface, this appears to have been a situation in which a responsible grandchild took in an elderly relative who needed support, but the circumstances are more complex than that. In the column for illness, Rita listed "falling numb," which was obviously dangerous, especially with a young child present. Maria Speed's presence was therefore mutually beneficial, for her and her grandson's family. This example supports Hunter's view that "extended family living arrangements, while having a direct impact on the household family economy, also must be viewed as a strategy that extends beyond the economic imperatives of the household to the survival of the larger kin group where families give as well as receive." The Pope family had entirely different circumstances, but it, too, underscored the importance of familial ties in the African American experience. Abraham Pope, a saloon owner and a future member of the village board of trustees, resided with his brother John and his family. He probably lived with his brother's family for personal reasons or to help them out, since he did not appear to need their financial help.[36]

Interestingly, many other Black politicians in Brooklyn lived in extended family relationships. Tazwell Bird, a member of the first village board of trustees and the school board, and his wife took in her great-grandmother, Sophia Carroll, for whom his wife was named. Carroll was a longtime Brooklyn resident. Twenty-year-old Isaac Carpenter also resided with the Birds. Carpenter had lived with Carroll in 1870 and most likely had been adopted by her and moved in with Tazwell and Sophia Bird when Carroll did. Fred Archer's mother and brother Joseph lived with him and his family. From 1874 to 1892, Fred served on the village board of trustees and the township board; Joseph was Brooklyn's treasurer from 1878 to 1882. John Henry Holliday, a fixture on Brooklyn's board of trustees between 1892 and 1904; his wife, Susan; and his young brother James Jones all lived together in the Holliday home. William Allison, who became mayor in 1894, had his mother, a laundress, living with him and his family. Anthony Speed, who became the treasurer of the Stites County Highway Commission and town marshal in the early 1900s, took in his father. Family was the foundation of Afro-Brooklyn. Its centrality predisposed the Black community to interpret "taking care of one's relatives" as a *personal virtue* and a *positive political value*. Black Brooklynites shared this family and community ethos with other Black-town residents.

According to Norman Crockett, Black-town politicians used their "past service to the community" and "concern for the common people" to appeal to
the electorate. The financial capability of these families to take in relatives
must also be considered. Most of these men were artisans, farmers, or merchants and were better situated to extend support to their relatives.[37]

After the migrations following the Civil War, fosterage and adoption became common in Brooklyn. McDaniel defined children as fostered when they
resided in a home headed by someone other than their mother or father.
Fosterage was a traditional African family arrangement that built on the
extended family and traditional African communalism. Adoption is simply
a legalization of fosterage. Adoption was also quite common among Afro-
Brooklynites for reasons that appear to be quite varied. For instance, Jesse
and Laura Keolunge, an apparently childless couple, adopted the fourteen-
month-old Florence Hawker. Jesse was forty-eight, and Laura was twenty-
four. Perhaps they were unable to have children. However, Harrison and
Parthium Dorsey, who had three small children, ages five, four, and twenty
months, and his 104-year-old great-grandmother, Phyllis Edwards, living with
them, adopted eleven-year-old Emma Newborn. Harrison Dorsey was a
forty-year-old common laborer and Parthium was a twenty-nine-year-old
housekeeper. Surely Emma helped with the children after she returned from
school, but her contributions to child rearing do not explain why the Dorseys adopted her. Eliza Hamilton adopted nine-year-old Eliza Shelly, perhaps
because there was a connection between them. Twenty-five year-old Beu
Hughes and his twenty-three-year-old wife, Sarah, adopted two children:
seventeen-year-old Wesley Campbell and eight-year-old Ellen Carper. It is
possible that Campbell was Sarah Hughes's brother. Yet her birth in Mississippi before the Civil War and his birth in Florida during the war did not fit
slave trading and postwar migration patterns. Adoption was not a middle-
class practice. All six Afro-Brooklynites who adopted were common laborers or laundresses. Again, it is possible that many of the young people being
adopted were related to those who adopted them. If so, the census takers failed
to record this relationship.[38]

The real change in Brooklyn's African American family structure was, of
course, the decline of two-parent families and the rise of augmented families. In 1880, two-parent families included 27 households, contained 128 persons, and accounted for 34.5 percent of the African American population (see
table 9). Augmented homes now numbered 20, housed 113 individuals, and
represented 30.46 percent of all Black Brooklynites. In Brooklyn, augmented families usually included more than one other family or another family
and a boarder. Typical of this pattern was the augmented household headed
by Virington Tillman. The Tillmans rented to Beu Hughes and Tauby Bowles
and their families. As noted earlier, two of the Hughes's three children were

adopted. The Bowles had two children. Worksite was a basis of unity for
Tillman, Hughes, and Bowles, who were all boat workers. Not so typical was
Elizabeth Joiner's household. Her son, Theodore, lived with her, and she rented a room to a single boarder. What made Elizabeth Joiner's home unusual
was that she was the only woman operator of a boardinghouse. Joiner was
quite enterprising, as she also took in laundry.[39]

Perhaps the most interesting illustration of an augmented relationship was
the one that existed between Matilda Anderson, the widow of the Reverend
John Anderson, and Nancy Brown. In 1870, Brown, her husband, and two
children lived with Anderson. There had been a series of property exchanges
between them beginning in 1868. Before the Reverend John Anderson died,
he transferred clear title to two properties, lots numbered 47 and 61, to his
wife. More than two years later, on 19 August 1868, Matilda Anderson and her
son Simon transferred lot 62 to Nancy Brown. On 24 April 1874, Nancy Brown
purchased by warrantee deed lot 47 from Mrs. Anderson. Perhaps Nancy
Brown was Matilda Anderson's daughter, but again the enumerator failed to
note this relationship. It is more likely, however, that Brown was the daughter of one of Anderson's friends from the days of slavery.[40]

In 1880, after Matilda Anderson's death, John R. Stites, the court-appointed
executor, appraised her real and personal property at $369.50. According to
his report, "one house and a lot in the town of Brooklyn" constituted $300.00
of this amount. She did not leave a will, and Stites oversaw the auction of her
personal effects. He submitted to the court a "Petition to Sell Personal Property at Private Sale." The executor rationalized the immediate sale because
"all the household and kitchen furniture, wearing apparel & c being in danger if not speedily disposed of, that the same may be stolen or destroyed."
No mention was made of what happened to her home, but her personal property valued at $69.55 by Stites brought only $61.25 at the sale. Unfortunately,
her estate's debts totaled $76.38, the largest being $28.55 for funeral costs,
which left a deficit of $15.13. The records do not reveal how Stites handled
this.[41]

The dwindling of two-parent households and the increase in extended
families and augmented homes suggest that Afro-Brooklynites were adapt-
ing their family and household structures to the changing socioeconomic
conditions (see tables 8 and 9).

Constructing a Freedom-Conscious Political Culture

The erosion of the family, especially married couples, increased the need for
meaningful relationships outside the home. The church partly filled this void.
The decline in ministerial leadership in community affairs was not a reflection of the quality of post-1870 ministers, nor did it indicate the withering

of religious influence. Rather, it was symptomatic of a trend toward seculariation rooted in the new socioeconomic environment. During the early 1870s, the African American church increased its power and status in the Black community. On 23 March 1873, the Antioch Baptist Church gave a supper, apparently to benefit its building fund, for within two years the congregation moved into a newly constructed building. The land for the new church building had been donated by the Reverend John Richard Anderson, Antioch's first pastor. The new church was the culmination of at least eight years of fund-raising activities. The *East St. Louis Gazette* covered the laying of the cornerstone. It is significant that the ceremony attracted newspaper coverage, but the *Gazette*'s reporter ignored the tremendous sacrifices made by the small adult population of Black Baptists to raise $1,500 to build a new church. Instead the writer focused on the arrest of four men who "got very nasty and troublesome." Five years later, at a cost of $2,500, the African Methodists also built a new church building.[42]

During this period, Brooklyn's growth and development was evidenced by the rebuilding of old institutions, the creation of new organizations, and the continued construction of a racially conscious political culture. In the mid-1870s, affiliates of national fraternal orders emerged as important social actors in Black Brooklyn. African American fraternal orders grew at such a rapid rate between 1870 and 1910 that some observers called this "the golden age of Negro secret societies." Brooklyn's array of lodges followed the national pattern. Essentially, these organizations sought to provide fellowship, mutual benefit, and recreation for their membership and the broader Black community. For instance, shortly after the formation of Brooklyn's International Order of the Odd Fellows, the organization purchased a lot and began construction of its own meeting hall. The newly formed Masonic Lodge, in keeping with its motto, "Brotherly love, relief, and truth," sponsored activities that served to cement community bonds. On Thursday morning, 10 September 1874, the Masons dedicated their hall and, according to the *East St. Louis Tribune,* "indulged in a picnic" on Bloody Island. The brothers and their guests had such a good time "eating, dancing and drinking" that they resumed the celebration Friday and carried it on into Saturday morning. The *Tribune* article's tone projects stereotypical images of irresponsible "darkies" partying their lives away. The reporter, blinded by his racial bias, missed the important fellowship functions performed by such social gatherings as this. The *Tribune*'s treatment of African American fraternal orders contrasts sharply with that of the *St. Louis Palladium,* an African American–owned paper. On 28 November 1903, the *Palladium* explained why Lewis Watkins, its Newport News distributor, had not disseminated the prior week's paper. In a playful tone, the author reported Watkins had "reveled so fully in the knighting hilarity on November 21, 1903 that he failed to deliver the

Palladium." Watkins and eighteen other candidates from the metro-east area had been knighted into the East St. Louis lodge of the Knights of Pythias. The depictions of these two events are ideological worlds apart. Although more than a quarter-century apart, racist representation may even have increased in the northern press during the nadir, 1890–1915. Yet, ironically, we are probably aware of Brooklyn's Masonic event only because of the reporter's racism. The *Tribune* was not alone in misrepresenting African American pleasure-seeking activities.[43]

The *Belleville Weekly Advocate* also promoted racism. For instance, on 19 March 1875, the paper printed a story about the murder of a Black man by a white bartender in Waverly, Missouri. After denying the Black man a drink, the saloon keeper expelled him from the bar. Sometime later the African American returned and read the Civil Rights Act of 1875 to the bartender. The 1875 Civil Rights Act granted Blacks equal access to public accommodations. After the man finished reading the act, the bartender murdered him in cold blood. Commenting on this event, "Enough," a columnist for the *Weekly Advocate,* wrote, "This ought to prove to all negroes what Enough has often alleged, that death lurks in the intoxicating cup." Given the prevalence of racist ideologies throughout St. Clair County, it is amazing that a few positive stories about the predominately Black town appeared in the *Belleville Weekly Advocate* or the *East St. Louis Tribune.*[44]

With this racist environment, it is not surprising that Brooklyn Blacks joined local lodges of national and international African American fraternal organizations and that its African Methodist Episcopal and African Baptist churches were plugged into broader networks. They also concentrated on celebrating their own achievements.

Festivals, celebrations, and commemorations have been part of the African American tradition since the early eighteenth century. Perhaps the most significant cultural expression of African Americans' freedom ethos was their celebration of Emancipation Day. Before emancipation, free African Americans commemorated three holidays that especially addressed the freedom of African people throughout the diaspora. Early in the nineteenth century, they celebrated New Year's Day in honor of the abolition of the slave trade on 1 January 1808 by the United States, England, and Denmark. They also celebrated New York's abolition of slavery on 4 July 1827 by holding festivities on 5 July (to distinguish it from American Independence Day). The third freedom celebration they commemorated was the abolition of slavery in the British Caribbean on 1 August. Emancipation Day probably incorporated various aspects of these celebrations instead of simply supplanting them. This may explain why some communities commemorated Emancipation Day during the summer.[45]

Emancipation Day celebrations were regionalized. Historically, African Americans in Alabama, Georgia, and Mississippi celebrated on 28 May. Blacks

in east Texas, western Louisiana, southwestern Arkansas, and southern Oklahoma commemorated on 19 June. Blacks in Ohio, Indiana, and Illinois celebrated 22 September, the day President Lincoln issued the Emancipation
Proclamation. Even within states, there was diversity. For instance, Blacks in
Chicago celebrated on 1 January, African Americans in Decatur celebrated
on 22 September, and Blacks in Springfield and southern Illinois traditionally held Emancipation Day celebrations in August. The first recorded participation of Afro-Brooklynites in Emancipation Day activities was on 25
August 1883, when they joined Blacks from across the state at Lincoln's tomb
in Springfield, Illinois. Blacks in the state capital and home of Lincoln began their commemorations in 1864. The first recorded observance of Emancipation Day in southern Illinois was in Elizabethtown in Hardin County on
the Illinois-Kentucky border in 1882. Emancipation Day was also celebrated
early in Metropolis and Brookport, which also border Kentucky. Brookport
was a transit point for several Blacks who eventually made their way to Brooklyn and probably was the source of Brooklyn's Emancipation Day activities.[46]

The 1870s witnessed the continued growth and development of Brooklyn's
two oldest institutions, Quinn Chapel and the Antioch Baptist Church, and
saw the creation of such new secular organizations as the Odd Fellows and
Masonic lodges. The need for new church and lodge buildings and the ability to build them suggest growing prosperity and a strengthening of indigenous institutions and organizations. Specifically, this implies an increase in
membership and revenue. New building construction was tangible evidence
of race advancement, but it also symbolically testified to African Americans'
emancipation from the Black Laws. Though the churches continued to influence community life, politics and the new social organizations and institutions challenged their hegemony over African American public life after
the town incorporated. The social organizations provided an arena in which
a new secular-based leadership was trained and emerged to contest white
political power. For instance, John Evans, the first African American mayor,
was a Mason. The emergence of these new institutions and organizations thus
laid the foundation for the rise of Black political power.[47]

Challenging White Political Supremacy

On the surface, it does not appear that race was either an organizing principle or a disorganizing appeal in the initial village board elections. Considering the lack of documentary evidence and confirming data that race was not
a factor in town politics, it would be quite naive to conclude it was not. Beginning with the struggle around the mixed school issue in 1875, race leapt
into town politics and surfaced as the most salient question undergirding
politics between 1875 and 1900.[48]

Brooklyn, like most incorporated Black villages and towns, adopted the mayor-council form of municipal government. Most Black towns and small working-class communities favored this form of government because they did not need a complex form of governmental organization. Under this form, the people in Brooklyn elected a board of trustees, usually six, and the trustees then selected a president, or mayor, from among themselves. The marshal, assessor, and justice of the peace were elected. Unlike most Black towns, Brooklyn adopted an at-large election system rather than an aldermanic one. Trustees served four years. Terms overlapped so that every two years three trustees were elected. The president and the board generally appointed a treasurer, a village clerk, at least one street commissioner, and other offices as needed to fulfill the demands of local government. Except for administrative appointments, the president, or mayor, could vote only in case of a tie, but he did have veto power over ordinances passed by the board. The trustees could override his veto with a two-thirds vote. Beginning with the 1890 election, Brooklynites chose to hold mayoral elections every four years, though Brooklyn had an election every other year for trustee positions. This ensured the prominence of politics in Brooklyn. It established the basis for an exciting exercise in self-government, but it also created the context for factionalism. Brooklyn, like most Black towns, was highly politicized.[49]

John R. Stites, John R. Doscher, William Wey, George Batchelor, Fred Archer, Henry McAllister, and Tazwell Bird composed Brooklyn's first board of trustees. The whites, Stites, Doscher, Wey, and Batchelor, held the majority of the seats and elected Stites as president. Since Stites had the power to decide tie votes, the posts of village clerk and village marshal went to whites. Clerk Henry Roundtree controlled Brooklyn's administrative functions, and Marshall William Hunt controlled the repressive apparatuses. Brooklyn did not have a treasurer at this time.[50]

John R. Stites was probably the most powerful man in Brooklyn. He was a wealthy tavern owner and one of the first property owners in Brooklyn. He was also Brooklyn's first justice of the peace. In 1888, St. Clair County officials removed Brooklyn from East St. Louis Precinct and incorporated it, along with the northwestern portion of Caseyville Precinct, into a new township as part of a political reorganization. They initially named the newly created township Brooklyn, after its only incorporated town, but soon they changed the name to Stites Township. John R. Stites was a judge at this time and was significant enough in county politics that the *St. Clair Tribune* reported his visits to East St. Louis. John Doscher was part of a politically influential family, and his brothers, Alex and George, would later serve as justices of the peace. Alex became the justice of peace when Stites left the post, and after Alex died, George "inherited" the office and still held it in 1912. William Wey, a German immigrant, was a twenty-eight-year-old saddler who owned real estate valued at $2,500 and personal property worth $350. George

Batchelor was an Illinois-born engineer who listed no real or personal wealth. William Hunt does not appear in the 1870 census or in the available city directories. Henry Roundtree was a thirty-year-old merchant from Alabama, and, like George Batchelor, he claimed no wealth.[51]

Archer, McAllister, and Bird were the Afro-Americans on Brooklyn's first village board. The Archers were pillars of the Black community. In 1870, Fred Archer was a thirty-five-year-old mulatto farmer from Alabama but between 1870 and 1880, he operated the "most extensive" of four groceries in Brooklyn. His grocery was housed in a "snug two story frame building." Archer, his brother, and his protege Frederick Vanderberg evolved into powerful political figures. The Archers' wives, Josephine and Elizabeth, were also influential members in Quinn Chapel and the community. Josephine was a prominent member of the church's Ladies' Sewing Circle. A pianist, Elizabeth Archer managed both the musical and literary departments and presided over the church's "Grand Fair and Bazaar" in April of 1898. During the fair, an aging Archer led the girls' drill team in a broom-jumping contest. Denied legal marriages, slaves symbolized their union by ritually "jumpin' the broom." After slavery, this ritual was transformed into a game rather than discarded. Its preservation represented an attempt to incorporate a previously meaningful cultural practice into a new situation by recasting it. The Archers seemed to have had a gendered approach to community service; the women focused their considerable leadership skills and energy on social and cultural affairs, while the men concentrated on business and politics. Josephine and Fred's son, Sylvester, took over the store, and though he was not a politician, like his father and uncle, he was involved in community affairs.[52]

Henry McAllister was a forty-four-year-old Black teacher when he was elected to the board of trustees. In 1860, his wealth amounted to $600 ($500 in real estate and $100 in personal property). McAllister does not appear in the 1870 census, but by 1880, he had become a Baptist preacher and was no longer teaching school.[53]

Tazwell Bird, a thirty-five-year-old Black plumber and a member of the village board, was the driving force behind African Americans' struggle for access to the public schools. In 1875, he mobilized a movement to form a school district free of segregation. Bird and other African American activists made separate schools unacceptable to Brooklyn's Black majority. Bird was subsequently elected to the board of education that presided over the new integrated school district. Bird was the first Brooklyn politician simultaneously to hold seats on the village board and the school board, which attests to his popularity.[54]

Bird was the first of the moderate, middle-class Black politicians to break with what Michael Chesson called middle-ground politics. Bird initiated his campaign to take advantage of new laws and court decisions, for example, the 1872 act "to establish and maintain a system of free schools" and the 1874 act "to protect colored children in their rights to attend Public school." The first act removed section 80 (84) and its discriminatory term white from the laws governing Illinois public education. Section 48 of the second piece of legislation mandated that a school district maintain enough schools to make a free public education available to all persons between the ages of six and twenty-one, but this section also contained a provision that allowed local boards to assign students to their schools. Robert McCaul maintains, correctly I believe, that this clause was not a progressive affirmation of local autonomy but a concession to racism that allowed segregation to replace exclusion.[55]

Across the state, African Americans responded by opposing separate schools. Even Governor Palmer believed that segregation in education was illegal and could exist only if African Americans voluntarily accepted it. In an 18 April 1874 article entitled "The Rights of Colored Children," the East St. Louis Gazette anticipated racial conflict in St. Clair County over interpretation of this act. Within a year, the Illinois Supreme Court went even further. The court maintained that operating two schools solely for maintaining racial separatism was wasteful of the taxpayers' money. It ordered the separate school for four Afro-American children in Danvers, McLean County, to be closed. However, the court did permit separate schools in areas with a "sufficiently large" African American student population.[56]

In Belleville, the St. Clair County seat, the school board passed a resolution to close Lincoln School, its school for Black children, because "the small number of pupils, is at present carried on at an unnecessary expense." The board declared, "Resolved: that the pupils of said school be distributed to other schools in accordance to their attainment." In this instance, the cost of maintaining two separate school systems so overburdened the school district that whites decided to abolish segregated schooling.[57]

In the midst of these changes, Bird began the struggle in Brooklyn. He, Charles O. Jennings, a thirty-six-year-old Black laborer, and James Boyd were elected to Brooklyn's first school board. In sharp contrast to the village board of trustees, the board of education was composed solely of Afro-Americans, apparently a result of Tazwell Bird's skillful mobilization around the issue of "mixed" schools and African Americans' greater interest in this arena. Bird initiated and mobilized a movement to form a school district free of segregation. He and other Black activists argued that separate schools were intolerable in Brooklyn. Because of Bird's activism, it became a public issue, and the community was forced to get involved. Bird, like other people of African descent throughout United States, saw education as the prerequisite for self-improvement, upward mobility, and collective Black social advancement. It appears that, at least initially, they viewed education as more important than majority rule. Afro-Brooklynites recognized education as an opportunity to obtain the skills necessary to advance in the society, especially for the children. African American control of the board of education predictably led to a dispute between African Americans and Euro-Americans over separate schools.[58]

A reporter from the *East St. Louis Republican* described the situation: "Considerable wrangling has ensued between white and colored populations in regard to mixed schools, in which a number of colored people (and they are in the majority) take the ground that a mixed school is the proper course for that locality, in which the whites object." The *Republican*'s description of this controversy suggests that European Americans unanimously opposed "mixed" schools but that not all African Americans supported school integration. Subsequent events reinforce this interpretation. The Black-controlled school board refused to fund separate schools. By ending public financing of separate educational facilities, Brooklyn became one of a few southern Illinois towns that did not maintain Jim Crow schools. The strife over school desegregation, however, sparked a split among Blacks themselves. This is not surprising since African Americans across the state were divided on this issue. African Americans in southern Illinois generally accepted segregated schools and focused their energies on obtaining Black teachers and equal funding for Black schools.[59]

In the midst of this controversy, John Watson, a farmer, storekeeper, and one of the wealthiest African Americans in Brooklyn, leased from the St. Louis–based owner of the school property the rights to the land on which the schoolhouse was built. Watson's real property was estimated at $1,200 in 1870, the same as Thomas Moore's and William Lorell's, two other African American farmers (see table 10). In addition, Watson owned personal property valued at $350, while Moore's and Lorell's were assessed at $500 and $175, respectively. Susan Henry was the wealthiest African American in Brooklyn. Her real property was valued at $3,000 and her personal wealth at $375. Watson was thus the third wealthiest African American in Brooklyn. In 1870, the forty-eight-year-old Watson resided on a farm on the fringe of town with his forty-five-year-old wife, Adalina, and their seventeen and fourteen-year-old daughters, Loucinda and Mary. Watson was physically isolated from the Black community: African Americans occupied only two of the thirty-two households nearest him. By 1880, Watson was a widower and had become a store owner; his youngest daughter, Mary, now twenty-four; her husband, William Parker; and their two preschool-aged daughters lived with him. Joseph Boyce, Watson's clerk, also lived with the Watson extended family. Although he lived next door to August George, the father of Lula George, a white schoolteacher, he now resided squarely in Black Brooklyn.[60]

After leasing the land in 1875, Watson demanded the keys to the school building. When Tazwell Bird, the board's leader, refused to hand them over,

Table 10. African American Property Owners in Brooklyn, 1870

Name	Color	Occupation	Value of Real Property	Value of Personal Property	Total
Moses Bellod	black	farmer	$ 150	$150	$ 300
Dann Clark	black	cook	—	75	75
Sophia Carroll	black	at home	175	50	225
Joseph Brown	black	saloonkeeper	—	175	175
Stephan Bell	black	farmer	150	250	400
Anthony Barnes	black	farmer	150	150	300
Thelda Brown	mulatto	at home	—	75	75
Daniel Wilson	black	laborer	150	100	250
Edward Williams	mulatto	carpenter	175	75	250
John Broady	black	farmer	175	250	425
James Boyd	mulatto	farmer	1,100	250	1,350
Alex Broady	black	whitener	100	75	175
Hubert Carper	black	farmer	275	175	450
John Lee	black	farmer	375	100	475
Susan Henry	black	keep house	3,000	375	3,375
Prudence Archer	mulatto	keep house	300	400	700
Nelson Nicholas	black	laborer	200	75	275
William Lorell	black	farmer	1,200	175	1,375
John Watson	black	farmer	1,200	375	1,575
Thomas Moore	black	farmer	1,200	500	1,700
			$10,075	$3,850	$13,925

Source: Population Schedules of the Ninth Census of the United States, 1870, Illinois, St. Clair County, Roll 280, 620–25.

Watson threatened to enforce his demand with a cudgel. He withdrew after Bird backed up his refusal with a shotgun. According to the *St. Clair Tribune,* Brooklyn crackled with tension as supporters of Bird and Watson squared off. Retreating to East St. Louis, Watson swore out a warrant "charging Bird with an assault with an intent to kill." In court, Bird claimed that he could not get a fair trial before Judge J. N. Ryan and obtained a change of venue. Bird believed Ryan was prejudiced against him, perhaps for his activism in the mixed school issue. This matter generated intense feelings on both sides. As the *Tribune* reported, "Half the male population . . . *both white and black,* came down with them either as witnesses or spectators." The reporter feared "the committing of an overt act by either side would be the signal for a pitched battle." How were the sides determined? Was race the primary dividing line, just as it was over mixed schools? After the physical confrontation between Watson and Bird, newspaper coverage focused on this aspect, claiming "the colored folks have fallen out among themselves," and failed to explore the underlying dimensions of the conflict between them. Nevertheless, the timing of Watson's lease, his attempt forcibly to take control of the school building, and the community's fervent interest in the trial strongly suggests the confrontation between them may have been a continuation of the racialized political struggle around mixed schools. However, Watson may have been motivated by personal gain as well.[61]

Watson had an extensive criminal file. He was convicted twice of selling liquor without a license in 1878, and in December of 1879, Watson again acted improperly regarding school issues. This time he attempted to sell the school and a large amount of wood belonging to it. This case did become part of the court record. State's Attorney George Brockhaud charged:[62]

> John Watson then and there and while he was a school director did sell the said building and the said lumber for the sum of $500.00 and did then and there receive and take the said sum of $500.00 unlawful money for the said building and lumber . . . and did then and there unlawfully, knowingly and fraudulently convert the said sum of money? to his own use . . . against the state and the dignity of the People of the state of Illinois.
>
> Geo. M. Brockhaud
States Atty.

On 6 January 1878, Judge George W. Wall impaneled a grand jury, which on 18 January issued the following indictment:[63]

> The People v. Watson   }
> Indictment for Converting School
> Monies to his own use.

> And now on the 18th day of January 1879, the Grand Jurors chosen, selected and sworn according to law, come in open court and by their foreman Amos Thompson report and return into Court an indictment in this cause endorsed "a true bill" against the defendant, and thereupon the court fixes the amount of bail to be required of said defendant at $300.00. And now the court orders that this cause be certified to the County Court of St. Clair County for further proceedings & c.

They delayed this matter several times. The grand jury had a difficult time getting witnesses to cooperate. All members of the school board were issued summonses. The grand jury ordered John Reushaw, the board's treasurer, to bring the district's books as well. Other city officials and prominent citizens subpoenaed included the mayor, John R. Stites; the city clerk, Henry Roundtree; Henry McAllister, a village trustee; and James A. Pettiford, the future town marshal. They tried three times but were unable to subpoena James M. Boyd. Watson's defense attempted to squelch the indictment before the grand jury during its July 1879 term on the following grounds:

> And now comes the said John Watson and moves the court to quash said indictment and each count thereof because no offense is charged therein.

2nd Because it does not sufficiently appear from *either* count of said indictment that *deft* [*sic*] was committed within the statute.

3rd Because it is not shown in either count of said indictment sufficiently what if any deft has [been] committed.

And *lastly* because said indictment and each count thereof is otherwise insufficient *in law* to require deft to plead the same.

By J. B. Nay Atty for Defendant.[64]

The court rejected Watson's motion for dismissal. Witnesses were subpoenaed throughout the July term of 1881. Court records do not show whether they ultimately convicted Watson, but we can speculate that he was because criminal files were kept open only if the accused was found guilty.[65]

At this time, Brooklyn did not have a justice of the peace. The *East St. Louis Gazette* pointed out the reasons for and the consequences of this problem in January of 1874. The *Gazette* claimed that the candidate for judge from Brooklyn would have been elected if "he had kept out of 'rings [political factions].'" Furthermore, the *Gazette*'s commentator projected that bringing disputes to East St. Louis cost Brooklyn citizens "time and money." It is possible that the *Gazette*'s editors were more desirous of keeping Brooklyn's disputes out of East St. Louis than concerned for equitable political treatment for the majority Black community.[66]

Mary Barnes, an African American woman, was the first educator hired by Brooklyn's school board. The hiring of Barnes appears unusual. According to Bettye Collier-Thomas, "Until the mid to late 1880s, black teachers found it extremely difficult to acquire teaching positions in black public schools, since a large number of these institutions employed white teachers only." Gender compounded this racialized hiring practice. Collier-Thomas maintains that initially when African American teachers replaced white teachers, "it was customary to replace them with male instructors." When Black women were fortunate enough to obtain teaching positions, they were usually in rural districts. Moreover, they were generally paid less than men, regardless of race, and less than white women, regardless of experience. Barnes's hiring was therefore unusual. In 1879, Brooklyn enacted a $3,000 bond and built a "fine, four room, two story brick schoolhouse." A year later, the twenty-two-year-old Charles B. Jones was promoted to principal, and Barnes was replaced by Lillian B. Turner, a nineteen-year-old mulatto. Turner was the stepdaughter of James Milton Turner, the resident minister and consul-general to the Republic of Liberia from 1872 to 1878 and Missouri's most outstanding African American leader during the nineteenth century.[67]

The Turners boarded in the home of Harrison Edwards, a forty-year-old Black farmer from Missouri. Edwards's wife, Fanny, was a twenty-year-old housekeeper. At the time of the census, between 1 June 1879 and 31 May 1880,

Fanny's mother and stepfather were also residing with the Edwardses. Why would James Milton Turner be living in Brooklyn? According to Gary R. Kremer, Turner's major biographer, after the fiasco surrounding Turner's attempt to find an Oklahoma settlement for the exodusters in 1879, Turner moved around throughout the Midwest. The records are sketchy, but James Milton Turner may have lived in Brooklyn for nearly a year.[68]

Turner was a prominent national African American leader, and his counsel would have been sought by Afro-Brooklynite leaders. A staunch advocate of Black political power, Turner may have influenced the African Americans to mobilize for greater power sharing in the 1882 village board election. Furthermore, his stay in Brooklyn had to have affected his thinking on racial advancement. In November of 1886, after Afro-Brooklynites had gained control of Brooklyn's municipal machinery, Turner began advocating the creation of a "colony" in Butler County, in the Missouri bootheel, where Blacks would "have an opportunity of getting both land and an education under the most favorable circumstances."[69]

Brooklyn Blacks took every opportunity to promote education. When they were unable to hire qualified Black teachers, the board of education hired Euro-Americans. Some of the early white teachers employed by District 188 included Lula George; C. B. Carroll, compiler of "C. B. Carroll's Brooklyn City Directory"; and Carroll's brother. In 1880, the eighteen-year-old George lived with her parents next door to John Watson. The George family lived in "Black Brooklyn"; they were separated from the nearest white household by four Black households on one side and seventy on the other.[70]

African Americans named the school Lovejoy in honor of the martyred abolitionist Elijah P. Lovejoy, whom a proslavery mob in nearby Alton, Illinois, had killed. While the naming of the school reflected the community's legacy as initially a settlement of free and fugitive African Americans, it also to some extent rejected the early all-Black settlement's history of self-reliance. Why did they not name the school building after Mother Baltimore, Bishop William Paul Quinn, or William Carper, Afro-Brooklyn's own martyred freedom fighter? Was it an effort to reach out to the whites still residing there? Had they obtained a freedom consciousness but not yet a Black national consciousness? Or did they genuinely believe that Elijah Lovejoy best represented the values they wanted to instill in their children? Lovejoy was clearly viewed as a patron saint in this Black community.

They did not name the school after the name of the town. During the nineteenth century, Afro-Brooklynites did not name any of their community or public institutions "Brooklyn." The *State Capital,* an African American newspaper published by S. B. Turner in Springfield, Illinois, captioned its news on the happenings in Brooklyn under the title "Lovejoy, Illinois." Even today, residents and nonresidents refer to the town by the name of the martyred abolitionist Elijah P. Lovejoy. This suggests that the Black majority may have preferred to use a town name that linked them to the town's antiracist heritage.

Conclusion

The combination of industrial development, abolition of the state's Black Laws, passage of the Thirteenth, Fourteenth, and Fifteenth amendments, and incorporation of the village created the conditions for a large migration of African Americans to Brooklyn. Between 1870 and 1880, southern African American migrants swelled Brooklyn's Black population as they sought work in the emerging factories in the surrounding predominantly white industrial suburbs. The social structure of Afro-Brooklynites was drastically changed by industrialization and proletarianization. First, Blacks significantly extended their numerical advantage. Racial segregation solidified as African Americans increased their percentage of the population. The increase in population also facilitated Blacks' challenge to racial exclusion in the public school and white political hegemony. Second, the family and household structures of Afro-Brooklynites began to change as Blacks adapted them to the new situation wrought by proletarianization: on the one hand, the incorporation of Black men into the factories of neighboring cities and on the other, the restriction of Black women to domestic service. This latter factor provided the major inducement for Black families to take in boarders. Third, although Brooklyn was bypassed as a site for industrialization, the population underwent rapid proletarianization. Industries chose to locate in the new towns of National City (1872) and Venice (1873), the communities that sandwiched Brooklyn on the south and north, respectively. Fourth, the increased population generated the construction of new social institutions, such as fraternal orders. Fifth, the rapid influx of a large number of single males accelerated the community's male to female ratio and began the erosion of Brooklyn's nuclear family structure and the transformation of its culture.

Enfranchisement and incorporation facilitated the creation of a class of Black politicians and social activists who would eventually supersede the ministers as the leaders of Afro-Brooklyn. First, the newly enfranchised Afro-Brooklynites fought for and won school desegregation and elected an all-Black school board. Second, beginning with the school challenge, the new class of Black leaders began a process of political mobilization that culminated in the overthrow of white minority rule and the installation of a Black power government.

4. Mobilizing the Race: John Evans and Black Political Power, 1878–1906

THE 1876 CAMPAIGN for "mixed" schools unveiled not only white racism but also the political possibilities for mobilizing African Americans along race lines by opposing white supremacy. The struggle around schooling galvanized the African American community and forged the foundation for their campaign to gain control of the village board of trustees. The school struggle helped clarify the political direction of Brooklyn's African American leadership and combined with long-term social processes to establish the trajectory the town would follow into the next historical period, 1886 to 1898. This development did not occur overnight. Most African Americans who lived in Brooklyn in 1870 to 1886 were recent migrants from the former slave states of Tennessee, Missouri, Mississippi, Kentucky, and Virginia. In the sixteen years between their acquisition of citizenship rights and their assumption of political power, African Americans strengthened their institutions, consolidated themselves around a freedom-conscious culture, shaped a new militant leadership, and molded themselves into a community. African American success at running their own institutions and organizations and a profound belief in their own efficacy, as the majority population, created enormous potential for them to take political control. Strong leaders, exemplified by Tazwell Bird and John Evans, enabled African Americans to mobilize their community resources and transform their consciousness into a movement for Black power.

The history of Brooklyn, Illinois, provides a rare opportunity to examine African American political mobilization in the late nineteenth century. This chapter reconstructs and analyzes the Black majority's struggle for political power and its efforts to *use* that power to develop the town. John Evans's political career provides a focal point around which we can connect Afro-Brooklynites' battle for Black power to statewide and national African American political movements. The struggle for Black power in Brooklyn was a movement for self-determination and decolonization. Black power meant activating the African American community to fight against the debilitating effects of internal colonialism. It was a strategy for gaining and maintaining political control of municipal government and for breaking the grip of economic underdevelopment. Black power in Brooklyn also had social and cultural implications. It reflected Afro-Brooklynites attempts to elevate Black people to positions of power and influence throughout the town and county, to build social and cultural institutions that affirmed their heritage, and to create and attract economic institutions that would promote development. Between 1886 and 1910, John Evans was the principal political figure advocating Black power. Under his leadership, African Americans won political control and struggled to construct a viable economy and to build a town that would exult the race. As the first Black mayor, he used the power of the office to modernize the town's infrastructure, institutionalize a freedom-conscious political culture, and encourage extra-electoral activism. For these reasons, John Evans is remembered as "the Father of Brooklyn."[1]

In many ways, Evans exemplified the trends of his era; in others, he shattered traditions. For instance, in 1870, a seventeen-year-old John Evans joined the stream of Blacks from Virginia and the border states who migrated North. Interestingly, the year Evans headed north was the apex of the postwar Black migration. Evans was probably a former slave who, like most southern migrants of this period, left the South for economic and noneconomic reasons. Whereas most immigrants from Virginia took the northeast migratory stream to the metropolitan areas of New York and Boston, where they were employed as cooks, domestic servants, or common laborers, Evans went against the current. He was part of a small group of young men who chose to migrate to the fledgling African American village of Brooklyn in St. Clair County, Illinois. Why John Evans chose to live in Brooklyn when other Afro-Virginian migrants, such as Phil Preston Logan, Joseph Johnson, and Mayo Lawson, decided to reside in predominantly white towns may never be known. Perhaps, Evans, James Ross, and other young migrants from Virginia settled in the African American town to reconnect with relatives or friends. Or maybe they were guided by a protonationalist consciousness.[2]

Though Evans's residential decisions contrasted with the migration patterns of Afro-Virginians, his experiences mirrored those of Brooklyn's African American male population. Perhaps the extraordinary political harmony that developed between Evans and Brooklyn's Black majority was because of this. For instance, in 1870, forty-eight of out of fifty-six African American males at least eighteen years old (nearly 86 percent) were born in the South (see table 4 in chapter 3).[3] His experiences reflected those of Brooklyn's Black males in other significant ways as well. Evans, like many Black men of this era, had joined the Masonic fraternal order. Moreover, like several other male Afro-Brooklynites during the 1880s, Evans owned a farm. After at least a decade as an unprosperous farmer, Evans was forced into the ranks of the industrial working class. By 1891, he was employed as a common laborer at the Wabash Railroad Car Repair Shop. Some Black men had briefly flourished as independent farmers, but by 1880, they were being forced from their farms and into the factories of the emerging industrial economy (see tables 6 and 7 in chapter 3). The percentage of farmers among Brooklyn's African American labor force plunged from 36.07 percent in 1870 to 13.37 percent in 1880. By 1900, it had dropped to 7.20 percent. Conversely, the percentage of common laborers exploded from more than 36 percent in 1870 to nearly 59 percent in 1880. Although it fell by 1900, common laborers still accounted for 50 percent of the Black male work force. In Brooklyn, Blacks did not experience the semi-proletarianization of sharecropping, though many worked as farm laborers before they joined the industrial labor force. John Evans, Anthony Barnes, and other Afro-Brooklynites were forced into wage labor because they were the most marginal members of St. Clair County's peasantry. For Evans and many other Blacks, the factories represented a step up from marginal land ownership, farm labor, or nonindustrial wage labor. Evans occupied an ambivalent class position, moving between what Thomas D. Boston called the "class segments" of the Black working class. By 1910, he had been promoted from a common laborer to shop floor supervisor.[4]

Evans is an amazingly elusive figure, especially for an African American leader. We know very little about his personal life. He married in 1878, and his wife, Elizabeth, and he were together until his death in 1910. During their thirty-two years of marriage, they had five children. Four were born between 1882 and 1894: two sons, Dennis and John L., and two daughters, Jessie and Evelyn. The birth of his children probably explains why he left farming for wage labor. John and Elizabeth Evans had another son who died on 29 March 1904 at the age of ten. Amazingly, their son's death notice in the *St. Louis Palladium,* an African American newspaper, was one of the few social appearances of John or Elizabeth Evans in the newspapers. Since he left no extant diary, memoir, or personal papers and village board minutes disappeared long ago, few of the sources associated with Euro-American or African American elites can be used to reconstruct his personal life. Evans's life, like that of nonelites, must be assembled primarily from such public sources as manuscript censuses, city directories, and property and probate records.[5] Though he rarely appeared in the newspapers as a social figure, Evans, as mayor of Brooklyn and as a prominent member of the Illinois Afro-American Protective League, often appeared in the newspapers in connection with political activities. Brooklyn did not have a newspaper during the nineteenth century, but African American papers throughout the state and newspapers from predominately white towns surrounding it did provide sporadic though often controversial coverage during this era.[6]

During his distinguished political career, Evans combined the strategy and tactics of an elected official with those of a social movement activist. In 1906, after losing the Republican primary, he ran as an independent candidate for state representative, and between 1892 and 1898, he was active in the Illinois Afro-American Protective League. His independent legislative campaign and his participation in the Afro-American Protective League illustrate how his political philosophy transcended electoralism. The Afro-American Protective League was the principal vehicle for Evans's social and political activism beyond Brooklyn's boundaries. The story of the Illinois Afro-American Protective League is therefore integral to the narrative of Evans's leadership. The story of the fight for Black political power, however, did not begin with John Evans.

The key transformations in this period included the proletarianization of Brooklyn's African American population, the continued declined of two-parent nuclear families, and the creation of new social organizations and institutions. These new social organizations and institutions birthed a new militant Black leadership. Their desire to free their community from white minority colonial domination fueled their drive for Black power in the 1880s.

John Evans, the "Father of Brooklyn": Decolonization and Black Power

In industrializing America, the transition from the nineteenth century to the twentieth encompassed all of the processes that compose modernization. Modernization is said to entail industrial development, greater social mobility, and an increased access to political participation. Brooklyn's incorporation into the emerging urban industrial economy of the St. Louis metro-east region, the enfranchisement of African American men, and the acquisition of municipal status led to political power.[7] These structural changes created the preconditions for African Americans to initiate a movement for Black power. The political mobilization model best explains the blossoming of Black power in Brooklyn between 1875 and 1886. Doug McAdam identified four factors that are critical to the successful development of a social movement. The first are long-term social processes, such as urbanization and proletarianization. Structural factors create either favorable or unfavorable environments for agency. Second, and the most crucial, is the oppressed community's level of internal organization because it is the basis on which self-activation occurs. Third is the extent to which the oppressed believe in their own efficacy. Not only must they believe in the righteousness of their cause but also they must believe they can win. Fourth is the structure of political opportunities open to the insurgents. McAdam posits that long-term social processes and expanding political opportunities interacting with the increasing institutional strength of the subordinated community create the "structural potential" for successful political mobilization. However, this potential is realized only if the oppressed are also undergoing the subjective process of "cognitive liberation." The conjuncture of structural and objective factors with a positive sense of efficacy generate a social movement, according to McAdam.[8]

When African-American leaders mobilized the Black community to gain political control of Brooklyn, their mobilization was akin to a decolonization movement. Decolonization, to paraphrase Frantz Fanon, is essentially the replacement of one type of people with another type of people. At this most basic level, decolonization is the transfer of political power from one people to another, who differ by race or nationality from the previous rulers. It is a return of a people's self-determination. With the reacquisition of political power, the formerly colonized complete a process of indigenization, that is, they systematically people the governing apparatus with their own nationality or ethnicity. Along with indigenization comes cultural reconversion, that is, a process of revitalizing the values, beliefs, and practices of the newly empowered people. The difference between decolonization and the rise of Black power in Brooklyn, Illinois, is a matter of degrees, albeit extreme degrees, rather than a question of kind. In many ways, Brooklyn's activated Black middle class behaved as a nationalist bourgeoisie. The emerging African American political elite was composed mainly of striving merchants, aspiring artisans and educators, and segments of the lower middle class. These petty bourgeois activists—African nationalists, on the one hand, and African-American protonationalists, on the other—launched movements that returned majority rule and self-determination to African peoples.[9]

Racism and its obverse, an appeal to racial unity or Black nationalism, gave them potent ideological weapons with which to mobilize their constituency. The 1875–76 campaign for mixed schools demonstrated the salience of "race" as an organizing principle and the effectiveness of an aroused African American community. It is instructive that African Americans first assembled themselves into a social movement to challenge school segregation and only afterwards formed an insurgent electoral political movement. During the 1878 board of trustee elections, Black politicians mobilized their constituency to gain control of Brooklyn's political apparatus. They were partly successful. Whites retained control of the board of trustees, with John R. Doscher, William Wey, and George Batchelor remaining as trustees. Fred Archer was the only African American reelected. New African American members included Charles O. Jennings, who had served on the original school board, and Abraham Pope, who owned a saloon. Henry Roundtree, white, was still town clerk, but Fred Archer's younger brother, Joseph, was appointed to the newly created post of town treasurer, and James Pettiford replaced William Hunt as town marshal. Slowly but surely Blacks were asserting their power. Whites retained the powerful positions of board president and town clerk, and through these positions, they controlled Brooklyn's administrative apparatus. However, the town's finances and repressive apparatus were now in African American hands. This arrangement held until 1886, when Blacks gained four of the six seats.[10]

Decolonization began in earnest in Brooklyn in 1886, when John Evans and Anthony Barnes joined Fred Archer and Frederick Vanderberg to form an African American majority on the village board of trustees. The Black majority elected Evans president of the village board. With his election as mayor of the village of Brooklyn, John Evans simultaneously became the first Black mayor of the nation's oldest Black town, possibly the first African American to govern a biracial town, and probably the first African American mayor of an incorporated American municipality. Blacks had acquired political control and would maintain it for the rest of Brooklyn's existence. Black political domination accelerated Brooklyn's transformation from a town with a Black majority into an all-Black town. Black power, the control of the town's political apparatuses, was far more threatening than the racial demographics of Brooklyn and may explain why Brooklyn failed to attract a major industrial plant.[11]

Within two years of Evans's victory, the East St. Louis City Council exercised its option to form a precinct limited to its corporate boundaries. During its December 1883 term, the St. Clair County Board of Supervisors, in accordance with the state's township organization statutes, changed the name and number of the county's political subdivisions from sixteen to nineteen townships. The ordinance on township organization allowed the East St. Louis City Council to abolish East St. Louis Precinct and to form a separate township limited to the city's corporate boundaries. East St. Louis did not exercise this option until 1888. Until then, Brooklyn had been part of East St. Louis Precinct. Afterward Brooklyn and the northwest section of Caseyville Township were reconstituted into Brooklyn Township. Soon after that, the township's name was changed to Stites Township, probably in honor of John R. Stites. African Americans composed a two-thirds majority of the new township.[12]

During Evans's first term, from 1886 to 1890, he consolidated Black control of the town's governing apparatus. In his final term, from 1890 to 1894, he presided over the modernizing of Brooklyn's infrastructure and repulsed the last desperate attempts by the white minority to "redeem" Brooklyn. Almost no record has survived of Evans's first term in office. The one extant document concerns his acquisition of land from the Wiggins Ferry Company, the major owner of real estate along the river. In June of 1888, he convinced the company to transfer land to the village of Brooklyn. The land transfer carried the following stipulation: it was for "public use for street purposes only all its interest in the tract of land that would be included in and between the line of Madison Street as shown on the plat of the Town of Brooklyn recorded in Book E page 3 of the St. Clair County records, if extended West to the East line of Water St. Excepting that portion heretofore deed to Railways." The town upheld its part of the bargain and built a new street. Evans also began to oil Brooklyn's streets. This was probably a quid pro quo agreement since less than two years later, the Brooklyn Village Board granted the Wiggins corporation a right-of-way on Water Street. Evans's first term must have been successful since the *Belleville Weekly Advocate,* the *East St. Louis Gazette,* and the *East St. Louis Journal* did not condemn his performance or report any scandal. Despite Evans's management of a scandal-free administration and modernization of Brooklyn's infrastructure, the town's white minority mobilized to reconstitute colonial domination.[13]

Whites and a few Black opponents manifested their disenchantment with Evans's policies during his reelection campaign. Newspaper coverage reflected the growing opposition to Black political power. For example, the *East St. Louis Journal* commented, "Lively times are expected in our neighboring colored village," as a coalition of "the few whites there assisted by dissatisfied negroes will attempt to wrest the management of the government from the present negro regime." Embedded in this brief statement are personal and socially shared attitudes and opinions about African Americans that reflect a white supremacist ideology. It is an excellent example of how racism is reproduced through discourse. When deciphered, it provides interesting insights into the racial climate in which John Evans and Brooklyn's new Black political leadership functioned. Teun A. Van Dijk noted that to understand fully the meaning of a discourse or a "text," it must be analyzed in its historical, sociocultural, and political contexts. What were the historical, sociocultural, and political contexts in which the *East St. Louis Journal* reporter made his remarks? The reporter's comments occurred on the cusp of the nadir, or the abyss, in race relations. These remarks were made during a historical moment in which St. Clair County papers routinely printed negative depictions of African Americans, especially southern Black migrants. Brooklyn, East St. Louis, and St. Clair County were boiling cauldrons of racial, ethnic, and class conflict. According to Van Dijk, textual analysis generally divides discourse structures into "*surface* structures and *deep* or *underlying* structures." Surface structures refer to the visible or audio forms of language, such as words, word order, active or passive usage, sounds, intonations, and gestures. Deep or meaning structures refer to perspective, implications, presuppositions, and coherence. The *Journal*'s characterization of Brooklyn's Black administration as a "regime" instead of a government represents an example of how word usage reproduces a negative and here a racist construction. The term *regime* is synonymous with the word *government*, but, according to the *Oxford Universal Dictionary*, regime also refers to the "old system or style of things" and is most often associated with the expression *anciens régime*, the prerevolutionary French monarchy. *Regime* therefore connotes a corrupt dictatorial form of government. The word *wrest* suggests the mayoral election was a war to "take back" political power rather than a democratically contested election. This election was a struggle between antagonistic political factions that were organized primarily on racial lines but perhaps party lines as well. The white minority could not hope to succeed without some Black support. The order in which the reporter listed the dissidents—whites first—and the description of Blacks as "assisting" them reveals the white minority as the active agents leading the opposition. This syntactic structure signals the reporter's white supremacist interpretation of these events. The election challenge is reported solely from the perspective of the whites and their Black junior partners.[14]

This brief newspaper account is all that survives of Brooklyn's pivotal 1890 mayoral campaign. Besides revealing external racial antipathy, it also exposes internal racial discord and intraracial factionalism. We do not know the margin of Evans's victory, but he was reelected president of the village board. The dissolution of East St. Louis Precinct and the creation of Stites Township two years earlier proved fortunate because Evans was also elected supervisor for Stites Township, thereby consolidating Black control of Brooklyn and the new township. The supervisorship included a seat on the St. Clair Country Board of Supervisors. John Evans thus became the first African American member of the St. Clair County Board of Supervisors and the representative of African American interests in the county. With the Black electorate now conscious of its political power, Brooklyn's white minority must have sensed that 1890 was its last opportunity to reclaim political control. The interracial alliance attempting to unseat John Evans represented a desperate effort to halt the advance of overwhelming historical forces, both structural and ideological. John Evans, an astute popular leader, skillfully molded the African American demographic advantage and surging militant Black consciousness to doom forever dreams of redemption and a return to white minority political rule.[15]

The escalating racial conflict in Brooklyn was a product of multiple causes. In the main, it represented Blacks' new capacity to use political power to advance their interests. Problems that before 1870 rumbled below the surface now erupted into the public arena. Racial political conflict was primarily a product of accelerating residential segregation. Antebellum residential patterns were determined mainly by class, though race was a factor. People dwelt near their place of employment. Between 1837 and 1870, Brooklyn conformed to the national pattern. The town was divided into "upper Brooklyn" and "lower Brooklyn," but this division reflected class more than race, although few African Americans lived in "upper Brooklyn." After emancipation and the post–Civil War migration, race superseded class as the basis for residential segregation. By 1880, the African American and European American communities almost formed two distinct towns. "White Brooklyn" and "Black Brooklyn" now replaced "upper Brooklyn" and "lower Brooklyn" as the metaphoric designations for residential segregation. "White Brooklyn" consisted of the first forty-four households enumerated by the census taker. It contained 45 families with 172 individuals, including 3 African American households with 10 members. "Black Brooklyn" consisted of 3 white households interspersed among the 88 African American homes, composed of 101 Black families with 371 people. Another 3 Euro-American households were on the fringe of the town. Most of the Euro-American households were on the periphery of town. Brooklyn was evolving the residential architecture that would come to characterize a late twentieth-century city, a Black core with a white exterior. Brooklyn's geography provided the material undergirding for the white population's response to Evans's reelection.[16]

In July of 1891, fifteen months after Mayor Evans handily won reelection, the remaining whites and their Afro-American allies confronted him with petitions to annex Brooklyn to East St. Louis. Unable to regain political control of Brooklyn, the white minority now conspired to vote the town out of existence. An *East St. Louis Gazette* reporter believed annexation was inevitable. As early as 1881, two historians predicted Brooklyn would eventually be incorporated into East St. Louis: "Brooklyn is so closely situated to the city of East St. Louis on the south, with Venice almost touching it on the north, that it has but little chance for its life . . . Indeed it might be considered as a suburb of East St. Louis, but the time is not far distant when it will be so in fact." It is questionable whether people in East St. Louis were interested in annexing Brooklyn. They never expressed a desire to do so. Perhaps the white-led dissidents drew encouragement from East St. Louis's annexation of New Brighton in 1887, but surely they remembered that a year later the industrial suburb divested itself politically from Brooklyn when it dissolved East St. Louis Precinct. Before the village board's decision, Evans polled the citizens to discover their will, an action displaying his commitment to democratic procedures. African Americans accurately viewed annexation as a white-led plot to demolish their power and readily rejected annexation.[17]

Would Afro-Brooklynites have benefited from annexation? In many ways, Brooklyn was a "dependent town." It was incorporated into the metro-east region's political economy as a commuter town, and consistent with the laws of uneven capitalist development, its economic development lagged behind that of its neighbors. Brooklyn's development, like the creation of Black towns, testifies to African Americans' ability to obtain a degree of political autonomy, but economic self-sufficiency proved far more elusive. Black political domination accelerated Brooklyn's transformation from a town with a Black majority into an all-Black town. Brooklyn was economically underdeveloped, partly because of the locational decisions of corporate managers and partly because of its subordinate relationship with external political units, such as the St. Clair County Board of Supervisors and the St. Clair County Sheriff's Office. The potential advantage of annexation was an improvement in municipal services. Brooklyn's citizens may have suffered a loss in the quality and extent of municipal services because of the town's failure to attract major industries that would have furnished tax revenue. Yet the history of East St. Louis specifically and industrial suburbs more generally suggests that since social welfare was a distant second to industrial profitability, industries in such cities usually were undertaxed. Annexation would have cost Brooklyn self-government, with at best meager improvement in municipal services. Ingo Walter and John E. Kramer, two political scientists who studied Black towns for the Department of Health, Education, and Welfare in the 1960s, concluded that Black political control increased economic dependence on larger white-controlled governmental units. Their theory suggests that Afro-Brooklynites would have benefited from annexation, but this line of reasoning presumes that municipalities distribute services equitably. A closer examination of the African American experience in urban enclaves reveals the blatant disparity between the delivery of city services to white and Black neighborhoods.[18]

In the aftermath of the first annexation crisis, Evans turned his attention to municipal improvements. During his second term, he embarked on an unprecedented building campaign. On 7 January 1891, he again extended the town's boundaries when he acquired two more acres from the Wiggins Ferry Company. This deed also carried stipulations regarding its use. The land was sold to the village "[p]rovided . . . the above described land shall be used and only used by the party of the second part for grave yard purposes only. . . ." Brooklyn's new cemetery was on Canal Street at the eastern edge of town. This was an extremely important acquisition since it meant that Blacks could now be buried in a cemetery of their own. Historically, American cemeteries were segregated, perhaps even more so than residential areas. When graveyards were "integrated," Blacks were normally relegated to the periphery or buried in the worst land near the section for paupers and strangers. American cemeteries were structured in a hierarchical manner designed to signify "race, class, age, gender, and religious distinctions," according to Agelika Kruger-Khloula. Legal segregation of the dead continued until 1968, when it was outlawed by the Jones v. Meyer decision. Nearly fifteen years after John

Evans obtained a cemetery for Brooklyn Blacks, St. Louis African Americans were struggling to do so. During the nadir, St. Louis area cemeteries were abandoning the old practice of separating Blacks and whites by "invisible walls and fences" and were simply refusing to sell burial plots to African Americans. The situation was so bad the *American Eagle,* a Black St. Louis newspaper, argued that a Black-owned cemetery "would prove a paying investment, stimulate enterprise and self-respect among Colored people of the city and the county." Evans's transaction carried great symbolic and material significance: it was a symbolic manifestation of Afro-Brooklynites control over their mortuary and memorial needs and provided another material example of racial accomplishment.[19]

In August 1891, the village board announced the installation of electric streetlights. Obtaining electric lights only a year after East St. Louis shows that Brooklyn was developing rapidly under Mayor Evans's leadership. On 18 August 1891, Evans opened a new post office, which was named in honor of Elijah P. Lovejoy, the white abolitionist. Subsequently, all mail leaving or entering Brooklyn was addressed to the "Lovejoy Post Office." Oral tradition claims the post office was named after Lovejoy because another town named Brooklyn existed in Schuyler County. Since zip codes did not exist in 1891, this probably explains why the post office was not named after the town, but it does not explain why it was named for an antislavery activist. The answer is found in Brooklyn's freedom-conscious political culture. Ironically, the consequence of honoring Lovejoy by naming the post office after him nearly obliterated the town's official name from public consciousness. Even today few people have heard of Brooklyn, Illinois, yet many are aware of Lovejoy. James Beasley, perhaps the only important white politician left in Brooklyn town politics at the time, was appointed to the new position of postmaster. Beasley and Alex Doscher, also white, were the town's justices of the peace. On the last day of October 1891, Evans dedicated a new two-story brick town hall, and in February of 1892, he contracted to have a fence built around the new city building. The new administrative building completed Evans's modernization of the town's infrastructure. Evans's success at enlarging the town's spatial boundaries and dramatically improving its infrastructure is evidence of his political skill and administrative ability. Just as important as his modernization campaign, however, was his role in the formation of a culture of affirmation and resistance that connected Brooklyn to broader Black political currents within the state and throughout the nation.[20]

Celebrating Freedom: Emancipation Day 1892

Afro-Brooklynites had probably been celebrating Emancipation Day since 1865, though their participation was not noted until 1883. The 1892 celebration is the only Emancipation Day observance on which we have detailed information. S. B. Turner, an Illinois assemblyman and the publisher and editor of the *State Capital,* a Black newspaper published in Springfield, Illinois, was the keynote speaker and reported on the festivities. Emancipation Day was part of an alternative political calendar created by Afro-Brooklynites, as was the celebration of Elijah P. Lovejoy's birthday. Afro-Brooklynites celebrated the traditional U.S. holidays, both secular and sacred. Quinn Chapel and Antioch Baptist churches and the various fraternal lodges also commemorated their foundings. Emancipation Day and Lovejoy's birthday, however, were special events because they were self-determined public holidays. The freedom-conscious political culture that gave birth to the town was expressed in these commemorative ceremonies. Under the banner "Grand Emancipation Celebration," the *State Capital* newspaper reported Brooklyn's Emancipation Day observance on 1 January 1892. According to Turner, John Evans and the town of Brooklyn "celebrated our emancipation in a grand and impressive manner." Blacks from St. Louis, Missouri, the metro-east region, and throughout the state attended this commemoration. By the 1890s, Emancipation Day ceremonies had developed a set of identifiable conventions. According to William W. Wiggins, Emancipation Day observances often included a parade through town led by a marching band. The marchers usually assembled at an African American church, frequently the largest Black church in the community. Ceremonies generally included the singing of freedom songs, the reading of the Emancipation Proclamation, and speeches assessing the state of the race. Wiggins described the Emancipation Day ceremonies as "sacred celebrations based upon the rituals and culture of the black church." Brooklyn's 1892 Emancipation Day celebration conformed to many of these conventions but departed from others.[21]

John Evans started Brooklyn's activities with a parade through the town. Marching to the beat of the Thomas Collins Band of St. Louis, the procession made its way through a heavy snow to the new town hall. Elsa Barkley Brown and Greg Kimball noted that in Richmond, Virginia, parades were often routed through the various sections of the Black community as a symbolic rite of unification. Parades in Brooklyn probably served similar purposes, but the 1892 procession was primarily designed to showcase municipal improvements, especially the new town hall, where the observance was held. The new post office and city building were monuments of civic and race pride. Fittingly, Turner commented on the electric streetlights and the new city building.[22]

The program began with a benediction given by the Reverend H. C. Burton, pastor of Quinn Chapel, Brooklyn's oldest church. Despite the opening, Brooklyn's 1892 Emancipation Day ceremony was not dominated by ministers or religious symbolism. The Reverend Burton and the Reverend Dr. Gar-

rett, the pastor of Antioch Missionary Baptist Church, were the only ministers scheduled to address the audience. Since they were pastors of the oldest
and largest churches in the community, it is not surprising that they were the
ministers chosen to participate. Both pastors were reputed to be excellent
orators. The Reverend Burton was often out of town preaching to other congregations and represented the Methodists in doctrinal debates with the Baptists. He was a rarity in post-incorporation Brooklyn—a politically active
minister. In February, he would be elected an alternate delegate from Stites
Township to the St. Clair County Republican Party Convention. In many ways,
the Reverend Burton continued the activist legacy of the African Methodist
Episcopal bishops William Paul Quinn and Jordan Winston Early.[23]

After the Reverend Burton's prayer, the keynote speaker, S. B. Turner, was
introduced. Turner addressed the "state of the race." Striking a positive note,
he concentrated on racial accomplishments since the end of slavery. Turner
was followed by Burton Washington, a teacher. Turner described Washington as "a young man of rare ability, reared and educated in Brooklyn." In early
December 1891, Washington filled the position of township clerk vacated
because of Henry Bletson's early death. Washington performed quite well in
the office and was elected clerk in the spring election. In 1906, Washington
would be elected mayor. Turner reported that Washington's speech was "frequently applauded." The Reverend Garrett, the next scheduled speaker, ex-
cused himself. Turner did not provide an explanation for Garrett's decision.
Professor Charles Jones spoke after Washington. Jones was principal of the
Lovejoy School and the revenue collector for Stites Township. In 1896, Jones
would be elected town treasurer and would serve as mayor from February
1903 to 1906. Turner credited him with giving "an eloquent and forceful address." The next speaker was postmaster James Beasley, the only Euro-American to address the audience and the last Euro-American to teach at Lovejoy
School in the nineteenth century. According to Turner, Beasley "made a
speech which reflected much credit on him and would have been appropriately received by any intelligent audience." Turner's comments suggest the
audience was unresponsive, perhaps even hostile, to Beasley's talk. Beasley
may not have been very popular. In 1898, Frederick Vanderberg would trounce
him in a contest for the school board. His address did not "move" the audience. It is possible that the crowd reacted to his style of presentation rather
the substance of his speech. Because of the oratorical tradition in African
American culture, audiences often place a greater emphasis on the style of
presentation than on the presentation's content. Oratory, according to Molefi
Kete Asante, is "the total oral tradition of Africans and African Americans."
The spoken word derives its significance in African American culture from
two sources. First, its power represents an Africanism, or a cultural continuity from African traditions. Second, and more important, it reflects the lin-

gering effect of slave-era antiliteracy laws. African Americans therefore prize the spoken word as an art form more than Euro-Americans do. Given Turner's positive assessment of Beasley's talk, it is likely Beasley appealed to the crowd's head, not its heart.[24]

In contrast, John Evans concluded the commemoration with a rousing speech. Evans, like Washington and Jones, realized that he had to "fire up" the crowd. Turner did not provide an excerpt from the speech, but he did summarize the audience's reaction. An exuberant Turner wrote, "The able, reliable and forceful speaker brought down the house at every word." The audience probably responded to the charismatic Evans's style of presentation as much as to the content of his address. Its response reflected the symmetry between Evans and Brooklyn's Black majority. The *East St. Louis Journal* described Evans as "an excellent orator—with a knowledge of the needs of his constituents" in its announcement of Brooklyn's 1894 Emancipation Day celebration. The article concluded that John Evans's remarks "will prove interesting to the audience and public. . . . And will receive a warm reception." Afro-Brooklynites' "warm" feelings for John Evans were not only because of his charisma but also because of his leadership role in ending colonial-style political domination, in modernizing Brooklyn's infrastructure, and in preserving a freedom-conscious political culture.[25]

The reception following the 1892 ceremony was hosted by Emma Vanderberg, wife of Frederick Vanderberg, a school board member who was the former town clerk and would become the mayor. Emma Vanderberg was the only woman mentioned as a part of the proceedings, and she was confined to a traditional woman's role. The Vanderbergs were probably the wealthiest Black Brooklynites. They owned a saloon, a billiard hall, and a restaurant. By having the reception at the Vanderberg's restaurant, Afro-Brooklynites were showcasing another "racial" accomplishment. In practical terms, their cafe was a private enterprise, but the politics of racial oppression symbolically converted their personal business into a "collective" accomplishment. Holding the reception in a Black-owned business was part of the same ethos that necessitated marching through town past the new post office and electric streetlights and holding the celebration in a modern, new town hall. Afro-Brooklynites took pride in these accomplishments. Summing up the activities, Turner wrote, the citizens of Brooklyn provided "an example worthy of imitation."[26]

This undoubtedly was true, yet Brooklyn's 1892 Emancipation Day celebration broke with tradition in several important ways. First, though these commemorations were usually sacred affairs, Brooklyn's was highly secularized. It occurred in the town hall rather than in a semipublic church, and the ministry played a minimal role. We cannot determine whether the celebration was structured according to "the rituals and culture of the black church."

We know the Thomas Collins Marching Band provided music, but we do not know what songs they played or whether church choirs sang spirituals or gospel songs. The newspaper accounts did not comment on the rituals and cultural aspects of the celebration. However, it would be extremely unusual if such spirituals as "Swing Low Sweet Chariot," "Free at Last," "Many Thousands Gone," and "Go Down Moses" were not sung. Second, it appears that the Emancipation Proclamation was not read. The reading of President Lincoln's decree was a special part of Emancipation Day observances. African American orators, usually young women, had developed its reading into an art form, according to Wiggins. He claimed that when "this stilted document" was "filtered through the filter of Afro-American culture," it was transformed "into a powerful statement of freedom." I doubt that the reporters would have failed to mention such an important part of the commemoration. Despite these differences, Brooklyn's 1892 Emancipation Day celebration was rooted in the African American oral tradition and conformed to a central convention of emancipation celebrations.[27]

The Emancipation Day speakers represented Brooklyn's political leadership. They were all male and African American except for one Euro-American speaker. Two of the presenters were ministers, though their role was marginal. One offered the benediction, and at the last minute the other declined to speak. Three of the orators were schoolteachers, one of whom was white. All three also held administrative positions in the community. Burton Washington had recently been appointed town clerk, Charles B. Jones was the tax collector for the township, and James A. Beasley was the new postmaster. Evans and Jones were the only "politicians" to address the crowd. That most of the speakers were educators is not surprising, since the school district offered the only readily available supply of professionals. John Evans was not a teacher but a laborer, as was most of the village board of trustees. His administration symbolized the rise of the working class and its teacher allies as elected and appointed public officials. The prominent role of educators in Brooklyn politics is consistent with Vincent P. Franklin's observation that educators have historically been the most active professionals in the African American community. Within six years, objective class distinctions and differences in strategy would divide Brooklyn's anticolonial militants into two warring political factions: the Republicans and the Peoples party. In 1892, however, they were united around the basic principle of Black power.[28]

Besides celebrating Emancipation Day, Afro-Brooklynites commemorated 31 March in honor of Elijah Lovejoy's martyrdom. Celebrating the birthdays of antiracist whites was not strange for African Americans. Blacks commemorated the birth of Abraham Lincoln as well as lesser-known figures. For example, Blacks in St. Louis observed William Lloyd Garrison's birthday. Though little is known about the commemoration ceremony for Lovejoy, it is reasonable to suppose that it followed conventions similar to Garrison Day ceremonies and other such occasions. We do know that Emancipation Day and Lovejoy Day represented Afro-Brooklynites' political calendar. Collectively, these celebrations affirmed the community's commitment to teach and preserve its antiracist heritage and to keep the community focused on freedom. The commemorations of Emancipation Day and the martyrdom of Elijah Lovejoy are poignant examples of Mayor John Evans's encouragement of a political culture of affirmation and resistance.[29]

In late February, Evans, Beasley, and Green Hart, a laborer, were elected delegates from Stites Township to the 1892 St. Clair County Republican Party Convention. During the nineteenth century, Hart was the only African American elected to a judgeship in St. Clair County. The delegates from Stites Township reflected the racial composition of the township. The delegates included two Afro-Americans, Evans and Hart, and one Euro-American, Beasley. Two African Americans—the Reverend H. C. Burton and Marshal James Pettiford—and one Euro-American—Samuel S. Hoffman—were the alternates. Stites Township's African American leadership practiced a form of proportional representation, making sure to include whites as minority participants. Although Blacks dominated Brooklyn and the township, they were marginalized at the county level. At the county convention in Belleville on 5 March 1892, John Evans was the only African American delegate elected to the state convention, and no African American was elected to attend the congressional convention.[30]

In mid-May of 1892, John Evans displayed his ability to communicate with non-Blacks. On 19 May 1892, Brooklyn was devastated by what the *Belleville Weekly Advocate* described as the "most destructive flood since 1844." Brooklyn was submerged under water, and its residents were forced to seek refuge on an island in the Mississippi River. Mayor Evans appealed to the East St. Louis City Council and the St. Clair County Board of Supervisors for aid. According to the *East St. Louis Journal,* his appeal was so moving that he returned to the encampment "loaded down with meats, bread, groceries, and all manner of provisions." Evans's persuasiveness had elicited a generous response from the county board and the residents of East St. Louis and Belleville. Evans was adept at conveying his message to both African and European Americans.[31]

After two successful terms as president of the village board, John Evans focused his considerable political energies on the Stites Township board, the St. Clair County board, and the Illinois Afro-American Protective League. In the spring of 1894, William Allison succeeded Evans as mayor. Allison, like many of Brooklyn's striving politicians, worked in several occupations. In 1880, when he was twenty-four, the manuscript censuses listed "works in shoe shop" as his occupation. During the 1890s, he was listed as a carpenter, a farmer, and the owner of a shoe store in city directories and newspapers. As mayor, Allison was essentially a caretaker. In January of 1895, Brooklyn sponsored another Emancipation Day, and at the end of January 1896, he renamed streets and renumbered dwelling places. Although his tenure as mayor was uneventful, a decision by the school board in 1894 would have tremendous ramifications.[32]

In 1894, white residents again exercised their right to petition government. Three years earlier, they had tried to annex Brooklyn out of existence. This time, they presented petitions to the all-Black school board requesting a return to segregated schooling. Amazingly, according to C. B. Carroll, "the school board composed entirely of negroes, in response to a petition from the white citizens of the town, provided for a separate school for the education of white children, and appointed Mr. Henry Hertel as its first principal." Consequently, as Carroll noted, Brooklyn became the only town in the country "governed by colored men" to have "a separate school for the education of white children, presided over by a white teacher." This was a dramatic reversal of Tazwell Bird's struggle to desegregate schooling nearly two decades before. Unable to regain control of the municipal government or abolish it, the town's remaining white residents targeted the schools for resegregation. Why did the Black community accommodate the exclusionary demands of its white minority? Besides strategic differences, it must be pointed out that the first two teachers at Sherman School, the white school, were Henry and Walter Hertel, the sons of Charles Hertel, the St. Clair County superintendent of schools. When Henry left teaching to become a physician, Walter inherited his position. Employment of the county superintendent of schools' sons suggests that patronage might have been involved or that St. Clair County school officials pressured members of Brooklyn's school board into accepting separate schooling for white children. The return of institutional segregation reflected the gaping holes in Black unity, the lack of a consensus on basic political and social questions, and a retreat from the legacy of Tazwell Bird. Evans, as his deep involvement in the Alton case demonstrated, opposed segregated schooling. The implications of the decision to resegregate would reverberate into the early twentieth century.[33]

In August 1898, Allison died, and funeral services were held at Corinthian Baptist Church. According to William Halliburton, a stringer for the *Illinois Record*, the "funeral was largely attended." Allison was succeeded by Frederick F. Vanderberg, who had been town clerk from 1882 to 1890. Evans held various elective offices through 1906, but increasingly his activism in the Illinois Afro-American Protective League moved him beyond the boundaries of the small Black town and electoral politics.[34]

From Politician to Afro-American Protective League Political Activist

On 3 January 1892, two days after he sponsored the town's largest Emancipation Day celebration, Evans hosted a state convention of the Illinois Afro-American Protective League. Illinois state president James Hale Potter and representatives from Alton, Bloomington, Cairo, Danville, Decatur, Jacksonville, Peoria, Rock Island, and Chicago met in Brooklyn. T. Thomas Fortune had conceived of the National Afro-American League in 1887. The National Afro-American League combined the preeminent philosophy of self-help and racial solidarity with the protest tactics of legal and direct action. The league movement rapidly spread throughout Black America. By 1889, enough state and local chapters had been established to call a national convention. In 1890, the league held its first national convention in Chicago, Illinois. In his presidential address, Fortune enunciated a strategy that merged legalism and self-defense:

> All those who have gotten profit by our disorganization and fattened on our labor by class and corporate legislation, will oppose this Afro-American League movement. In the intensity of their opposition they may resort to cowardly argument of violence; but are we to remain forever inactive, the victims of extortion and duplicity on this account? No, sir. We propose to accomplish our purposes by the peaceful methods of agitation, through the ballot and the courts, but if others use the weapon of violence to combat our peaceful arguments, it is not for us to run away from violence. "A man's a man," and what is worth having is worth fighting for.[35]

Besides advocating the right to self-defense, bloc voting, and litigation, the Afro-American League targeted areas for protest: the discriminatory structure of public education, the brutalization and exploitation of convicts, segregation of public facilities, and labor exploitation. The league movement also called for self-development initiatives, such as organizing banks and business enterprises and establishing an emigration bureau to move Afro-Americans throughout the United States. The National Afro-American League practiced a dialectical strategy that involved, in Lerone Bennett's words, "a double and reciprocal struggle for Black development and *against* white restrictions on that development."[36]

By 1893, the Afro-American League movement had begun to fracture because of ideological, strategic, and personal differences. Factionalism incapacitated most of the league chapters between 1893 and 1898. In Illinois, however, several league chapters continued to function. These local chapters were organized into two different leagues: the Illinois Afro-American Protective League, led by the Reverend Jordan Chavis of Quincy, and the Afro-American State Protective League of Illinois, led by John G. Jones of Chicago. John Evans was the state treasurer of the former league, which represented most of the downstate Afro-American communities. During November of 1897, the Illinois Afro-American Protective League held a conference in Springfield. In a letter to the *Illinois Record,* whose masthead declared it was "the official organ of the Illinois Afro-American Protective League," the Reverend Chavis explained the necessity for the league:

> It is evident that the prejudice to our people in many localities is growing worse each year. This in my opinion is due to the rapid progress of the Negro rather than to his former condition. The whites therefore inaugurate impediments to the progress out of fear of Negro supremacy, therefore to overcome these impediments it is highly necessary that the thinking, the educated and loving men and women of the race come together not for notoriety, self-aggrandizement, nor political trickery, but to systematize efforts, to manifest the strength, and encourage the weak of the race to meet constant opposition manly and unfaltering. Hence the greatest necessity for the Afro-American Protective League.[37]

Despite the irony of calling on men and women to engage in "manly" resistance, Chavis, unlike most male spokespersons then, did explicitly include women in his analysis. He was probably unaware of this contradiction. Though his notion of bourgeois leadership is equally troubling, Chavis clearly articulated the continuing need for the league. Further, since he did not call for revitalization or reorganization, his statement suggests that at least one Illinois league was functioning in 1897.

The year 1898 was particularly harrowing for African Americans in Illinois. Across the state, Blacks found themselves under increasing physical, political, and social attack. In Decatur, Springfield, and Chicago and in Pulaski and St. Clair counties, African American activists challenged local Republican parties for their fair share of political offices and civil service appointments. Derisively, African Americans began to call the Republican party the "party of promises" or the "*Grand Old Lilly White Party.*" Violence against African Americans reached a peak when a Black man was lynched in Logan. Beginning on 1 September, sporadic racial violence flared as mine owners imported Black miners into Pana and Virden to break a strike by white miners. On 12 October, open warfare erupted as armed whites attacked a train attempting to unload Black miners in Virden. Eleven people were killed, none of which were African American, but several Blacks were among the thirty injured. The next day, the National Guard restored order and generally retained it until the spring of 1899. In March of 1899, at their annual convention, the United Mine Workers passed a resolution requesting Governor John R. Tanner to "remove the State troops and disarm all Negroes in Pana and force said operators and miners of Pana to make . . . A settlement." The Illinois National Guard was withdrawn. On 10 April 1899, Deputy Sheriff Frank Cheney ar-

rested "Big Henry" Stevens, a leader among African American miners. In the
resulting racial clash, seven people were killed, and fourteen were wounded.
Four of the seven dead and seven of the fourteen injured were Black. The
National Guard was sent back to quell the violence. Samuel Brush, an op-
portunistic mine operator in Carterville, responded to a strike at his mine
by attempting to move about forty of the Black miners from Pana to his facilities. On 30 June, the train carrying the Black miners was attacked before
it could reach Carterville. The National Guard arrived on 2 July. On 17 September, six days after the National Guard was recalled, five African American miners were murdered as racial violence erupted again. The National
Guard returned to Carterville. By October, the Pana mining company began
negotiating with the United Mine Workers. It subsequently dismissed its
Black employees and rehired the white union miners.[38]

In Alton and Centralia, Blacks went to court to end school segregation. In
1897, the city of Alton had decided to return to its early 1870s policy of segregated public education for the elementary grades. Alton's Mayor Henry
Brueggemann was particularly anti-Black. Using white supremacist rhetoric, Brueggemann callously manipulated this issue to his political advantage.
Blacks responded to Brueggemann's racism by suing the city. August Meier
referred to *The People of Illinois, ex rel, Scott Bibb v. the Mayor and Common
Council of the City of Alton* as one of the first court cases challenging segregated schooling after the *Plessey v. Ferguson* decision. In 1908, after eleven
years, seven jury trials, and five appeals, the Illinois Supreme Court finally
ruled in favor of the Bibb family's suit. In this climate of racial warfare, political betrayal, and efforts to reinstate policies reminiscent of the antebellum era Black Laws, George E. Hall, the managing editor of the *Illinois Record,*
considered unification of the Illinois leagues a necessity if African Americans
were to weather this racist blizzard.[39]

John Evans took the lead in formulating African Americans' response to
their worsening conditions. In late January 1898, Evans convened a meeting
on the Alton school crisis. He appointed a committee, headed by Sylvester T.
Archer, a Black grocer and son of former Brooklyn politician Frederick Archer, and charged it "to devise ways and means to support the Alton struggle." The Brooklyn committee decided to raise monies for the Alton struggle
by soliciting funds from church congregations. Archer immediately published
a letter in the *Illinois Record* urging statewide support for the suit against school
segregation in Alton. He stated, "We hope to be of some benefit to the citizens of Alton though the conflict does not reach us directly as individuals, but
it does indirectly as a nation." This meeting was very timely since the court
had scheduled a hearing for February on the Afro-American protesters' writ
of mandamus requesting that Mayor Brueggemann, the city council, and the
board of education rescind the order segregating Alton's schools. Evans's ini-

tiative was immediately duplicated throughout the state. In February, the Decatur chapter of the Illinois Afro-American Protective League held rallies protesting segregated schooling in Alton. At one rally the keynote speaker, Waymon Wilkerson, told the audience, "Those who put their trust in legislation as a sure means of receiving good and preventing evil are no wiser than those of today who have implicit confidence in the saving power of corporations, trusts and monopolies." Wilkerson's observation reminds us of the anticapitalist sentiments Fortune had articulated. As the Alton crisis simmered during the summer, African American communities in the northern and central sections of the state established special committees. Springfield Blacks sponsored a statewide rally on the Fourth of July. The special committees that sprung up around the state were modeled after Brooklyn's.[40]

Perhaps Alton's proximity to Brooklyn made this case special for Evans, but his opposition to his school board's reestablishment of segregated schooling in 1894 probably motivated him as much as anything else. From 1876 to 1894, Brooklyn maintained a desegregated school system, but Brooklyn whites, like most other white southern Illinoisans, opposed "mixed" schools. Alton, East St. Louis, Edwardsville, and most other towns in St. Clair County drew the color line in education. In 1875, when Tazwell Bird led the struggle for "mixed" schools, some Blacks opposed desegregation. Most Afro-Americans in southern Illinois communities accepted segregated schools, even though Blacks in the central and northern parts of the state did not. Downstate Blacks often focused their energies on obtaining equality within the contours of segregation. That is, they fought for equal funding for Black schools and for the employment of Black teachers. Consequently, there was always some support for separate schools among Afro-Brooklynites. This sentiment manifested itself in 1894, when Brooklyn's all-Black school board capitulated to whites' petition for "a separate school for the education of white children" by building Sherman School in 1901.[41]

In March 1898, Hall urged Blacks to support African American candidates and to participate in the Republican primary to ensure that party candidates were not "anti-Black" and "to get their fair numerical share of delegates to the State Republican Convention." He estimated that eighty-one Afro-American delegates, including three from St. Clair County, should be elected to the state convention.[42] In September 1898, Hall reported that African American activists in Brooklyn were challenging the St. Clair County Republican party for positions and patronage. Evans and league activists published the following statement in the *Illinois Record:* "The colored voters of this county deserve political recognition and the sooner the leaders make up their minds to give us justice, the better will be the results. Promises don't go. We have lived on them for many years.'By your deeds ye are known.'"[43] This challenge reflected Evans's success at propagating the Afro-American

League's philosophy and methods throughout St. Clair County. Similar efforts were occurring in Decatur and Springfield and in Pulaski County. In Decatur, Blacks openly opposed Isaac R. Mills, the Republican nominee for Congress, and Harry Midkiff, the Republican candidate for Macon County sheriff because they believed the men were either negligent or culpable in the lynching of Samuel J. Bush in 1893. Reports of similar challenges to Republican hegemony are abundant during 1897–98. Oscar Duncan, a Black candidate, lost a campaign for the Springfield City Council because not enough white Republicans voted for him. According to Shirley Portwood, African Americans in Pulaski County were threatening to bolt the party if their demands for power sharing were not met. After white Republicans failed to support Black Republican candidates in the 1898 elections, many Blacks left the party, and Democrats won the 1898 county elections. Pulaski County's white Republicans were subsequently forced to appoint Blacks to civil service positions and to support African American candidates in the 1900 elections.[44]

As Fortune was agitating for the revival and reorganization of the national league, Hall was pushing for the reactivation and unification of the two Illinois associations. Responding to Hall's initiative and perhaps his criticisms, the Reverend Chavis called a meeting of the Illinois Afro-American Protective League's executive board. In a statement dated 23 March 1898, Chavis announced an executive meeting in Bloomington on 23 April. Negotiations began with the Chicago league after the April meeting. In July, while the Reverend Chavis was in Cuba serving as chaplain of the Eighth United States Regiment, the two associations announced a joint convention for September "to unite the various sections of the Illinois Afro-American League."[45] Representatives from both factions issued the following statement:

> By the power invested in us as President and Secretaries of the two branches of the Afro-American League we jointly call the convention to convene in Springfield Tuesday, September 27, at noon. We urgently request every part of the state to be represented, as the conditions demand action at once. The Alton and Centralia School questions and the potter's field for the Negro warrants your attention in compliance to the constitution.
>
> John G. Jones, Chicago, President, Jacob Amos,
> Cairo, Secretary; Rev. George A. Browne,
> Springfield, First Vice-President; Dr. M. A. Majors,
> Decatur, Secretary

A merger was now merely a formality. Hall issued the call for the convention in banner headlines: "COME IN LARGE NUMBERS TO THE CONVENTION." In bold language, Hall repeated his calls for insurgent politics, stating, "The time demands organization. . . . The time has come when we must stand on our merits as men and not as tools in the hands of political sycophants who don't know you after the election is over."[46]

The decision to hold a reunification conference was timely, for on 1 September striking white miners attacked Black mine workers in Pana and on 1 November a Black man was murdered in Logan. Hall quickly condemned Republican governor John R. Tanner for responding slowly to the racial violence engulfing Pana and Virden and the lynching of the African American in Logan.[47] At its unification convention, the Afro-American League, composed of the old Illinois Afro-American Protective League and the Afro-American State Protective League of Illinois, formed special committees on the race riots and the Alton and Centralia school controversies. John Evans, who initiated support activities for the Alton struggle, was joined on the committee by Lem Taylor of Centralia, C. Johnson from Watseka, and Albert O'Leary of Jacksonville. The Reverend George Browne, former vice-president of the downstate chapter, was appointed chair of the statewide committee, and Lawrence A. Newby, president of Cook County's Colored Democratic League, was appointed secretary.[48]

The return of segregated schooling in Alton and Centralia was viewed by the Afro-American League as a significant reversal. The Alton case was particularly odious because the town's police force abused protesting Afro-American youth. The reunited league represented the views of northern, central, and radical Afro-Illinoisans. Since the struggles against the Black Laws in the 1850s, northern and central Illinois Blacks had been more aggressive in challenging racial restrictions. Southern Illinois Black leaders had long ago acquiesced to segregated education. The Wood River Baptist Association's opposition to Scott Bibb's suit against segregated schooling in Alton underscores the regionalized political division among Illinois Blacks regarding mixed schooling. The league supported Bibb's suit through rallies and fundraising efforts for the remainder of its existence, but the case dragged on long after the league had disbanded.[49]

Probably because of the reunification, the Illinois Afro-American League was chosen to hold the National Afro-American League's annual convention on 17–18 August 1899 in Chicago. At the convention, the activists who had worked to unite the organization's northern and southern factions were replaced by nationally renowned activist-intellectuals. Ida B. Wells-Barnett, then residing in Chicago, was the only Illinoisan who played a major public role in the conference. Wells-Barnett and T. Thomas Fortune, the founder of the organization, were in charge of the program. On 5–7 October 1899, the Illinois state chapter of the Afro-American League held its annual meeting in Chicago. The *Broadax* expected a large crowd, but on the same weekend Chicago hosted the National Association of Colored Women. Unfortunately, the reunited Afro-American League never became the force for African

Americans in the state that John Evans and other local activists envisioned, but it did educate a core group of activists who would continue the battle into the twentieth century.[50]

Independent Challenge to the Republican Party Hegemony

A decade after he left the mayor's office, John Evans decided to run for Brooklyn's board of trustees. In 1904, he joined the reform government of Charles Jones. Why did Evans run for the village board? During 1903, Brooklyn was rocked by two devastating events. On 19 February 1903, Frederick Vanderberg, leader of the local Peoples party, had his mayorship interrupted by a criminal conviction for embezzlement. Four months later, on 6 June 6 1903, David Wyatt, a teacher at Lovejoy School and the secretary of the Brooklyn Republican party, was lynched after he shot the St. Clair County school superintendent, Charles Hertel. Things were going so badly in Brooklyn that the *St. Louis Palladium* predicted, "Next year the mayor of that village will be white. Next year Brooklyn will be governed by a white man and such as Dr. Arthur will be the cause of it." Dr. W. R. Arthur, Brooklyn's postmaster, was described by John Wheeler, editor of the *Palladium*, as "a low down owner of a saloon-dance-hall." Wheeler's animus toward Arthur was based on his belief that Arthur was a con man who had been set up in the saloon business by Euro-American brewers. Wheeler dedicated himself to exposing Arthur. Vanderberg, also the owner of a saloon, was arrested often between 1899 and 1915 for selling liquor without a license and running an illegal gambling parlor. Perhaps concern for the quality of local government and fear of an invasion by white mobs from the surrounding communities led Evans to rejoin the board of trustees.[51]

During the spring campaign, the Evans family was struck with tragedy when their ten-year-old son died. Mysteriously, John and Elizabeth Evans chose to bury their youngest child in St. Peter's Cemetery in St. Louis. This is peculiar because during his tenure as mayor Evans had negotiated the return of a section of land from Wiggins Ferry Company expressly for a cemetery in Brooklyn. Despite the tragedy of his son's death, Evans went on to win a place on the village board.[52]

In 1906, two years after helping install a city leadership untainted by corruption, Evans sought elective office beyond the borders of Brooklyn and Black-dominated Stites Township. He sought the Republican party's nomination for state representative from St. Clair County. Getting on the ballot was no easy task. Drawing on his local political organization and statewide contacts, Evans succeeded in collecting the necessary 25,000 signatures. This was a bold move, for if he won, he would become the first African American outside Chicago to sit in the Illinois General Assembly. Evans had several strong points in his favor. Most important, he had held elective office for six-teen years. He had been mayor of Brooklyn from 1886 to 1894 and supervi-sor from Stites Township from 1892 to 1900. Evans had established a record as an honest, hard-working politician. Still, in the eyes of St. Clair County's white Republican party leadership, Evans had disadvantages. He was Black; he had led the African American political insurgency in Brooklyn; he was a militant Afro-American Protective League activist, who had supported the Alton desegregation case; and he came from a town noted for political cor-ruption. To win, he would need more than the Black vote. This was a daunt-ing challenge considering the racial climate in St. Clair County during the spring of 1906.

Two incidents convey the racial climate. On Monday night, 26 March 1906, George White, an African American, went to the home of Carrie Brown, a white woman, to confront her after learning at work that she had accused him of assaulting her Sunday night. Allegedly after seeing White on her porch, Brown began screaming. White packing-house workers saw White running from Brown's house and gave chase, eventually cornering him at 700 Bow-man Street. Four African Americans, John Hickman, John Joiner, J. Lewis, and J. Miles, who lived nearby saved White and, firing gunshots and wield-ing clubs, effected a standoff with the mob until the police arrived. Police officers fired riot guns and dispersed the mob described by the *East St. Louis Journal* as "150 foreigners, Polanders and Armenians." After dispersing the mob, the officers arrested all five African Americans. White was held on $1,000 bond and bound over to the grand jury. The actions of George White, John Hickman, John Joiner, J. Lewis, and J. Miles demonstrate African Amer-icans' transgression of acceptable racial etiquette. Less than a week after this event, on Saturday, 31 March, the Citizens party filed two complaints with the East St. Louis Election Commission. First, it complained that its support-ers, "particularly the colored voters," were being intimidated to keep them from voting. Second, it alleged that "colonization of voters for illegal voting" was occurring. The absence of race from the second charge strongly suggests the Citizens party believed white voters were being brought into East St. Louis. The election board issued this resolution:

> It is hereby ordered by the Board of Election Commissioners, of the City of East
> St. Louis, that the Chief of Police of this City, be requested to instruct Police
> officers who will be on duty at the respective polling places on next Tuesday
> the 3rd day of April 1996, to see that the peace is duly preserved and that said
> Police Officers see to it that there shall be no electioneering or soliciting of voters
> on Election day within 100 feet of any polling place, and that no voter while
> approaching or leaving the polling place, shall be interrupted, intimidated, or
> interfered with, and to arrest any and all persons who may be found intimi-
> dating or interfering with voters whether within or without the 100-foot limit,

and that the sheriff of St. Clair County be requested to have his local force of deputies on hand and subject to the orders of this Board on election day to assist the Police on that day, if necessary in preserving the peace, and enforcing the laws, regulating elections.

It is further ordered that the Clerk of this Board furnish the Chief of Police, and the Sheriff a copy of this order.

Benj. H. Canby
E. S. Coddington
P. Flannery
Board of Election Commissioners,
Attest: Chas. S. Lambert[53]

Though the racialization of the mayoral campaign in East St. Louis and the near lynching of George White on the eve of the primary election were not linked to Evans's campaign for the Illinois legislature, these events did not endear his candidacy to white St. Clair County voters.

Perhaps because of St. Clair County's heated racial atmosphere, the *Forum*, an African American newspaper published in Springfield, initially adopted a political strategy that today would be known as "deracialization." "Deracialization, as applied to American electoral politics, is," according to Huey L. Perry, "the conduction of an electoral campaign in which racial issues and themes are minimized, if not avoided, in order to attract increased white electoral support." The *Forum* described Evans as "a staunch Republican" who "stands high in his county." E. L. Rogers, the editor, tried to establish Evans's credentials as a loyal Republican to distinguish him from Blacks who had aligned themselves with the Peoples party. After commending the "idea of competent Negroes aspiring to office," the newspaper pledged to "render Mr. Evans all the services at our command." Rogers ended the endorsement by declaring, "The readers of the *Forum* in Brooklyn know our stand and therefore have our cooperation for Evans."[54]

Like most African American candidates throughout the state and across the country, Evans lost in the primary. Illinois had adopted a primary system in 1898. The meager success African Americans had in obtaining party nominations and election to office under the previous party convention system was reversed by the adoption of the primary method of candidate selection. Urban politics dictated that African Americans be placed on the ballot in areas where the African American vote was important, and the convention system had facilitated the development of a racially integrated ticket because party conventions tended to "rubber stamp" the nominating committee's choices. For example, under the old convention system Abraham Pope, an African American from Brooklyn, was nominated for a seat in the legislature in 1874. Pope, like most African American candidates, did not benefit from party loyalty after nomination, however. He won only East St.

Louis Precinct 3 (Brooklyn) and one other precinct. Adoption of the primary system at the turn of the century forced African American candidates to run first against white fellow Republicans in the primary contests and then against a white Democrat in the general election. Harold Gosnell points out how this change affected Black Republicans vying for seats on the Cook County Board of Supervisors. He discovered that out of ten cases, whites defeated black candidates four times in the Republican primary, and in the six instances in which African Americans won the primary they were defeated by white Democrats in the general election. The historical evidence indicates that not many whites were willing to vote for a Black man, even a nominee of their party. Though the reformers claimed they were expanding the democratic process by abolishing the arbitrary and corrupt practices of the conventions, many scholars see racial and class motivations behind many Progressive Era reforms, such as direct primaries and citywide elections.[55]

After Evans's defeat in the Republican primary, he decided to run as an independent candidate. The *Forum* reassessed its deracialization policy and began to use subtle racial appeals. Apparently, the editor thought their new policy was not working because in the middle of May the paper was again deemphasizing race, declaring that Evans "will make the race on his merits." By July, however, it seemed clear that white Republicans were not supporting Evans. In response to the Republican party's refusal to support African American candidates, the Black newspaper advocated an independent, race-conscious, political line. The new perspective recalled the *Illinois Record*'s 1898 call for the election of "race men" to the General Assembly. In late July, Rogers boldly stated, "John Evans . . . should receive a solid Republican vote— they had better support Evans, for the Negro has declared henceforth, 'way down in their hearts, that an eye shall be given for an eye, and a tooth for a tooth.'" The *Forum*'s Old Testament imagery served several purposes. First, it gave religious sanction to independent Black politics. Second, it challenged the Republican party to return the loyalty that African Americans had shown the party. Third, it articulated a return to independent Black politics. By drawing on the religious traditions of African Americans, the *Forum*'s editor used the biblical language as an "inherent ideology," a cultural resource, with which to mobilize African American voters and to threaten the traitorous Republican party.[56]

Responding to what they termed the Republican party's disrespect, African Americans resolved to stand for "manhood." That is, they agreed to support independent African American candidates. The relationship between independence and manhood suggested in the formation of the new political stance is consistent with the tenor of the times. African American men recognized the connection between the concepts of manhood and independence and attempted to recast manhood into a weapon for Black advancement, although accepting its gender implications. During the nineteenth century, African American usage of *manhood* was equivalent to workers' use of *manliness*. It had multiple meanings. The term conveyed the refusal to bow to white America's dictum "that the Black man has no rights that the white man is bound to respect." It embodied the dignity of defiance and self-reliance, but it also reflected African American men's desire to emulate Euro-American's gender relations.[57]

Curiously, the *Forum,* the *East St. Louis Journal,* and the *Belleville Weekly Advocate* did not cover Evans's campaign rallies or fund-raising events. The lack of coverage from the *Journal* and the *Advocate* is understandable, since neither saw Evans as a creditable candidate. The *Forum* diligently promoted his candidacy but did not address his identification of the issues or his stance on them. We may never know what John Evans's positions were or whether he endorsed the shifting strategies of the *Forum,* but the evidence strongly suggests that the aggressive race-conscious policy reflected Evans's sentiment. First, the militant biblical language in the *Forum*'s July editorial mirrored the tenor and tone of an open letter from Brooklyn Blacks to the St. Clair County Republican party. The letter appeared in the 10 September 1898 issue of the *Illinois Record.* John Evans was most likely the author of this statement. Second, Evans's decision to run as an independent candidate after losing the Republican party primary illustrated his position on the question of race and party loyalty.[58]

In response to the defeat of John Evans and other highly respected African American activist politicians, Blacks in Chicago talked about breaking with both major white capitalist parties and forming their own party. However, Blacks in central and southern Illinois went beyond words and formed the Independent League "to work in their own interests." With three seats at stake in the legislative race, John Evans chose to continue the fight for Black political representation as an independent candidate. He challenged two Democratic candidates, Lincoln Wright and George F. Smith, and Fred Keck and John L. Flannigan, who had defeated him in the Republican primary. The *Forum,* having failed to rally whites to Evans's campaign, returned to appeals for racial unity. Rogers declared, "Mr. Evans should receive every Negro vote in that county . . . We hope our people will not be frustrated and fooled. Vote for John Evans and you will be glad of it in the future. Pave the way for yourselves and your children. Will you do it?"[59]

Evans lost his independent bid for the legislature. He received only 1,200 votes in the legislative district, including 555 in East St. Louis. Evans came in last, finishing behind Keck, Flannigan, and Smith, who were elected to the state House of Representatives, and Wright, the other Democratic candidate.[60]

Conclusion

On 30 July 1910, four years after his independent run for the state legislature, John Evans died a relatively poor man in Hot Springs, Arkansas, at the age of fifty-five.[61] Evans was never elected to public office outside Brooklyn, but he was one of the most outstanding Black political leaders in Illinois during this period. Evans left a complex legacy. Between 1886 and 1906, he struggled to build Black power in Brooklyn; he was the central force behind the Black community's mobilization against white minority colonial domination. He used the prestige of his office to promote a freedom-conscious African American culture. From the mayor's office, he preached and practiced protest politics. He also modernized Brooklyn's infrastructure. During his tenure as mayor, Brooklyn acquired electric streetlights and built a post office and new town hall. He also engaged in statewide politics. He was the state treasurer of the Illinois Afro-American Protective League, and his early activism in support of the plaintiffs of the Alton school case sparked similar actions across the state. In 1905–6, Evans challenged white Republican hegemony in St. Clair County by running as an independent candidate for state representative.

Evans was an anomaly among Black mayors. Whereas many Black mayors were entrepreneurs who profited from their offices, he was a common laborer during most of his tenure as mayor. This working-class political activist became the first African American mayor of the oldest Black town and the first Black chief executive of an American municipality. Further, Evans offers a sharp contrast to Isaiah T. Montgomery, T. B. Armstrong, and the other conservative Black-town mayors who practiced the accommodationist politics of Booker T. Washington, the "Wizard of Tuskeegee." Evans was a working-class mayor of a majority-Black town whose internal politics was shaped by the industrial proletarianization process. John Evans's life offers a model of the dedicated and defiant African American political activist.

PART 3

Proletarianization, Dependency, and the Limits of Black Political Power, 1886–1915

5. Proletarianization, Dependency, and Underdevelopment, 1886–1910

THE TWENTY-YEAR PERIOD from 1890 to 1910 was the critical time during which Brooklyn's role as a site for commuter labor in the metro-east's political economy was determined. These years span parts of the third period (1886–97) and fourth period (1898–1915) of Brooklyn's history and are encompassed by the metro-east region's "golden age" of industrialization, 1890–1919. This era represents the culmination of fundamental economic and social changes that began in the metro-east's third period of industrialization, 1875 to 1890. Rapid proletarianization affected Brooklyn's development in many ways. It shaped its demographic, occupational, social, and family structures and influenced its culture and politics. In the wake of these structural changes, Brooklyn's population soared to 1,577. However, the population increase was uneven, in not only nativity but also race, gender, and age. Racially, the Euro-American population fell about 7 percent, from 207 in 1880 to 194 in 1910, while the Afro-American population nearly quadrupled, from 371 to 1,384. Much of the African American growth occurred among adults. The adult population rose from 208 in 1880 to 485 in 1900 and 996 in 1910. In 1880, Afro-American adults constituted 56 percent of Black Brooklyn's population; by 1910, they were nearly 72 percent. Afro-American women numbered 102 in 1880, 237 in 1900, and 462 in 1910. Nevertheless, their percentage of the adult Black population declined slightly, from more than 49 percent in 1880 to less than 47 percent in 1910. Meanwhile, Black men totaled 106 in 1880, 248 in 1900, and 533 in 1910. Correspondingly, Black men's share of the adult Black population increased from less than 51 percent in 1880 to more than 53 percent in 1910.[1]

During this period, the migration of southern Blacks to Brooklyn both conformed to and differed from the Afro-American migratory stream to Il-

linois. Before the great migration, most Black migrants to Illinois came from
the border states; after 1915, they came mainly from the Deep South. Brooklyn's Black migrants followed this pattern. In 1900, 179 (more than 42 percent) of employed Black males were born in Tennessee (81), Missouri (63),
and Kentucky (35). Although most Blacks continued to migrate from the
former slaves states bordering Illinois, by 1910 many Afro-Brooklynite males
came from the southern states of Alabama, Arkansas, Georgia, Louisiana, and
Mississippi. By 1910, Mississippi supplied the third largest group of African
American male migrants (42). One hundred twenty-nine (24.29 percent)
came from the Deep South. Afro-Brooklynite males migrated to Brooklyn
from twenty-one different states, the Indian Territory, Africa, and Canada,
while Black females came from eighteen different states, Africa, and Canada
(see table 11). Black migrants who settled in Brooklyn were like other Afro-
Americans migrating to Illinois in another significant way. Between 1860 and
1890, most Black migrants to Illinois settled in rural areas or in small towns.
Jack Blocker suggests this preference may be because they were familiar with
farm labor. Nonetheless, like most of their fellow migrants, Black and white,
they were unable to acquire farmland. However, Blacks migrating to Brooklyn also diverged from the mainstream in several ways. First, by 1890, it is
unlikely that migrants to Brooklyn held fantasies of becoming a freeholder.
Second, before 1890, more Black men than women migrated to Illinois; after 1890, the reverse was true. Brooklyn, however, contradicted this pattern.
The 1870 and 1880 censuses report a slight majority of Afro-American women
migrating to Brooklyn, 165 to 163 (see tables 4 and 5 in chapter 3). Finally, in
1910, in contrast to the statewide pattern, at least 382 Black men relocated to
Brooklyn compared with 289 Afro-American women.[2]

Why did Brooklyn's African American migrants diverge from the dominant Black migration stream to Illinois? Brooklyn was unique in two major
ways. First, although it was a small town, it was located in one of the most
rapidly industrializing regions in Illinois. Second, it was one of the few Black
communities in Illinois. The migrants were part of a labor migration, what
Carole Marks defined as a movement of people from less industrialized areas to core areas of the economy to fill low-skilled jobs that indigenous workers were loath to take. Although a substantial number of women continued
to migrate there, most of Brooklyn's surging population was due to the inmigration of young Black men after 1890 (see table 11). The men were incorporated into the region's industrial proletariat; they took jobs at the plants
in East St. Louis, Granite City, and other manufacturing suburbs in the
metro-east. Black women migrants who worked outside the home worked
in domestic service, just as they had in the South. These men and women
migrated to Brooklyn primarily for employment, but they left the South for
a variety of other reasons as well, including the intense racial oppression

Table 11. Place of Birth of Adult Afro-Brooklynites, 1910

	Men	Women	Total
Africa	1	1	2
Canada	1	1	2
South and Deep South			
Alabama	14	6	20
Arkansas	23	14	37
Georgia	22	8	30
Louisiana	28	23	51
Mississippi	42	33	75
South Carolina	7	3	10
North Carolina	7	5	12
Virginia	10	7	17
	153	99	252
Contiguous southern states			
Kentucky	35	25	60
Missouri	63	63	126
Tennessee	81	82	163
	179	170	349
Illinois	137	138	275
Contiguous and midwestern states			
Indiana	6	8	14
Iowa	5	0	5
Ohio	4	0	4
Kansas	9	2	11
Minnesota	0	1	1
	24	11	35
Southwestern and western states			
Colorado	2	0	2
California	1	1	2
Texas	14	4	18
	17	5	22
Northeastern states			
Pennsylvania	2	0	2
New York	1	0	1
Massachusetts	1	1	2
Connecticut	0	1	1
	4	2	6
Indian Territory	1	0	1
Unknown	2	0	2
Grand totals	519	427	946

Source: *Population Schedules of the Thirteenth Census of the United States, 1910, Illinois, St. Clair County,* Roll 323, 151–66.

endemic to the plantation economy and the desire to reconnect with family and friends. That they were pushed from the rural and urban South and pulled to the urban North summarizes the essential truth of the migration's structural basis, yet it masks the specific details motivating individuals to alter their lives. The decision to respond to these structural forces by leaving familiar, even if uncomfortable, surroundings and circumstances was a personal and a collective decision that reflected great courage. That these men and women took their own destiny into their hands and dared to re-create their lives is not in question. The migrants responded to "conditions not of their own choosing" with a self-determined agency, yet the magnet that drew them to the metro-east was the prospect of industrial jobs. Although Blacks who moved to the metro-east were motivated mainly by economic reasons, the decision to live in Brooklyn, instead of East St. Louis or another industrial suburb, was determined primarily by race and racism.[3]

In this chapter, I emphasize socioeconomic relations in Brooklyn. I use the 1900 and 1910 federal manuscript censuses to reconstruct its occupational and social structures. I considered using the 1891 East St. Louis city directory as a replacement for the 1890 manuscript census but found it inadequate. For instance, it listed only 80 employed African American men, about half the number listed in the 1880 manuscript census (see table 7 in chapter 3). Its problems were both endemic to city directories and specific to Brooklyn's relationship with East St. Louis. Like all city directories, it overrepresented the wealthy and underrepresented the poor and women. Moreover, it did not include a separate listing for Brooklyn. Instead, it listed metro-east residents with their town of residence in parentheses.[4]

The Afro-American Community: Work and Business, 1890–1910

Joe William Trotter Jr. identified three periods in the African American urban experience: 1870 to 1914, 1915 to 1932, and from the Great Depression until the end of World War II. Essentially, Trotter's periodization reflects the modern incorporation of African Americans into the urban industrial proletariat. He further claimed that the second period, 1915–32, represented the period during which "the black industrial working class fully emerged," that is, "acquired its most characteristic expression." According to Trotter, other social processes accompanied the proletarianization of African Americans, such as ghettoization, acceleration of racial polarization, and increased class stratification. This, of course, is true of Brooklyn as well. Ultimately, proletarianization, while supplying an income, also negatively affected social development in the town. Brooklyn's demographic changes were driven by a dialectic between proletarianization and migration, on one hand, and the forces undergirding the rise and consolidation of Black political power, on the other. Afro-Brooklyn's class structure consisted of a large wage-laboring industrial proletariat and a minuscule petty bourgeoisie that consisted mainly of saloon owners, schoolteachers, and a small coterie of local government bureaucrats. Brooklyn's class structure reflected the town's underdevelopment. Dependency would over time distort and undermine Black political power. Proletarianization and underdevelopment provided the structural basis for the skewed male to female ratio that led to a phenomenal reduction in the percentage of two-parent households and subsequently an extremely small median family size. These changes negatively affected the community's social and economic institutions and sped the transmutation of Brooklyn from a family, church, and fraternal-based community into one in which saloons and vice became a major part of the social environment. The interrelated but contradictory forces of Black political empowerment and economic underdevelopment characterized Brooklyn during these years. Afro-Brooklynites underwent proletarianization during Trotter's first period, 1870–1914, more than a generation before this process became the definitive modal experience for Black urban residents. Moreover, Afro-Brooklynites were fully incorporated into the industrial working class while residing in an overwhelmingly African American community that Blacks controlled politically.[5]

Why were Black Brooklynites incorporated into the industrial working class a generation before most other Afro-Americans? First, the South was economically underdeveloped, and Blacks' opportunities for leaving the South were severely limited during this period. Second, industrialists in the metro-east had developed a tradition of incorporating African Americans into the region's emerging industrial economy. Third, Brooklyn's existence minimized the "intrusions" on the "rights" of white labor because white workers only had to work with Blacks, not live with them. Fourth, residing in an all-Black town offered Blacks greater security and a chance for self-determination and self-development. The horrors, traumas, and routine oppressions that led Rayford Logan to term this period "the nadir" were the major impetuses for Afro-Americans to leave the South during these years. Yet most of the North was closed off to Black southern migrants before the "Great Migration." Before the closing of European immigration on the cusp of World War I, Black southern migrants received little inducement and found few of the accommodations that would be available a generation later. Moreover, Black migration northward was inhibited by the lack of an infrastructure. Few railroads connected the South to the North before the 1880s. It was not until 1889 that Illinois was finally linked with the Deep South by a through rail line. The metro-east region was a rare exception to this pattern. Moreover, it was one of the few industrializing regions that bordered the South during this stage of industrialization. Industrial development had begun early in the metro-east, but between 1890 and 1919, industrialization accelerated, and East St. Louis and the other predominately white communities surrounding Brooklyn became the sites of immense manufacturing complexes. During this historical period, industrial development in the metro-east region surpassed that of St. Louis. Robert A. Harper called this period the "golden age" of metro-east manufacturing. In 1893, the Western Cartridge Company, a munitions plant, opened in East Alton. Two years after the city of Madison incorporated, Merchants Bridge was built by the Madison Land Syndicate. A year later, in 1890, the American Car and Foundry Company began operations in Madison. In 1894, the brothers William and Frederick Niedringhaus founded Granite City. By 1896, Granite City was home to the Markel Lead Works, American Steel Foundry, St. Louis Stamping Works, and the Niedringhauses' own Granite City Steel Works. East St. Louis remained the metro-east's major industrial suburb as numerous major companies, such as Obear (Nester) Glass Works, Missouri Mallable Iron, Memphan Paint, American Steel, Aluminum Ore, and Key Boiler, established production facilities there by 1900. Between 1890 and 1919, 20,972 new wage workers began working in factories throughout the metro-east. Many new proletarians streaming into the metro-east were African Americans. East St. Louis and Belleville were hostile environments for Blacks. According to Russell De Bow, a Brooklyn resident, Blacks were excluded from living in Granite City, Madison, and Venice. De Bow told Arthur Moore, a field-worker for the Works Progress Administration, that "many moved to Brooklyn to be near their work." Brooklyn thus facilitated both the racist exclusionary aspirations of white industrialists and white proletarians and Blacks' dreams of self-determination. Brooklyn's existence in the metro-east allowed capitalists to incorporate Blacks directly into industrial production without accruing unwanted costs. It also permitted white workers to exclude Blacks from their communities, thereby severely restricting the public spaces they shared with them. With few enticements to "come North," Blacks who sought escape from the South re-created a strategy popularized by the "exodusters," who founded approximately sixty Black towns in the South and West between 1890 and 1910. With the availability of industrial jobs in the metro-east region, the restrictions on Black northern migration, and the rise of the African American town movement, it is not surprising that a Black-governed town in a northern industrial complex would witness its greatest population growth during this period. Furthermore, Brooklyn offered Blacks an opportunity to determine their political destiny in an environment relatively safe from racial violence. A significant percentage of St. Clair County Blacks thus chose to reside in a Black town rather than an African American enclave.[6]

The migration accelerated occupational trends evident since the 1870s. For instance, in 1900, there were only nineteen African American farmers and six farm laborers. They constituted 7.20 percent and 2.20 percent of employed Afro-American men, respectively (see table 12). This represented a continuing decline from 1870 and contrasted sharply with the national trend as well as the experience of Blacks in other Illinois communities. For instance, in Pulaski County between 1880 and 1900, the number of Black farmers increased from 283 to 384, though their percentage of the African American labor force declined from 34.7 percent to 24.8 percent. Nevertheless, their decline was not nearly as severe as the one in Brooklyn. In 1880, farmers and farm laborers had numbered 42 and represented 26.74 percent of the male Afro-American occupational force, yet in about a generation, they had totally disappeared. Consequently, Brooklyn barely resembled the Black towns of the West and South. Promiseland, South Carolina; Mound Bayou, Mississippi; Boley, Oklahoma; and the other Black towns were farming communities or service centers for farming communities. Nationally, in 1910, 57 percent of African American men worked in agriculture, forestry, and fishing. However, according to the 1910 federal manuscript census, not one African American male in Brooklyn listed his occupation as farming or farm labor. As the number of African Americans making their living as farmers plummeted, the number and percentage of African American craftspeople, supervisors, and common laborers skyrocketed. Thus, during the national heyday of the African American peasantry, Afro-Brooklynites had already been converted into an industrial proletariat.[7]

Afro-Brooklyn's class structure was reconfigured during the last part of

Table 12. Occupations of African American Males in Brooklyn, 1900 and 1910

	1900		1910	
Occupation	Number	Percentage	Number	Percentage
Professional persons	9	3.40	9	1.50
Farmer	19	7.20	—	—
Proprietors, managers, and officials	5	1.90	25	4.10
Clerical workers	2	0.80	3	0.50
Skilled workers and foremen	68	25.80	57	9.40
Semiskilled workers	11	4.20	10	1.70
Farm laborers	6	2.20	—	—
Unskilled laborers	132	50.00	496[a]	82.10
Personal and domestic servants	12	4.50	4	0.70
	264	100.00	604	100.00

Sources: Population Schedules of the Twelfth Census of the United States, 1900, Illinois, St. Clair County, Roll 342, 264–76; *Population Schedules of the Thirteenth Census of the United States, 1910, Illinois, St. Clair County,* Roll 323, Roll 151–66.

a. This figure includes 430 industrial workers, 40 men age 18 or over who worked odd jobs, and 26 employed males between the ages of 10 and 17.

Brooklyn's third period and the first part of its fourth period. From its origins until the 1890s, most Afro-Brooklynite men had been common laborers; many had been river workers working for the Wiggins Ferry Company or another employer in the river transportation industry. They were mainly roustabouts at the bottom of the industry, performing the hardest and most dangerous work for the least pay. The metro-east's work force was reorganized during the 1890s as the region's political economy shifted to manufacturing. The new manufacturing plants combined with bridge construction to liberate industrialists from the dominance of Wiggins Ferry's monopoly over river transportation. The river transportation industry was severely affected. According to Nancy Bertaux, Black men in Cincinnati bore a disproportionate share of the economic dislocation resulting from the transition to an industrialized economy. In Brooklyn, the situation was quite different. There, the Black work force was incorporated into manufacturing and shifted smoothly from employment in the river transportation industry to the railroads. By the time Terminal Railroad Association absorbed Wiggins Ferry Company, most Afro-Brooklynites were employed in the railroad industry, working for Terminal Railroad, St. Louis Car Works, or American Car and Foundry Company. Hundreds of others worked for Commonwealth Steel, Granite City Steel, or the National Stamping Company. In 1910, 200 (46.51 percent) of the 430 male Afro-Brooklynites in industry worked for the railroads, while only 2 still worked in the river transportation industry (see table 13).

More impressive was the phenomenal increase in African Americans employed in industry as unskilled laborers. In 1900, they had declined to 50 percent of Black men in the work force, but their numbers had risen from 92 in 1880 to 132 in 1900. When examined against the national context, the significance becomes readily apparent. David M. Katzman found that in Detroit in 1900, only 139 of the 36,598 men who worked in "manufacturing and mechanical pursuits" were African American, but Black men made up 49.4 percent of personal or domestic servants. The rapid influx into Brooklyn increased the Black male labor force from 264 in 1900 to 604 in 1910, of which 496 (82 percent) were employed as unskilled laborers (see table 12). The migrants overwhelmingly filled the ranks of common labor. Between 1900 and 1910, they nearly quadrupled the number of unskilled workers, from 132 to 496. Furthermore, 487 Afro-Brooklynite males (430 unskilled workers and 57 skilled workers and foremen) worked in industry; nearly 81 percent were employed in the railroad yards, steel mills, and slaughterhouses, and the like of the metro-east (see tables 12 and 13). Nationally at this time, only 18 percent of Black males were similarly employed. This startling surge in the employment of southern migrants as unskilled laborers in part explains the dwindling percentage of African Americans employed in the skilled, semiskilled, supervisory, and service categories between 1900 and 1910 (see table 12).[8]

Table 13. Industrial Employment Sites of Afro-American Males in Brooklyn, 1910

	Number	Percentage
Railroads		
Railroads	62	
Carshop	135	
Roundhouse	3	
	200	46.50
Steel mills/rolling mills	120	27.90
Meatpacking		
Slaughterhouses	80	
Stock yards	15	
	95	22.10
Oil mills	6	1.30
Bridge works	5	1.10
Cooper shop	2	0.55
River transportation	2	0.55
Grand totals	430	100.00

Source: *Population Schedules of the Thirteenth Census of the United States, 1910, Illinois, St. Clair County,* Roll 323, 151–66.

The proletarianization of Black laborers in Brooklyn cut in multiple and conflicting directions. The concentration of African Americans *even* in the lowest strata of the industrial proletariat represented an advancement over employment in the southern plantation economy and domestic and personal service. Even though Black industrial workers were restricted to the hardest and dirtiest work, sharecropping and service jobs were more oppressive in many ways. The social relations connected to these jobs were more degrading, and they also paid less. James C. Davis, mayor of Brooklyn during the late 1980s, worked thirty-eight years for American Steel Foundry. When he began working there in 1936, Blacks and whites worked together on the shop floor and received the same wages for the same work, even though, as Davis recalled, they "did not eat together or use the same rest rooms." Davis also remembered that the menial jobs were reserved for Blacks, Mexicans, and Polish. According to him, Blacks always did the "chipping," that is, using an air hammer to knock off excess steel. Chipping was considered the hardest job in the foundry. Davis claimed that Blacks had always had the hardest jobs at the foundries in Granite City and at the packing houses in National City.[9]

Suzanne Model noted several factors that account for ethnic (racial) job segregation. One reason was a matter of agency. For example, a "co-ethnic" often facilitated the hiring of a new immigrant or migrant. Another related to structural factors. Because of residential segregation, different racial and national groups were often near particular industries. Finally, employers had a predetermined belief about each racial and ethnic group's occupational suitability. As mentioned in the introduction, the meat-packers at Swift employed Blacks because they believed, according to Elliott Rudwick, that "Negroes did not object to performing low-paying, dirty, unpleasant tasks involved in fertilizer manufacturing and hog-killing." An advertisement for Monsanto Chemical Company proclaimed "colored workers are available here in large numbers" and are "especially useful for different kinds of *rough or disagreeable work.*" Racism worked on both structural and ideological levels to restrict Blacks to the "hot, dirty, and dangerous jobs." According to George Wright, a white person doing the same job as a Black person may have been listed as a skilled worker, while the Black person was categorized as a common laborer. Ron Bailey contended that Black men in general earned about two-thirds what white men made doing the same job during this historical stage. Even so, Afro-Brooklyn proletarians were a rung above most Black workers, who were restricted to servile "negro jobs" in the service sector of the economy in southern and northern urban communities. This was so because, as George Wright reported, "the vast majority of Afro-Americans found employment as servants and common laborers, marginal positions that paid very poor wages and were vulnerable to economic slowdowns." For example, in 1890, Black men constituted nearly 42 percent of the common laborers in Louisville, Kentucky, and in 1910, they made up 77 percent of the waiters. In Buffalo, New York, industries did not begin to hire African Americans until a strike occurred in 1916. This was the rule rather than the exception. Nearly 60 percent of Black men worked in service in New York City in 1890, although by 1910, only 30 percent were similarly employed. In 1910, 29.6 percent of Black men in Cleveland were service workers. Blacks composed 46.3 percent of Detroit's service workers in 1910. In 1900, Black male domestic workers composed 4.5 percent of Brooklyn's Black male labor force, but by 1910, they barely existed, composing a meager 0.7 percent. According to Trotter, "the movement of Blacks into northern industries represented an upward thrust in economic status."[10]

The labor process was reorganized as the dominance shifted from river transportation to meat-packing and then to railroads and steel production. The transformation of labor facilitated the restructuring of Black Brooklyn's class structure and created for the first time a significant skilled labor force. By 1900, 68 African American craftspeople and supervisors were employed in the plants surrounding Brooklyn. Between 1880 and 1900, Afro-Americans employed as skilled workers and supervisors nearly tripled, rising from less than 9 percent to nearly 26 percent (see table 7 in chapter 3 and table 12). In 1910, the number of Black supervisors and skilled workers had dropped to

57, but the most significant change was their reduction from 25.8 percent in 1900 to only 9.4 percent of Brooklyn's employed Black males (see table 12). Butchers composed the bulk of Black skilled workers, but a few Afro-Brooklynites were carpenters, coopers, painters, and, of course, barbers. The number of butchers reflected employment in the slaughterhouses of the various meat-packers. A few Afro-Brooklynite artisans were self-employed, but most worked at an industrial plant. Most of the self-employed Black artisans lived a tenuous existence, enjoying few of the fruits generally associated with the artisan middle class. For example, seventy-two-year-old Hemp Johnson and his forty-three-year-old son, Hatch, were self-employed carpenters from Mississippi who worked odd jobs and rented their home. Their insecure economic status was typical of Brooklyn's self-employed Black skilled tradesmen. The number of semiskilled workers also declined from 11 in 1900 to 10 in 1910 (see table 12). However, as in the skilled and "foremen" category, the most significant statistical change occurred in the percentage rather than in the raw numbers. In 1900, they constituted 4.2 percent but only 1.7 percent in 1910 (see table 12). Nevertheless, a labor force in which 26 percent, or even 9 percent, of African American men occupied skilled or supervisory positions was high for the urban North, though not for the urban South. As William H. Harris claimed, this was because southern free African Americans were far more likely to have been skilled during the era of slavery.[11]

In Brooklyn, the phenomenal expansion of African Americans into the industrial proletariat was also accompanied by what Harry Braverman called the "deskilling of labor." Again, this process cut in contrary directions for Black workers. The first generation of Black butchers experienced it much as their white counterparts did. In 1900, butchers made up the bulk of Black men in the skilled and supervisors category, numbering 37 and constituting 54.41 percent. It must also be pointed out that by 1900, the work process in the packing industry had been reorganized so that as many as "330 men" had replaced the all-round butcher, "each person doing the same minute manipulation a thousand times during a full workday," according to James R. Barrett. "This dramatic reorganization of work," Barrett continued, "seriously undermined the power and control of the skilled butcher and greatly increased production speed." Not only were the number and percentage of Black artisans falling, but also they exercised less power than they had in previous years. The "deskilling" of the "butcher workmen" was, however, the precondition for the numerical expansion of the butcher category. The dramatic rise in the number of Black butchers thus corresponded to the downgrading of the butchers. Although the new workers were not the powerful butchers of old, for most Blacks it was a better job than was previously available, especially outside the metro-east. In this sense, then, the inclusion of the butchers as skilled laborers may be illusionary. African American butchers consisted of two types, older residents and new migrants. For example, fifty-seven-year-old Oscar Bletson and fifty-three-year-old Anthony Speed represented the older residents. Speed, Bletson, and other old-timers had been butchers when the "butcher workmen" controlled the labor process. William and Sam Allen, nineteen- and seventeen-year-old brothers, represented the new migrants, those who had joined the occupation after the butchers had been deskilled. Most African American butchers were recent migrants from the South, like the Allen brothers. The elimination of farmers and the decline in semiskilled laborers and skilled workers and supervisors served to create a less occupationally diverse class structure in Brooklyn.[12]

Furthermore, although entrance into the ranks of the urban proletariat lessened African Americans' oppression in some ways, their labor exploitation increased with their incorporation into the industrial proletariat because African American common laborers had higher rates of productivity than did sharecroppers or cooks. Many African American Marxists have labeled this phenomenon superexploitation. Labor exploitation is a Marxist concept that explains how capitalists appropriate surplus value from the labor of workers. According to Marx, although capitalists purchased workers' labor power at a price equal to its value, exploitation occurred in a capitalist political economy because during production the capitalist extracted labor beyond the wage paid the worker. Many Marxist scholars and some political economists believe Afro-American workers have historically been superexploited.

The superexploitation thesis posits that surplus value was extracted from Black proletarians at a higher rate than from white workers. Superexploitation, according to Donald J. Harris, can only occur if "there is a systematic pattern of underpayment of Black labor relative to whites *for the same task, same level of skill and same level of productivity.*" Harris offered two contemporary scenarios that could produce situations of superexploitation. First, superexploitation could occur if the collective bargaining strength of Black workers relative to white workers was such that capitalists could pay them differential wages within the same job classifications. This could happen, Harris speculated, if Blacks were less unionized than whites or if the size of the Afro-American reserve army of labor in particular regions was large enough to reduce Black workers' bargaining power relative to white proletarians'. Second, superexploitation could take place if the state intervened in ways that disadvantaged African American workers in the wage-determination process. Writing during the 1970s, he concluded that historical evidence supported both cases, but that neither scenario represented the general condition of Black workers then.[13]

Richard Child Hill identified two different situations of superexploitation. The first corresponded to Harris's scenario, and the second encompassed moments in which a split labor market existed. A split labor market refers to the division of the labor force along ethnic or racial lines. According to Hill, a fraction of the work force is superexploited when "(1) that group wholly or disproportionately comprises the labor force in certain job categories, firms, industries on selected localities or regions and (2) because this segment of the workforce is unable to freely move from one job or sphere of production to another, it (3) produces a higher rate of surplus value than would be the case if the labor force were in fact 'homogeneous, transferable, continuously in competition and freely mobile.'" Discrimination facilitates superexploitation of Afro-American laborers because their disproportionate position among the unemployed fosters lower wages, poorer work conditions, and the like in occupational categories, plants, and industries in which Blacks predominate. Hill thereby contended the connections between exploitation, discrimination, and the high concentration of African American workers among the labor reserve combined to produce superexploitation. He concluded that the racially segmented labor force benefited both white capitalists and white workers. Some capitalists accumulated higher profit rates by underpaying all or some Black laborers, while some white workers received better-paying and more prestigious jobs, as well as measures of job protection, because of the racially stratified labor market.[14]

The existence of a split labor market is also the basis of Warren Whatley's apparent support for the superexploitation thesis. For Whatley, three situations demonstrate the existence of a racially divided labor market and the implicit existence of wage differentials. He argued "wage differentials" were often manifested in the exclusion of Blacks from supervisory and skilled jobs. Blacks also experienced lower promotion rates into these categories. Whatley cited exclusion from unions as evidence of the existence of a split labor market. Moreover, he claimed racial discrimination in wages was masked by a regional division of labor.[15]

Afro-Brooklynites were among the small number of African Americans incorporated into industrial capitalist production during the period from 1890 to 1915. For most, it was an advancement, but they still experienced racial discrimination in the social relations encompassing the work experience and superexploitation in their production relations. Social discrimination manifested itself in many ways. Residential segregation amounted to an additional "racial tax." Because Blacks were denied the option of living in most of the industrial suburbs in which their jobs were located, they were forced to incur travel expenses to and from work.

Black women also suffered from a split labor market and superexploitation. In 1910, for the first time, a large number of Afro-Brooklynite women listed an occupation, but their labor participation rate was far below that of Black men. This was consistent with the national trend. According to Sharon Harley, the national labor participation rate of Afro-American men in 1910 was 87 percent, while Black women's was only 55 percent. Moreover, unlike Black men, Afro-Brooklynite women were not finding new kinds of work. They were still frozen in the traditional job categories of laundress, cook, and waitress. Nationally, few Black women were employed outside the repressive confines of domestic service, except in agriculture. In Louisville, Kentucky, about 72 percent of Black women employees were servants in 1910. Approximately 64 percent of Black women were employed in the three servant categories in Milwaukee in 1910. Nearly 87 percent of Black women in Detroit in 1910 were employed in service occupations. In Brooklyn, 97 (more than 82 percent) of the 118 Black women in the labor force worked in domestic service occupations as laundresses, cooks, dishwashers, or servants (see table 14). Sixty-one (more than 51 percent) worked as laundresses. Forty-six (nearly 41 percent) worked in private homes. Many of these women, like Afro-American males, worked outside Brooklyn. The tradition of the Black domestic doing day work for white families predates this period and certainly continued long after it. Ruthie Bennett claimed she and many other Black women rode the streetcars to the homes of white families in the predomi-

Table 14. Occupational Structure of Afro-American Women, 1910

Occupation	Number	Percentage
Laundry		
Private family	51	
Laundry	10	
	61	51.60
Cook		
Boardinghouse	11	
Private family	8	
Hotels/restaurants	4	
Unspecified	2	
	25	21.20
Labor	8	6.77
Waitress/dishwasher	7	6.00
Proprietor	7	6.00
Servant	4	3.38
Education	3	2.50
Clerk/sales	2	1.70
Seamstress	1	0.85
Grand totals	118	100.00

Source: *Population Schedules of the Twelfth Census of the United States, 1910, Illinois, St. Clair County,* Roll 323, 151–66.

nately white towns surrounding Brooklyn to do day work during the 1940s. At least three Black women worked in factories in 1910. Thirty-seven-year-old Amanda James and her twenty-three-year-old brother worked as laborers at the carshop. Since she was much older than her brother, she probably helped him secure his job. Charlotte Mansfield was a forty-year-old single woman who worked as a butcher in a slaughterhouse and owned her own home. Bell Allen was a thirty-six-year-old widow who worked as a laborer in a rolling mill. The increase in working African American women was the result of economic transformation, urbanization, and proletarianization. The increase in laundresses was especially a result of this process. A small percentage of Black women did succeed in escaping the limitations of service work, however.[16]

In the early years of the twentieth century, the process of proletarianization was uneven and in one significant way diverged sharply from national patterns. Historically, Black women, whether married or unmarried, worked. Nationally, nearly 50 percent of all Black women were in the labor force in 1910. Conversely, less than 16 percent of white women worked for wages. Harley found that 23 percent of married African American women worked in 1890, while only 3 percent of white women did. In the District of Columbia, approximately 43 percent of married Black women were employed in 1890, and by 1920 the proportion increased to 50 percent. Earl Lewis noted that in Norfolk, Virginia, in 1920, the low wages paid Black men in nonindustrial jobs forced "a disproportionate number of their wives and children to work for wages." Despite the economic pressure on Black women to work, Harley observed that "even in the poorest black families, husbands and fathers, not wives and mothers, were considered the primary breadwinners, regardless of the duration of their employment. . . . Since a married woman's proper place, even in the black community, was considered to be in the home caring for her children and her husband, black men were more likely to engage in work than women." Eventually, Black women would construct countervailing cultural norms to rationalize their working outside the home, but women's wage labor would remain a source of tension in African American families and communities.[17]

The meager number of working wives in Brooklyn contrasted sharply with national norms. In the 1910 census, only 8 (3.6 percent) of the 222 married Black women in Brooklyn claimed an occupation other than "housewife." Moreover, there was no discernible pattern among the families in which wives worked. For instance, Minnie and Anderson Bolden Jr. and their sons, twenty-three-year-old James and twenty-one-year-old King, all worked. Fifty-seven-year-old Anderson was a clerk for Stites Township. Thirty-four-year-old Minnie, the boys' stepmother, worked as a cook at a hotel, and James and King were both employed as butchers at a slaughterhouse. Twenty-eight-year-old

Leathy Ann Doss worked as a waitress, and her forty-five-year-old husband, Henry, was a laborer at a rolling mill. Catherine, Henry's sixteen-year-old daughter, attended school. Although Leathy Ann and Henry both worked, they also took in three boarders. Abraham and Mary Pope also both worked. Fifty-eight-year-old Abraham was a prominent politician who had previously owned a saloon and worked as a butcher at a slaughterhouse. Forty-year-old Mary was employed as a cook at a hotel. The Popes had no children residing with them. Both twenty-nine-year-old Johnson Wakefield and twenty-seven-year-old Jennie Wakefield were laborers. Johnson worked at the roundhouse and Jennie at a slaughterhouse. They had three adolescent children. These families varied in type, size, number of employed household members, and the source of the additional income. Most were nuclear family units, none were extended, and only one was augmented. Only the Dosses and Wakefields had dependent children; the Boldens had other family members working. There may be no common thread connecting families in which the wives worked for wages or distinguishing them from families in which the wives did not.[18]

Although Brooklyn departed from the national pattern on wives employed outside the home, in other, perhaps more significant ways, Afro-Brooklynites conformed to national *racial gender* patterns. Despite the social developments and technological advances that culminated in the inclusion of white women in office work, Black women were largely excluded from the reorganization of the office. Furthermore, according to Carole Marks, "They were barred from virtually all clerical and retail sales positions and traditional fields of nursing and social work." The deployment of labor in Brooklyn's administrative sector, both public and private, reflected the previous era's preference for male clerks. Men dominated the administrative sector of the Black middle class, except in teaching. In Brooklyn, only ten African American women (less than 8 percent) worked as educators or were self-employed in 1910, but three of Brooklyn's four teachers were women. Thirty-year-old Jessie Barnes, twenty-seven-year-old Flora Howard, and twenty-four-year-old Anna A. Butler, along with Burton Washington, composed Brooklyn's teaching staff. The principal, however, was a male. In a reversal of roles, fifty-six-year-old Elizabeth Baker was the school janitor. Where women broke with tradition, it often appeared to have been because of the aid of powerful male loved ones. For instance, the postmaster, Anna Arthur, replaced her deceased husband. Hattie Washington and Alice Gaston were the *only* African American women employed as clerks in Brooklyn; Washington was the twenty-one-year-old sister of former mayor Burton Washington, and Gaston was the eighteen-year-old sister of Edward Gaston Jr., a former member of the village board of trustees.[19]

Arthur, Barnes, Howard, Butler, Washington, and Gaston were rare Afro-

Brooklyn women employed outside domestic service. By 1910, both African American women and men had been incorporated into the ranks of the proletariat. However, whereas Black men became part of the first generation of African American males to join the ranks of the industrial proletariat, Black women remained mired in the traditional occupations reserved for them in the service sector of the economy. Essentially, the only way for Black women to avoid the intense social oppression associated with domestic service was marriage to a man employed in industrial labor.

Social Transformation and Black Community Development, 1890–1910

In 1906, three commentators described Brooklyn: Newton Bateman and Paul Selby, two white historians, examined the town's economic conditions, and an unknown Black journalist surveyed Brooklyn's business ownership, race relations, and governance. Bateman and Selby characterized Brooklyn as "a small thriving industrial center." They based their observation on the presence of the machine shops of the Wabash Railroad Company and the terminal, or the roundhouse, of the Chicago and Alton Railroad Company, but these enterprises were actually located just outside Brooklyn. Brooklyn existed on the periphery of an expanding industrial economy. Its proximity to the huge plants established in nearby towns throughout the metro-east between 1875 and 1919 gave the illusion that Brooklyn was also a developing industrial town. The truth is that during the region's "golden era of manufacturing," not one of the forty-seven new plants built in the American Bottoms was in Brooklyn.[20]

A staff correspondent for the *Forum* was a more astute observer of economic relations in Brooklyn than the two historians were. In May 1906, he toured African American communities in the metro-east and submitted weekly reports of their conditions to the *Forum*. In "The Evolution of Lovejoy: The Efficiency of Its Government," he wrote, "Now comes Lovejoy, a beautiful little village. The assertion that no white people live there is erroneous. Some of the finest residences here are occupied by white people and the largest and only dry goods business is conducted by white people. The town is governed by Negroes. They have separate schools in a Negro town! Now who is drawing the color line? Surely the white people can't make us do what we don't want when we are boss. The Negroes govern the town well though. They get along like lambs together and are waking up to industry."[21] The correspondent's observations provide brief but significant observations about Brooklyn. City directories, county deed records, and community memory support his observations on business ownership. A business directory for 1906, the only year for which one is available for Brooklyn, reveals that African American business ownership mirrored Black business ownership in the metropolitan enclaves instead of other Black towns. For instance, Blacks owned all three barber shops, but Euro-Americans owned four of the six groceries and five of the eight saloons. Brooklyn was not an anomaly in this. Amazingly, Euro-Americans sometimes dominated business ownership in Black towns. For example, whites operated the most profitable businesses in Nicodemus, Kansas, including the Bank of Nicodemus. Brooklyn was developing, although not to the extent Bateman and Selby alleged. Furthermore, the white minority disproportionately benefited from the development that did occur. The portrait of business ownership depicted by the *Forum*'s staff correspondent and Gould's 1906 business directory reveals white dominance of Brooklyn's retail businesses. African Americans had obtained political power, but the white minority had retained economic power.[22]

Between 1900 and 1910, Black business ownership grew dramatically. Although the numbers remained small, proprietors rose from only five in 1900, representing less than 2 percent of the African American labor force, to twenty-five in 1910, more than 4 percent of the Black work force. Whites still dominated Brooklyn's business sector in 1910, but the pattern of business ownership had changed significantly. Half Brooklyn's grocery stores had closed by 1910. The two main groceries were owned by the Maher brothers and James J. Dowling and his son Henry. There were four Maher brothers. John and Thomas co-owned John Maher and Company, which included a grocery, meat market, and drugstore. Their older brother, Russ, worked for them as a butcher. Edward and John were extensively involved in real estate as well. Marion Tally, an African American, operated the other grocery store. Abram Davis, a thirty-six-year-old African American from Missouri, owned one of the two dry-goods shops. The other was owned by Antonia Purgley, a white woman. Louis J. Costly, Ollie Green, and Freeman Price, all African Americans, were the proprietors of the town's three barbershops. Four African Americans worked as self-employed contractors. Most significant, African Americans now owned four of the six saloons and liquor stores.[23]

Tavern ownership was popular with Brooklyn's Black political elite. The literature on saloons in the Black community has exposed the nexus between Black votes and liquor licenses that linked unscrupulous white and Black politicians and mercenary Black saloon operators. For instance, the *Cleveland Gazette,* an African American newspaper, often denounced the "politician-businessman alliance" that permitted gambling dens and "other vice in the central area because of 'police protection' provided by the local councilman." I am uncertain whether this type of alliance existed between Afro-Brooklyn politicians and white county officials. However, the evidence is overwhelming concerning an alliance between Brooklyn's saloon operators and Afro-Brooklynite politicians, because they were often the same. This tradition of merging the roles of tavern owner and politician goes back to the 1870s. Abraham Pope, a Republican candidate for the state legislature in 1874, owned a tavern. So did John Watson, the political activist who opposed mixed schools in 1875. Saloon ownership was especially popular with the leadership of Brooklyn's Peoples party. The Peoples party was a local political party founded by Frederick Vanderberg in 1898 and led by Afro-American and Euro-American entrepreneurs. Abraham Pope was one of the Peoples party members who operated saloons. Pope eventually sold part ownership to Edward Gaston, who became the speaker of the village board in 1902. Clement T. Reid, popularly known as "Captain" because he managed the Brooklyn Robins semiprofessional baseball team, owned the Manhattan Hotel and Cafe and was a member of the village board from 1901 to 1903. Charles Daniels, also a trustee between 1902 and 1904, was also engaged in the saloon business. By 1910, the Peoples party had collapsed, and Vanderberg was the only former party leader operating a tavern. He was joined in the saloon business by fellow African Americans Lewis Perryman, E. L. "Pops" Gates, Edward Green, and Steve Glass. Green and Glass were partners who boarded with Green's sister, Nellie Epps. Thomas Dorn and John Hasslip were the Euro-American tavern owners.[24]

Saloon ownership was the pillar of the nascent Black petty bourgeoisie. They were the only African American–owned businesses that employed several people. Sixteen (more than 59 percent) of the twenty-seven Black men employed in the retail sector worked in either a saloon or a liquor store in 1910. Most were bartenders. For example, sixty-two-year-old Charles Jones and forty-five-year-old Jeff Harris, who were next-door neighbors, both worked as bartenders. Twenty-year-old Sam Turner, who also worked in a saloon, listed his occupation as "porter." Of the remaining eleven Black men working in retail businesses, five worked in either a clothing store or tailor shop; three were self-employed barbers; and three, including the proprietor, worked in the grocery industry. Thirty-two African American women worked as cooks or waitresses in hotels and restaurants throughout the area in 1910 (see table 14). Frederick Vanderberg and Katie Grider were the only African Americans operating restaurants in Brooklyn. Vanderberg was a well-known saloon-owning politician. Grider was a successful Black woman entrepreneur. In 1910, she was a fifty-two-year-old widow from Kentucky. Besides a tavern and restaurant, she operated a boardinghouse. Vanderberg and Grider probably employed all six of the Black women working as waitresses. Eight of the twenty-five Black women who worked as cooks worked in private homes. Of the remaining nineteen African American female cooks, eleven worked in boardinghouses and four at hotels or restaurants. The remaining two most likely worked for Vanderberg or Grider. No Black women were proprietors of retail businesses, and only two were employed in retail sales, the previously mentioned Alice Gaston and Hattie Washington. Tally probably employed Alice Gaston since she listed her place of employment as a "grocery." Hattie Washington most likely worked as a clerk in Davis's dry-goods store. Apparently, owning a saloon was one of the few opportunities open to enterprising Afro-Americans.[25]

Few African American entrepreneurs could transcend the boundaries of service enterprises. Most had to choose between operating "legitimate" businesses or running enterprises connected with the vice industry. Brooklyn quickly became the preferred site for the reproduction of the metro-east's Black labor force. Over time, it also came to supplement "Black Valley," East St. Louis's ghetto and vice district. Elliott Rudwick described Black Valley as "a congested district of saloons, gambling parlors, and houses of prostitution," and the historian Irving Dillard contended that "similar conditions existed in the town of Brooklyn." The popular notion of Brooklyn as an "all-night town" derived from this situation. According to regional folklore, one could "party all-night" in Brooklyn. This arrangement was sanctioned because Brooklyn's Black political leaders, like their East St. Louis counterparts, owned and operated most of the legal and illegal establishments. For Brooklyn, this arrangement cut both ways. It provided an occupational alternative to common labor for a few residents, most notably politicians, and it provided the town with much-needed revenue. The town derived a significant portion of its revenue from liquor licenses. Nevertheless, as Irving Dillard noted just before the 1917 East St. Louis race riot, Brooklyn's "dens of iniquity" were the habitual resorts of white men from the surrounding communities. The dominant-subordinate relationship between East St. Louis and Brooklyn ultimately undermined the possibility of creating a viable internal economy in Brooklyn. Blacks controlled town politics, but economically they were trapped in the confines of service businesses.[26]

The success of saloons and illegal activities, such as gambling and prostitution, was largely premised on the rapid influx of single men. New migrants were generally young men, but as the population increased, women became a slight majority. As previously stated, this was not Brooklyn's experience during the four decades between 1870 and 1910. In 1870, Black women outnumbered Black men; the ratio of Black men to Black women was 1:1.12. By 1880, these proportions had begun to reverse themselves; the ratio of African American men to African American women was 1:0.96. By 1900, the effects of the migration could clearly be seen in the 1.04:1 ratio. In the first decade of the twentieth century, the Black men to Black women ratio increased to 1.15:1.[27]

The saloons were businesses, but they were also places of amusement for Brooklyn's working class. African American social drinking patterns differed from those of European Americans. Black taverns were not exclusively male refuges, even though they were predominately male places. The African American saloon was a place to drink, meet people, and dance. Brooklyn's "vice dens" were different from the traditional African American tavern, though. In Brooklyn, the clientele included many white men who were looking for prostitutes. The town's primary role in the metro-east regional political economy was not only to provide cheap labor-power but also to fulfill the pleasure needs of white "tourists." Running a tavern in an "all night town" could be hazardous. In 1892, a white tavern owner, John Lesuly, was "fatally shot" by A. D. Beaver, a Black man. In the 1920s, a dissatisfied patron murdered E. L. "Pops" Gates in his saloon. Perhaps Vanderberg and Grider are the "best" symbols of what the saloon business came to represent in Brooklyn. That is, although they were successful businesspeople, they catered to vice.[28]

Perhaps Brooklyn's location in an urban area explains why it differed from southern and western Black towns—such as Mound Bayou, Mississippi; Nicodemus, Kansas; and Boley, Oklahoma—concerning "vice." Many Black towns enacted strict moral codes and rigidly enforced bourgeois Victorian values. The Nicodemus town charter contained a provision prohibiting taverns and saloons. Nicodemus also banned gambling houses and pool parlors. Kenneth Hamilton reported an extraordinary case in Mound Bayou in which a committee of Baptist and Methodist churches identified forty unmarried couples who lived together. The town council ordered these "moral offenders" to marry or leave town. These examples highlight the Black middle class's hegemony. According to Norman L. Crockett, bourgeois Black-town leaders successfully argued that "antisocial" behavior undermined the community's efforts to overcome racial stereotypes. Victorianism was an integral strand of the prevailing philosophical tapestry of racial uplift. This quasi-nationalist philosophy served to cement bourgeois hegemony in most Black towns. However, Black-town residents also supported the temperance movement for practical reasons. Many residents argued that alcoholism often afflicted the poorer members of the community. Moreover, they contended that saloons attracted white men desirous of Black women. This certainly was the case in Brooklyn. Brooklyn's Black Victorians were unable to impose Victorian morality on the town, though one segment of them did try. (In the next chapter one such effort under Charles B. Jones's leadership is examined.) In 1904, Brooklyn's Victorians did succeed in passing an ordinance banning women from "hanging outside" of saloons.[29]

The growth of boardinghouses was also a direct response to the rapid inmigration of single Black men. The boardinghouse operators were part of a small struggling community of African American entrepreneurs. Interestingly, all of the individuals who appear in the census as "boarding house operators" were unmarried women. This is not surprising since studies reveal that 80 percent of Black-owned boardinghouses were female-headed homes from

1900 to 1950. Seven enterprising Black women and one white woman identified their trade or profession as "boarding house" operator in the 1910 census. These women were obviously attempting to free themselves from the traditional work relations open to African American women in the metro-east region. However, this figure misrepresents the extent of Brooklyn's boardinghouse operations. First, it grossly underrepresents the number and percentage of Afro-Brooklynites who rented to boarders. Ninety-six (nearly 24 percent) of the Afro-Brooklynite households rented to boarders in 1910. Although this percentage is below the 33 percent of Black families who let rooms in large northern cities, it is still substantial. Second, it distorts the character of boardinghouse operators. Boardinghouse operators were mainly women, but these households came in a variety of forms, including forty married-couples' households and twenty-one male-headed households. Many enterprising Afro-Brooklynites worked at a factory or for another family and also took in boarders. For example, Robert Manlors was a thirty-three-year-old who worked on the railroad but had five boarders living with him, including thirty-three-year-old Lillie Jones, whom he employed as a cook. Mary Terry, a thirty-one-year-old who worked as a laundress for a family, also took in five boarders. Fred and Elizabeth Vanderberg rented to Todd Jamison, an eighteen-year-old migrant from Arkansas who worked at the carshop. George and Emma Moore had three boarders, yet he appears in the census as a laborer who worked at a steel mill, and the census taker listed "none" for her occupation. Obviously, Emma Moore operated a boardinghouse.[30]

Some Black women boardinghouse operators ran more than one business. For instance, Laura Smith, a twenty-three-year-old widow, ran a boardinghouse and took in laundry to support herself and her three-year-old son. Lewis Perryman owned a liquor store and operated a boardinghouse. Perryman's two adult sons worked at the liquor store, and he employed three female servants who listed their places of employment as "boarding house." The boardinghouses not only supplied additional income for their operators but also provided jobs for many women. Besides the seven proprietors, eleven cooks and one porter were employed in the seven homes listed as boardinghouses. More Afro-Brooklynite women worked as cooks in Brooklyn's boardinghouses than in the hotels or restaurants throughout the metro-east. The eleven women whose occupations were listed as cooks at the boardinghouses represented 44 percent of the twenty-five Black Brooklyn women who worked as cooks in the metro-east (see table 14). Yet, strangely, these boardinghouses had few boarders. Only sixteen people lived in the seven boardinghouses owned by African Americans, and none resided with Clara Thomas, the Euro-American boardinghouse owner. Only Birdie Barnes had as many as three boarders, and she had no live-in cook. Barnes was also the only boardinghouse operator who owned her home. Moreover, four cooks were included among the sixteen boarders. Perryman employed three live-in female servants but had only one boarder at the time of the census. The cooks in the boardinghouses were mainly young women in their twenties. Why were there so many young women employed at the nearly empty boardinghouses? Katie Grider may hold the clue to this question. Grider lived with her twenty-three-year-old daughter and two boarders. George Dorman, one of her boarders, worked in her saloon/restaurant as a bartender. However, Grider's real business was prostitution. According to former mayor James C. Davis, Grider ran a "good time house." He claimed she "sold homemade liquor, beer, and women." Grider was probably not the only entrepreneur who used a boardinghouse as a cover for prostitution. Laura Green, a thirty-two-year-old single woman, is a case in point. Green's only boarders were the three young women who boarded with her. All were cooks who worked at the boardinghouse.[31]

At first glance, the increase in Black proprietors and managers appears as one of the few beacons of progress; however, their growth did not produce a diversification of businesses. Whereas such Black towns as Mound Bayou, Mississippi; Boley, Oklahoma; and Nicodemus, Kansas, developed diverse business establishments, including banks, newspapers, ice plants, brickyards, and lumberyards, in Brooklyn Blacks remained restricted to racial service enterprises. Why were western Black towns able to develop diverse local economies, but not Brooklyn? Western Black towns were spatially separated from neighboring white communities. Moreover, because of racism, the western Black towns were often disconnected from the essential transportation networks linking neighboring communities. Spatial distance and lack of integration into the emerging transportation networks helped provide space for Black entrepreneurs to develop an indigenous retail sector. Brooklyn's retail business sector, however, was circumscribed by its proximity to East St. Louis. For example, the trolley system that transported Afro-Brooklynites to work in the plants and homes in white communities also took them to the stores in those same communities. Because goods and most services were less expensive in East St. Louis than in Brooklyn, Afro-Brooklynites chose to spend their meager and hard-earned cash there.

Community Building: Family and Social Institutions

When the reporter for the *Forum* described Brooklyn as "a beautiful little village," he suggested the community was well kept, with a minimum of substandard housing. This is amazing, considering that substandard housing is inversely correlated with home ownership. Rental property is the source of most substandard housing. Although the reporter did not comment specifically on Brooklyn's housing, the lack of a comment in this context should be read as a positive statement. Moreover, few Afro-Brooklynites owned their own homes at the turn of the century. William Terry, the census enumerator, recorded only about 18 percent of Black Brooklynites (63 out of 348) as owning their homes in 1910. Afro-Brooklynites' percentage of home ownership is among the highest for northern Blacks but was far below that of their white neighbors, over 47 percent of whom owned their homes. More than 81 percent of Afro-Brooklynite families rented their homes, whereas only about 53 percent of white families rented.[32]

If Afro-Brooklynites did not own the homes they lived in, who did? Davis claimed James J. Dowling, a white merchant, "owned most homes in Brooklyn" well into the 1930s. Dowling was a significant landlord in 1910 and perhaps an even more significant one afterward, but in 1910, he was surpassed by two of the Maher brothers. John and Edward Maher were extensively involved in real estate. John was a prominent member of Frederick Vanderberg's Peoples party, and from 1901 to 1903, he served on the village board of trustees, chairing the Committee on Streets and Alleys. Between 1904 and 1908, the Maher brothers were involved in leasing or selling by warranty deed eleven pieces of property. They also transferred several pieces of property between themselves and their wives by "quick claim deed." Quick claim deeds are land transactions that do not involve the exchange of money. Perhaps because of John's political involvement, Edward was more active in real estate transactions. For instance, on 16 November 1907, John and his wife transferred lot "24 and more" to his brother Edward by a quick claim deed. On the same date, Edward leased this property to James Claybrooks. On at least one occasion, Edward had a renter removed from his property by court order. On 6 July 1908, one of Brooklyn's founding pioneers, the elderly Hardy Roberts, was served a "decree of relief," or in today's terminology an eviction notice.[33]

White petty capitalists owned the town's housing stock. A much greater proportion of whites owned their own homes than Blacks, yet the 1910 housing patterns barely resembled those of 1880. Claiming race no longer mattered would be wrong, however. Even though whites were almost completely diffused among the Black population, 70 (36 percent) of the 194 Euro-Americans lived in three clusters, two of which were toward the periphery of town. The largest white cluster included 16 households and 45 people. However, the more prominent Euro-Americans, such as merchants J. J. Dowling, the Maher brothers, and Judge James Beasley, did not live in these enclaves. For instance, Thomas Maher lived on Jefferson Street between George and Anna Calhoun and Frederick and Elizabeth Vanderberg. George Calhoun was a thirty-one-year-old Black man who worked on the railroad. He and his wife, Anna, lived in an extended family relationship that included their son and her sister and brother. Most of Maher's immediate neighbors were working-class African Americans, but a section of Jefferson Street was one area in which most African Americans owned their homes. This area was one block from "upper Brooklyn," the historic site of the middle class. It most likely represented the expansion of the middle class beyond the boundaries of "upper Brooklyn." Several prominent African Americans lived there. Besides Vanderberg, Anderson Bolden Jr., Marion Tally, and Lewis Perryman lived in this one-block area. Bolden was the township clerk, Tally owned a grocery, and Perryman had a liquor store. Black families owned nineteen of the thirty-one homes, including the next ten after Maher's. Surprisingly, Thomas Maher did not own his own home. He most likely rented from either Edward or John. Dowling lived on Eighth Street, one door from Katie Grider and two doors from Edward Gaston. Yet this was not a middle-class neighborhood; all of his immediate neighbors except Grider were African American workers. Furthermore, only four of the nearest ten homes on either side of him were owned by their occupants.[34]

Although African Americans did not own their homes, they did structure their neighborhoods and households. Small clusters of the middle class existed, but they were surrounded by the large working-class population. In addition to the small enclave on Jefferson Street between Washington and Madison, another middle-class cluster existed on Fifth Street. James A. Beasley, Dr. Earle Williams, Anna Arthur, John Henry Holliday, and the Reverends Anderson Langford and Columbus Smith all lived in a section of seven homes on Fifth. Williams was Brooklyn's only physician, Arthur was the postmaster, Holliday was a perennial member of the village board, Langford pastored Quinn Chapel, and Smith was the pastor at the Antioch Baptist Church. The section of Fifth Street west of Madison was in "upper Brooklyn." Both Quinn Chapel and the Antioch Baptist Church were in that area, which would explain the presence of the Reverends Langford and Smith. Class was an important variable in social relationships and perhaps the most important element in politics, but by 1910, it was negligible in determining residence. Nativity no longer played a dominant role in neighborhood formation either. Occasionally, a small cluster of Tennesseans could be found, but overall Afro-Brooklynites no longer clustered together on the basis of their state of origin. Illinoisans appeared to be grouped in several clusters, but this was more likely a consequence of their numerical dominance than of a tendency to cluster together. They composed nearly 29 percent of the 946 African American adults living in Brooklyn in 1910 (see table 11). Nor was occupation any longer a component in residential choice, as it had been before industrialization. When the railroads replaced river transportation as the town's major employer, the connection between worksite and residence was severed. Very few people were employed in town. Except for a handful of bureaucrats and police officers who worked for the town government and a few merchants, clerks, and boardinghouse operators, almost everyone else was employed beyond Brooklyn's borders. The streetcar line made it just as easy for them to get to work from one part of town as from another. If race, nativity, and occupation were no longer determinants in community building, what was?[35]

Family, church, social clubs, and politics were the dominant arenas by which Afro-Brooklynites organized themselves. These social institutions did not function in a vacuum; they existed in a social context structured by an industrializing capitalist political economy and white supremacy. Proletarianization affected household and family structure. Changes in Brooklyn's household and family structures were complex and uneven, but in general, they reflected structural changes generated in response to economic transformations and new socioeconomic conditions. Afro-Brooklynites responded to these new conditions much the same way Blacks did in metropolitan areas. Some families took in boarders; others continued or adopted extended family arrangements; still others did both; and a few sent children into the work force. The rapid development of the boardinghouse industry was a direct response to proletarianization and impoverished socioeconomic conditions. Augmented households or "taking people in" was one part of Black families' survival strategy. The multigenerational extended family and fosterage were others. To accommodate the influx of Black industrial workers seeking a place to live, Brooklyn's African American community responded by taking in boarders. It was a mutually beneficial arrangement, but was it a choice they made in "conditions not of their choosing"? Black workers were basically confined to living in East St. Louis's "Black Valley" district or in Brooklyn. Since Brooklyn had very little space for new housing construction and no possibility of expansion, converting single-family dwellings into boardinghouses was a reasonable accommodation. In time, this would have a deleterious effect on the quality of the housing stock. For instance, using reports compiled from the 1960 federal census, Harold Rose found Brooklyn's housing "substandardness percentage" was 81 percent, more than double that of its nearest neighbor, Venice, and 14 percent higher than East St. Louis's. Its impact on household and family structure was also immediate.[36]

Augmented households increased dramatically, surpassing extended family households. In 1880, augmented households numbered 20, represented 21.28 percent of Afro-Brooklyn households, and housed 113 people, who represented 30.46 percent of Afro-Brooklynites. The number of augmented homes in 1900 rose to 30, but their percentage of households declined to 12.24 (see table 15). The number of Afro-Brooklynites residing in augmented homes increased slightly, to 117, but now they represented only 15.87 of Afro-Brooklynites, or about half their percentage in 1880. In 1910, augmented Afro-Brooklynite households had more than tripled, to 95 (see table 16). They now constituted 23.63 percent of Afro-Brooklynite households. The number of

Table 15. Household Structure of Brooklyn's African American Population, 1900

	No. of Households (%)	No. of People (%)
Nuclear		
Married couple, children	58 (23.67)	307 (41.60)
Male-headed	8 (3.28)	26 (3.52)
Female-headed	23 (9.39)	77 (10.43)
Married couple, no children	34 (13.88)	68 (9.21)
	123 (50.22)	478 (64.76)
Single-person residences		
Female	19 (7.75)	19 (2.57)
Male	46 (18.78)	46 (6.23)
	65 (26.53)	65 (8.80)
Non-Black residences	1 (0.41)	1 (0.14)
Extended		
Married couple	16 (6.53)	36 (4.88)
Female-headed	9 (3.67)	38 (5.15)
Male-headed	1 (0.41)	3 (0.41)
	26 (10.61)	77 (10.44)
Augmented		
Married couple	20 (8.16)	80 (10.84)
Female-headed	10 (4.08)	37 (5.01)
	30 (12.24)	117 (15.85)
Grand totals	245 (100.01)	738 (99.99)

Source: Population Schedules of the Twelfth Census of the United States, 1900, Illinois, St. Clair County, Roll 342, 264–76.

people residing in these homes had also more than tripled, numbering 397 and composing nearly 29 percent of Black Brooklynites. Predictably, the boarders were young, single, recent migrants, most often men in their twenties and early thirties who worked in one of the nearby plants. There were 23 Black women boarders. These women boarded equally in the homes of married couples, female-headed households, and, surprisingly, single-male or male-headed households. Their demographic patterns were similar to the men's, but they tended to work as domestics for private families outside Brooklyn. Besides the 23 Black women boarders, there were 4 Black women who were listed in the census as servants. Almost all worked for single Black men, most of whom were factory workers. One might think the female servants would have been employed by the few Black men who occupied middle-class positions, but most of these men were married and were not in the market for a domestic servant. Fifty-one-year-old Fannie Hunter was unique in that she worked for an extended family of five headed by John and Anna Hall. Hall worked at a rolling mill, and his sister worked at the carshop. Black

Table 16. Household Structure of Brooklyn's African American Population, 1910

	No. of Households (%)	No. of People (%)
Nuclear		
Married couple, children	115 (28.61)	529 (38.22)
Male-headed	11 (2.74)	33 (2.38)
Female-headed	16 (3.98)	48 (3.47)
Married couple, no children	61 (15.17)	122 (8.82)
	203 (50.50)	732 (52.89)
Single-person residences		
Female	18 (4.48)	18 (1.30)
Male	34 (8.46)	34 (2.45)
	52 (12.94)	52 (3.75)
Individuals living in non-Black residences	3 (0.74)	3 (0.21)
Extended		
Married couple	24 (5.97)	110 (7.95)
Female-headed	15 (3.73)	56 (4.05)
Male-headed	10 (2.49)	34 (2.46)
	49 (12.19)	200 (14.46)
Augmented		
Married couple	40 (9.95)	204 (14.74)
Female-headed	34 (8.46)	130 (9.39)
Male-headed	21 (5.22)	63 (4.55)
	95 (23.63)	397 (28.68)
Grand totals	402 (100.00)	1,384 (99.99)

Source: Population Schedules of the Thirteenth Census of the United States, 1910, Illinois, St. Clair County, Roll 323, 151–66.

factory workers worked ten to twelve hours a day, and the domestic servants relieved these men of household chores. The proletarianization of Black men and to some extent women created the main context for the expansion of augmented households and facilitated the incorporation of a small number of Black women into wage employment as domestics.[37]

The number of single-person homes declined by 20 percent between 1900 and 1910. In 1900, 65 Afro-Brooklynites lived alone; by 1910, only 52 did. Furthermore, the drop was sharply gendered. Single-person homes headed by Black women decreased by one, from 19 to 18, but those of Black men declined by 26 percent, from 46 to 34. Some of these men married or moved away, but most took in boarders, thus contributing to the increase in augmented households. In 1900, there were only 9 male-headed households, none of which was augmented. By 1910, however, the number of male-headed households had nearly quintupled, to 42, of which half were augmented. It is likely that many single-male homes followed this pattern.[38]

Proletarianization drastically altered the traditional relationship between augmented and extended family households. Augmented households had always enjoyed a slight edge, but by 1910, they greatly outnumbered extended family arrangements. In 1880, the 15 extended families accounted for 20.22 percent of Afro-Brooklyn's population compared with 12 augmented homes with 30.46 percent (see table 9 in chapter 3). In 1900, there were 26 extended families and 30 augmented households. Extended family households accounted for 10.44 percent of the Black population, while 15.87 percent resided in augmented households (see table 15). By 1910, the number of augmented homes almost doubled the number of extended families in both number of residents and population percentage. There were 49 extended family households and 95 augmented ones in 1910. Two hundred (14.46 percent) of the Afro-Brooklynite population lived in extended family relationships, compared with 397 (28.68 percent) who resided in augmented households (see table 16). A caveat must be mentioned here. The number and percentage of relatives who lived in extended family relationships were much greater than the data initially reveal. Several households could be classified as augmented and extended. These were homes in which two or more relatives resided along with one or more boarders. A case in point involves John H. and Susan Holliday. Maria Woods, John's mother, and John Bohannon, a forty-six-year-old minister, boarded with them. The household of Minnie Barnes is another example. William Scott, a thirty-seven-year-old laborer, resided with her and Clarence, her five-year-old son, and Bell Travis, her fifty-three-year-old mother. Since the 1870s, proletarianization had been a major factor in increasing the number of extended family households. Nevertheless, by the turn of the century proletarianization, along with racism, was a major cause for the declining percentage of extended family households, because it increased the augmented households.[39]

In many ways, the augmented and extended families and their hybrids represented continuations of African cultural practices as well as socioeconomic adaptations. One example is fosterage, which Antonio McDaniel posited was a general phenomenon in Africa that granted family members "some responsibility and control for relatives' children." As mentioned in chapter 3, fosterage was common in Brooklyn, especially after the post–Civil War migrations. In 1880, a number of families adopted young people, most of whom were relatives. McDaniel discovered that children of African descent were "more than twice as likely" as Euro-American children to live with relatives other than their parents and three times as likely to be fostered. The 1910 census does not indicate any adoptions in Brooklyn, but it does include many young grandchildren, nieces, nephews, and cousins who lived with relatives independent of their biological parents. Women often left their children with relatives when they migrated to a new area or sent their children to family members better situated to care for them. For example, ten-year-old Magnolia Glover lived with her twenty-four-year-old cousin Font Moore and his twenty-four-year-old wife, Hattie. Fifty-year-old Johanna Richardson was raising her sixteen-year-old grandson and nine-year-old granddaughter. The extended family was also used to help young people, including married couples, get on their feet. Andrew Harris, Dr. Earle Williams's unemployed eighteen-year-old nephew from Indiana, lived with Williams; his wife, Alberta; and their five-year-old son, Earle Jr. Hugh Farris and Josephine, his bride of two years, continued to live with his mother, Alice Smith, who also rented to boarders. The Black family and households were transformed by the intertwined forces of proletarianization and African American adaptive culture. The multigenerational extended family reflected both socioeconomic need and historic cultural practices.[40]

The nuclear family was the household formation that was most greatly affected by proletarianization. In 1870, the 31 nuclear families represented 65.96 percent of households, included 116 Afro-Brooklynites, and represented 55.77 percent of the African American population. By 1880, the 50 nuclear families represented only 53.19 percent of Black homes. They consisted of 174 people but represented only 46.90 percent of Afro-Brooklynites. By 1900, the pattern had become contradictory. Nuclear homes had more than doubled, to 123. Yet the downward spiral continued in percent of households; it had now fallen to 50.22 percent, even though the number of both nuclear households and the people residing in them continued to increase. Four-hundred and seventy-eight (64.85 percent) of the Afro-American population now lived in nuclear family relationships. This trend did not last, however. The number of nuclear homes continued to increase, by 1910 numbering 203, and the number of people living in nuclear homes also increased, to 732. As a percentage of all households nuclear families remained fairly stable, increasing by only 0.32 percent, to 50.50 percent. However, between 1900 and 1910, the percentage of Afro-Brooklynites living in nuclear homes plunged drastically, from 64.76 to 52.89. Over a forty-year period, nuclear families had fallen from 65.96 percent of Black Brooklyn households to 50.50 percent. However, the decline had not been even and steady. Rather, it had occurred in an oscillating pattern, a huge drop and then a large increase. The decline during the first decade of the twentieth century mirrored the decline for the forty-year period.[41]

An explanation for this pattern can perhaps be found in the tendency of African American migrants to send one family member north initially. Most southern Black families could not afford to move intact, so men often left their wives and children in the security of extended family relationships "down south" while they explored the new environment. This was a common practice in Promiseland, South Carolina, another Black town. According to Elizabeth Rauh Bethel, men going north to find a better life often left "their families behind in the safety and security they knew to be there until they were established in the cities." Carole Marks identifies sustaining the family as one of three invisible but essential functions Black women performed during labor migrations. James R. Grossman suggests this practice reflected both a strategy of caution and a creative response to a lack of capital. Perhaps the dramatic increase in nuclear families in 1900 is because men, after working for several years, had saved enough money to move their families to Brooklyn. William Terry, the census taker is another example. Terry lived with his sister and brother-in-law, while his wife remained behind in Tennessee.[42]

Between 1900 and 1910, the percentage of African Americans living in two-parent households declined as well. In 1900, two-parent homes included nearly 42 percent of African Americans, but by 1910, only about 39 percent of African Americans lived in two-parent households (see tables 15 and 16). This trend was partly because of the increase in particular forms of female-headed households. In 1900, nearly 21 percent of Blacks lived in 42 female-headed homes. These homes constituted more than 16 percent of African American households. Female-headed households had increased to 65 by 1910 but had declined to about 16 percent of the total number of Black households. Seventeen percent of Afro-Brooklynites lived in female-headed homes in 1910. Moreover, whereas in 1900 the predominant form of female-headed households was the nuclear family home containing a mother and her children, in 1910 augmented female-headed households more than doubled. However, 20 (nearly 31 percent) of the 65 women who headed homes were widows. Married women separated from their husbands were another source of female-headed households. Minnie Barnes is an example. Barnes was a thirty-seven-year-old widow from Kentucky who had been married twenty-two years. Barnes had had two children, but only twenty-year-old Clarence was still living. Barnes listed no employment. The economic hardship on Barnes was compounded by the presence of her fifty-three-old mother, Bell Travis, who also was unemployed. They coped with the situation by constructing an augmented household. Although the census recorded her as unemployed, Barnes obviously ran a boardinghouse. They supported themselves from Clarence's job at a rolling mill and the rent paid by such boarders as William Scott. Lucy Reed is another example. Separated from her husband, Reed supported herself, her five-year-old son, and twelve-year-old cousin by running a boardinghouse.[43]

Conclusion

By 1910, Afro-Brooklyn's family structure diverged sharply from the African American national pattern. Using data from the 1910 Public Use Samples, one group of researchers found the "nuclear family structure was the prominent form" of African American families, but they revealed that 16 percent of Black families were extended, 10 percent were augmented, and 3 percent were extended and augmented. Nationally, 71 percent of African American homes were nuclear home units, compared with less than 51 percent of Afro-Brooklynite households. Whereas 16 percent of Black families nationally were extended, less than 13 percent of Afro-Brooklynite homes were. Only 10 percent of Black households were augmented nationally, but nearly 24 percent were in Brooklyn (see table 16). Afro-Brooklynites had more than double the percentage of augmented households that Blacks had nationally. The structure of Brooklyn's Black families demonstrated the extent to which they had been shaped by a process in which the forces of industrialization—chiefly proletarianization—racial oppression, and African American cultural practices interacted in both harmonious and conflicting ways. The prominence of the augmented household form in Brooklyn derived from this dialectical process. Southern Blacks were pulled to the metro-east by the possibility of industrial jobs. Once in the region, they found themselves largely limited to residing in Brooklyn or East St. Louis's "Black Valley" district. To accommodate the rapid influx of southern migrants, single-family homes were converted into boardinghouses and single individuals and families took in boarders. This cut both ways. On the one hand, some boardinghouses became sites for prostitution; on the other, the rent collected from boarders supplied many families, especially women and children, with a living wage.[44]

Proletarianization produced conditions in which the saloon business prospered in Brooklyn, but it also generated the base on which the churches and social clubs were built. In 1910, the seven saloons represented a stark contrast to the town's three churches, but the growth of the vice industry did not mean the churches stagnated or were inactive. On the contrary, the churches grew in number and were an extremely active force in community social life. For instance, a third church, the Corinthian Baptist, was formed around 1892 after a dispute among members of the Antioch Baptist Church. The *State Capital,* the *Illinois Record,* and the *Forum* reveal a rich and vibrant church life in Brooklyn during this period. Brooklyn hosted quarterly meetings of the AME Church. All three churches sponsored fund-raising events. The Brooklyn AME Church (Quinn Chapel) established a literary society, formed a women's sewing circle, and sponsored drill teams for both boys and girls. Brooklyn church leaders got involved in trying to rid Newport News, a neighboring Black community, of vice. The church remained a vital institution, but proletarianization and economic underdevelopment worked to undermine its traditional role. Nevertheless, Afro-Brooklynites used their cultural resources to mitigate the effects of proletarianization and racial oppression.

Some traditional values and practices were discarded, some were transformed, and others were revitalized. This process of cultural loss, transformation, and retention was in many ways similar to the process that African captives underwent during slavery. The evidence suggests that Black families endured strains and made adjustments to cope with the environmental factors. During the period from 1890 to 1910, however, it appears that the massive migration and proletarianization of the new migrants, mostly young single males, did work to undermine traditional institutions and community values.

6. The Black Municipality and the White Colonial County, 1898–1915

THE PERIOD FROM the acquisition of governmental control by African Americans in 1886 until the end of John Evans's mayorship in 1894 was a time of extraordinary development for the small town of Brooklyn. Evans's long tenure and remarkable leadership produced the political stability in which the leadership modernized the infrastructure, consolidated a political culture of freedom and self-determination, and began to project independent Black political power throughout St. Clair County. After 1890, Brooklyn underwent tremendous social transformation, especially between 1900 and 1910. The African American community nearly doubled in population as southern migrants streamed into the small Black town. Most migrants were young, single men attracted to the metro-east by the booming industries. Because they could not live in most other communities, they were forced to settle in Brooklyn. Their presence had a dramatic impact on community development, especially politics. Politics began to reflect the instability of the town. John Evans had presided over the town from 1886 until 1894. In the eight years after he left office, Brooklyn had three different mayors. Political turmoil became the norm.[1]

This chapter surveys Brooklyn's fourth period, 1898–1915. Frederick Vanderberg dominated this period, but his years in office were marred by scandal. Vanderberg was the mayor from 1896 to 1900 and from 1902 until his conviction and sentencing in February of 1903. He was also a member and clerk of the school board from 1898 to 1900. Under Vanderberg and the interracial Peoples party, whites were briefly brought back into Brooklyn politics, but Vanderberg's involvement in various illegal activities and political corruption exacerbated Black Brooklyn's already hostile relationships with

St. Clair County's white officials. Brooklyn's internal political crises represent one aspect of the story of its escalating conflicts with its surrounding white populations and the county government. Rising racism in the metroeast region represents another piece of this drama.[2]

This chapter also chronicles John Evans's and the Republican Club's continuing opposition to Vanderberg and the Peoples party. In 1904, John Evans and his allies, Charles B. Jones and Burton Washington, recaptured the reins of local government. From 1904 until 1912, Brooklyn's governmental affairs were free of scandal. Between 1912 and 1915, political instability peaked when a clique of elected and appointed officials conspired to rob the city treasury and to prevent a slate of candidates from the new Peoples Improvement party headed by John Evans's son, John L. Evans, from appearing on the official ballot. The election resulted in two antagonistic factions claiming the mayorship and creating dual governments. Each "mayor" appointed a police chief, and in early May the separate police forces attempted to resolve the crisis by "military" means. On 8 May 1915, the St. Clair County sheriff, Logan P. Mellon, ended the crisis by declaring martial law. He imposed a curfew, confiscated all firearms, and closed the saloons.[3]

The circumstances that culminated in Sheriff Mellon's imposing martial law were conditioned by racial capitalism and had been building since Vanderberg's first term in office. Frederick Vanderberg, born in Edwardsville, Illinois, in 1860, was the grandson of Samuel Vanderberg, a member of a group of free Blacks who settled in Pin Oak Township independent of the group freed by Edward Coles. In 1880, Frederick Vanderberg worked as a store clerk for Frederick Archer, who was on the village board of trustees. On 17 October 1882, Vanderberg married Emma Belle Woods, who had been born in Little Rock, Arkansas. In the marriage ledger, the clerk noted Vanderberg's and Woods's color. Vanderberg was described as "brown," while Woods was described as "dark." (This was a common practice in the St. Clair County Clerk's Office. The range of racial characterizations included "African," "African descent," "Negro," and "Colored." Descriptions of color ranged from "black" to "dark" to "brown" to "copper.") In 1882, at the age of twenty-two, Vanderberg was elected town clerk, replacing Henry Rentry, a Euro-American. Frederick Archer exercised tremendous influence over the town's administrative apparatus now that his protégé was clerk and his younger brother, Joseph, was town treasurer. Four years later, Vanderberg and his mentor were reelected as part of John Evans's insurgent Black majority.[4]

The initial African American administration of 1886 represented an alliance of necessity between an entrenched group of mulatto leaders and an insurgent group of blacks. The Archer brothers and Vanderberg constituted the mulatto leadership, while John Evans, Anthony Barnes, and Charles Jennings exemplified the blacks. In predominately Black Brooklyn, color was embedded in class in much the same way that race and class were intertwined in majority white environments. The Archers were farmers and merchants, and Vanderberg was their clerk, while Evans, Barnes, and Jennings were common laborers. In 1890, Vanderberg was replaced by Henry Bletson as clerk. Between 1890 and 1898, the Evans machine banished the Archers and Vanderberg to the periphery of Brooklyn politics. Vanderberg and the Archers may have been leaders among "the disaffected" African Americans who joined the small group of remaining whites seeking Brooklyn's dissolution after the 1890 election.[5]

With his ascension to the mayor's office in 1896, Vanderberg inaugurated an exciting but problematic era in Brooklyn's history. Sometime before the election, Vanderberg formed the Peoples party. The rise of Vanderberg and the Peoples party forced Evans and the Republican Club from municipal office. Between 1896 and 1900, Evans and his political allies, Jones and Washington, operated from the township board, while Vanderberg and the Peoples party controlled municipal government. The mayorship and dominance on the village board rotated between these political rivals as they battled for power. In 1900, Washington gained the mayor's office but lost it to Vanderberg in 1902. After Vanderberg was convicted the next year, Charles B. Jones completed his term, serving until 1906, when Washington regained the mayorship. Evans served in the Jones administration and the second Washington administration as a village trustee.[6]

John R. Stites and John Evans had simultaneously held the offices of Brooklyn mayor and supervisor for Stites Township, but Evans prevented Vanderberg from obtaining the supervisorship. Consequently, in March 1898, Vanderberg turned his attention to the District 188 school board elections. Vanderberg was opposed by James A. Beasley, a former teacher and justice of the peace. Beasley, now a grocer and the postmaster, was attempting to become the first European American to sit on Brooklyn's school board. The election was not even close. Vanderberg demolished Beasley 254 votes to 95 and joined William D. West Sr. and Isaac Gower on both the school board and village board of trustees. The board of education elected Vanderberg clerk. Brooklyn was probably the only town in American history in which an all-Black school board governed a segregated school system. Blacks determined funding and hiring for European American students attending the all-white Sherman School. In 1901, under leadership of the Peoples party, the school board built a new school for the European American students, which was described as a "neat frame structure, with a capacity for seventy students."[7] It is ironic that the African American leader who brought whites back into Brooklyn politics thwarted the only serious bid by a European American politician to obtain a seat on the board of education.

The Social Composition of the Peoples Party of Brooklyn, Illinois, 1898–1903

Vanderberg completed his takeover of Brooklyn town politics when the newly formed Peoples party swept the April 1898 elections. In 1896, the Vanderberg-led village board consisted of the following members: Anderson Bolden, Oscar Bletson, Isaac Gower, Jesse Holman, Abraham Pope, and William West Sr. In 1898, Peoples party candidates won the seats formerly held by Bletson, Holman, and West. Vanderberg pulled Jesse Holdman and Richard Hoard into office on his coattails. John Henry Holliday was most likely elected on his own reputation. Andrew Jackson was again elected clerk. Vanderberg's Peoples party now controlled the village board, and he was the dominant member on the board of education.[8]

The Peoples party was strictly a local party. Its membership epitomized the cliché "politics make strange bedfellows." Included within its ranks were such people as John Henry Holliday, who was described as "a straight Republican," and Charles Daniels, who was characterized as an "uncompromising Democrat." The Peoples party was an interesting amalgamation of elite Black and white merchants, managers and clerks, and common Black laborers. By 1891, Vanderberg had left Archer's employment and had become a successful entrepreneur. His proprietorships included a tavern with a pool hall and a cafe. Vanderberg was perhaps the most prosperous Black businessperson in Brooklyn. He employed Benjamin F. Jones as his private secretary and manager of his enterprises. John Maher, a Euro-American and eventually a village trustee, operated the post office and was the executive officer of John Maher and Company, which he owned with his brother Edward. The Maher brothers also owned a grocery, a meat market, a drugstore, and a "large amount of real estate in Brooklyn." John's share of their operations was estimated at $20,000. Although small by St. Louis standards, this was a substantial amount of money in Brooklyn. Charles Daniels, soon to become Stites Township tax collector and a village trustee from 1901 to 1903, also was reputed to own "considerable improved real estate in Brooklyn." Like Vanderberg and many other Afro-Brooklyn politicians, Daniels owned a saloon. Daniels was known as "captain" because he sponsored the Brooklyn Stars, a semiprofessional baseball team. John Henry Holliday was a security guard for the Madison Ferry Company. In 1899, he became a meat inspector for Swift Packing Company. Andrew Jackson was a supervisor at this time, but by 1899, he had been pushed back into the proletariat. Jesse Holdman was a white clerk, as was Richard Hoard, who had previously been constable for Stites Township. William West Sr. was a teamster.[9]

Through the Peoples party, Vanderberg brought whites back into Brooklyn town politics. Holdman and Hoard, elected on Vanderberg's ticket in 1898, were the first Euro-Americans to sit on Brooklyn's board of trustees since John Evans led the Black takeover in 1886. John W. Maher was appointed Brooklyn's postmaster by Vanderberg shortly after Maher moved there in 1900. He replaced James Beasley, an Evans ally, whom Vanderberg had defeated in the 1898 school board contest. Maher was elected to the village board on the Peoples party ticket in 1901. Mayor Vanderberg immediately appointed him the chair of the Committee on Streets and Alleys. In this position, he pursued the construction of a paved road between Brooklyn and East St. Louis. He was the last white man to hold a seat on the board of trustees. While such whites as James Beasley were allied with John Evans, the Evans group ran Black slates in village board elections, though it supported mixed slates in township elections. The key to understanding this apparent contradiction lies in the demography of Brooklyn and Stites Township. Evans and Brooklyn's Republican Club believed that Blacks should dominate Brooklyn politics because they were the overwhelming majority but that they should share power in the township because whites were a significant numerical presence there. Evans's practice of proportional representation presaged the political theory of Black power articulated by Kwame Toure (Stokely Carmichael) in 1967: "where black people have a majority, they will attempt to use power to exercise control . . . when black people lack a majority, Black Power means proper representation and sharing of control." The demography of Stites Township departed from the scenario described by Toure. Blacks remained the majority there, although the percentage of whites was higher in the township than in Brooklyn. Vanderberg's rapprochement with the white elite was a serious refutation of the kind of Black power politics John Evans practiced.[10]

Although there are no extant records of the Peoples party's critique of Brooklyn's Republican Club or vice versa, it is interesting that this local party emerged when the Republican party was under attack by Black activists in Illinois and several other states. The *Broadax* in Chicago published numerous articles between 1 May 1897 and 19 May 1900 in which it called the Republican party the "*Grand Old Lilly White Party.*" For example, on 1 May 1897, it reprinted "Against the Colored Brother" from the *Colored American.* According to the author, "a certain class of people want the Republican Party to become a white man's party when there are offices to be given out, but they are satisfied for the negro to do the voting, and the other hard and mean work of the campaign, and especially if there is any danger attached to it." On 18 November 1899, the *Broadax* ran an article in which Bishop Alexander Walters, president of the National Afro-American Council, posited that Blacks were no longer under an obligation to support the Republican party. Although Brooklyn's Peoples party may have grown in this climate, it did not appear to articulate these sentiments. It would have been very difficult for two reasons. First, the Peoples party was interracial and was responsible for reintroducing whites back into Brooklyn's municipal politics. Second, John Evans was one of the Illinois Black Republicans who was leading the charge against racism in the party. As discussed in chapter 4, Evans had challenged discrimination in office holding and patronage as early as September 1898.[11]

Evans and Vanderberg practiced different political strategies largely because they represented different classes. The base of each group was probably working class, but their leaders were drawn from different class strata and classes. Entrepreneurs composed the leadership of the Peoples party. Vanderberg was a solid member of the entrepreneurial strata of the Black middle class, and so was Daniels. Maher may have been the wealthiest person in Brooklyn. Holliday, Jackson, Holdman, Hoard, and West Sr. were middle-class supervisors or clerks. In contrast, the Republican Club's leadership was working class and petty bourgeois. Evans's class position was much more fluid. Evans was part of an upwardly mobile working class. Between 1880 and 1910, Evans worked as a farmer, a contractor, a common laborer, and a supervisor at a car repair shop. His closest political allies, Charles B. Jones and Burton Washington, were schoolteachers. The rival groups' leaders also embodied color, or subethnic, divisions within the African American community. Vanderberg was a mulatto; Evans was black. Extant records suggest that color differences never became politicized, but undoubtedly color conflict was a subtext that erratically influenced individuals and issues. In addition, the two parties represented polar opposite positions regarding the participation of whites in town politics. Political corruption and failure to promote town development were the other major issues that distinguished the Peoples party from the Republican Club.[12]

The Troubled Regimes of Frederick F. Vanderberg

Vanderberg's first two years in office were undistinguished, but they were also without scandal, an accomplishment that he would never again achieve. Perhaps a civil disturbance in January of 1898 presaged the turmoil that would engulf Brooklyn during Vanderberg's second term as mayor. In late January, before the Peoples party's victorious campaign of 1898, Brooklyn was shaken by a riot that exposed the inadequacy of its police force. A central figure in the riot was Edward Green. While visiting his sister, Ophelia Overshaw, Edward Green, a future member of the board of trustees, became embroiled in a dispute with Ben Lucas. They decided to settle their differences outside. Once out of the home, Green drew a pistol and shot Lucas through the chest. Lucas's brother, Dan, then hit Green over the head with a tree branch he found on the ground. He continued to pummel Green until he was shot by William Epps, a friend of Green. Hearing the commotion, residents arrived in droves. They took sides, and a riot ensued. According to the *East St. Louis Journal,* Constable James H. Thomas "issued a riot call and with the assistance of some of the cooler heads, they finally restored order." Green, the Lucas brothers, and Epps were charged with disorderly conduct and starting a riot. The riot sparked a move to upgrade the city's protective capacity. In 1896, town marshal had been a part-time position in Brooklyn, but by 1899, it was a full-time position. By 1905, the marshal had an assistant, and in 1906, a second assistant was hired. James H. Thomas Sr. was the marshal of Brooklyn during much of the period from 1896 to 1902. Brooklyn's chief law enforcement officer was known as the town marshal from 1873 until 1906, but after 1906, the position was renamed chief of police. The title upgrade highlighted the changed role of the law-keeping force. The new enlarged police force soon became a source of controversy.[13]

Vanderberg, like John Watson during the 1870s, would find himself repeatedly in trouble with the law, partly because of his saloon business. Between 1894 and 1913, Vanderberg was indicted twenty times by three different St. Clair County state's attorneys, Martin Dann, F. J. Tecklenberg, and Charles Webb. Several times, the charges were far more serious than selling liquor without a license. Dann indicted him three times for embezzlement in the winter of 1898–99. On 1 December 1898, a grand jury indicted him for allegedly "fraudulently and feloniously" secreting $700 of public money for his own use. A month later, on 1 January 1899, it charged Vanderberg, Isaac L. Gower, and William West Sr. with scheming to defraud Daniel Sullivan, the township treasurer, of $125. In another indictment, the grand jury charged Vanderberg, Gower, and West with conspiring to "fraudulently issue $3000 worth of school bonds." On 11 February 1899, Vanderberg posted bond and was released from custody for "the penal sum of Five Hundred Dollars." After missing his first court date and forfeiting his bond, he was surrendered to the country sheriff by Brooklyn's city attorney, Alexander Flannigan. Vanderberg went to trial during the April term of 1899. In a sworn statement on 8 May, his attorney requested a continuance because he had not had sufficient time to prepare for trial. Flannigan was replaced as Vanderberg's attorney by Frank Hannah of the Oscar Becherer and W. W. Halbert law firm. Hannah claimed that he, too, had had insufficient time to consult with his client. The judge refused Hannah's request. On 8 May, in a surprising verdict, the jury found Vanderberg not guilty of all three counts of embezzlement. He still faced the second charge of conspiracy. During the September term of the grand jury, Vanderberg's new attorneys, Webb and Webb, attempted to quash the indictment because it was not "sufficient in the law." On 1 September, the state's attorney presented another charge, this time for selling liquor without a license. The two cases were heard during the September term. The jury acquitted him on the conspiracy charge, just as it had on the three counts

of embezzlement. Vanderberg waived his right to a trial on the liquor indictment and entered a plea of guilty. The court fined him $100.[14]

Alexander Flannigan, the Brooklyn city attorney under Vanderberg, was a
notorious character. He was an East St. Louis lawyer and political boss. In 1892,
Flannigan reconstituted the political network of East St. Louis's founding
mayor, John Bowman. The corrupt Bowman had been assassinated seven years
earlier in a dispute between local and corporate interests over raising East St.
Louis's grading. Flannigan named his political supporters the Peoples party.
His position as Brooklyn city attorney suggests a relationship between the two
Peoples parties. Years later, Flannigan's racially charged speech before the East
St. Louis Labor Council helped incite the 1917 East St. Louis riot.[15]

Vanderberg's brush with the law helped Burton Washington win election
in April 1900. Abraham Pope was reelected, and Benton Bracy and Elisha
Gilliam replaced Andrew Bolden and Isaac Gower as trustees. Gower, like
Vanderberg, had been politically damaged by the charges of attempting to
defraud the school board. Bracy was an African American laborer. Gilliam
was the son of Stephen Gilliam, Brooklyn's butcher for the last twenty-seven
years. Elisha Gilliam was also butcher, but in the changed economic environment, he worked for Swift Packing Company instead of owning his own meat
market. Gilliam and Pope were described as "pure in heart" Republicans.
Peoples party members Hoard, Holdman, and John Henry Holliday continued to serve their terms. As mayor, Washington had the right to break ties,
which gave the Republican Club control of the board of trustees.[16]

Seven months after the return to a Black administration, a new scheme to
annex Brooklyn to East St. Louis was initiated. In November, nine hundred
Brooklyn residents residing "south of the Madison County line" circulated
a petition to have "that part of the village annexed to East St. Louis." Since
the northwest periphery of Brooklyn was located just south of the Madison
County line, this phrase must refer to Brooklyn residents who lived closest
to Venice. What made this annexation drive unique was that it sought to
annex only part of Brooklyn. It is strange that the residents who lived in the
section furthest from East St. Louis would want to be annexed to that city.
The timing of this petition is also interesting because it came shortly after
the Black slate defeated the interracial Peoples party. The newspaper article
reporting the annexation scheme did not name any of the petitioners, but
the circumstances suggest that they may have been members of dissatisfied
white minority and their Black allies, the same group that proposed annexation in 1890. The *East St. Louis Journal* reporter commented that "annexation would greatly increase the Republican vote" in East St. Louis. This statement offers another window into the racial politics of the *Journal;* shortly
before the riot of 1917, it also charged that annexation was a "Republican-
inspired plot" to colonize African Americans in East St. Louis.[17]

The only annexation proposal that, at least on the surface, appeared to have higher motives was the East St. Louis Real Estate Exchange's 1905 proposal to consolidate Granite City, Madison, Venice, Brooklyn, National City, and East St. Louis into a new metropolis, to be named Illinois City. It also called for the creation of a new county. The proposition emphasized economic development. The Real Estate Exchange cited three reasons for its recommendation. The first and second concerned mutual protection from the annual flooding of the Mississippi and cooperation in draining the lowlands lying between the cities and the bluffs to aid eastward growth. The third reason was to free East St. Louis of the "stigma" of being considered a suburb of St. Louis. The movement got nowhere. For our purposes, it was important because it was the only annexation proposal that was not racially motivated, although objectively it would have ended Black Brooklynites' political independence.[18]

Consolidation failed, but the Black power government of Burton Washington two years later gave way to the Black and tan (white) politics of the Peoples party. In 1902, Vanderberg regained the mayor's office. John Maher, John Henry Holliday, and Charles Daniels, all members of the Peoples party, were elected along with him. The Peoples party again dominated the village board. They chaired the most influential committees and appointed the commissioners who administered the day-to-day operations of town agencies. John Maher chaired the Streets and Alleys Committee; Thomas Stricklyn, a former laborer, was street commissioner; and William Doug West Jr., a schoolteacher, was town clerk. John Henry Holliday, a trustee since 1892 except in 1896–97, chaired the influential License Committee, which controlled the issuance of liquor licenses, one of the town's major sources of revenue. Brooklyn, like East St. Louis, received a substantial amount from saloon license fees. Historically, liquor licenses in many communities were granted to individuals with political connections or to those willing to enter kickback schemes. Tavern and saloon operations were therefore often a source of graft. Brooklyn was no different. Restricted to racial enterprises, ambitious Black Brooklynites found tavern ownership one of the few lucrative avenues easily accessible to them. Political leaders were attracted to the business because of its opportunities, or saloon owners became politicians because their wealth gave them a degree of economic independence and political influence. Many of Brooklyn's political leaders, such as John Watson, Abraham Pope, Edward Green, and especially such Peoples party leaders as Vanderberg, Benjamin Jones, and Charles Daniels had liquor licenses and operated saloons.[19]

Vanderberg lasted hardly a year before he, Thomas Stricklyn, and William Doug West Jr. were indicted for conspiracy. The grand jury charged them with plotting to defraud the village of Brooklyn on 5 February. The grand jury alleged that on 5 February 1902, Vanderberg, as president of the board of trustees, and West, as town clerk, issued an unauthorized $241 warrant payable to Stricklyn, who collected the money the next day. The draft given Stricklyn read as follows:

No. *243* $241.00. Village of Brooklyn, Ill. Feb. 5ᵗʰ 1902.
TREASURER VILLAGE OF BROOKLYN
Pay to *Thomas Stricklyn*
for labor on the streets with teams and men
Two Hundred and Forty-One Dollars

F. F. Vanderberg   *Wm. D. West Jr.*
President   Clerk[20]

Besides being charged with paying Stricklyn for work not performed, they were charged with carrying "straw men" on the town's payroll. After several trials, Vanderberg and Stricklyn were finally convicted. West's turning state's evidence was the key to the convictions. The prosecuting attorney granted West immunity in exchange for his testimony against Vanderberg and Stricklyn. On 19 February 1903, Circuit Court Judge M. W. Schaefer overruled a motion for a new trial and sentenced Vanderberg and Stricklyn to jail.[21]

Two William Wests lived in Brooklyn at this time. They were father and son. In the city directories for the period 1897–98 to 1912, they appear as William West and William Douglas West. William West Sr. was a Black teamster who worked for Swift Packing Company. By 1910, he was a self-employed contractor operating a hauling business. William D. West Jr., known as Doug West, taught at Lovejoy School during the 1897–98 school year but appears as a laborer in the 1898–99, 1900, and 1906 directories. In 1902, he was Brooklyn's town clerk. The 1903 directory identifies him as a cattle driver employed at the St. Louis National Stock Yards. By 1912, he was again working in a middle-class job as a clerk.[22]

At first glance, the continuing prosecution of Vanderberg by St. Clair County state's attorneys may appear as persecution of a powerful African American political leader, but a more sustained analysis reveals that this was not a simple case of racially motivated political harassment. The involvement of the senior and junior Wests and the similarities between the 1898–99 and 1902 embezzlement cases suggest that Vanderberg was engaged in political corruption. His influence remained even after he was incarcerated. Unfortunately, Vanderberg succeeded in establishing a corrupt political culture that became the dominant ethos in Brooklyn political life.

After Vanderberg's incarceration, the Peoples party was swept from power by the "pure in heart" Republicans. In April of 1903, Charles B. Jones replaced Vanderberg as mayor. Edward Maher, who had been elected in 1902, served only one term. Although he was not implicated in the embezzlement scheme, he was the chair of the Committee on Streets and Alleys when Vanderberg, West Jr., and Stricklyn conducted their scheme to defraud the town. Maher was the last white person to hold a position on the Brooklyn board of trustees. It seems logical that when Afro-Brooklynites ousted Vanderberg from political office for the last time, they would put out the lone elected white official with him. After 1903, the Peoples party disappeared from Brooklyn politics. Yet despite or perhaps because of his difficulties with St. Clair County state's attorneys, Frederick Vanderberg remained a popular figure in Brooklyn. The Peoples party, like its founder, had a brief and controversial career. In its five years of political activity, its leader was charged with several criminal violations, two of its elected officials were incarcerated, and scandals drove at least two other members from public life.[23]

The Lynching and Burning of David F. Wyatt

Charles Jones became mayor during a critical moment in Brooklyn's history. The mayor and street commissioner had been incarcerated, and William Doug West Jr., the town clerk and a schoolteacher, had been driven from public life in disgrace. Less than two months after Jones's election, the man he had replaced as principal of Lovejoy School, David F. Wyatt, was lynched. Within a week of Wyatt's lynching, Brooklyn and the rest of the metro-east were devastated by floods.

Saturday night, 6 June 1903, a mob took Lovejoy's schoolteacher David Wyatt from the St. Clair County jail and lynched him. Wyatt was lynched after he shot Charles Hertel, the St. Clair County superintendent of schools, allegedly for not renewing his teaching certificate. After Wyatt's lynching, the *East St. Louis Journal* asserted, "The dead criminal bore a bad reputation and Superintendent Hertel was amply justified in refusing him a certificate." The author claimed that "grievous complaints of his conduct" were made when Wyatt taught at Cahokia and Alta Sita. However, the newspaper did not delineate those complaints or even charge that his work at Lovejoy School was substandard. Although the paper reported that after a decade of teaching in the Brooklyn school system, Wyatt was dismissed for supposedly extreme brutality toward his students, it never interviewed members of Brooklyn's school board, fellow teachers, or parents of students concerning Wyatt's teaching or behavior. In perhaps the most bizarre commentary on this tragedy, the *Chicago Tribune* attributed Wyatt's behavior to his supposed "mulatto" status. The paper stated, "The wretched creature who was thus hurried to death undoubtedly suffered because he was not wholly a Caucasian. Whether the black or the white strain in his veins controlled him to commit the crime—cannot positively be said." These and other wild speculations and unsubstantiated accusations about Wyatt's character and work appeared in the white press. At a rally organized by Chicago-based African American activists, including the indomitable Ida B. Wells-Barnett, Samuel T. Archer claimed that Wyatt, who was his brother-in-law, was an "intelligent, upright, and valuable citizen." Since there are such contrasting images of David Wyatt, it is instructive to examine depictions of him before the lynching. Wyatt appeared several times in the Illinois African American press as well in the local white newspapers during the decade in which he was principal or taught in Brooklyn. These earlier presentations provide a more rounded view of David Wyatt.[24]

David F. Wyatt was one of Brooklyn's corps of young African American teachers. He held a master's degree from the University of Michigan. Wyatt came to Illinois from Ann Arbor, Michigan, and had been principal of "colored schools" at East Carondelet, Illinois, before coming to Brooklyn. Prior to the lynching, African Americans in Brooklyn and throughout the state seemed to hold Wyatt in high esteem. He was active both in the community and in the statewide Afro-American Teachers Association. At the organization's second annual meeting, on 28–30 December 1892 in Carbondale, Illinois, Wyatt was among a few teachers singled out as a "race educator" who had "contributed to the success" of the conference. Service in statewide organizations and causes appears to have been a hallmark of Wyatt's activism. Six years later, in 1898, he was also one of the statewide vice presidents selected to organize the commemoration ceremony for John Mercer Langston upon his death on 25 January 1898. The *Illinois Record* described the services held at the House of Representatives as "the grandest outpouring of the Negro race in the history of the state of Illinois."[25]

Wyatt was also extremely active in Brooklyn. For two years, he served as principal of Lovejoy School. In February of 1898, Principal Wyatt started a night school for adults, another example of his educational activism and his commitment to abolish illiteracy among Blacks in Brooklyn. In March of 1898, Vanderberg defeated the Republican James A. Beasley for the vacant seat on the school board, and under his leadership, the board replaced Wyatt with Charles B. Jones. Perhaps Wyatt was replaced by Vanderberg because Wyatt was secretary of Brooklyn's Republican Club. As secretary of the Brooklyn Republican Club, he had been involved in organizing what the *East St. Louis Journal* noted in 1896 was "decidedly the largest and most effective meeting of the present campaign, held in St. Clair County." The *Journal* described his closing speech at an election rally sponsored by the club in 1896 as "an eloquent address." Wyatt was the only club member and Brooklynite among an outstanding roster of politicians who spoke. John A. Waller, a Kansan and a former U.S. consul to Madagascar, gave the keynote address; he was followed by Judge Launtz and Colonel John Robinson of East St. Louis.[26]

The contrast between the snippets of information found in the Black and the white press concerning David Wyatt and the picture painted of him after his gibbeting suggests that the *Journal* too easily accepted Superintendent

Hertel's evaluation of Wyatt's character and work record. Reports from other sources suggest there was much behind the shooting and lynching.

Wyatt had taught in the Brooklyn school district from 1893 until his lynching. After ten years of employment, Superintendent Hertel did not renew his teaching certificate, allegedly because he was "in bad repute amongst the school patrons." Wyatt went to the superintendent's office in Belleville late Saturday afternoon to convince Hertel to renew his teaching certificate, which Hertel refused to do. Hertel, his son Garfield, and his assistant George Fiedler claimed Wyatt then pulled a revolver and shot the superintendent. We may never know what happened, but the fact that Wyatt had a revolver suggests he anticipated trouble. The gunshot or shots attracted two police officers and a crowd to the courthouse, where the county education department was housed. Wyatt was immediately captured and arrested; Hertel was taken to a nearby hospital for treatment. Before the police could escort Wyatt to the county jail, a crowd of several hundred gathered at the courthouse. After the arrival of reinforcements, police officers rushed Wyatt through the crowd to the jail four blocks away.[27]

They made it safely to the jail and locked Wyatt away in a cell. From this point on, the events closely conformed to standard lynching behavior. Rumors of Hertel's death fueled the crowd's size and aggressiveness. According to the *St. Louis Post-Dispatch,* someone cried, "Let's hang the negro." Another responded, "Of course." A third demanded Wyatt be lynched. The crowd's increasing anger was partly spurred by liquor, as the would-be lynchers renewed their resolution with frequent trips to the near saloons. One hardware store owner sold out his entire supply of revolvers, while another gave away numerous handguns. The crowd continued to grow. About 6:00 P.M., Fred J. Kern, a former congressperson and the current mayor of Belleville, addressed the crowd. Kern's speech and subsequent behavior were crucial in determining the night's events. Kern gave an ambiguous speech that the *Post-Dispatch* claimed "inflamed, rather than quieted the crowd." Mayor Kern stated a community that "would not be aroused to a frenzy by what the negro did would not be made of the right stuff," though he also implored the crowd to "permit the law to take its course." After his brief speech, the mob belted Kern with rocks and stormed the jail. Mayor Kern quickly retreated inside the jailhouse. As the mob battered down the outer door, Kern, State's Attorney James Farmer, and an ex-judge named M.W. Schaefer decided a course of action. They agreed not to use force against the mob. The police officers were told to stand down if the mob broke through the inner door. Kern would later rationalize his actions by stating he did not want "to see innocent blood flow on account of the guilty wretch in jail." Farmer or Schaefer suggested having the fire department use firehoses to disperse the mob. Although Kern opposed this sug-

gestion, someone rang the fire bell. The subsequent events had a tragicom-
ic effect. The fire fighters rushed toward the mob unraveling their hose, but
they did not turn on the water. They were unwilling to spray a crowd composed of their fellow white citizens. Apparently, they thought they could
bluff the mob into dispersing. Instead, the mob coolly cut the waterhose into
sections and tied them into bowknots. Humiliated, the fire fighters departed with however much hose they could gather from the crowd.[28]

About 8:00 P.M., Mayor Kern left the scene. According the reporters, it was
quite a festive atmosphere. In the perverse tradition of lynching spectacles,
the crowd, which by then numbered in the thousands, included a cross section of Belleville's white community: men, women, and youths of the middle and working classes. The lynchers, as usual, consisted of a small group
of men and boys, estimated by the press at no more than fifteen. Cheering
them on and laughing at every depraved racist joke were well-dressed wom-
en with baby buggies, respectable men, and their entire families. According
to the *Post-Dispatch,* around 10:30 A.M., the crowd learned that the police
would not use force to prevent Wyatt's lynching. After five hours of work,
the mob finally broke the inner door down. Meeting no resistance from the
police, by 11:20 the men had broken through to Wyatt's cell. They forced a
rope around his neck and dragged him down the stairs into the street. Wyatt
was choking to death as his assailants dragged him through a gauntlet of
white men, who beat and kicked him. When they reached the public square,
they strung him up on a telephone pole.[29]

An *East St. Louis Journal* reporter described what happened next:

> When the body swung free, a mighty shout arose from the assembled thousands.
> The mob's revenge was not completed with the death of the negro. Oil was
> procured and poured over the remains. This was touched off and soon the body
> was wrapped in flames. Still, no mercy was shown. With clubs and stones the
> body was beaten into a shapeless mass. Within a half an hour of the terrible deed
> not enough was left of the body to tell that it had ever borne human form. . . .
> From time to time more oil was fed to the flames and the square was lit up in
> the luridest and most tragic light it has ever seen in its existence. . . . Their wild
> night's work done, the mob dispersed quietly, letting the charred and mutilat-
> ed remains burn in the heart of the city. . . . Before the body was entirely con-
> sumed the police managed to work up sufficient energy to bring up a few pails
> of water. The flames were extinguished and what was left of the body was gath-
> ered up and taken to Holdener & Co. undertaking company.[30]

The reporter mildly condemned "the lynching, and particularly the mutilation and burning of the body" as an "*unfortunate* affair," but he quickly added
that "the negro richly deserved punishment." Concluding his remarks, he
claimed the punishment should have been dispensed by the courts. In the
metro-east, the reporter's views were quite liberal.[31]

The *Journal's* reporter ignored the role the press played in creating the charged atmosphere. For instance, the day before Wyatt was lynched, the *Journal* printed a front-page story of a lynching entitled "Asked for Time to Pray." This article irresponsibly reported the lynching of a Black man in Greenville, Mississippi, without condemning this racialized form of political terror. Also on 5 June, the *Belleville Weekly Advocate* ran a story entitled "Killed by a Negro" about a white East St. Louis man who was killed in an altercation with an African American. These two stories appearing the day before Wyatt's lynching no doubt encouraged the vigilantes' action by helping establish a permissive environment. Collectively, these articles conveyed to St. Clair County whites that Blacks were out of control and that lynching was a legitimate antidote for "uppity" African Americans.[32]

Mayor Kern blamed the lynching on Wyatt himself and Pastor Charles Thomas, whom he described as a "vicious negro agitator." Thomas had sued a barbershop proprietor, Henry Baumgaten, for refusing him a shoe shine. Thomas lost his suit, but his actions gravely offended many Belleville whites. Mayor Kern alleged the hostile feelings unleashed by Thomas's suit "had much to do with the lynching of Wyatt." It obviously exacerbated existing anti-Black sentiment, but Belleville was known among Blacks as an extremely racist community. Thomas proved very prescient. Because of several threats on his life, Thomas wrote Governor Richard Yates days before Wyatt's lynching, asserting his life and "the lives and property of other colored citizens of Belleville were in danger." Three days before Wyatt's lynching, Attorney General H. J. Hamlin responded for Governor Yates. Hamlin advised Wyatt to see the St. Clair County state's attorney, James Farmer. After the lynching, Belleville and county officials increased their harassment of Thomas.[33]

Pastor Thomas used his Sunday sermon the morning after Wyatt's lynching to denounce the murder of David F. Wyatt and racial oppression in Belleville. It was alleged Thomas hoisted a pistol before his congregation and offered to help them obtain firearms. Monday he was arrested and charged with having given Alonzo Hendricks a revolver with which to defend himself on Saturday night. He was released for lack of evidence. Thomas was not the only African American subjected to threats and harassment. In the days after the lynching, Blacks in Belleville were menaced and molested on the streets. Thomas consulted an attorney about the harassment, especially the number of threatening letters he had received. The lawyer advised him to leave town. By Wednesday, Thomas was gone. The *Post-Dispatch* claimed Thomas "deserted his flock." Thomas left Belleville, but he did not abandon the struggle for racial justice. He joined Samuel T. Archer and Ida B. Wells-Barnett at several rallies in Black churches throughout Chicago. Once in Chicago, the Reverend Thomas challenged the official story of Wyatt's lynching. He and Wells-Barnett claimed Wyatt acted in self-defense. According to them, Hertel or Fielder fired first. It is unclear who or what their source was.[34]

The regional and national press also denounced the lynching. On 9 and 10 June, the *Post-Dispatch* criticized the lynching, Mayor Kern, and the ruling of the coroner's inquest. Even though Wyatt was lynched in front of thousands of people by unmasked men and boys, the inquest predictably determined he died "at the hands of persons unknown." The *East St. Louis Journal*'s editorial represented the ambiguity and contradictions that characterized the press's reaction to the lynching. In a belated editorial on 12 June, the *Journal* condemned the lynching in forceful language but equated Wyatt's shooting of Hertel with his murder and mutilation by the mob. The editorial did, however, conclude that all vigilante actions undermine law and order. On 13 June, John W. Wheeler and Kate Jackson, publisher and editor, respectively, of the *St. Louis Palladium,* an African American weekly, carefully condemned the lynching and admonished Mayor Kern for cowardice. Wheeler and Jackson called for prosecution of the murderers and claimed the governor should act if the mayor failed to perform his duties.[35]

The article in the *Palladium* reflected the ambiguities of the moderate African American middle class. Besides their moderate reaction, Wheeler and Jackson devoted a sparse amount of space to Wyatt's lynching. Their commentary was surprisingly short and appeared at the bottom of the paper's first page. They condemned the lynching but made it clear they "were not defending the negro." The *Palladium* did not try to humanize Wyatt. It provided no background information on him, and like the Euro-American press, it ignored his accomplishments, his status in Brooklyn, and his role in the county's Republican party and in the state's African American educational association. Wheeler and Jackson avoided the language of moral outrage. After a lynching in Decatur, Illinois, in 1893, Wilson Woodford, a Black attorney, published an "indignation letter" in Decatur's three white newspapers. Whereas Woodford condemned "the cowardly mob of human fiends," Wheeler and Jackson politely noted that "all intelligent and law-abiding citizens" condemned the lynching of "the school teacher Wyatt." Wheeler and Jackson's response was consistent with the position of many middle-class African American race men and women. To their credit, however, their moderate response did not attempt to move the issue away from the lynching and onto the moral behavior of African Americans, as the Chicago-based *Broadax* did after the lynching of "Click" Mitchell in Ohio. The *Broadax* declared, "If the members of our race desire to escape the vengeance of mob and lynch law they must refrain from violating the laws of the land; and must also remember that it is not the white man who is on trial, but that it is the negro. And everytime a negro falls by the wayside, it has a tendency of lowering every negro in the estimation of our enemies and our friends." Though Wheeler and Jackson did not say so, they were in complete agreement with this sentiment.[36]

The lynching drew mixed reactions from Belleville's white community. Predictably, liberal citizens condemned the lynching. Belleville's white Christian ministers rebuked the lynchers in Sunday morning sermons. In contrast, Belleville's white political and business leaders most often defended the lynching. Mayor Fred Kern called the lynching an "irregular execution." The St. Clair County Board of Supervisors claimed it was too busy with the flood to comment on the lynching. The Commercial Club and the Retail Merchants Association followed the lead of the board of supervisors. George R. Long, president of the Good Government League, expressed the dominant sentiment of the white community. Echoing Mayor Kern, Long stated, "I think the matter better be dropped. I am tired of the vilification of Belleville. I am against mob law under all circumstances, but I believe the negro got what he deserved. It is better that the brute who came here to do what he did should have been lynched than that a dozen innocent men should have been killed by the officials firing on the mob." A day after Long's comments, representatives of the "better class"—the Reverend A. J. Gallaher, pastor of the Presbyterian church; and George W. Detharding, president of the Commercial Club—condemned the lynching and called for a special grand jury. Encouraged by Attorney General Hamlin, State's Attorney James Farmer sought to impanel a special grand jury. Judge R. D. W. Holder, who allegedly had witnessed the lynching, indicated his reluctance to call a special grand jury. Holder claimed, "It would be hard on many of our farmers to ask them to leave their work now and the expense to the county would be considerable." Holder's views were victorious. Despite some desire for a special impaneling, nothing was done until the regular grand jury convened in September.[37]

The grand jury met secretly during September and October, and in November indictments were issued. By issuing fourteen indictments, the grand jury exposed the duplicity of the corner's inquest. However, because witnesses had been unwilling to identify those who placed the rope around Wyatt's neck, the indictments were for rioting and assault rather than murder. On 18 December, in an apparent plea bargain, the attorney Charles Webb pled eleven of the indictees guilty on the charge of rioting. Judge Holder accepted their pleas and fined them fifty dollars and court costs. Before the spring session, two other defendants accepted similar arrangements. In April 1904, the last defendant accepted the original plea bargain.

The lynching, mutilation, and burning of David Wyatt conformed to many features of the lynching cycle posited by the black sociologist Oliver C. Cox. Cox theorized that lynching was a systematic process of repression rather than "primarily a spontaneous act of mob violence." Cox's lynching cycle consisted of eight elements: (1) an emerging consensus among whites that African Americans were rapidly "moving out of their place," which could be accelerated by an economic downturn; (2) a "continuing critical discussion" about Black and white interaction that led to "racial antagonism and tension"; (3) an alleged or an actual violent act committed by a Black person;

(4) the formation of a lynch mob and the lynching of the accused, usually in the shadow of the courthouse, followed by mutilating, burning, and dragging the body through the Black community; (5) Blacks forced into hiding, often seeking the protection of powerful whites rather than law officers; (6) white liberal condemnation of the lynching as the action of a few lawless men and then the demand for a legal investigation, which finds that death "occurred at the hands of parties unknown"; (7) the coercion of Blacks into a new racial accommodation as the lynchers are lionized in the white community and militant Blacks are censored in the Black community; and (8) the restoration of racial etiquette, as diffidence replaces self-assertion among Blacks and the lynching cycle begins anew.[38]

Several components of Wyatt's lynching fit neatly into Cox's lynching cycle. First, there was the contentious history in Brooklyn around "mixed" schooling. Battles between Black and white Brooklynites over this issue had been going on for a generation. In 1876, Blacks led by Tazwell Bird had won a heated community struggle to integrate Brooklyn's schools. They not only succeeded in desegregating the public schools but also gained control of the educational process by electing an all-Black school board. This rift was never healed. After the Black community enacted a school bond, the Tazwell Bird–led board built a new school building in 1879, but white parents refused to send their children to the new public school. In 1894, the Black school board reversed its predecessors and reenshrined racial segregation when it built Sherman School for Brooklyn's remaining whites. Superintendent Charles Hertel's sons taught at Sherman School.

After the election of John Evans, whites tried to undermine the Black government by attempting to annex Brooklyn to East St. Louis, a predominately white city. Furthermore, inflammatory articles critical of African American behavior were often published in the *East St. Louis Journal* and the *Belleville Weekly Advocate*. Fred Vanderberg's recurring difficulties appeared to provide evidence to support "the white man's burden" thesis. Finally, the discrimination suit filed by Pastor Thomas brought racial animosities to the surface.

Wyatt's alleged assault on Hertel became the trigger that unleashed longstanding white resentment against Blacks in St. Clair County. Two newspapers, the *East St. Louis Journal* and the *Belleville Weekly Advocate*, inflamed the already charged atmosphere with their racialized reportage of Hertel's shooting. Their incendiary language legitimized a discourse that encouraged a crowd of thousands to gather at the St. Clair County courthouse. Wyatt suffered the full brutality of an enraged racist mob. Its lust for blood was not sated by lynching him; the mob also wanted the perverse satisfaction of mutilating and burning his body. The "better class"—white ministers and some business leaders—and local newspapers did condemn the lynching, but the murderers received what amounted to a slap on the wrist. Whites did not attack Brooklyn, but Black leaders had reason for apprehension because pillaging and plundering of the Black community often accompanied a lynching. Although the mob did not attempt to carry its fury into Brooklyn, whites did threaten Blacks in Belleville, including harassing the Reverend Thomas and others until they left town. The mob did not drag Wyatt's body through Brooklyn or the Black community in Belleville, but evidence suggests a "new racial accommodation" was imposed on African Americans in Belleville.

Victorian Soldiers: Middle-Class Moral Reformers

During his first year in office, Mayor Charles B. Jones launched an offensive against prostitution. Like many middle-class "race men and women," Jones probably feared the activities in the saloons, gambling, and jook joints undermined the moral fiber of the community and created circumstances that could provoke an attack by Brooklyn's white neighbors. In the aftermath of Wyatt's lynching, this fear was probably heightened and likely contributed to his determination to purge Brooklyn of prostitution and vice. During this era, many middle-class African Americans feared that the "good and decent people" would one day have to pay for the "acts of the lawless." The Black petty bourgeoisie reacted to these crises primarily in two ways. Sometimes they launched moral crusades to "clean up" the Black community, and sometimes they adopted a discourse designed to distinguish *for whites* "middle class Christian Colored people" from the "degenerate lower class negroes." For instance, in the aftermath of the 1908 race riot in Springfield, Blacks who had fled to Decatur for safety formed the Colored People's Law and Order League of Central Illinois. The Reverend James H. Magee, a leader of the Black community in Springfield and president of the league, blamed the riot on the poor and the moral degenerates of both races. The purpose of the protective association, according to Magee, "was to distinguish the better class of law-abiding colored people from the low class." This strategy was usually directed at the Black working class to chide them into respectable behavior.[39]

In Brooklyn, Mayor Jones initiated an antiprostitution campaign, the first strategy. The specifics of his crusade against prostitution have, like so much of Brooklyn's history, eluded the extant record. Nevertheless, one piece of evidence, an excerpt from a speech by Brooklyn trustee John Henry Holliday, offers an interesting and suggestive tidbit. Holliday was one of several Brooklyn politicians and ministers who responded to a request from the Booker T. Washington Improvement League (BTWIL), an aptly named community self-help organization, to help them halt "the shooting and disgraceful conduct about the streets of Newport." Newport News was a Black community in the western part of Madison, north of Brooklyn. In January 1904,

Holliday described to a rally in Newport News how Mayor Charles B. Jones "had stamped out the disgrace of women hanging in and around the saloons" in Brooklyn. Less than a year after Vanderberg's removal from office, Brooklyn's Black leaders obviously felt confident enough to help launch a moral crusade in Newport News. When "Essence," a local columnist for the *St. Louis Palladium,* queried "Cannot colored communities be decent as well as white?" he answered his own question affirmatively, stating, "Brooklyn enjoys a society of quite a good class of intelligent people. Newport is going to reform and do well."[40]

Using the pseudonym "Essence," Professor Wilhite chronicled in his weekly *Palladium* column, "Newport Notes," the campaign to shut down saloons and gambling dives in Newport News. Wilhite was not an unbiased source. As head of the Booker T. Washington Improvement League, he led the moral crusade in Newport News. Although named after the "Wizard of Tuskegee," the league reflected the contradictory views of Wilhite more than those of the arch accommodationist. The league practiced a combination of moral suasion, self-help, and direct action. Under Wilhite, the Booker T. Washington Improvement League aimed its fire at whites and Blacks alike. In his own idiosyncratic way, Wilhite condemned racist politicians, African American saloon owners, narrow-minded Black Christian ministers, and the Black middle class. Nevertheless, Wilhite was best positioned to analyze the dynamics of the struggle in Newport News, including the role played by Brooklyn's moral reformers. His analysis provides insight into how Brooklyn's moral crusaders conceptualized these issues. It also sheds light on how their approach to fighting vice was structured by Brooklyn's context.

Newport News suffered from extreme neglect as well as vice and violence. For example, on 9 January 1904, the *Palladium* noted that Newport News that was "populated for the most part by Colored people has scarcely a sidewalk." The Booker T. Washington Improvement League mobilized Black residents to build a sidewalk to the "colored school." On 29 August 1903, after a white man attempted to rape a sixteen-year-old Black girl near one of the community's numerous saloons, "Essence" launched his crusade to clean up Newport News. In a scathing editorial, he challenged the alleged connection between "purity and white women," condemned the Belleville mayor's action during David Wyatt's lynching, and called on the Black community to mobilize against the "thieves and crap-shooters." Within two weeks, a committee of the BTWIL met with Madison's mayor about the saloons, schools, and streets. Apparently, the BTWIL was dissatisfied with the meeting because invitations were soon issued to ministers and political leaders from Brooklyn to come to Newport News. During the week of 19 September, "quite a number of visitors from Brooklyn" attended rallies sponsored by the Free Will and Missionary Baptist churches. During the week of 26 September,

Brooklyn's Reverend Thomas Threadway brought the moral crusade to New-port News. Coincidentally, that night a white man was "beaten in a Colored joint." The following Monday night, approximately twenty-five Black men fled Newport News when the village was "threatened by a ravaging mob" of white men. Essence's fears that "the good decent people" would one day "pay for the acts of lawlessness" committed by "Negro criminals" had been real-ized. Less than four months after Wyatt's lynching, white terrorists again threatened the lives of African Americans.[41]

Responding to these crises, the BTWIL continued its dual strategy of de-manding municipal action and initiating Black self-help activities. Simulta-neously, the league announced the appointment of a truant officer by the Madison school district and civics classes sponsored by the BTWIL. Mean-while, the Reverend Green Price of Brooklyn's AME Church took charge of efforts to organize an AME church in Newport News. The Reverend Price held joint services with Elder Gibson of the Missionary Baptist Church in Brooklyn and sponsored meetings at the George Washington Young Masonic Hall in Newport News. By November, the Reverend Price had succeeded in forming an AME congregation in Newport News. By March, the *Palladium* reported the Reverend Price was "having great success," especially in attract-ing young people. The success of the churches shifted the crusade from a dual strategy toward one in which the moral regeneration of the Black commu-nity became the primary focus. After 3 October 1903, criticisms of the white city government's neglect waned and criticisms of Blacks accelerated. The descent from protest into morality was perhaps pushed by the desire to com-pete with the ministry, but moralism was also an essential aspect of Profes-sor Wilhite's worldview. During September and early October, this element had been submerged as the league organized against injustices. In mid-October, when the initiative was seized by Brooklyn ministers, a moral fa-naticism began to appear in Wilhite's writings. Between October 10 and early November, the league receded from public view. By 7 November 1903, Wil-hite declared the Booker T. Washington Improvement League was not "dead" but had been undergoing a process of "self-resurrection."[42]

Besides attempting to out-moralize the ministers, "Essence" questioned the Reverend Price's motivations and strategy. During the fall of 1903 and the winter and spring of 1904, Wilhite implied that the AME elder was accept-ing "anybody with money" into the church. He further charged that his "Rev-erence" had recommended "White Wall Trickster" and "Mrs. Sneak Plotter" for teachers and officers in the church's Sunday school. For his part, the Rev-erend Price praised Wilhite's mastery of "dialectical [Hegelian] logic" but alleged Wilhite held "erroneous ideas regarding Christianity," and he there-fore refused to assign Wilhite a Sunday school class. Nonetheless, the attrac-tion of young people into the church and away from the saloons was a victory of sorts since one of the community's major problems according to the Booker T. Washington Improvement League was that youth often visited the saloons instead of attending school. The logic of Wilhite's actions suggests that he desired a secular or, more accurately, a *political* solution to the problem posed by the saloons. This explains why the league sponsored a talk by Brooklyn trustee John Henry Holliday in late January 1904. The BTWIL developed a twofold strategy to confront this problem: political action and self-help. It lobbied city officials to close the saloons or, failing that, to exercise their influence on the youth of Newport News. In his *Palladium* editorials, Wilhite often called on "the respectable citizens to invoke the aid of the state" in shutting down the joints and dives. John Wheeler, publisher of the *Palladium,* in his editorials wondered why Madison officials allowed saloons in which "young men and young women hang out" to operate. The BTWIL convinced Madison school district officials to appoint a truant officer to roust youth away from the saloons and back to school. The BTWIL employed more traditional self-help tactics as well, such as sponsoring civic classes.[43]

"Essence" and the Booker T. Washington Improvement League often mixed rational and effective political strategies with irrational exhortations and unreasonable bourgeois expectations. For instance, he often blamed Black parents for the lack of books and teaching materials at the "Colored school," accusing them of irresponsibility and neglect. He also indiscriminately lumped together criminals and people who rejected his puritanical values. For instance, after condemning "adulterers, gamblers, and perjured dive-runners," "Essence" complained about the failure of the "so-called decent people" to support the BTWIL's effort to "bring to justice Negro criminals." For all his reputed training in the dialectic, "Essence" failed to dig beneath the "appearance" of things and approached the struggle against the saloon keepers one-dimensionally. He allowed his notion of morality to supersede his political common sense. In his condemnations of working-class Black parents, Wilhite ignored material factors, such as "the closing of plants employing hundreds of laborers." He behaved as a zealot. In an attempt to rally a sputtering Booker T. Washington Improvement League, he wrote, "Charge brave soldiers for order and decency in this Negro community, and never call retreat until every adulter leaves Newport." The dispute between the Reverend Price and "Essence" was perhaps because of the elder's apparent success and the BTWIL's failure. Despite their different approaches, the Reverend Price and "Essence" and the BTWIL operated from a similar set of petty bourgeois moral values and were incapable of seeing the positive role saloons and dance halls played for the working class. Katrina Hazzard-Gordon recognized one essential function of jook joints when she stated, "Working-class dance arenas provided African Americans with a bulwark against white cultural domination." According to her, the jook was a site in which the formation and transformation of core black cultural forms—"food, language, community fellowship, mate selection, music, and dance—found sanctuary." Such moral reformers as the Reverend Price and "Essence" simply overlooked the positive role the joints played in providing Black workers with havens from white culture and sites for Black cultural creativity where they could rejuvenate after a long day in the plants.[44]

The goals of Mayor Jones were seemingly much more limited than the Booker T. Washington Improvement League's. According to John Henry Holliday, the Jones administration had eliminated the town's "embarrassment" of having women gather outside the saloons. Jones apparently succeeded in curtailing open prostitution, not in shutting down the dives and gambling halls. Another difference in the antivice campaigns in Brooklyn and in Newport News was their gender target. Holliday's statement implied that the antivice campaign in Brooklyn targeted the prostitutes rather than the men who owned the saloons (Katie Grider was the only female saloon owner). Targeting the saloon owners would have been extremely difficult since a significant portion of Afro-Brooklyn's political and economic elite owned saloons. By targeting impoverished and disfranchised women rather than the enfranchised male owners of the taverns and "dives," Brooklyn's Black male leaders sought to accomplish two related goals. First, like most antiprostitution campaigners during this era, they apparently were operating from the ideology of separate spheres, which relegated women to the home and reserved public space for men. Prostitutes objectively challenged this gendered division of space and in so doing reaffirmed, for bourgeois men *and* women, the correctness of the ideological construction of separate spheres. Since Black men in Brooklyn accepted most, if not all, bourgeois gender conventions, they restricted women's activities in the public domain to church, school, and social welfare activities. Racial pride was a second consideration for Brooklyn's Black male leadership. Elite Afro-Brooklynites were very conscious of their position as the only Black-controlled government in the metro-east region and in the state of Illinois and the racial responsibility this placed on them. Prostitutes were an embarrassment to them and their community. Their intervention into the moral politics of Newport News was an example of how seriously they took their responsibility. Black control of government in Brooklyn further differentiated the Brooklyn and Newport News antivice campaigns. In Brooklyn, the campaign was initiated by the mayor, whereas in Newport News, it was led by a Black civic organization and the ministry. In Brooklyn, Mayor Jones was praised for his actions. In Newport News, "Essence" was assaulted by men allegedly hired by saloon operators. Finally, the Booker T. Washington Improvement League waged an antivice campaign, although over zealously, while Mayor Jones and Brooklyn's town government waged an antiprostitution campaign, at best.[45]

Jones's reforms were not considered very extensive by "Snake Soosa," a fictional social critic created by John Wheeler, publisher of the *St. Louis Palladium*. Wheeler styled himself variously as the "Palladium man" and the "political preacher."[46] However, it was as "Snake Soosa" that he issued his most biting social commentaries. Wheeler wrote "Soosa's" column in dialect. He believed Jones should have extended his actions to such saloon owners as Dr. W. R. Arthur, a saloon operator who became Brooklyn's postmaster and, according to Wheeler, was a swindler. Wheeler thought that saloon owners like Dr. Arthur would bring whites back into control of Brooklyn's government. At times, Wheeler seemed obsessed with Dr. Arthur. For example, in an editorial condemning Madison's city government for not arresting the saloon owner who had "Essence" beaten, Wheeler swiftly shifted the article into a critique of Dr. Arthur. Nevertheless, "Snake Soosa" could offer an incisive analysis of white supremacy, racial oppression, and African Americans' entrepreneurial aspirations. In a column entitled "Echoes from Brooklyn," he wrote, "Dese old BREWERS WILL SET UP ten thousand dollars any day to ENCOURAGE NIGGERS to RUN DIVES THAT'S AGETTING 'EM LYNCHED. THAT'S AGETTING CULLUD PEOPLE'S HOUSES BURNED and THEM RUN OUT OF TOWN. Yet these same BREWERS would not put up TEN CENTS to start a respectable nigger in a respectable business among us. It is jest another way to make a slave of niggers an jest such men as Dr. Arthur jump at such a chance, jes' so he makes a little money."[47] The literature on saloons in the Black community has exposed the nexus between Black votes and liquor licenses that linked unscrupulous white politicians and mercenary Black saloon operators, yet few writers have discussed the role of white capitalists in establishing saloons in the African American community. Though Wheeler's critique is marred by his petty bourgeois worldview, he raises an issue that needs far more historical investigation.

Wheeler, Wilhite, and most middle-class "race men and women" during this period shared a belief that the behavior of working-class Blacks was partly responsible for lynching, riots, and the denial of Blacks' civil rights. Wheeler, like Wilhite, was an extreme moralist, who, unlike Wilhite, was a member of the ministry. His obsession with Arthur was rooted in his moralistic worldview. He once wrote, "To a race attempting to climb the ladder of the public's good opinion, and reach the pinnacle of success in being recognized as a race worthy of a chance, the exposure of any person whose morals are not what they ought to be is just as essential as the removal of a rotten apple from a barrel of good ones."[48] Though Wheeler's accusations may have been true, his subjectivity makes some of his interpretations highly questionable. For instance, in an article written after a visit to the "village of Aunt Hagar's children," he continued his attack on Dr. Arthur but claimed that Frederick Vanderberg was one of Brooklyn's old respected and well-liked citizens. How

Wheeler distinguished between Arthur's alleged larceny and Vanderberg's documented criminality is questionable. Furthermore, that he could speculate Arthur's behavior would lead to whites' regaining political control yet ignore Vanderberg's role in bringing whites back into Brooklyn town politics is disturbing.[49]

The threat of white violence and domination hung over Brooklyn. The lynching of David Wyatt and the intimidation of Blacks in Belleville and Newport News justified Afro-Brooklynites' fears of invasion. Wyatt's lynching was at least a catalyst for Brooklyn officials' concern with protecting prisoners from possible vigilante actions by nearby predominantly white communities. Three years after David Wyatt's lynching, Brooklyn's board of trustees, under the leadership of Burton Washington, passed the following resolution: "Resolved that Bert Washington, mayor of the Village, be empowered to instruct Village Marshall C. S. Dorman and his assistant Geo. Hicks to visit St. Louis and ascertain the price of twelve riot guns, which may be kept in the Brooklyn City Hall for the use of the officials and the citizens of Brooklyn, so that they could protect anyone that they might arrest and save them from any threatened mob violence from Venice, Madison, Granite City, East St. Louis or Belleville."[50] This resolution clearly shows that Brooklyn's city officials believed whites from the surrounding communities might invade their town. It has the air of a beleaguered town attempting to alert those contemplating an impending assault that Brooklyn would be prepared for them. The phrase "for the use of the officials and the citizens of Brooklyn" implies the organization of a civilian militia. Perhaps they planned to deputize citizens to help repulse an attack by a white racist mob. Precedence existed for such an act. African Americans in the Black town of Langston, Oklahoma, had formed a seventy-five-man militia in 1891. Black men from Boley, Oklahoma, forcibly freed Louis Young from jail after white authorities in nearby Progue arrested him for allegedly raping a white girl. The memory of the failure of law enforcement officials to act to protect the life of David Wyatt was still fresh in their minds.[51]

Political Crises: The Scandals of 1912–13 and Dual Government and Martial Law in 1915

The year 1912 introduced a very traumatic three years for Brooklyn politicians. First, Randall J. Cole, who had become mayor in 1910, members of the police department, and the village treasurer were charged with conspiracy to defraud the town. Second, former mayor Frederick Vanderberg was indicted again for selling liquor without a license and charged in a separate indictment with operating a gaming house. Third, without a doubt the most significant of the political crises, a violent battle between rival political factions in

1915 resulted in the St. Clair County Sheriff Mellon's declaring martial law. These scandals shattered seven years of exemplary government conducted by Brooklyn's political leaders.

Charles Webb, the state's attorney, alleged that Mayor Randall J. Cole; Oscar Bletson, the chief of police; Robert Jackson, a police officer; and Louis J. Costly, the village treasurer, conspired to defraud the village of $350. Cole, a janitor, began his political career in 1906, when he was appointed town treasurer. Bletson, a former member of the village board of trustees, had been a laborer before his appointment; so had Jackson. Costly owned a barbershop. The case began when Robert Jackson submitted a request for back pay for alleged employment as a police officer from 1 June 1910 to 1 May 1911. Jackson claimed his attorneys had sued the village "some months prior to the incumbency [sic] of office of the present administration," but because he was "so closely connected and identified with the same," he "thought it would be much better for all concerned if the matter could be adjusted outside of the court, as the case comes up this term if an agreement cannot be reached." Jackson "magnanimously" offered to settle out of court for seven months' salary, totaling $350. Mayor Cole ordered William Terry, the village clerk, to issue a warrant of $350 to Robert Jackson. Terry refused, contending that Jackson had been employed elsewhere during the period covered by the warrant. Terry was relieved of his office, and trustee Edward Green was appointed clerk by Mayor Cole. Either Green also refused or the defendants did not approach him with their scheme. They convinced Percy Hemingway, a mentally disabled person, that he was the town clerk, and he signed the warrant for Jackson. Former clerk William Terry exposed the plot to the state's attorney and the grand jury.[52]

The grand jury issued a three-count indictment against the defendants. At the beginning of the January term, the defendant's attorney, W. L. Coley, demanded that Webb provide them with a "bill of particulars." Webb responded with the following charges, "The People will claim and prove in support of the charge of false pretense set out in the indictment and each count thereof in the above entitled cause that the defendants falsely pretended that Robert Jackson had rendered services as Assistant Marshall of the Village of Brooklyn from June 1, 1910 to May 1, 1911." Webb further alleged "that said Defendants falsely pretended that a suit was pending in the Circuit Court at Belleville, wherein the said Robert Jackson was Plaintiff and the Village of Brooklyn was Defendant to recover the amount of such alleged claims." According to the prosecuting attorney, the defendants claimed that Jackson agreed to withdraw the suit in exchange for a compromise of $350. Cole and company had tricked Percy Hemingway into signing the warrant by promising him they would appoint him village treasurer if he successfully passed this test.[53]

Attorney Coley presented a motion to quash the indictment and to dismiss the charges because they "were not sufficient in law to require them to plead thereto." The court refused. During the trial, Coley presented several motions for instructions to the jury that the court declined to render. On 13 February 1913, the jury made the following ruling:

> We the jury find the defendants Randall Cole, Robert Jackson and Louis J. Costly guilty as charged in the indictment . . .

> We fix the punishment of the defendant Randall Cole at a fine of Five Hundred Dollars ($500.00)

> We fix the punishment of the defendant Robert Jackson at a fine of Five Hundred Dollars ($500.00)

> We fix the punishment of the defendant L. G. Costly at a fine of Five Hundred Dollars ($500.00)[54]

Bletson was found not guilty. After the verdict, Attorney Coley filed a motion requesting that the judge set aside the jury's decision and order a new trial for everyone except Bletson. He alleged that improper evidence was admitted while proper evidence was withheld, that instructions were denied that should have been approved, and that the verdict was contrary to the evidence and the law. The motion was rejected, and the conviction stood.[55]

The second political scandal during this era entailed the continuing legal problems of Frederick Vanderberg. Vanderberg was charged with selling liquor without a license on 20 September, 25 September, and 5 October 1912. While these proceedings were underway, Vanderberg was charged again with committing the same offense. The warrant alleged that on 1 January 1913, he did "unlawfully sell intoxicating liquor, in less quantity than one gallon, to be drunk upon the premises, located in Brooklyn Illinois." On 19 January, Vanderberg was cited for operating a "gaming house." The court heard all of Vanderberg's cases during the January term. On 3 January, Vanderberg waived his right to a jury trial and pled guilty in the first set of liquor cases. He was fined $100. The court documents are incomplete and do not reveal what happened in the other liquor cases or in the gambling case.[56]

This continued pattern of arresting Vanderberg on minor liquor violations, long after his political career was over, suggests that St. Clair County officials were out to get him. However, Vanderberg's problems involved more than just racism. John Evans, Charles Jones, and Burton Washington were never harassed in this manner. Yet by 1912, Vanderberg had become the object of a campaign of legal repression. On the surface, it seems odd that the white power structure in St. Clair County would aim their legal weapons at the one Black politician in Brooklyn who had encouraged white participation in town politics. The language used in the indictments contains an excess of pejoratives that are more appropriate in a sermon than as part of a statement of charges. Vanderberg, however, had come to symbolize the epitome of the "corrupt negro politician." This distorted and negative image of African American political leadership was popularized in the aftermath of Reconstruction and served, as W. E. B. Du Bois pointed out, to "prove" Blacks were incapable of self-government. Vanderberg's behavior reinforced this stereotype, and the county's campaign against him kept this image before the public.[57]

Between January of 1898 and May of 1915, sixteen articles about Brooklyn appeared in the *East St. Louis Journal:* eight focused on political corruption, one concerned a riot, another was about citizens who wanted to secede from the Black town, another discussed the village board's decision to purchase shotguns, and one was headlined "Trying To Oust Dark Town Mayor."[58] Eleven of the sixteen newspaper articles reinforced negative stereotypes, especially of African Americans' alleged propensity for violence and their supposed limited capacity for self-government.

The other factor that must be considered is the possibility of a personal vendetta against Vanderberg by the prosecuting attorneys—Martin Dann, F. J. Tecklenberg, and Charles Webb. Since three different state's attorneys prosecuted Vanderberg, I doubt that they were motivated mainly by personal animus. Dann's prosecution of Vanderberg in the winter and spring of 1899 was overzealous, if not persecutory. Dann had already charged Vanderberg with three counts of embezzlement, and while these cases were in process, he had him arrested for selling liquor without a license. This additional charge suggests that the police were watching Vanderberg. Charles Webb had a prior relationship with Vanderberg. Webb's firm had successfully defended Vanderberg in 1899 against Dann's charge of embezzlement, after Frank Hannah resigned as his attorney. At Webb's insistence, Vanderberg entered a guilty plea to the charge of selling liquor without a license. Webb was a crusader against political corruption and crime, and Vanderberg was only one of several politicians Webb indicted during his tenure as state's attorney. Webb prosecuted Vanderberg three times on liquor violations and once on gambling. In the winter of 1912–13, Webb personally led several raids in "Black Valley." Brooklyn was an extension of East St. Louis's "Black Valley." In most cities, the vice district incorporated or abutted the "Black belt," but in Brooklyn a whole town was corrupted as vice became one of the few viable industries. It must be emphasized that these forays were primarily aimed at shutting down the illegal sources of white East St. Louis bosses' wealth. African Americans owned few of the taverns and gambling dens in Black Valley, and most of the prostitutes and criminals who worked Black Valley were not Black. Brooklyn, however, was different; there Black politicians owned or at least controlled most of the saloons, gambling halls, and houses of prostitution. Webb's raids resulted in almost three hundred indictments handed

down by a special grand jury impaneled for gambling. Vanderberg was arrested on 1 January 1913 for a liquor violation and on 19 January for running
a gaming house. His indictments were part of the crusade Webb waged
against vice between March 1912 and April 1913. Did Webb go after Vanderberg and other corrupt Black Brooklyn politicians more than he did East St.
Louis's unscrupulous Euro-American politicians? This does not appear to
have been the case since Webb indicted a police commissioner, a former police
chief, and an alderman from East St. Louis. His zealousness led to St. Clair
County's Democratic and Republican leaders coalescing to defeat him in 1916.
Charles Webb was attempting to eliminate vice in East St. Louis and St. Clair
County, and Frederick Vanderberg was one of several corrupt politicians
caught in the crusading state's attorney's web.[59]

In the political history of Brooklyn, 1913 stands as a disastrous year—a year
in which a mayor, former mayor, city treasurer, and police officer were convicted of criminal activity. While these actions by elected and appointed officials were deplorable, Brooklyn's African American political leaders were
engaged in a larger pattern of corruption in St. Clair County. The monies that
Afro-Brooklynite politicians were charged with embezzling were exceedingly
meager, generally amounting to no more than a few hundred dollars at a time.
Perhaps the poverty of Brooklyn reduced the graft that could be taken in the
Black town. As pale as things looked in 1913 for Black Brooklyn, they would
grow more pallid in 1915.[60]

The major crisis in Brooklyn during this era began in April of 1915, when
elected officials conspired to keep the Peoples Improvement party off the
official ballot. This action set in motion a series of events that undermined
the legitimacy of the April elections and established the context in which
different political cliques declared themselves the authentic government. John
Evans's youngest son, John L. was the new political party's mayoral candidate, and John De Bow, Dr. Earle Williams, and Robert Boatner were the
party's candidates for the village board of trustees. The junior Evans, a car
repairer, was a member of the school board; De Bow was a car repairer, who
also worked for the Wabash Railroad Company; Williams was a surgeon and
president of the school board; and Boatner was a porter. All were African
Americans. The Peoples Improvement party's supporters included former
mayors Frederick F. Vanderberg, Charles B. Jones, and Burton Washington;
former village board members Edward Gaston and Henry Sanford; and
former town clerk William Terry. Black businesspeople signing their nominating petition included barbershop owner James Freeman Price and tavern
operators Vanderberg and Thomas Koen. Ada Butler joined her fellow teachers Jones, Washington, and Terry in the new political party. The Peoples
Improvement party represented a realignment of Brooklyn politics as the
Republican Club merged with remnants of the Peoples party. The bulk of

those signing the nominating petition were workers. This slate continued the senior Evans's policy of uniting the teachers and the African American working class into a political alliance under working-class leadership.[61]

In 1915, John L. Evans and Williams, along with their ally Henry Sanford, a trustee during Jones's mayorship, were members of the District 188 school board. In 1913, the board of education had begun building a new $18,000 school. This was the first new school building for Brooklyn's African American students since 1888, when Evans's father was in office and had made the town's infrastructure a priority. A victory in the village board elections would have consolidated political power in the hands of John L. Evans and the Peoples Improvement party. This certainly was not lost on the other political organizations, headed by Randall J. Cole and James H. Thomas Sr.[62]

William Terry had the Peoples Improvement party's petition certified by Edward Green, a former trustee and a notary public, before submitting it to James H. Thomas Jr., the town clerk. Apparently everything was in order. Charles Webb, the state's attorney, later alleged that on 9 April 1915, James H. Thomas Jr., William Colbert, James Shaw, Ernest L. Dixon, and Elijah J. Jackson entered into a complex conspiracy. The junior Thomas was town clerk, and Colbert and Dixon were trustees. According to the indictment, Shaw challenged the Peoples party's petition, though he knew the petition conformed to the statute. Mayor Cole then formed a special committee to hear the challenge. The committee consisted of the mayor, the town clerk, and a member of the board of trustees to be chosen by lot. Each member of the village board was to have his name written on a slip of paper and placed in a hat, from which the clerk would draw the name of the third member of the special committee. The clerk drew William Colbert's name. The committee then ruled the petition invalid. Webb later charged that Thomas Jr. had written Colbert's name on all the pieces of paper. Webb also charged that on the night of 14 April, the younger Thomas had printed the ballots before board approval. Webb claimed the ballots contained

> only the names of the said James H. Thomas, Sr., as candidate for President of said Village of Brooklyn, and the said Henry Hunter, said Dave Ferguson and said Richard Evans, as candidates for members of the Board of Trustees of the said Village of Brooklyn, and had caused the said ballots to be printed so . . . closely together that there was not and is not a blank space on said ticket under each of said name wherein aid electors might write in another name, or names for election to said offices, or either of them, and to make a X opposite thereto as provided by law.[63]

Mayor Cole had previously appointed Jackson and Dixon election judges. Thirty minutes before the polls opened on election day, 20 April, Jackson and Dixon decided to replace A. J. Bowers, the third poll judge, with Shaw. According to the indictment, Dixon, Jackson, and Shaw refused to assist or allow any illiterate person to vote unless the person agreed to vote for James H. Thomas Sr. Webb alleged that this illegal act prevented many voters, who would have voted for John L. Evans and the Peoples Improvement party, from voting. The Thomas forces deprived illiterate citizens of their voting rights because they believed they would vote for Evans and the new Peoples Improvement party.[64]

Thomas's faction succeeded in preventing the election of the Peoples Improvement party, but it lost by a plurality to Randall Cole, the incumbent. There is no indication that Cole was part of the conspiracy, but Evans and the Peoples Improvement party challenged the election.[65] A trial was scheduled for 26 April 1915, but Thomas got a continuance. On the afternoon of Thursday, 6 May 1915, Sheriff Logan P. Mellon confiscated the town seal and the municipal records. The St. Clair County Sheriff's Office retained possession of them until the court ruled on the legality of the election. Though Cole had more votes, Thomas was advised by unidentified person(s) to claim the office until the courts rendered a decision. On Friday, 7 May, Mayor Cole appointed his police force. He named Lemanuel G. Costly police chief, and he appointed Napoleon B. West, Robert Jackson, and Henry Gaston as police officers. Thomas also named his police officers on 7 May. He appointed former marshal Anthony Speed police chief and named former chief Oscar Bletson, Louis Perryman, and Joseph H. Doss as police officers. Consequently, on 7 May 1915, Brooklyn, Illinois, had dual governments, each with its own armed forces, and these contending factions fought each other for the right to govern Brooklyn.[66]

Many of the principals had questionable histories. Perryman was a saloon operator. Speed, who had been town marshal, constable for Stites Township, and treasurer of the Highway Commission, had been indicted for embezzlement. After the April 1905 township election, he was replaced as treasurer of the Highway Commission by George P. Doscher, a member of Brooklyn's first village board. On 22 and 24 April, Speed refused to turn the commission's balance of $4,3122.79 over to Doscher. After State's Attorney Tecklenberg issued a warrant for his arrest for embezzlement, Speed fled. On 12 May, Speed surrendered to the county sheriff. On 2 June, the grand jury issued a "true bill" charging Speed with "withholding money" and ordered the sheriff to rearrest him. The "withholding money" charge was a lesser charge than embezzlement. The court records do not indicate whether Speed was found guilty.[67]

In 1913, Cole and Jackson had been convicted of conspiring to defraud Brooklyn. Bletson, then the chief of police, was indicted with them but was cleared of all charges. Perhaps bad blood still existed between Bletson and his former allies—Cole and Jackson. Whatever the case, a confrontation occurred on Friday afternoon, when Chief Costly's police force arrested Chief Speed and his squad for "posing as officers of the law." Speed and his men were released on bond, and their weapons and "other police property was restored to them." After leaving the jail, Speed and his officers were joined by Thomas Sr. This force now included three former police chiefs—Thomas, Speed, and Bletson. Around seven o'clock, the armed squadron walked to the center of Madison Street in front of James J. Dowling's general store, where they confronted Costly, Jackson, Gaston, and West. In an affidavit given from St. Mary's Hospital in East St. Louis, Robert Jackson described the violent conflict:

> They were coming along up the street, Speed and the whole bunch, they were coming toward [?] and Bletson said "I got a warrant for Costly." When he said that Mr. Costly stepped toward the middle of the street and Speed fired the first shot then and Mr. Costly fell. Then there was more shots and Doss came running up to me and threw his gun right on me. I got two shots, one in my leg and one in my stomach. When we were coming along Pole West and Henry Gaston, Mr. Costly and me and I saw Speed first. He had a gun on his arm. We were at the rear end of Dowling's store. Speed, he shot a rifle and I saw Mr. Costly fall. There was no reason to shoot. We were going on by to get out of the way when they started to shoot, and I got it worse than any of them. I was just about 25 feet from Speed when he shot Costly. Speed, Perryman, Oscar Bletson, Dorman and old Thomas were all there and they all had guns and shot. I had just come home from work and gone up town and got my star and be killed my first and Doss did it. That's about all!—I don't want to talk to make my condition worse. Is it a fact that Perryman is dead?[68]

Jackson's wounds were fatal, as he feared they would be. He died on 9 May 1915. Most observers claimed Louis Perryman, not Speed, fired the first shot at Costly. Perryman was killed during the shootout. Four other combatants were injured. Costly was shot in the neck, and Speed was shot twice, in the chest and in the hand. Both were in serious condition, but they lived. Emmitt Dorman and George Campbell, according to the *East St. Louis Journal,* received serious wounds when hit by stray bullets. State's Attorney Webb charged that Dorman and Campbell had fought on the side of Thomas and Speed. An ambulance took the wounded to St. Mary's Hospital and Perryman's body to Kurrus Morgue. Both were in East St. Louis.[69]

Upon learning of the disturbance, Sheriff Mellon and several deputies rushed to Brooklyn from Belleville, the county seat. They immediately closed the saloons and began to round up all firearms. Mellon assigned four deputy sheriffs to patrol Brooklyn. In effect, the sheriff imposed martial law on the Black town. Saturday, Chief Deputy Sheriff Stuart Campbell arrested Tobias Crittenden and George Campbell on charges of carrying concealed weapons, and they were incarcerated in Belleville in the county jail. On 30 May, when State's Attorney Charles Webb filed a "quo warranto suit to oust J. H. Thomas as mayor," Brooklyn was still under martial law.[70]

On 11 May, the coroner conducted an inquest into the cause of Robert Jackson's and Louis Perryman's death. St. Clair County Coroner C. P. Renner concluded, "It appears probable from the evidence of witnesses sworn and examined before me at said inquest, that Louis Perryman and Robert Jackson came to their death from a gun shot wound made by one John H. Doss with murderous intent." The coroner's jury found that Speed and the elder Thomas were also "responsible for the deaths of the said Louis Perryman & Robert Jackson." The next day, 13 May, the court issued a writ of habeas corpus for the arrest of Doss, Speed, and Thomas Sr. Thomas filed a petition with Judge George A. Crow requesting that he be released because his incarceration was based on "wholly insufficient evidence" delivered at the coroner's inquest, but the court records do not reveal whether he was released.[71]

Prosecuting attorney Webb secured indictments against Thomas Sr., Speed, Doss, Bletson, George Campbell, Dorman, William McCoy, and George Parks for murder. He also obtained indictments against the Thomases, William Colbert, Ernest Dixon, Elijah Jackson, and James H. Shaw for conspiracy. The sequence of events, the ordering of both trials, their continuances, and new trials are quite confusing. To reduce the confusion, I will discuss the conspiracy trial first. The grand jury returned a "true bill" on 25 June, after testimony from the following witnesses: Charles B. Jones, Dr. Earle Williams, Randall J. Cole, Henry Gaston, Nancy King, Julie Kegler, and W. L. Coley. Nancy King apparently was the wife of Bedford King, a Black laborer who had signed Evans's nominating petition, and Julie Kegler was a white widow. Coley, of course, had represented Vanderberg in 1899 and Cole and his colleagues in 1913.[72]

The indictment handed down by the grand jury began a sequence of trials that continued into 1918. The defendants were arrested for conspiracy and posted bail of $400 each on 21 July 1915. Their attorney, former St. Clair County State's Attorney F. J. Tecklenberg, moved to quash the indictments, claiming the four counts were insufficient in law because they were not specific or were not stated in the language of the statutes. On 7 December, the court ruled for the defendants in *The People of the State of Illinois v. James H. Thomas et al.* They were released on a technicality. Webb immediately pursued another indictment. On 11 December, after hearing from Charles B. Jones, W. L. Coley, Burton Washington, Randall J. Cole, L. G. Costly, Henry Gaston, and William Terry, the grand jury issued another indictment. The new indictment included the missing specifics that had earlier led to the case's dismissal. Webb had Thomas, Speed, Campbell, Rowe, Doss, Dorman, Bletson, McCoy, and Parks rearrested on 15 December 1915. He also increased their bail to $500 each. The case was continued in 1918 under a completely new file number. I was unable to find the final verdict of the conspiracy case because the 1918 file includes only two pages, the criminal file numbers, and the charge.[73]

Simultaneous with the murder trial, Webb charged the defendants with conspiracy to commit assault with the intent to kill Lemanuel G. Costly and Robert Jackson. On 3 August 1915, the jury found James H. Thomas Sr., Anthony Speed, George Campbell, George Rowe, Joseph Doss, and Emmitt Dorman guilty of murder and sentenced each of them to fourteen years in the penitentiary. Oscar Bletson, William McCoy, and George Parks were found not guilty. Alexander Flannigan, attorney for the defendants and former attorney for the town of Brooklyn, asked the court to set aside the jury's verdict and grant a new trial on the grounds that the verdict resulted from "passion and prejudice erected in the minds of the jury by the improper and irrelevant evidence admitted for the people and by the improper and misleading arguments of the counsel of the people." The judge refused the motion. Flannigan appealed the case to the Illinois Supreme Court, and a year after the election, on 20 April 1916, the Illinois High Court ruled that there was "Manifest Error" (though it did not specify what that might have been) and remanded the case back to the Circuit Court of St. Clair County. Unfortunately, the trail ends here, because St. Clair County criminal records do not include any other files under the name James H. Thomas Sr. et al.[74]

In the April 1916 elections, Charles Webb was defeated by Hubert Schaumleffel, whom East St. Louis's political bosses considered more "broad-minded," that is, less aggressive in prosecuting corrupt politicians. It is possible that Schaumleffel simply dropped the case. The records are not any better in informing us about the outcome of the conspiracy trial or the quo warranto suit to remove the elder Thomas from office. This leaves mostly unanswered questions, and these issues transcend the Thomas-Speed clique's guilt or innocence. Eyewitnesses' accounts of this incident found the Thomas-Speed faction at fault. It appears that they decided to acquire with the bullet what they did not win with the ballot. Nevertheless, the evidence indicates that Louis Perryman initiated the hostilities. Nothing in the newspaper accounts or in the state's attorney's charges proves conclusively that there was a conspiracy to assassinate Costly and Jackson, though the Thomas-Speed faction acted improperly.

At first glance, the existence of dual governments in Brooklyn and the armed conflict between them seem incredible. Yet in the metro-east, dual governments and politically motivated violence was not unusual. In 1877, after successfully amending East St. Louis's charter, John Bowman won the mayorship in a special election, but a faction of the village board led by former mayor Ernest W. Wider refused to recognize Bowman's victory. Wider refused to turn over the city's administration to Bowman while the case was being contested in the courts. Both Wider and Bowman appointed police forces. On 30 June 1878, Bowman's "city marshals" attacked the headquarters of Wider's "metropolitan police," and during the assault, two of the marshals were killed. On 23 July, another shootout occurred between the city marshals and the metropolitan police, after Bowmanites attempted to destroy railroad tracks being laid in accordance with a right-of-way granted the Illinois and St. Louis Railroad by the Wider administration. This action ended a monopoly enjoyed by the Cairo Short Line that Bowman was determined to preserve. The metropolitan police suffered fatalities during this confrontation. In 1885, Bowman was assassinated in another bid for the mayorship. These incidents from East St. Louis's tumultuous political past demonstrate that Brooklyn's descent into political violence was not without precedence in the metro-east.[75]

Conclusion

As late as 1906, Brooklyn was considered well governed. Its plunge from a family community into a local state of warring armed factions in less than a decade was a product of more than the personal corruption of individual politicians. Vanderberg, Speed, Cole, and Thomas were no more the cause of Brooklyn's problems than the series of crooked political bosses who ruled East St. Louis during the same era were solely to blame for that city's problems. Andrew Theising contended that corruption was a structural component of industrial suburbs. Political corruption flourished in East St. Louis because the absentee industrialists encouraged it. According to Theising, "Because industrial suburbs rely on the host city for infrastructure and institutions, it becomes imperative that industry have some hand in the host city's operations. This is most easily accomplished when host city officials are capable of being influenced by money, power, or some other exchange. Therefore, industrial suburbs and the host cities on which they rely condone corruption and vice for purposes of profitability. By keeping everyone in the process happy, a measure of stability which ensures profitability of industry exists." East St. Louis politicians were vulnerable because of the path and pace of its industrialization. Brooklyn politicians were open to corruption partly because of Brooklyn's failure to attract major industries. Just as East St. Louis was a dumping ground for the industrial noise, smoke, disease, and congestion no longer deemed acceptable in St. Louis, Brooklyn was an outlet for the overflow of taverns, gambling, prostitution, and the like from East St. Louis. Because the African American entrepreneurial class was restricted to service and liquor enterprises, it was vulnerable to the lure of easy profits from the vice industry. Although these entrepreneurs often appear as villains, this role was thrust on them because of the way Brooklyn was incorporated into the political economy of the metro-east region. Vice was not only condoned but also encouraged in Brooklyn because it was the dominant industry.[76]

We cannot begin to know how much graft occurred in Brooklyn, but it must have been substantial to induce the type and extent of corruption in Brooklyn between 1913 and 1915. Certainly, Charles Webb thought so. Webb vigorously pursued the Thomas forces, as he had Cole's clique two years earlier and Vanderberg's in the preceding decade. What is certain is that under the corrupt regimes of Vanderberg, Cole, and Thomas, little was done to improve the town's infrastructure or to promote cultural development. Newspapers no longer reported the celebration of Emancipation Day, the creation of new social organizations, or the modernization of the town's infrastructure. During this era, virtually all reported news concerned either church functions or the indictments of political leaders. Celebrations and commemoration—such as Emancipation Day; meetings of statewide organizations, such as the Afro-American League; and Lovejoy's birthday—had been occasions for citizens to reaffirm their freedom-conscious heritage, but the antidemocratic character of the degenerate regimes disempowered Brooklyn's citizenry. Unlike John Evans, none of the Vanderberg-era political bosses ever elevated themselves to the stature of a political activist or became a statewide African American leader. They remained just politicians. Although corrupt government officials ruled Brooklyn for only about half this seventeen-year period, their actions so perverted the practice of municipal government that Brooklyn could be compared with East St. Louis, then considered one of the most corrupt city governments in the United States.[77]

Conclusion

BROOKLYN, ILLINOIS, stands at the nexus of a number of underdeveloped areas in African American historical scholarship. Brooklyn is unique in several ways. It is the oldest Black town in the United States. The town began as one of a small number of freedom villages organized by fugitive slaves and free African Americans during the first part of the nineteenth century. In 1873, it became the first majority-Black community to incorporate as a municipality. Brooklyn is also one of a handful of such communities to survive into the twentieth century. Most Black towns were formed on the western frontier or in the rural south. Brooklyn was the first predominately Black community to develop in an urban industrial complex. By the mid-twentieth century, similar communities would be formed on the suburban rings of industrial cities throughout the Midwest. When scholars have taken note of Black towns, the rural western and southern towns have received the bulk of their attention, however.[1]

Although important as examples of Black nationalism, the western and southern towns evolved against the grain of American historical development. These communities founded between 1890 and 1910 reflected the social beliefs of an earlier era. Their peasant philosophy located "independence" and "manhood" in land ownership. By 1890, however, land ownership was no longer possible for most Americans, Black or white. It had been effectively closed off by the rise of urban- and industrial-based monopoly capitalism. That is, during the era of urbanization and industrialization, African Americans' efforts to create small, self-sufficient rural towns were doomed to failure. Because of their different political economies, the occupational, class, and family structures of these agrarian towns differed profoundly from those of Black towns emerging in the industrial complexes. Although Brooklyn,

Illinois; Urban Crest, Ohio; Kinloch, Missouri; Robbins, Illinois; Lincoln Heights, Ohio; Fairmount and Glenarden, Maryland, also sprouted from African Americans' aspirations for autonomy, the metropolitan-area African American towns either presaged or reflected the national trend of migration to urban industrial areas. For instance, Urban Crest and Kinloch developed during the 1890s and initially were unincorporated "pseudo towns" located on the outskirts of Cincinnati, Ohio, and St. Louis, Missouri. Robbins, Illinois; Lincoln Heights, Ohio; Fairmount and Glenarden, Maryland, were products of the great migration. The Black commuter suburbs, like their rural counterparts, were concrete manifestations of Black nationalism, but, unlike the rural towns, they were created by the newly dominant processes of industrial capitalism. Brooklyn and the Black worker communities of the great migration era were the creations of labor migration, proletarianization, and racial oppression.

Brooklyn was the first town in which the politics of Black power produced Black majority rule. After Black people gained control of the government, class-based intraracial conflict slowly replaced racial warfare as the dominant contradiction in the predominately Black town. The struggles between the Evans forces and the Vanderberg clique revolved around questions of infrastructural development, political culture, political alliances, patronage, and involvement in statewide African American issues. The battles of these contending Black political fractions call into serious question the Mozell Hill–Thelma Ackiss thesis that racial unity eclipsed class conflict in all-Black towns. The merger of color and class was an unarticulated, subterranean factor in Brooklyn's intraracial disputes. In this respect, Brooklyn town politics was just an extreme example of Black-town politics.

After Blacks assumed political power, whites began to emigrate, a process that over time converted the community back into an all-Black settlement. One could claim that after Blacks gained control of the government in 1886, Brooklyn was transmuted into a neocolony. This process transpired between 1886 and 1910, coinciding with the industrial explosion taking place in the metro-east. It seems that whites fled Brooklyn because of their fear of "Negro domination." The consequence of the racialized manner in which African Americans were absorbed into the regional political economy made it improbable that they could create an economically viable community. On the surface, Ingo Walter and John E. Kramer's theory that Black political independence meant economic dependence for all-Black towns appears true. Of course, Walter and Kramer did not articulate the role of the racist capitalist system in structuring economic dependence for all-Black towns. The two political scientists undervalued structural factors in favor of an analysis that focused on individual explanations. Specifically, they focused on such individual factors as low educational attainment and poor job skills—factors that were not so much explanations as consequences of earlier racial-economic determinations.[2]

Afro-Brooklynites were incorporated into industrial proletarian occupations when most Blacks were still restricted to the agricultural sector. Unlike most Black towns, Brooklyn was not a remote rural agricultural service center but a town centrally located in a booming industrial region. Proletarianization had mixed effects on the life and culture of Afro-Brooklynites. On the one hand, industrial employment was the magnet that attracted African Americans to Brooklyn; the plants in the metro-east region were responsible for the population boom. On the other hand, proletarianization served to warp Brooklyn's male to female ratio because the nature of the jobs pulled a predominately male labor force. A decrease in nuclear families was accompanied by a rise in extended and augmented households. The plants needed common laborers, and this demand worked to undermine the social structure of Brooklyn. The number and percentage of farmers, skilled and semi-skilled workers, and supervisors dropped drastically during this period. Businesses catering to an overwhelming male population thrived, while other types of enterprises failed to develop. No major industry located in Brooklyn, although the Wabash Railroad Company did locate a roundhouse and machine shops on Brooklyn's periphery, between Brooklyn and Venice. Economic dependency worsened as vice and corruption grew. Political factions often battled one another over the spoils of political office holding. These factors combined to accelerate Brooklyn's deterioration. Finally, the decline of this once thriving community was a result of the way in which Brooklyn was incorporated into the metro-east's political economy—as a source of unskilled labor.

Many of the same processes that transformed Brooklyn between 1886 and 1910—industrial capitalism, proletarianization, African American migration, acquisition of political power, and white flight—would work similar effects on East St. Louis, Illinois; Gary, Indiana; and Detroit, Michigan, between 1950 and 1980. The Black experience in Brooklyn thus presaged the post-1960s African American urban experience. While Afro-Brooklynites saw much of their vision of autonomy wither under the pressure of economic exploitation, racism, underdevelopment, and political corruption, they still managed to sustain a semi-independent community in which at least the dream of Black self-government was kept alive. Though the community was not "Founded by Chance," it certainly was "Sustained by Courage."

Notes

Introduction

1. Lafayette S. White Sr., "Lovejoy's History," in *Brooklyn Homecoming, 1987* (Brooklyn, Ill.: Helping Hands Organization of Brooklyn, 1987), 3 (White is recognized as the community's historian); Harold Rose, "The All-Negro Town: Its Evolution and Function," *Geographic Review* 55, no. 3 (1965): 354.

Kendleton and Broad House, Texas, the second oldest all-Black towns, were founded on 8 June 1869. Kenneth M. Hamilton lists Kendleton and Broad House as the first Black towns in the Trans-Appalachian West. See Kenneth L. Hamilton, *Black Towns and Profit: Promotion and Development in the Trans-Appalachian West, 1877–1915* (Urbana: University of Illinois Press, 1990), 2, 4n2. See also Alwyn Barr, *Black Texans: A History of African Americans in Texas, 1528–1995* (Austin, Tex.: Jenkins, 1973), 65.

Scholars disagree on the definition of a Black town. Two geographers, Harold Rose and Robert Thomas Ernest, use a minimum of 1,000 residents as part of their definition. Obviously, there is a threshold below which the Black population can not fall. For Rose, that figure was 95 percent; for Ernest and Norman L. Crockett it was 90 percent. W. Sherman Savage maintained the most important factor was the purpose of the town's founding. He therefore classified towns with nearly 50 percent white populations, such as Douglasville, Texas, as Black towns. Juliet E. K. Walker considered the race of the town founder(s) the most critical element, while Crockett considered Black political control the most critical variable. I have constructed a definition based on incorporation, purpose of founding, and political control. I define a Black town as a municipality whose origins involved a distinct "racial" or protonationalist purpose in which nearly 90 percent of the population is Black and the reins of government are controlled by Blacks. See Rose, "All-Negro Town," 352; Robert Thomas Ernest, "Factors of Isolation and Interaction in an All-Black City: Kinloch, Missouri" (Ph.D. diss., University of Florida, 1973), 17; Norman L. Crockett, *The Black Towns* (Lawrence: Regents Press of Kansas, 1979), xiii; W. Sherman Savage, *Blacks in the West* (Westport, Conn.: Greenwood, 1976), 103; and Juliet E. K. Walker, *Free Frank: A Black Pioneer on the Ante-Bellum Frontier* (Lexington: University Press of Kentucky, 1983).

2. Organized on 27 April 1790 by Arthur St. Clair, the territorial governor, St. Clair County was the first county formed in the territory that became the state of Illinois. For information on Brooklyn's early history, see White, "Lovejoy's History," 3; Newton Bate-

man and Paul Selby, eds., *Historical Encyclopedia of Illinois: St. Clair County*, vol. 2 (Chicago: Munsell, 1907), 9; U.S. Department of Labor, Federal Writers' Project, *Illinois: A Descriptive and Historical Guide*, American Guide Series (Chicago: A. C. McClurg, 1947), 490–91; St. Clair County Recorder of Deeds, *Book J*, 272, St. Clair County Courthouse, Belleville, Illinois; St. Clair County Recorder of Deeds, *Incorporation Index Book*, 310–11; *History of St. Clair County, Illinois* (Philadelphia: Brink, McDonough, 1881); *Belleville Weekly Advocate*, 6 September 1873; and "C. B. Carroll's Brooklyn City Directory, 1903," in *East St. Louis City Directory* (East St. Louis: East St. Louis City Directory Publishing, 1903), 232.

For discussion of "organized black communities," see William Pease and Jane Pease, *Black Utopia: Negro Communal Experiments in America* (Madison: State Historical Society of Wisconsin, 1963).

Some scholars consider Lewis, the Woodson's oldest child, the "father of African American nationalism." See Floyd J. Miller, "The 'Father of Black Nationalism': Another Contender," *Civil War History* 17, no. 4 (1971): 310–19; Floyd J. Miller, *The Search for a Black Nationality: Black Emigration and Colonization, 1787–1863* (Urbana: University of Illinois Press, 1975); and Ellen N. Lawson, "Sarah Woodson Early: 19th Century Black Nationalist 'Sister,'" in *Black Women in United States History*, ed. Darlene Clark Hine (Brooklyn, N.Y.: Carlson, 1990), 820–21.

3. For information on other Black towns, see Janet Sharp Hermann, *The Pursuit of a Dream* (New York: Oxford University Press, 1981); Janet Sharp Hermann, "Isaiah T. Montgomery's Balancing Act," in *Black Leaders of the Nineteenth Century*, ed. Leon Litwack and August Meier (Urbana: University of Illinois Press, 1988), 291–304; Elizabeth Rauh Bethel, *Promiseland: A Century of Life in a Negro Community* (Philadelphia: Temple University Press, 1981); Thomas Knight, *Sunset on Utopian Dreams: An Experiment of Black Separatism on the American Frontier* (Washington, D.C.: University Press of America, 1977); and Ronald Love, "Community in Transition: A Study of Mound Bayou, Mississippi" (Ph. diss., Boston University, 1982), 17.

4. Mozell C. Hill, "The All-Negro Communities of Oklahoma: The Natural History of a Social Movement," *Journal of Negro History* 31 (Summer 1946): 257 (quote).

Menifee, Arkansas, was destroyed by a tornado in 1965, and Lyles Station's population has dwindled to about fifty. For information on these two communities, see Ramla Bandele, "The Underdevelopment of Black Towns" (M.A. thesis, University of Illinois, 1984), 12–13, 16, 18; Pease and Pease, *Black Utopia;* Andrew Wiese, "Places of Our Own: Suburban Black Towns before 1960," *Journal of Urban History* 19 (May 1993): 30–54; and Andrew Wiese, "The Other Suburbanites: African American Suburbanization in the North before 1950," *Journal of American History* 85 (March 1999): 1495–1524.

For information on the economic development of Brooklyn and the metro-east region, see Robert A. Harper, *The Metro-East: Heavy Industry in the St. Louis Metropolitan Area* (Carbondale: Department of Geography, Southern Illinois University, 1958); Bateman and Selby, *Historical Encyclopedia of Illinois,* 172; Karen Saffel, "The Founding of Caseyville," *Journal of St. Clair County Historical Society* 3, no. 3 (1977): 29–35; Harry M. Dixon, "The Illinois Coal Mining Industry" (Ph.D. diss., University of Illinois, 1951); Elin Schoen, *Tales of an All-Night Town* (New York: Harcourt Brace Jovanovich, 1979), 11; A. Doyne Horsely, *Illinois: A Geography* (Boulder, Colo.: Westview, 1986), 133; Carl Baldwin, "East St. Louis," in *St. Louis: Its Neighbors, Landmarks and Milestones*, ed. Robert E. Hannon (St. Louis: St. Louis Regional Commerce and Growth Association, 1986), 240–51; U.S. Bureau of the Census, *Population Schedules of the Thirteenth Census of the United States, 1910, Illinois, St. Clair County,* Roll 323, 151–66, National Archives and Records Service, Washington, D.C.

5. Mozell C. Hill, "The All-Negro Society in Oklahoma" (Ph.D. diss., University of Chicago, 1946), 124. In his pioneering studies of Black towns, Mozell C. Hill posited that

racial oppression and the desire for autonomy formed the basis for the construction of Black towns. Kenneth Hamilton disputed Hill's thesis, claiming instead that economic considerations were the primary factors in Black town formation. See M. C. Hill, "All-Negro Society in Oklahoma," 124; M. C. Hill, "All-Negro Communities of Oklahoma," 254–68; Hamilton, *Black Towns and Profit*, 155–64; and Sundiata Keita Cha-Jua, "Racism, Nationalism and Black Town Development: A Review of *Black Towns and Profit: Promotion and Development in the Trans-Appalachian West, 1877–1915*," *Journal of the West* 32 (April 1993): 96. See also Bandele, "Underdevelopment of Black Towns," 23–24; David Joseph Organ, "The Historical Geography of African American Frontier Settlements" (Ph.D. diss., University of California at Berkeley, 1995); Ernest, "Factors of Isolation and Interaction in an All-Black City"; Hermann, *Pursuit of a Dream;* Crockett, *Black Towns,* 104–13; Ingo Walter and John E. Kramer, "Politics in an All-Negro City," *Urban Affairs Quarterly* 4 (September 1968): 65–87; and Ingo Walter and John E. Kramer, "Political Autonomy and Economic Dependence in an All-Negro Municipality," *American Journal of Economics and Sociology* 28 (July 1969): 225–48; and Joseph Taylor, "Mound Bayou—Past and Present," *Negro History Bulletin* 3 (July 1940): 105–11.

For racial captialism, see Cedric Robinson, *Black Marxism: The Making of the Black Radical Tradition* (London: Zed, 1983), 3.

6. See Harold Cruse, *The Crisis of the Negro Intellectual* (New York: William and Morrow, 1967); Essien Udosen Essien-Udom, *Black Nationalism: A Search for an Identity in America* (Chicago: University of Chicago Press, 1962); James Turner, "The Sociology of Black Nationalism," *Black Scholar* 1 (December 1969): 17–37; Alphonso Pinkney, *Red, Black, and Green: Black Nationalism in the United States* (Cambridge: Cambridge University Press, 1976); Raymond Hall, *Black Separatism in the United States* (Hanover, N.J.: University Press of New England, 1978); and Manning Marable, *Blackwater: Historical Studies in Race, Class Consciousness, and Revolution* (Dayton, Ohio: Black Praxis, 1981), 93–128.

7. *Webster's New Collegiate Dictionary* defines a *maroon* as "a fugitive Negro slave of the West Indies and Guiana in the 17th and 18th centuries." Other dictionaries offer similar meanings. For instance, *Longman Dictionary of Contemporary English* describes a maroon as "a slave of black West Indian origin who has run away from his master." Herbert Aptheker contends that these definitions are temporally and spatially inaccurate. James A. Gerschwender offers an alternative definition. According to him, maroons were "groups of fugitive slaves who escaped and established relatively permanent communities." See *Webster's New Collegiate Dictionary; Longman Dictionary of Contemporary English* (Brunt Mill, England: Longman Group Limited, 1978), 667; Herbert Aptheker, "Maroons within the Present Limits of the United States," *Journal of Negro History* 24 (April 1939): 167–84; Herbert Aptheker, "Slave Revolts, Resistance, Maroonage, and Implications for Post-Emancipation Society," *Annals of the New York Academy of Sciences* 292 (1977): 491–95; Herbert Aptheker, "Resistance and Afro-American History," in *Resistance: Studies in African, Caribbean, and Afro-American History,* ed. Gary Y. Okihiro (Amherst: University of Massachusetts Press, 1986), 10–20; James A. Gerschwender, *Racial Stratification in America* (Dubuque, Iowa: Wm. C. Brown, 1978), 272; and Eugene Genovese, *From Rebellion to Revolution: Afro-American Slave Revolts in the Making of the New World* (New York: Vintage, 1979), 68–81. For the only book published on organized Black communities, see Pease and Pease, *Black Utopia.*

8. Rayford Logan, *The Negro in American Life and Thought: The Nadir, 1877–1901* (New York: Dial, 1954).

9. John Bracey, August Meier, and Elliott Rudwick, *Black Nationalism in America* (New York: Bobbs-Merrill, 1968), 157.

10. M. C. Hill, "All-Negro Society in Oklahoma," 5; William Bittle and Gilbert Geis, "Racial Self-Fulfillment and the Rise of an All-Negro Community in Oklahoma," *Phylon* 18 (September 1957): 247; Wiese, "Places of Our Own," 30.

Mozell C. Hill is the premier scholar of Black towns. See also his "All-Negro Communities of Oklahoma," 261; *Culture of a Contemporary All-Negro Community* (Langston, Okla.: Langston University, 1943); "Basic Racial Attitudes toward Whites in the Oklahoma All-Negro Community," *American Journal of Sociology* 49 (May 1944): 519–22; "A Comparative Study of Race Attitudes in the All-Negro Community in Oklahoma," *Phylon* 7 (March 1946): 260–68; "A Comparative Analysis of the Social Organization of the All-Negro Society in Oklahoma," *Social Forces* 25 (October 1946): 70–77; and, with Thelma Ackiss, "Social Classes: A Frame of Reference for the Study of Negro Society," *Social Forces* 22 (October 1943): 92–98.

11. For the few scholarly examinations of Black nationalism before the late 1960s, see August Meier, "Booker T. Washington and the Town of Mound Bayou," *Phylon* 15 (December 1954): 396–401; Bill McAdoo, *Pre–Civil War Black Nationalism* (1964; reprint, New York: David Walker, 1983); Howard H. Bell, "Chicago Negroes in the Reform Movement, 1847–1853," *Negro History Bulletin* 21 (April 1958): 153–54; Howard H. Bell, "The Negro Emigration Movement, 1849–1854: A Phase of Negro Nationalism," *Phylon* 20 (June 1959): 132–42; Bittle and Geis, "Racial Self-Fulfillment and the Rise of an All-Negro Community in Oklahoma," 247–60; William Bittle and Gilbert Geis, "Alfred Charles Sam and an African Return: A Case Study in Negro Despair," *Phylon* 23 (Summer 1962): 178–96; William Bittle and Gilbert Geis, *The Longest Way Home: Chief Alfred Sam's Back-to-Africa Movement* (Detroit: Wayne State University Press, 1964); Essien-Udom, *Black Nationalism;* A. J. Gregory, "Black Nationalism: A Preliminary Analysis of Negro Radicalism," *Science and Society* 27 (Winter 1963): 415–32; Pease and Pease, *Black Utopia;* Rose, "All-Negro Town," 352–67; and Taylor, "Mound Bayou," 105–11.

12. Theodore Draper, *The Rediscovery of Black Nationalism* (New York: Viking, 1969); Walter and Kramer, "Politics in an All-Negro City," 65–87; Walter and Kramer, "Political Autonomy and Economic Dependence in an All-Negro Municipality," 225–48; Ernest, "Factors of Isolation and Interaction in an All-Black City"; Kenneth Hamilton, "The Origin and Early Development of Langston, Oklahoma," *Journal of Negro History* 62 (July 1977): 270–87; Kenneth Hamilton, "Townsite Speculation and the Origin of Boley, Oklahoma," *Chronicles of Oklahoma* 55, no. 3 (1977): 180–89; Joseph G. Mannard, "Black Company Town: A Peculiar Institution in Pierce, Florida," *Tampa Bay History* 1, no. 1 (1979): 61–66; and Crockett, *Black Towns.* See also Cruse, *Crisis of the Negro Intellectual;* Robert Allen, *Black Awakening in Capitalist America* (Garden City, N.Y.: Doubleday, 1969); and Edwin Redkey, *Black Exodus: Black Nationalist and Back-to-Africa Movements, 1890–1910* (New Haven, Conn.: Yale University Press, 1969).

White scholars investigating Black nationalism included Theodore Draper, August Meier, Elliott Rudwick, Howard H. Bell, William Bittle, Gilbert Geis, A. J. Gregory, William Pease, and Mary Pease, among others. Black scholars included Essien Udosen Essien-Udom, Kenneth Hamilton, Edwin Redkey, Robert Allen, and Harold Cruse.

13. Draper, *Rediscovery of Black Nationalism;* Herbert Aptheker, "Consciousness of Negro Nationality to 1900," in *Afro-American History: The Modern Era* (New York: Citadel, 1971), 109–17 (this essay was originally published in *Political Affairs,* June 1949); Eugene Genovese, *In Red and Black: Marxian Explorations in Southern and Afro-American History* (New York: Pantheon, 1971), 128–57, 230–55; Bell, "Negro Emigration Movement," 132–42; Gregory, "Black Nationalism," 415–32; Cruse, *Crisis of the Negro Intellectual;* Harold Cruse, *Rebellion or Revolution?* (New York: William Morrow, 1968); Essien-Udom, *Black Nationalism;* McAdoo, *Pre–Civil War Black Nationalism;* Allen, *Black Awakening in Capitalist America;* Rodney P. Carlisle, *The Roots of Black Nationalism* (Port Washington, N.Y.: Kennikat, 1975); Pinkney, *Red, Black, and Green;* Hall, *Black Separatism in the United States;* Theodore Vincent, *Black Power and the Garvey Movement* (San Francisco: Ramparts, 1972); Tony Martin, *Race First: The Ideological and Organizational Struggles of Marcus Garvey and the Universal Improvement Association* (Westport, Conn.: Greenwood, 1976); and Tony Martin, *The Pan-African Connection* (Boston: Schenkman, 1983); Robert A. Hill, *The*

Marcus Garvey Papers, vols. 1, 2, and 3 (Berkeley: University of California Press, 1986); Judith Stein, *The World of Marcus Garvey: Race and Class in Modern Society* (Baton Rouge: Louisiana State University Press, 1986).

14. Draper, *Rediscovery of Black Nationalism*, 59; Redkey, *Black Exodus;* Wilson Jeremiah Moses, *The Golden Age of Black Nationalism, 1850–1925* (London: Oxford University Press, 1988); Sterling Stuckey, *Slave Culture: Nationalist Theory and the Foundations of Black America* (New York: Oxford University Press, 1987). See also Wilson Jeremiah Moses, *Classical Black Nationalism: From the American Revolution to Marcus Garvey* (New York: New York University Press, 1998); and William L. Van Deburg, *Modern Black Nationalism: From Marcus Garvey to Louis Farrakhan* (New York: New York University Press, 1997).

William Pease and Jane Pease's *Black Utopia* is the only major study of the efforts to build organized black communities during the antebellum era. Furthermore, Bill McAdoo maintains that emigrationism was reactionary because it encouraged a nascent African American middle class to abandon its enslaved brethren to embark on embryonic imperialist schemes in Africa. See Pease and Pease, *Black Utopia*, 106; and McAdoo, *Pre–Civil War Black Nationalism*, 23–31.

15. For Hill's six articles, see note 10; Bethel, *Promiseland;* Knight, *Sunset on Utopian Dreams;* Crockett, *Black Towns;* Hamilton, *Black Towns and Profit;* Hermann, *Pursuit of a Dream.*

16. Hill and Ackiss, "Social Classes"; Taylor, "Mound Bayou," 105–11; Bandele, "Underdevelopment of Black Towns."

17. Walter Rodney, *How Europe Underdeveloped Africa* (Dar-es-Salaam: Bogle-L'Overture, 1972), 15; Michael Hechter, *Internal Colonialism: The Celtic Fringe in British National Development, 1536–1966* (Berkeley: University of California Press, 1975), 32; Paul Kantor, *The Dependent City Revisited* (Boulder, Colo.: Westview, 1995), 44.

18. Karl Marx, *Capital*, vol. 1, *A Critical Analysis of Capitalist Production* (1967; reprint, New York: International, 1987), 714–15.

19. Joe William Trotter Jr., *Black Milwaukee: The Making of an Industrial Proletariat, 1915–45* (Urbana: University of Illinois Press, 1985), 226.

20. This periodization is a reformulation of Robert A. Harper's periodization and is based on Andrew Theising's insights. Harper identified five periods of industrialization of the metro-east between 1830 and 1960: (1) the beginning of manufacturing, 1830–50; (2) modern industrial expansion, 1850–75; (3) the rise of St. Louis as a major industrial center, 1875–90; (4) the "golden era" of metro-east manufacturing, 1890–1919; and (5) slow growth and maturation, 1919–60. See Harper, *Metro-East*, 3; and Andrew Theising, "Profitable Boundaries: Incorporating the Industrial Suburb" (Ph.D. diss., University of Missouri–St. Louis, 1997).

21. Harper, *Metro-East;* Theising, "Profitable Boundaries," ii (first quote), 2 (second quote), 83–101; Doris Rose Henle Beuttenmuller, "The Granite City Steel Company: History of an American Enterprise," *Bulletin of the Missouri Historical Society* 10 (January 1954): 135–55, 199–282.

22. David Gordon, "Capitalist Development and the History of American Cities," in *Marxism and the Metropolis: New Perspectives in Urban Political Economy*, ed. William K. Tabb and Larry Sawers (New York: Oxford University Press, 1984), 21–53; Harper, *Metro-East*, 308; Sam Bass Warner, *The Private City: Philadelphia in Three Periods of Its Growth* (Philadelphia: University of Pennsylvania Press, 1968); Sam Bass Warner, *The Urban Wilderness: A History of the American City* (New York: Harper and Row, 1972).

23. Theising, "Profitable Boundaries," 83–101; Niedringhaus quoted in Beuttenmuller, "Granite City Steel Company," 152.

24. Harper, *Metro-East*, 52–67, 95–39; Dixon, "Illinois Coal Mining Industry," 76; Horsely, *Illinois*, 134; Theising, "Profitable Boundaries," 5–7, 58–74, 78–84; Beuttenmuller, "Granite City Steel Company," 148–52.

25. Oliver C. Cox, *Caste, Class, and Race* (1948; reprint, New York: Monthly Review,

1970), 321–45; Harold M. Baron, "Racism Transformed: The 1960s," *Review of Radical Political Economics* 17 (Fall 1985): 10–33; Al Szymanski, "The Structure of Race," *Review of Radical Political Economics* 17 (Fall 1985): 106–20; Paul Liem and Eric Montague, ed., "Toward a Marxist Theory of Racism: Two Essays by Harry Chang," *Review of Radical Political Economics* 17 (Fall 1985): 34–45; Michael Banton, "Epistemological Assumptions in the Study of Racial Differentiation," in *Theories of Race and Ethnic Relations*, ed. John Rex and David Mason (New York: Cambridge University Press, 1988), 20–41; E. J. San Juan Jr., "Problems in the Marxist Project of Theorizing Race," *Rethinking Marxism* 2 (Summer 1989): 58–80; Charles W. Mills, *The Racial Contract* (Ithaca, N.Y.: Cornell University Press, 1997).

26. Theising, "Profitable Boundaries," 33, 116; NAACP, *Thirty Years of Lynching in the United States, 1889–1918* (1919; reprint, New York: Arno, 1969), 29; Sundiata Keita Cha-Jua, "'A Warlike Demonstration': Legalism, Armed Resistance, and Black Political Mobilization in Decatur, Illinois, 1894–1898," *Journal of Negro History* 83 (Winter 1998): 52–72; Elliott Rudwick, *Race Riot at East St. Louis, July 2, 1917* (1964; reprint, Urbana: University of Illinois Press, 1982), 22; Monsanto Chemical Works, *Monsanto, Illinois* (St. Louis: Privately published, 1929), 17 (emphasis added). Harold Rose termed communities like Brooklyn "dormitory towns," that is, communities whose proletarian populations must commute to work. See Rose, "All-Negro Town," 355.

27. Elmer Gertz, "The Black Laws of Illinois," *Journal of the Illinois Historical Society* 56 (Autumn 1963): 457. See also Mason Fishback, "Illinois Legislation on Slavery and Free Negroes, 1818–1865," *Transactions of the Illinois State Historical Society* 9 (1904): 414–32; and Paul Finkelman, "Slavery, the 'More Perfect Union' and the Prairie State," *Illinois Historical Journal* 80 (Winter 1987): 248–69.

28. St. Clair County Recorder of Deeds, *Incorporation Index Book E-2*, 240; Bateman and Selby, *Historical Encyclopedia of Illinois*, 762; Dixon, "Illinois Coal Mining Industry," 76; Baldwin, "East St. Louis," 242; Harper, *Metro-East*, 55; Horsely, *Illinois*, 134.

29. Donald William Clements, "The Economic Nature of Some Small Towns Near East St. Louis, Illinois: A Study of Metropolitan Dominance" (M.A. thesis, Southern Illinois University, 1964), 21.

30. *Population Schedules of the Seventh Census of the United States, 1850, Illinois, St. Clair County*, Roll 94, 118–27.

31. Theising, "Profitable Boundaries," 31.

32. Harper, *Metro-East*, 200; Beuttenmuller, "Granite City Steel Company," 148; "Over the River," *East St. Louis Gazette*, 18 April 1874, 2; James N. Adams, comp., and William E. Keller, ed., *Illinois Place Names*, Occasional Publications, No. 54 (Springfield: Illinois State Historical Society, 1968), 448.

33. Control of river transportation allowed the Terminal Railroad Association and Wiggins Ferry Company to charge the coal merchants twenty cents more per ton to transport coal across the Mississippi than to any location on the Illinois side. Doris Beuttenmuller reported "that the rate on a ton of coal from the Illinois bituminous mines within one hundred miles from St. Louis, some of them less than ten miles away, was fifty-two cents to St. Louis and thirty-two cents to any point on the east side of the Mississippi." Incorporation of Madison, Illinois, was designed to protect their investment by securing control of the land bordering the bridge site. See Theising, "Profitable Boundaries," 2, 83–101; and Beuttenmuller, "Granite City Steel Company," 148.

34. *Population Schedules of the Thirteenth Census of the United States, 1910, Illinois, St. Clair County*, Roll 323, 151–66.

35. Horsely, *Illinois*, 133; Baldwin, "East St. Louis," 240–51; Harper, *Metro-East*, 77, 308; Thomas J. Sugrue, *The Origins of the Urban Crisis: Race and Inequality in Postwar Detroit* (Princeton, N.J.: Princeton University Press, 1996), 5.

36. Jack O'Dell, "A Special Variety of Colonialism," *Freedomways* 7 (Winter 1967): 7–15; Jack O'Dell, "Colonialism and the Negro American Experience," ibid. 6 (Fall 1966):

296–308; Jack O'Dell, "The July Rebellions and the 'Military State,'" ibid. 7 (Fall 1967): 288–301; Jack O'Dell, "The Contours of the 'Black Revolution' in the 1970s," ibid. 10 (Fall 1970): 104–14; Stokely Carmichael and Charles V. Hamilton, *Black Power: The Politics of Liberation in America* (1967; reprint, New York: Vintage, 1992); Allen, *Black Awakening in Capitalist America;* William Tabb, *The Political Economy of the Black Ghetto* (New York: W. W. Norton, 1970); Robert Blauner, *Racial Oppression in America* (New York: Harper and Row, 1972); Robert Staples, *The Urban Plantation* (San Francisco: Black Scholar, 1986), 6. See also Richard Child Hill, "Race, Class, and the State: The Metropolitan Enclave System in the United States," *Insurgent Sociologist* 10 (Fall 1980): 45–57; Charles P. Henry, *Culture and African-American Politics* (Bloomington: Indiana University Press, 1990), 105–7; and Rose, "All-Negro Town," 354. Allen subsequently abandoned the internal colonial thesis. See Robert Allen, "Racism and the Black Nation Thesis," *Socialist Revolution* 27 (January–March 1976): 145–50. For critiques of the internal colonial thesis, see Donald J. Harris, "The Black Ghetto as Colony: A Theoretical Critique and an Alternative Formulation," *Review of Black Political Economy* 2 (Summer 1972): 3–33; and Michael Burawoy, "Race, Class, and Colonialism," *Social and Economic Studies* 24 (December 1974): 521–50.

37. Walter and Kramer, "Political Autonomy and Economic Dependence in an All-Negro Municipality," 246–47.

38. Sugrue, *Origins of the Urban Crisis;* Theising, "Profitable Boundaries," 38. See also Baron, "Racism Transformed," 23; Kantor, *Dependent City Revisited,* 141–56; William Julius Wilson, *The Truly Disadvantaged: The Inner City, the Under Class, and Public Policy* (Chicago: University of Chicago Press, 1987); Henry Louis Taylor Jr., ed., *Race and the City: Work, Community, and Protest in Cincinnati, 1820–1970* (Urbana: University of Illinois Press, 1993); Henry Louis Taylor Jr., *African Americans and the Rise of Buffalo's Post-Industrial City, 1940 to Present,* vol. 1, *An Introduction to a Research Report* (Buffalo, N.Y.: Buffalo Urban League, 1990); and Kenneth L. Kusmer, "African Americans in the City since World War II: From the Industrial to the Postindustrial Era," in *The New African American Urban History,* ed. Kenneth Goings and Raymond A. Mohl (Thousand Oaks, Calif.: Sage, 1996), 320–68.

39. Walter and Kramer, "Political Autonomy and Economic Dependence in an All-Negro Municipality," 246–47.

40. Rose, "All-Negro Town," 355–60.

41. Rudwick, *Race Riot at East St. Louis,* 191; Theising, "Profitable Boundaries," 109–10; Irving Dillard, "Civil Liberties of Negroes in Illinois since 1865," *Journal of the Illinois State Historical Society* 56 (Autumn 1963): 608.

42. Andrew Wiese discusses the development of some of these towns. He also identifies communities that conform to Rose's concept of a "pseudo town." Wiese engages Rose in a debate about the application of the concept suburban to these types of Black towns. See Wiese, "Places of Our Own," 30–54.

43. Ted Gurr and Desmond King developed the approach I take to the "local state," and I have worked some of their understandings into my definition of a dependent town. See Ted Gurr and Desmond King, *The State and the City* (Chicago: University of Chicago Press, 1987), 51–52. See also Gordon, "Capitalist Development and the History of American Cities," 21–53; Ira Katznelson, *Marxism and the City* (New York: Oxford University Press, 1994); R. C. Hill, "Race, Class, and the State," 46; and Henry, *Culture and African-American Politics,* 105–7.

Chapter 1: From Separate Settlement to Biracial Town, 1830–60

1. U.S. Department of Labor, Federal Writers' Project, *Illinois,* 490–91; Anthony Speed, interview by Arthur Moore, 20 March 1936, transcript, U.S. Department of Labor, Works Progress Administration, Federal Writers' Project, in folder for Brooklyn, Illinois, Madi-

son County, District 7, Archives of the State of Illinois, Springfield, Ill.; Schoen, *Tales of an All-Night Town,* 11; *History of St. Clair County,* 308. On 1 May 1837, County Recorder John H. Day entered the plat of the town of Brooklyn into the record. See St. Clair County Recorder of Deeds, *Book J,* 272.

2. "C. B. Carroll's Brooklyn City Directory, 1903," 232 (quotes); *History of St. Clair County,* 308; *Population Schedules of the Ninth Census of the United States, 1870, Illinois, St. Clair County,* Roll 280, 623; White, "Lovejoy's History," 3.

Thomas Osburn; John R. Stites, whose family name the township would later bear; and George H. Lewis were among the first European Americans to reside in Brooklyn. Charles Woodworth, Alfred Sparks, Hardy Roberts, and Mrs. Newell were also listed as early Black residents of the town of Brooklyn. Mrs. Wyatt was probably Charlotte Wyatt, who was eighty years old in 1870. I was unable to verify the others, however. The WPA writers erroneously listed Brooklyn in Madison rather than St. Clair County. See U.S. Department of Labor, Federal Writers' Project, *Illinois,* 490–91.

The best sources for information on Brooklyn's history are the introductions to the town's 1903 and 1905 city directories. C. B. Carroll, the compiler of Brooklyn's city directory during these years, had taught in Brooklyn during the late 1870s.

3. According to Eugene Genovese, the salient features of maroons were (1) they were escaped slaves; (2) they built agricultural communities and were dependent on others for industrial products; (3) family and social patterns hearkened back to Africa; and (4) they sought to integrate Euro-American practices. Genovese claimed that Africans, as opposed to creoles (Afro-Americans born in the new world), composed the bulk of maroons. This, of course, was true in general, but it certainly was not true in the United States during the early nineteenth century. He also emphasized maroons' military conflicts with the slaveholding regimes, though he pointed out that they sometimes were able to preserve peace. The Afro-Americans who founded Brooklyn included many fugitives; certainly the culture they cultivated was more American than African, but like free African American culture elsewhere in the United States, it included Africanisms in muted form. Finally, the maroons' activities against slavery, while not reaching the state of warfare, does suggests that they led expeditions into Missouri to liberate those still held in captivity. I therefore believe the term *maroon* can be applied to these escaped slaves prior to Brooklyn's platting. See Genovese, *From Rebellion to Revolution,* 52–54, 69.

4. For more on the Black Laws, see Leon Litwack, *North of Slavery: The Negro in the Free States, 1790–1860* (Chicago: University of Chicago Press, 1961); Leonard P. Curry, *The Free Black in Urban America, 1800–1850: The Shadow of the Dream* (Chicago: University of Chicago Press, 1981); V. Jacque Voegeli, *Free but Not Equal* (Chicago: University of Chicago Press, 1967). Among the several works that examine the African American experience in antebellum Illinois are Robert L. McCaul, *The Black Struggle for Public Schooling in Nineteenth-Century Illinois* (Carbondale: Southern Illinois University Press, 1987); Walker, *Free Frank;* Shirley J. Carlson, "The Black Community in the Rural North: Pulaski County, Illinois, 1860–1900" (Ph.D. diss., Washington University, 1982); Don Harrison Doyle, *The Social Order of a Frontier Community: Jacksonville, Illinois, 1825–1870* (Urbana: University of Illinois Press, 1978); and N. Dwight Harris, *The History of Negro Servitude in Illinois and the Slavery Agitation in That State, 1719–1864* (Chicago: A. C. McClurg, 1904).

5. Cox, *Caste, Class, and Race,* 554; Robert Chrisman, "Black Prisoners, White Law," *Black Scholar* 2 (April–May 1971): 45; John Hope Franklin, *From Slavery to Freedom,* 7th ed. (New York: Alfred A. Knopf, 1998), 148–70.

6. Peter S. Onuf, *Statehood and Union: A History of the Northwest Ordinance* (Bloomington: Indiana University Press, 1987); Paul Finkelman, "Evading the Ordinance: The Persistence of Bondage in Indiana and Illinois," *Journal of the Early Republic* 9 (Spring 1989): 21–51; Walker, *Free Frank;* Edgar A. Love, "Registration of Free Blacks in Ohio: The Slaves

of George Mendenhall," *Journal of Negro History* 69, no. 1 (1984): 38–47; David A. Gerber, *Black Ohio and the Color Line, 1860–1915* (Urbana: University of Illinois Press, 1976).

7. Pease and Pease, *Black Utopia,* 22–23.

8. Ellen Nore and Dick Norrish, *Edwardsville: An Illustrated History* (St. Louis: G. Bradley, 1996), 34. See also Ellen Nore, "African Americans in Edwardsville City History" (Paper presented at the "Community Building and Resistance: African Americans in the Land of Lincoln" Conference, 17 April 1997, Southern Illinois University at Edwardsville, in author's possession).

9. Quoted in E. B. Washburne, *Sketch of Edward Coles* (1882; reprint, New York: Negro Universities Press, 1969), 50. See also Pease and Pease, *Black Utopia,* 23; and Carl G. Hodges and Helene H. Levene, *Illinois Negro Historymakers* (Chicago: Illinois Emancipation Centennial Commission, 1964), 11.

10. Nore and Norrish, *Edwardsville,* 34 (quote); Nore, "African Americans in Edwardsville City History"; Pease and Pease, *Black Utopia,* 22–23. Nore's source was Frieda Lewis, a longtime African American resident of Edwardsville.

11. Rose, "All-Negro Town," 355.

12. "C. B. Carroll's Brooklyn City Directory, 1903," 232; *Population Schedules of the Sixth Census of the United States, 1840, Illinois, St. Clair County,* Roll 290, 252–94; John Buecher, comp., *St. Clair County, Illinois Census, 1840* (Thomson, Ill.: Heritage House, n.d.), 28; M. W. Beckly, "The African Methodist Episcopal Church," in *History of Madison County* (Chicago: W. R. Brink, 1882), 293; W. T. Norton, ed., *Centennial History of Madison County and Its People, 1812–1912* (Chicago: Lewis Publishing, 1912), 343; Miles Mark Fisher, "Negro Churches in Illinois: A Fragmentary History with Emphasis on Chicago," *Journal of the Illinois State Historical Society* 56 (Autumn 1963): 553–54; Doyle, *Social Order of a Frontier Community,* 145–53.

13. *Population Schedules of the Seventh Census of the United States, 1850, Illinois, St. Clair County,* Roll 94, 125; Hyman Alterman, *Counting People: The Census in History* (New York: Harcourt Brace and World, 1969); George A. Singleton, *The Romance of African Methodism: A Study of the African Methodist Episcopal Church* (New York: Exposition, n.d.), 73.

14. Singleton, *Romance of African Methodism,* 71 (quote), 74; Charles S. Smith, *A History of the African Methodist Episcopal Church,* vol. 2 (New York: Johnson Reprint, 1968), 16, 34; Lawson, "Sarah Woodson Early," 820–21.

15. Quoted in Fishback, "Illinois Legislation on Slavery and Free Negroes," 422. See also Finkelman, "Slavery, the 'More Perfect Union' and the Prairie State," 248–69.

16. Larry Gara, "The Underground Railroad in Illinois," *Journal of the Illinois State Historical Society* 56 (Autumn 1963): 519 (quote); C. S. Smith, *History of the African Methodist Episcopal Church,* 35; Lawson, "Sarah Woodson Early," 820–21.

17. Singleton, *Romance of African Methodism,* 73; Edna C. McKenzie, "Self-Hire among Slaves, 1820–1860: Institutional Variation or Aberration?" (Ph.D. diss., University of Pittsburgh, 1973), 24; Elizabeth Keckley, *Behind the Scenes* (New York: G. W. Carlson, 1968); Judy Day and M. James Kedro, "Free Blacks in St. Louis: Antebellum Conditions, Emancipation, and the Postwar Era," *Bulletin of the Missouri Historical Society* 30 (January 1974): 117–35.

18. Charles A. Smith and George A. Singleton claimed Priscilla Baltimore rowed Bishop Quinn to the shores of Missouri, but Elaine Welch asserts that Isaac Donica performed this task. Donica was an exhorter and a member of the St. Paul AME Church in St. Louis. In all likelihood, Baltimore and Donica shared this assignment. See C. S. Smith, *History of the African Methodist Episcopal Church,* 17; Singleton, *Romance of African Methodism,* 72; and Elaine Welch *William Paul Quinn: A Militant Churchman* (Chicago: By the author, 1933), 30.

19. Hodges and Levene, *Illinois Negro Historymakers,* 15–17; Gara, "Underground Railroad in Illinois," 519–20; William Still, *The Underground Railroad* (1877; reprint, Chica-

go: Johnson, 1970); William Wells Brown, "The Narrative of William Wells Brown: A Fugitive Slave," in *Four Fugitive Slave Narratives*, ed. Robin W. Winks (Menlo Park, Calif.: Addison-Wesley, 1969), 29; and Benjamin Quarles, *Black Abolitionists* (London: Oxford University Press, 1969).

Magnolia Johnson, one of Quinn Chapel's oldest members, recounted that as a child she was told the church's rebuilt (1836) basement was often used to house fugitives. See Magnolia Johnson, interview by author, 1 August 1989. Given its proximity to the slave states of Missouri, Kentucky, Tennessee, and Arkansas, the six thousand figure probably underestimates the number of fugitives who fled into or through Illinois. The underground railroad in Illinois was reportedly a poorly organized operation, but a fugitive from a border state, such as Missouri, could reach "quasi-freedom" with very little aid.

20. Laura Mary Gard, "East St. Louis and the Railroads to 1875" (Ph.D. diss., Washington University, 1947), 12–13; Juliet E. K. Walker, "Entrepreneurial Ventures in the Origin of Nineteenth-Century Agricultural Towns: Pike County, 1823–1880," *Illinois Historical Journal* 78 (Spring 1985): 57; Saffel, "Founding of Caseyville," 29–35; U.S. Department of Labor, Federal Writers' Project, *Illinois*, 490.

21. *Belleville Advocate*, 12 January 1866, quoted in Harper, *Metro-East*, 72; Walker, *Free Frank*, 165–67; Hamilton, *Black Towns and Profit*, 35.

Samuel B. Chandler, George Walker, Vital Jarrot, and Daniel Pierce were the other investors in the Illinois and St. Louis Line. Illinoistown was actually dissolved and incorporated into the newer community of East St. Louis. See "East St. Louis," 9, 11–13, 15, box 19, Illinois Historical Library, Springfield; Dixon, "Illinois Coal Mining Industry," 76; Baldwin, "East St. Louis," 242; Gard, "East St. Louis and the Railroads to 1875," 20–21; Harper, *Metro-East*, 55; Saffel, "Founding of Caseyville," 28–29; Horsely, *Illinois*, 134; and St. Clair County Recorder of Deeds, *Incorporation Index Book E-2*, 240.

22. St. Clair County Recorder of Deeds, *Book L*, 58; Walker, "Entrepreneurial Ventures in the Origin of Nineteenth-Century Agricultural Towns," 57; Gard, "East St. Louis and the Railroads to 1875," 175; Josephine Boylan, "Illinois Highways, 1700–1848: Roads, Rivers, Ferries and Canals," *Illinois Historical Journal* 26 (April–July 1933): 54.

23. St. Clair Recorder of Deeds, *Book M*, 228.

24. Quoted in Walker, *Free Frank*, 105. The regulation requiring free Blacks to post bonds was not always enforced.

25. St. Clair Recorder of Deeds, *Book M*, 228. Between 2 March 1866 and 25 August 1869, Priscilla Baltimore sold six properties. On 2 March 1866, she sold a lot in block 50 to Richard Christian, and on 21 July, she sold a lot in block 40 to Madison Jones, both by warrantee deed. A warrantee deed means that a mortgage was left on the property. Nearly two years later, on 30 May 1868, she sold by deed lot number 420 to Edward Williams and lot 419 to Oliver Carroll. Both of these lots were in block 40, which faced Madison Street and encompassed the block between Fifth and Sixth streets. On 23 March 1869, Mother Baltimore sold another lot, this time by warrantee deed to Joseph W. Parker. On 25 August 1869, she sold lot 380 in block twenty-eight on Madison Street to Thomas Henry in the same manner. See St. Clair County Recorder of Deeds, *Book E-4*, 107, *Book F-4*, 598, *Book V-4*, 148, 196, *Book Y-4*, 464, and *Book Z-4*, 62; and John Hinchcliffe, *Illustrated History of St. Clair County, Illinois* (Chicago: Warner and Beers, 1874), 51.

26. The 1840 census does not list Nicholas Carper, though a Miller Carper does appear as the head of a family of six. Perhaps he was Nicholas's father or his older brother. See *History of St. Clair County*, 308; and "C. B. Carroll's Brooklyn City Directory, 1903," 234. For information on vigilance committees, see Stephen Middleton, "The Fugitive Slave Crisis in Cincinnati, 1850–1890: Resistance, Enforcement, and Black Refugees," *Journal of Negro History* 72 (Winter–Spring 1987): 20–32; Vincent Harding, *There Is a River: The Black Struggle for Freedom in America* (New York: Vintage, 1981): 121–23; Quarles, *Black Abolitionists*, 197–222; and Robert P. Smith, "William Cooper Nell: Crusading Black Abolition-

ist," *Journal of Negro History* 55 (Spring 1970): 182–99. For a discussion of white slave res-cuers, see Stanley Harrold, "John Brown's Forerunners: Slave Rescue Attempts and the Abolitionists, 1841–51," *Radical History Review* 55 (Winter 1993): 89–110; and Stanley Harrold, "Freeing the Weems Family: A New Look at the Underground Railroad," *Civil War History* 42, no. 4 (1996): 289–306. For a discussion of the role of Black women abolition-ists, see Shirley J. Yee, "Organizing for Racial Justice: Black Women and the Dynamics of Race and Sex in Female Antislavery Societies, 1832–1860," in *Black Women in America*, ed. Kim Marie Vaz (Thousand Oaks, Calif.: Sage, 1995), 38–53; and Shirley J. Yee, *Black Women Abolitionists: A Study in Activism, 1828–1860* (Knoxville: University of Tennessee Press, 1992).

27. Quoted in Herbert Aptheker, *Documentary History of the Negro People in the United States*, vol. 1 (New York: Citadel, 1951), 159. See also Harding, *There Is a River*, 121. Al-though the masters preferred to view slaves as strictly chattel, the inherent contradictions in this view constantly manifested themselves, enabling the slave's humanity to emerge. According to Paul E. Lovejoy, this duality could be fashioned into a weapon by slaves that could undermine their value as chattel, if not their status as slaves. Through various forms of day-to-day resistance, slaves could use their humanness to devalue themselves as chattel. However, it was not necessarily beneficial for a master to acknowledge a slave's humani-ty. In a brilliant discussion of rape and seduction, Saidiya V. Hartman illuminated the oppressive side of this dialectic. She contended slave masters exploited the slave's humani-ty, turning their basic human fragilities against them for their own sexual and psycho-logical pleasure. See Paul E. Lovejoy, "Fugitive Slaves: Resistance to Slavery in the Sokoto Caliphate," in *Resistance*, ed. Okihiro, 71–95; and Saidiya V. Hartman, *Scenes of Subjection: Terror, Slavery, and Self-Making in Nineteenth-Century America* (Oxford: Oxford Univer-sity Press, 1997), 4–5, 79–112.

28. "C. B. Carroll's Brooklyn City Directory, 1903," 234.

29. *St. Louis Post-Dispatch*, 9 July 1911, 5. This interview with Turner is reprinted in Gary R. Kremer, *James Milton Turner and the Promise of America: The Public Life of a Post–Civil War Black Leader* (Columbia: University of Missouri Press, 1991), 201–10. See also Irv-ing Dillard, "James Milton Turner: A Little Known Benefactor of His People," *Journal of Negro History* 19 (October 1934): 377.

30. The 1850 federal manuscript census surveyed District 6, the American Bottoms, which included Brooklyn and the predominately white village of Illinoistown. It is difficult to identify Brooklyn as a corporate entity, so I identified the contiguous clusters of Afri-can Americans. See Hinchcliffe, *Illustrated History of St. Clair County*, 8; and Hodges and Levene, *Illinois Negro Historymakers*, 57–58.

Chapter 2: Uncovering Brooklyn's African American Population, 1850

1. Hinchcliffe, *Illustrated History of St. Clair County*, 8; James O. Horton, "Shades of Color: The Mulatto in Three Antebellum Northern Communities," *Afro-Americans in New York Life and History* 8 (Spring 1984): 37–53; Theodore Hershberg and Henry Williams, "Mulattoes and Blacks: Intra-group Color Differences and Social Stratification in Nine-teenth-Century Philadelphia," in *Work, Space, Family, and Group Experience in the Nine-teenth Century*, ed. Theodore Hershberg (New York: Oxford University Press, 1981), 392–431; Curry, *Free Black in Urban America*; John G. Mencke, *Mulattoes and Race Mixture: American Attitudes and Images, 1865–1918* ([Ann Arbor, Mich.]: UMI Research Press, 1979). Richard Seltzer and Robert C. Smith have demonstrated the continuing significance of color in determining access to such social goods as education and income and as an aes-thetic preference. See Robert C. Smith, *Racism in the Post–Civil Rights Era: Now You See It, Now You Don't* (Albany: State University of New York Press, 1995): 96–100; and Rich-

ard Seltzer and Robert C. Smith, "Color Differences in the Afro-American Community and the Differences They Make," *Journal of Black Studies* 21 (March 1991): 279–86.

2. Thomas Bender, *Community and Social Change in America* (Baltimore: Johns Hopkins University Press, 1978; Craig Calhoun, "Community: Toward a Variable Conceptualization for Comparative Research," in *History and Class: Essential Readings in Theory and Interpretation*, ed. R. S. Neale (New York: Basil Blackwell, 1983), 86–110.

3. Henry Louis Taylor Jr. and Vicky Dula, "The Black Residential Experience and Community Formation in Antebellum Cincinnati," in *Race and the City*, ed. Taylor, 102.

4. Hill and Ackiss, "Social Classes," 94.

5. *Black Towns and Profit* by Kenneth M. Hamilton is the most recent work of historical scholarship on Black towns. Although it is an advancement in the use of public records, such as manuscript censuses and city directories, Hamilton still underutilized these sources. Hamilton used census information only to present aggregate racial population statistics. He did not use the census or city directories to reconstruct occupational or family structures. For further discussion of this point, see Cha-Jua, "Racism, Nationalism and Black Town Development," 96.

6. Albert Szymanski, *Class Structure: A Critical Perspective* (New York: Praeger, 1983), 2–7, 76–84; Thomas D. Boston, *Race, Class, and Conservatism* (Boston: Unwin Hyman, 1988), 1–21; Allin Cottrell, *Social Classes in Marxist Theory* (London: Routledge and Kegan Paul, 1984), 33–93.

7. V. I. Lenin, *Collected Works*, vol. 29 (Moscow: Progress, 1974), 421.

8. Matthew Sobek, "Class Analysis and the U.S. Census Public Use Samples," *Historical Methods* 24 (Fall 1991): 179 (first quote), 173 (second quote); Nancy Bertaux, "Structural Economic Change and Occupational Decline among Black Workers in Nineteenth-Century Cincinnati," in *Race and the City*, ed. Taylor, 126.

9. Alterman, *Counting People*.

10. St. Clair County Recorder of Deeds, *Book U*, 480, and *Book W-2*, 439. Monographs and articles that address the racial composition of urban housing patterns in antebellum America include James Borchert, *Alley Life in Washington: Family, Community, Religion, and Folklife in the City, 1850–1970* (Urbana: University of Illinois Press, 1980); Curry, *Free Black in Urban America;* Douglas H. Daniels, *Pioneer Urbanites: A Social and Cultural History of Black San Francisco* (Philadelphia: Temple University Press, 1980); James O. Horton, "Blacks in Antebellum Boston: The Migrant and the Community," *Southern Studies* 21, no. 3 (1982): 277–93; James O. Horton and Elizabeth E. Horton, *Black Bostonians: Family Life and Community Struggle in the Antebellum North* (New York: Holmes and Meier, 1979); William D. Piersen, *Black Yankees: The Development of an African American Subculture in Eighteenth-Century New England* (Amherst: University of Massachusetts Press, 1988); and Theodore Hershberg, Alan Burstein, Eugene P. Ericksen, Stephine Greenberg, and William L. Yancey, "A Tale of Three Cities: Blacks and Immigrants in Philadelphia, 1850–1880, 1930, and 1970," *Annals of the American Academy of Political and Social Science* 441 (January 1979): 55–81.

11. *Population Schedules of the Seventh Census of the United States, 1850, Illinois, St. Clair County*, Roll 94, 118–19.

12. Ibid., 118–27; St. Clair County Recorder of Deeds, *Incorporation Index Book E-2*, 240.

13. "East St. Louis," 2, 10, 15; *Population Schedules of the Seventh Census of the United States, 1850, Illinois, St. Clair County*, Roll 94, 118–27; Curry, *Free Black in Urban America*, especially chap. 2; Philip S. Foner, *Organized Labor and the Black Worker, 1619–1981*, 2d ed. (New York: International, 1981).

14. *Population Schedules of the Seventh Census of the United States, 1850, Illinois*, Roll 94, 118–27. Theodore Hershberg and Henry Williams found that the color designation of a third of African Americans changed from census to census. Moreover, the change was connected to job classification. Mulattoes who experienced occupational downgrading

were also "reduced" to "black" in later censuses; conversely, some blacks who improved their occupational and social status lightened over time. See Hershberg and Williams, "Mulattoes and Blacks"; Mencke, *Mulattoes and Race Mixture*, 2; and Horton, "Shades of Color," 41.

15. *Population Schedules of the Seventh Census of the United States, 1850, Illinois, St. Clair County*, Roll 94, 127.

16. Ibid., 127–28.

17. Hallie Hawkins, interview by author, 2 August 1989 (Hawkins is Quinn Chapel's historian and a former elementary schoolteacher at Lovejoy School); "History of Quinn Chapel," n.p. (Unpublished mimeograph, in author's possession); *History of St. Clair County*, 309; St. Clair County Recorder of Deeds, *Book K-4*, 198; *Population Schedules of the Seventh Census of the United States, 1850, Illinois, St. Clair County*, Roll 94, 127. The church's history does not provide a date for when Brooklyn AME Church changed its name to Quinn Chapel. See "Brief Synopsis of the History of Quinn Chapel A.M.E. Church," August 1988 (163rd Anniversary Booklet of the Quinn Chapel AME Church, in author's possession).

18. *Population Schedules of the Seventh Census of the United States, 1850, Illinois, St. Clair County*, Roll 94, 118–27.

19. Ibid.

20. Ibid.; Bertaux, "Structural Economic Change and Occupational Decline among Black Workers in Nineteenth-Century Cincinnati," 126–55; Taylor and Dula, "Black Residential Experience and Community Formation in Antebellum Cincinnati," 106. Frederick Trautmann recounts Johann Koler's experience as a farm laborer in St. Clair County in 1851. See Frederick Trautmann, "Eight Weeks on a St. Clair County Farm in 1851," *Journal of the Illinois Historical Society* 75 (Autumn 1982): 178.

21. St. Clair County Recorder of Deeds, *Book K-4*, 198; Taylor and Dula, "Black Residential Experience and Community Formation in Antebellum Cincinnati," 110–27.

22. *Population Schedules of the Seventh Census of the United States, 1850, Illinois, St. Clair County*, Roll 94, 121–27. The other two white owners of real estate were Henry Vague, a French immigrant farmer who owned $1,000 worth of real property, and James Thornton, an immigrant English laborer who owned property valued at $700.

23. Ibid., 126; Curry, *Free Black in Urban America*, 44; Orville Vernon Burton, *In My Father's House Are Many Mansions: Family and Community in Edgefield, South Carolina* (Chapel Hill: University of North Carolina Press, 1985), 215. For the origins of the "quasi-free" Black strata and the disproportionate percentage of mulattoes within its ranks, see Curry, *Free Black in Urban America*, 44, 269; Burton, *In My Father's House Are Many Mansions*, 214–17, 318–23; Litwack, *North of Slavery*, 1961; Richard Wade, *Slavery in the Cities: The South, 1820–1860* (London: Oxford University Press, 1964); Carl N. Degler, *Neither Black nor White* (New York: Oxford University Press, 1971); Ira Berlin, *Slaves without Masters: The Free Negro in the Antebellum South* (London: Oxford University Press, 1974); Ira Berlin, "The Structure of the Free Negro Caste in the Antebellum United States," *Journal of Social History* 9 (May 1976): 297–317; Joel Williamson, *New People* (New York: Oxford University Press, 1980); Hershberg and Williams, "Mulattoes and Blacks," 392–431; Suzanne Lebsock, "Free Black Women and the Question of Matriarchy," in *Sex and Class in Women's History*, ed. Judith Newton, Mary P. Ryan, and Judith Walkowitz (London: Routledge and Kegan Paul, 1983), 146–66; Dorothy Sterling, ed., *We Are Your Sisters: Black Women in the Nineteenth Century* (New York: W. W. Norton, 1984), 26–31; Robert Brent Toplin, "Between Black and White," *Journal of Southern History* 45 (May 1979): 185–200; and Horton, "Shades of Color," 37–59.

24. Trautmann, "Eight Weeks on a St. Clair County Farm in 1851," 178; Florence Young Barnes, *Wilhelm Dorr (Doerr), 1821–1891: Early German Immigrant to St. Clair County, Illinois*, (Champaign, Ill.: By the author, 1965), 2.

25. Paul J. Lammermeier, "The Urban Black Family of the Nineteenth Century: A Study of Black Family Structure in the Ohio Valley, 1850–1880," *Journal of Marriage and the Family* 35 (August 1973): 442–43.

26. *Population Schedules of the Seventh Census of the United States, 1850, Illinois, St. Clair County,* Roll 94, 118–27. For information on free Black family structures, see Theodore Hershberg, "Free Blacks in Antebellum Philadelphia: A Study of Ex-slaves, Freeborn, and Socio-Economic Decline," *Journal of Social History* 5, no. 2 (1971–72): 183–209; Curry, *Free Black in Urban America;* Lammermeier, "Urban Black Family of the Nineteenth Century," 440–56; and William H. Harris, "Work and the Family in Black Atlanta, 1880," *Journal of Social History* 9 (May 1976): 319–30.

27. *Population Schedules of the Seventh Census of the United States, 1850, Illinois, St. Clair County,* Roll 94, 118–27. The median household size of Afro-Brooklyn was larger than in six of the seven towns and cities examined by Lammermeier. Pittsburgh and the four smaller towns of Steubenville, Wheeling, Portsmouth, and Marietta had an average of 4.8 members per African American household, while Cincinnati and Louisville had 4.6 and 3.8, respectively. See Lammermeier, "Urban Black Family of the Nineteenth Century," 440–56.

28. *Population Schedules of the Seventh Census of the United States, 1850, Illinois, St. Clair County,* Roll 94, 118–27; Herbert G. Gutman, *The Black Family in Slavery and in Freedom, 1750–1925* (New York: Vintage, 1976), 185–201.

29. *Population Schedules of the Seventh Census of the United States, 1850, Illinois, St. Clair County,* Roll 94, 119, 126; Lammermeier, "Urban Black Family of the Nineteenth Century," 442–43; Burton, *In My Father's House Are Many Mansions,* 206, 214; Taylor and Dula, "Black Residential Experience and Community Formation in Ante-bellum Cincinnati," 108. Lammermeier's study is one of a very small number that examine the structure of the African American family at midcentury. Most studies are based on the 1870 and 1880 censuses. One hundred and thirty-seven Blacks lived in Steubenville, 206 in Wheeling, 145 in Portsmouth, and 59 in Marietta.

30. *Population Schedules of the Seventh United States Census, 1850, Illinois, St. Clair County,* Roll 94, 119, 126; Lammermeier, "Urban Black Family in the Nineteenth Century," 440–56. See also Hershberg, "Free Blacks in Antebellum Philadelphia," 183–209; and Curry, *Free Black in Urban America,* 8–14.

31. Curry, *Free Black in Urban America,* 10–14. See also Burton, *In My Father's House Are Many Mansions,* 318–19.

32. James H. Magee, *The Night of Affliction and Morning of Recovery: An Autobiography* (Cincinnati: By the author, 1878), 17–18.

33. *Population Schedules of the Seventh Census of the United States, 1850, Illinois, St. Clair County,* Roll 94, 118–27.

34. Illinois General Assembly, *Laws and Statutes, 19th* (1855), 85, quoted in McCaul, *Black Struggle for Public Schooling in Nineteenth-Century Illinois,* 29.

35. Ibid., 30–31.

36. John Blassingame, *Black New Orleans, 1860–1880* (Chicago: University of Chicago Press, 1973), 21–22; Mencke, *Mulattoes and Race Mixture,* 2; Horton, "Shades of Color," 41.

37. Michael Omi and Howard Winant, *Racial Formation in the United States,* 2d ed. (New York: Routledge and Kegan Paul, 1994); Hershberg and Williams, "Mulattoes and Blacks," 392–431.

38. Berlin, "Structure of the Free Negro Caste in the Antebellum United States," 300; *Negro Population in the United States, 1790–1915* (Washington D.C.: Government Printing Office, 1918), 221; Mencke, *Mulattoes and Race Mixture,* 19.

39. Wade, *Slavery in the Cities,* 124; Blassingame, *Black New Orleans,* 9; Berlin, *Slaves without Masters,* 110–11, 178.

40. Blassingame, *Black New Orleans*, 21–22.

41. Horton, "Shades of Color," 41.

42. *Population Schedules of the Seventh Census of the United States, 1850, Illinois, St. Clair County*, Roll 94, 118–27; Horton, "Shades of Color," 41.

43. Hawkins, interview by author, 2 August 1989; "Brief Synopsis of the History of Quinn Chapel A.M.E. Church"; *Population Schedules of the Seventh Census of the United States, 1850, Illinois, St. Clair County*, Roll 94, 118–27.

44. Bell, "Chicago Negroes in the Reform Movement," 153–54; Sylvester C. Watkins Sr., "Some of Illinois' Free Negroes," *Journal of the Illinois State Historical Society* 56 (Autumn 1963): 495–507; Charles A. Gliozzo, "John Jones and the Black Convention Movement, 1848–1856," *Journal of Black Studies* 3 (March 1972): 227–36.

45. *Population Schedules of the Seventh Census of the United States, 1850, Illinois, St. Clair County*, Roll 94, 118–27.

Chapter 3: From Outlaws to Lawmakers, 1870–80

1. *Population Schedules of the Ninth Census of the United States, 1870, Illinois, St. Clair County*, Roll 280, 620–25; *Population Schedules of the Tenth Census of the United States, 1880, Illinois, St. Clair County*, Roll 246, 19–24.

2. For a discussion of the effects of proletarianization on African Americans, see Trotter, *Black Milwaukee*, xii–xiv, 226–41; and Joe W. Trotter, *Coal, Class, and Color: Blacks in Southern West Virginia, 1915–32* (Urbana: University of Illinois Press, 1990), 1–6, 263–70; Richard Walter Thomas, *Life for Us Is What We Make It: Building Black Community in Detroit, 1915–1945* (Bloomington: Indiana University Press, 1993); and Ronald L. Lewis, "From Peasant to Proletarian: The Migration of Southern Blacks to the Central Appalachian Coalfields," *Journal of Southern History* 55 (February 1989): 77–102.

3. Roger D. Bridges, "Equality Deferred: Civil Rights for Illinois Blacks, 1865–1885," *Journal of the Illinois State Historical Society* 74 (Summer 1981): 84.

4. Quoted in ibid., 87. See also McCaul, *Black Struggle for Public Schooling in Nineteenth-Century Illinois*, especially chap. 6.

5. McCaul, *Black Struggle for Public Schooling in Nineteenth-Century Illinois*, 83.

6. Neil F. Garvey, *The Government and Administration of Illinois* (New York: Thomas Y. Crowell, 1958), 488; St. Clair County Recorder of Deeds, *Incorporation Index Book*, 310–11.

7. St. Clair County Recorder of Deeds, *Incorporation Index Book*, 310–11.

8. At the time of its incorporation, thirty-two of the fifty-four African American men who appeared in the census could neither read nor write, compared with only five of the European Americans. The more than 59 percent illiteracy rate of African American men in Brooklyn was, however, significantly below the African American national figure of nearly 80 percent. Afro-Brooklynites' literacy rate of 41 percent also was better than that of Blacks in Nicodemus, Kansas, ten years later. There, 39 percent of African Americans could read, but only 25 percent could write. Though literacy was probably not a factor in political participation, many whites were unable to vote because they were not yet citizens. *Population Schedules of the Ninth Census of the United States, 1870, Illinois, St. Clair County*, Roll 280, 620–25; Hamilton, *Black Towns and Profit*, 17.

9. Harper, *Metro-East*, 200; Margaret Walsh, *The Rise of the Midwestern Meat Packing Industry* (Lexington: University Press of Kentucky, 1982), 74 (quotes); "Over the River," *St. Louis Republican*, 15 April 1974, reprinted in *East St. Louis Gazette*, 18 April 1974, p. 2, col. 3; Theising, "Profitable Boundaries," 85–89; Adams and Keller, *Illinois Place Names*, 448.

10. Bateman and Selby, *Historical Encyclopedia of Illinois*, 172; John H. Keiser, *Building for the Centuries: Illinois, 1865 to 1898* (Urbana: University of Illinois Press, 1977), 201, 203–4; Saffel, "Founding of Caseyville," 29; St. Clair County Recorder of Deeds, *Incorporation Index Book E-2*, 240.

11. Harper, *Metro-East*, 77. Blacks in Halifax County and a few other Black-majority counties in southern states dominated office holding in their areas, but they always had to share power with the white minority, as Afro-Brooklynites did until 1886. Since Promiseland, South Carolina, was unincorporated, its citizens did not exercise self-government, and since they were a minority in the county, they were prevented from holding political office. See Eric Anderson, "James O'Hara of North Carolina: Black Leadership and Local Government," in *Southern Black Leaders of the Reconstruction Era*, ed. Howard N. Rabinowitz (Urbana: University of Illinois Press, 1982), 102–3; and Bethel, *Promiseland*, 1981.

12. Black Brooklynites followed a pattern of community formation replicated by African Americans during each migration period and in each migratory stream. See Jon Butler, "Communities and Congregations: The Black Church in St. Paul, Minnesota, 1860–1900," *Journal of Negro History* 56 (Spring 1971): 118–34; Joanne D. Wheeler, "Together in Little Egypt: A Pattern of Race Relations in Cairo, Illinois, 1865–1915," in *Toward a New South? Studies in Post–Civil War Southern Communities*, ed. O. Vernon Burton and Robert C. McMath Jr. (Westport, Conn.: Greenwood, 1982), 103–34; Carlson, "Black Community in the Rural North"; and Shirley J. Portwood, "Black Migration to Pulaski County, Illinois, 1860–1900," *Illinois Historical Journal* 80 (Spring 1987): 37–46. Shirley J. Carlson and Shirley J. Portwood are the same person. Portwood is her married name.

13. "Over the River," *St. Louis Republican*, 15 April 1974, reprinted in *East St. Louis Gazette*, 18 April 1974, p. 2, col. 3; *Population Schedules of the Ninth Census of the United States, 1870, Illinois, St. Clair County*, Roll 280, 620–25; "C. B. Carroll's Brooklyn City Directory, 1903," 234.

14. *Population Schedules of the Tenth Census of the United States, 1880, Illinois, St. Clair County*, Roll 246, 19–25. For works on segregation, see Kenneth Clark, *The Dark Ghetto* (New York: Harper and Row, 1965); Blauner, *Racial Oppression in America*; James R. Grossman, *Land of Hope: Chicago, Black Southerners, and the Great Migration* (Chicago: University of Chicago Press, 1989); Arnold R. Hirsch, *Making the Second Ghetto: Race and Housing in Chicago, 1940–1960* (Cambridge, Mass.: Harvard University Press, 1983); Henry Taylor Jr., "City Building, Public Policy, the Rise of the Industrial City, and Black Ghetto-Slum Formation in Cincinnati, 1850–1940," in *Race and the City*, ed. Taylor, 156–92; Charles F. Casey-Leininger, "Making the Second Ghetto in Cincinnati: Avondale, 1925–70," in *Race and the City*, ed. Taylor, 232–57; and Raymond Mohl, "Making the Second Ghetto in Metropolitan Miami, 1940–1960," in *New African American Urban History*, ed. Goings and Mohl, 266–98.

15. *Population Schedules of the Ninth Census of the United States, 1870, Illinois, St. Clair County*, Roll 280, 620–25; *Population Schedules of the Tenth Census of the United States, 1880, Illinois, St. Clair County*, Roll 246, 17–18; *Directory of the City of East St. Louis for 1891–92*, vol. 2 (East St. Louis: East St. Louis Directory Publishing, 1891); "C. B. Carroll's Brooklyn City Directory, 1903," 249; Crockett, *Black Towns*, 116–17; Hamilton, *Black Towns and Profit*, 50–51. There are a number of contradictions between the 1870 and 1880 censuses, two of which concern the Haneys. In 1870, Richard Haney is listed as forty-three years old; a decade later the census listed him as fifty-five years old. Nancy Haney's age was listed as twenty-three in 1870 and as twenty-four in 1880.

16. *Population Schedules of the Seventh Census of the United States, 1850, Illinois, St. Clair County*, Roll 94, 118–27; *Population Schedules of the Ninth Census of the United States, 1870, Illinois, St. Clair County*, Roll 280, 620–25; and *Population Schedules of the Tenth Census of the United States, 1880, Illinois, St. Clair County*, Roll 246, 19–24. The manuscript census for 1870 lists twenty-two Black farmers but included personal or real property values for only ten. Perhaps they were sharecroppers or share renters.

Joe W. Trotter conceives of proletarianization as the "making of an industrial working class," but Karl Marx saw the initial proletarianization process as the conversion of serfs and peasants into a rural proletariat; therefore, I include farm laborers and industrial workers under the headings proletariat and worker. See Trotter, *Black Milwaukee*, 22; and Marx, *Capital*, 669–70. See also David Levine, ed., *Proletarianization and Family History* (Orlando, Fla.: Academic, 1984), 4.

17. *Population Schedules of the Ninth Census of the United States, 1870, Illinois, St. Clair County*, Roll 280, 620–25; *Population Schedules of the Tenth Census of the United States, 1880, Illinois, St. Clair County*, Roll 246, 19–24.

18. Faye Dudden, *Serving Women: Household Service in Nineteenth-Century America* (Middletown, Conn: Wesleyan University Press, 1983), 6; *Population Schedules of the Ninth Census of the United States, 1870, Illinois, St. Clair County*, Roll 280, 620–25; *Population Schedules of the Tenth Census of the United States, 1880, Illinois, St. Clair County*, Roll 246, 19–24. See also Carter G. Woodson, *Free Negro Owners of Slaves in the United States in 1830* (Washington, D. C.: Associated, 1924), 24–26; John Hope Franklin, *The Free Negro in North Carolina, 1790–1860* (New York: W. W. Norton, 1971), 159–61; and Berlin, *Slaves without Masters*, 272–75.

19. *Population Schedules of the Seventh Census of the United States, 1850, Illinois, St. Clair County*, Roll 94, 118–27; *Population Schedules of the Ninth Census of the United States, 1870, Illinois, St. Clair County*, Roll 280, 620–25; *Population Schedules of the Tenth Census of the United States, 1880, Illinois, St. Clair County*, Roll 246, 23; *Directory of the City of East St. Louis for 1891–92*, 5, 10.

20. *Population Schedules of the Seventh Census of the United States, 1850, Illinois, St. Clair County*, Roll 94, 118–27; *Population Schedules of the Ninth Census of the United States, 1870, Illinois, St. Clair County*, Roll 280, 620–25; and *Population Schedules of the Tenth Census of the United States, 1880, Illinois, St. Clair County*, Roll 246, 19–24.

21. *Belleville Weekly Advocate*, 20 February 1874, p. 1, col. 6; John H. Keiser, "Black Strikebreakers and Racism in Illinois, 1865–1900," *Journal of the Illinois State Historical Society* 65 (Autumn 1972): 315; William H. Harris, *The Harder We Run: Black Workers since the Civil War* (New York: Oxford University Press, 1982), 21–22; Warren C. Whatley, "African-American Strikebreaking from the Civil War to the New Deal," *Social Science History* 17 (Winter 1993): 530–36, table 1, 542 (quote).

22. *Population Schedules of the Tenth Census of the United States, 1880, Illinois, St. Clair County*, Roll 246, 20–24.

23. Ibid., 19–24.

24. Ibid.; W. H. Harris, *Harder We Run*; David M. Gordon, Richard Edwards, and Michael Reich, *Segmented Work, Divided Workers: The Historical Transformation of Labor in the United States* (New York: Cambridge University Press, 1982).

Self-activity refers to resistance, cultural development, institutional construction, or any actions taken by a group to further their interests. Examples of Black self-activity in transforming themselves from sharecroppers into wage workers include migration and the help of relatives, friends, Black churches, fraternal lodges, and the Urban League in job acquisition. Push and pull factors established the conditions in which Blacks made their decision to migrate north or to remain in the South, but the decision to migrate was an act of self-activity. Blacks often migrated en masse. Sometimes whole churches relocated. Often the wives and children of men who went north moved in with relatives. Meanwhile, male migrants often moved in with kin or friends who had already gone north. Churches, the Urban League, and fraternal lodges helped imigrants find jobs, housing, and social outlets.

25. *Population Schedules of the Ninth Census of the United States, 1870, Illinois, St. Clair County*, Roll 280, 620–25.

26. *Population Schedules of the Tenth Census of the United States, 1880, Illinois, St. Clair County*, Roll 246, 22–23; *Population Schedules of the Ninth Census of the United States, 1870, Illinois, St. Clair County*, Roll 280, 620–25.

27. Taylor and Dula, "Black Residential Experience and Community Formation in Antebellum Cincinnati," 107; *State Capital* (Springfield), 13 February 1892, p. 1, col. 7; Grossman, *Land of Hope.*

28. *Population Schedules of the Seventh Census of the United States, 1850, Illinois, St. Clair County,* Roll 94, 118–27; *Population Schedules of the Eighth Census of the United States, 1860, Illinois, St. Clair County,* Roll 333, 62–72; *Population Schedules of the Ninth Census of the United States, 1870, Illinois, St. Clair County,* Roll 280, 622; *Population Schedules of the Tenth Census of the United States, 1880, Illinois, St. Clair County,* Roll 246, 21.

29. Lammermeier, "Urban Black Family of the Nineteenth Century," 453; *Population Schedules of the Ninth Census of the United States, 1870, Illinois, St. Clair County,* Roll 280, 622. For a discussion of Black women's role in farming and sharecropping, see Susan A. Mann, "Slavery, Sharecropping, and Sexual Inequality," *Signs: Journal of Women in Culture and Society* 14 (Summer 1989): 784–86.

30. *Population Schedules of the Eighth Census of the United States, 1860, Illinois, St. Clair County,* Roll 333, 62–72; *Population Schedules of the Ninth Census of the United States, 1870, Illinois, St. Clair County,* Roll 280, 622; Mann, "Slavery, Sharecropping, and Sexual Inequality."

On 25 February 1853, Prudence Archer brought lot 316 and more, on the southwest corner of Fourth and Jefferson streets from Wilbur N. McLean. Three days later, she purchased lot 310 and more, which was located a block further north from Milton McClain on Fourth Street. Frederick purchased two lots, 29 and 30, located along Water Street from Nicholas Honeyer on 25 September 1865. For Prudence Archer's transactions, see St. Clair County Recorder of Deeds, *Incorporation Index Book E-2,* 316; for Frederick's transactions, see St. Clair County Recorder of Deeds, *Book D-4,* 574.

Frederick Archer had owned two town lots in 1865, but the manuscript census does not list real or personal values for his property in 1870. Perhaps he no longer owned property in 1870. Stephen Gilliam, William Ballad, James Lyngin, James Smith, Frederick Archer, Joseph Archer, James Cooper, Richard Haney, Strickland Parker, Benjamin Chambers, James A. Pettiford, and John Lee were all listed as "farmers," but none had monetary values listed for real or personal property.

31. *History of St. Clair County,* 308; *Population Schedules of the Tenth Census of the United States, 1880, Illinois, St. Clair County,* Roll 246, 21. It may have been common for employers to house employees since Joseph Boyce, a twenty-three-year-old mulatto clerk, also boarded with John Watson. Watson was the only other African American retail merchant listed in the 1880 census.

32. *Population Schedules of the Tenth Census of the United States, 1880, Illinois, St. Clair County,* Roll 246, 22–25. See also Evelyn Nakano Glenn, "Racial Ethnic Women's Labor," *Review of Radical Political Economics* 17 (Fall 1985): 86–108; Evelyn Nakano Glenn, "From Servitude to Service Work: Historical Continuities in the Racial Division of Paid Reproductive Labor," *Signs: Journal of Women in Culture and Society* 18 (Autumn 1982): 1–43; and Mann, "Slavery, Sharecropping, and Sexual Inequality," 774–98.

33. Gutman, *Black Family in Slavery and in Freedom,* 444–45; *Population Schedules of the Ninth Census of the United States, 1870, Illinois, St. Clair County,* Roll 280, 620–25; *Population Schedules of the Tenth Census of the United States, 1880, Illinois, St. Clair County,* Roll 246, 23.

34. *Population Schedules of the Tenth Census of the United States, 1880, Illinois, St. Clair County,* Roll 246, 19–24, especially 24; Gutman, *Black Family in Slavery and in Freedom,* 443–44; Andrea G. Hunter, "Making a Way: Strategies of Southern Urban African-American Families, 1900 and 1936," *Journal of Family History* 18, no. 3 (1993): 238.

35. Antonio McDaniel, "The Power of Culture: A Review of the Idea of Africa's Influence on Family Structure in Antebellum America," *Journal of Family History* 15, no. 3 (1990): 231–32; Niara Sudarkasa, "Interpreting the African Heritage in Afro-American Family

Organization," in *Black Families*, 2d ed., ed. Harriette Pipes McAdoo (Newbury Park, Calif: Sage, 1988), 37–53; W. E. B. Du Bois, *The Negro Church: Report of a Social Study Made under the Direction of Atlanta University* (1903; reprint, New York: Octagon Books, 1968), 2–6; Gutman, *Black Family in Slavery and in Freedom*; Stuckey, *Slave Culture.*

36. *Population Schedules of the Tenth Census of the United States, 1880, Illinois, St. Clair County*, Roll 246, 21–22; Hunter, "Making a Way," 233; *East St. Louis Gazette*, 21 November 1874, p. 3, col. 3; "C. B. Carroll's Brooklyn City Directory, 1903," 238–39.

37. *Population Schedules of the Tenth Census of the United States, 1880, Illinois, St. Clair County*, Roll 246, 19–24; *History of St. Clair County*, 308; *East St.Louis Gazette*, 1 May 1886, p. 3, col. 3; Crockett, *Black Towns*, 85.

38. *Population Schedules of the Tenth Census of the United States, 1880, Illinois, St. Clair County*, Roll 246, 19–24.

39. Ibid., 22–23.

40. *Population Schedules of the Seventh Census of the United States, 1850, Illinois, St. Clair County*, Roll 94, 118–27; *Population Schedules of the Ninth Census of the United States, 1870, Illinois, St. Clair County*, Roll 280, 620–25; *Population Schedules of the Tenth Census of the United States, 1880, Illinois, St. Clair County*, Roll 246, 19–24; St. Clair County Recorder of Deeds, *Book E-4*, 368 (granter, John Anderson; grantee, Matilda Anderson); St. Clair County Recorder of Deeds, *Book V-4*, 338 (grantor, Simon P. Anderson and wife; grantee Nancy Brown); St. Clair County Recorder of Deeds, *Book W-5*, 211 (grantor, Matilda Anderson; grantee, Nancy Brown); St. Clair County Recorder of Deeds, *Book X-5*, 553 (grantor, Matilda Anderson; grantee, Mary Jackson).

41. Probate Records, St. Clair County, Box 451, Roll No. 000159, Sequence No. 400059, Case No. 000387 (1880).

42. *East St. Louis Gazette*, 21 November 1874, p. 2, col. 3; *History of St. Clair County*, 308.

43. George Wright, *Life behind a Veil: Blacks in Louisville, Kentucky, 1865–1930* (Baton Rouge: Louisiana State University Press, 1985), 14; *East St. Louis Tribune*, 24 March 1876, p. 2, col. 3; *St. Louis Palladium*, 28 November 1903, p. 8, col. 2; Logan, *Negro in American Life and Thought.*

44. *Belleville Weekly Advocate*, 19 March 1875, p. 4, col. 2.

45. For more on these celebrations, see William H. Wiggins Jr., "'Lift Every Voice': A Study of Afro-American Emancipation Celebrations," in *Discovering Afro-America*. ed. Roger D. Abrahams and John Szwed (Leiden: E. J. Brill, 1975), 45–57; and William H. Wiggins Jr., *O Freedom! Afro-American Emancipation Celebrations* (Knoxville: University of Tennessee Press, 1987), 25–48. See also Lorenzo J. Greene, *The Negro in Colonial New England* (1942; reprint, New York: Athenum, 1968), 255; Joseph P. Reidy, "'Negro Election Day' and Black Community Life in New England, 1750–1860," *Marxist Perspectives* 1 (Fall 1978): 106–10; Wright, *Life behind a Veil*, 14; William D. Pierson, *Black Yankees: The Development of an Afro-American Subculture in Eighteenth-Century New England* (Amherst: University of Massachusetts Press, 1988), 118–40; William B. Gravely, "The Dialectic of Double Consciousness in Black American Freedom Celebrations, 1808–1863," *Journal of Negro History* 17 (Winter 1982): 302–17; Shane White, "'It Was a Proud Day': African Americans, Festivals and Parades in the North 1741–1827," in *New African American Urban History*, ed. Goings and Mohl, 13–50; and Genevieve Fabre, "African-American Commemorative Celebrations in the Nineteenth Century," in *History and Memory in African-American Culture*, ed. Genevieve Fabre and Robert O'Mally (New York: Oxford University Press, 1994), 72–91.

46. An article in *Broadax* noted that Senator T. T. Allain left for Decatur, Illinois, on Thursday, 21 September 1899, to address the Emancipation Day Celebration on Friday, 22 September. In 1882, the *Conservator* announced Emancipation Day Celebration for 1 January. See *Broadax* (Chicago), 23 September 1899, p. 1, col. 2; and *Conservator* (Chicago), 23 December 1882, p. 3, col. 1. See also *Forum* (Springfield), 23 July 1906, p. 1, col. 3;

History of St. Clair County, 309; and John W. Allen, "Emancipation Day Has about Vanished" and "It Happened in Southern Illinois," 7 July 1957, Bulletin No. 212, Southern Illinois University, Illinois Negroes Vertical File, Illinois State Historical Library, Springfield. Allen was unaware of the celebrations held in Springfield.

47. Anne Firor Scott contends that the line separating the church-based and the new secular organizations was dotted and incomplete. Nevertheless, she posits that secular organizations emerged in the 1890s to promote self-education and community improvement. In an important article on the Alton school crisis, Shirley J. Portwood reports that church members participated heavily in the formation of the Alton Citizens Committee, although ministers played a very circumscribed role. See Anne Firor Scott, "Most Invisible of All: Black Women's Voluntary Associations," *Journal of Southern History* 56 (February 1990): 9; and Shirley J. Portwood, "The Alton School Case and African American Community Consciousness, 1897–1908," *Illinois Historical Journal* 91 (Spring 1998): 3–4.

48. For the growth of Black secular leadership during this period, see Nell Irvin Painter, *Exodusters: Black Migration to Kansas after Reconstruction* (1976; reprint, New York: W. W. Norton, 1992); Thomas Holt, *Black over White: Negro Political Leadership in South Carolina during Reconstruction* (Urbana: University of Illinois Press, 1977); and Eric Anderson, *Race and Politics in North Carolina, 1872–1901* (Baton Rouge: Louisiana State University Press, 1981).

49. Garvey, *Government and Administration of Illinois,* 496–99; Crockett, *Black Towns,* 81–86.

50. "C. B. Carroll's Brooklyn City Directory, 1903," 230–44.

51. *Population Schedules of the Seventh Census of the United States, 1850, Illinois, St. Clair County,* Roll 94, 110–27; *Population Schedules of the Eighth Census of the United States, 1860, Illinois, St. Clair County,* Roll 333, 62–72; *Population Schedules of the Ninth Census of the United States, 1870, Illinois, St. Clair County,* Roll 280, 622; "C. B. Carroll's Brooklyn City Directory, 1897–98," in *East St. Louis City Directory* (East St. Louis: East St. Louis Directory Publishing, 1897–98), 388; *St. Clair Tribune* (East St. Louis), 3 March 1875, p. 3; *History of St. Clair County,* 308; and Bateman and Selby, *Historical Encyclopedia of Illinois,* 707.

52. *Population Schedules of the Ninth Census of the United States, 1870, Illinois, St. Clair County,* Roll 280, 622; *Population Schedules of the Tenth Census of the United States, 1880, Illinois, St. Clair County,* Roll 246, 19; *Illinois Record* (Springfield), 9 April 1898, p. 3, col. 4, 23 March 1898, p. 3, col. 2, and 20 August 1898, p. 3, col. 3.

53. *Population Schedules of the Ninth Census of the United States, 1870, Illinois, St. Clair County,* Roll 280, 622; *Population Schedules of the Tenth Census of the United States, 1880, Illinois, St. Clair County,* Roll 246, 19.

54. *Population Schedules of the Tenth Census of the United States, 1880, Illinois, St. Clair County,* Roll 246, 8; "C. B. Carroll's Brooklyn City Directory, 1903," 234.

55. Michael B. Chesson, "Richmond's Black Councilmen, 1871–96," in *Southern Black Leaders of the Reconstruction Era,* ed. Rabinowitz, 191–222; McCaul, *Black Struggle for Public Schooling in Nineteenth-Century Illinois,* 83 (first quote), 84 (second quote), 127–35.

56. *East St. Louis Gazette,* 18 April 1874, p. 4, col. 5; McCaul, *Black Struggle for Public Schooling in Nineteenth-Century Illinois,* 127–36; Bridges, "Equality Deferred," 96–97.

57. Quoted in Thomas O. Jewett, "Belleville's School for Blacks," *St. Clair County Historical Journal* 3, no. 10 (1985): 20.

58. McCaul, *Black Struggle for Public Schooling in Nineteenth-Century Illinois,* 234; Robert A. Goldberg, *Grassroots Resistance: Social Movements in Twentieth-Century America* (Belmont, Calif.: Wadsworth, 1991), 12.

59. "White vs. Black," *St. Clair Tribune,* 24 August 1876, p. 3, col. 5, reprinted from the *East St. Louis Republican;* McCaul, *Black Struggle for Public Schooling in Nineteenth-Century Illinois,* 22–32, 150–53; Carlson, "Black Community in the Rural North," 99–104; Portwood, "Alton School Case and African American Community Consciousness," 4;

Michael W. Homel, *Down from Equality: Black Chicagoans and the Public Schools, 1920–41* (Urbana: University of Illinois Press, 1984), 1–26; August Meier and Elliott Rudwick, "Early Boycotts of Segregated Schools: The Alton, Illinois, Case, 1897–1908," *Journal of Negro Education* 36 (Winter 1967): 400.

60. *Population Schedules of the Ninth Census of the United States, 1870, Illinois, St. Clair County,* Roll 280, 620–25; *Population Schedules of the Tenth Census of the United States, 1880, Illinois, St. Clair County,* Roll 246, 21.

61. *St. Clair Tribune,* 24 August 1876, p. 3, col. 5, reprinted from the *East St. Louis Republican* (emphasis added).

Fortunately, the predicted physical struggle never occurred, but this was only the beginning of a protracted dispute. Apparently the charges were withdrawn, since Bird has no criminal record and they do not include this incident in Watson's criminal file.

62. John Watson Criminal Case Files, St. Clair County, Roll No. 000226, Sequence No. 100165, Case No. 000265 (1878).

The records are extremely difficult to read and at various points cite both January of 1878 and January of 1879 as the date when John Watson was indicted, but they do agree that the crime was committed in December of 1877. See also John Watson Criminal Case Files, St. Clair County, Roll No. 000213, Sequence No. 100026, Case No. 000011 (1878), and Roll No. 254, Sequence No. 100071, Case No. 000138 (1878).

63. John Watson Criminal Case Files, St. Clair County, Roll No. 000226, Sequence No. 100165, Case No. 000265 (1878).

64. Ibid. Boyd was Watson's neighbor and perhaps friend and supporter.

65. Ibid.

66. *East St. Louis Gazette,* 21 November 1874, p. 2, col. 3.

67. Bettye Collier-Thomas, "The Impact of Black Women in Education: An Historical Overview," *Journal of Negro Education* 51 (Summer 1982): 176 (first two quotes); "C. B. Carroll's Brooklyn City Directory, 1905," in *East St. Louis City Directory* (East St. Louis: East St. Louis Directory Publishing, 1905), 19; Kremer, *James Milton Turner and the Promise of America;* Dillard, "James Milton Turner," 372–411; Lawrence Christensen, "J. Milton Turner: An Appraisal," *Missouri Historical Review* 70 (November 1975): 1–19; *History of St. Clair County,* 309 (third quote); *Population Schedules of the Tenth Census of the United States, 1880, Illinois, St. Clair County,* Roll 246, 19–24; Gary R. Kremer, professor of history at William Woods College, interview by author, 3 December 1997.

68. *Population Schedules of the Tenth Census of the United States, 1880, Illinois, St. Clair County,* Roll 246, 19–24; Kremer, interview by author, 3 December 1997.

69. *Population Schedules of the Tenth Census of the United States, 1880, Illinois, St. Clair County,* Roll 246, 22; *St. Louis Post-Dispatch,* 19 November 1886, p. 4, col. 3; Kremer, *James Milton Turner and the Promise of America,* 143.

70. *Population Schedules of the Tenth Census of the United States, 1880, Illinois, St. Clair County,* Roll 246, 21. Willie Wilson, whom the census taker listed as August George's five-year-old grandson, also lived in the household. He may have been Lula George's child.

Chapter 4: Mobilizing the Race, 1878–1906

1. *East St. Louis Journal,* 29 December 1894, p. 3, col. 3. Lerone Bennett used the term *Black power* to refer to Reconstruction governments. See Lerone Bennett, *Black Power U.S.A.: The Human Side of Reconstruction, 1867–1877* (Chicago: Johnson, 1967). For contemporary discussions of its meaning, see Carmichael and Hamilton, *Black Power,* 46; Robert Smith, "Black Power and Transformation from Protest to Politics," *Political Science Quarterly* 96 (Fall 1981): 431–43; Cruse, *Revolution or Rebellion?* 193–258; James Boggs, *Racism and the Class Struggle* (New York: Monthly Review, 1970), 51–62; Manning Marable, *Race, Reform, and Rebellion: The Second Reconstruction in Black America, 1945–1982*

(Jackson: University Press of Mississippi, 1984), 104–10; William L. Van Deburg, *New Day in Babylon* (Chicago: University of Chicago Press, 1992), 112–91; and John T. McCartney, *Black Power Ideologies: An Essay in African-American Political Thought* (Philadelphia: Temple University Press, 1992), 111–32.

2. *Population Schedules of the Ninth Census of the United States, 1870, Illinois, St. Clair County,* Roll 280, 620–25; St. Clair County Recorder, *St. Clair County Marriage Licenses, 1876–78,* 66, 191; St. Clair County Recorder, *St. Clair County Index to Marriages, 1878–87, Book 1;* Daniel M. Johnson and Rex R. Campbell, *Black Migration in America: A Social Demographic History* (Durham, N.C.: Duke University Press, 1981), 46.

3. *Population Schedules of the Ninth Census of the United States, 1870, Illinois, St. Clair County,* Roll 280, 620–25.

4. John Evans Probate Record, St. Clair County, Roll No. 269, Sequence No. 100041, Case No. 899 (1910); *Population Schedules of the Tenth Census of the United States, 1880, Illinois, St. Clair County,* Roll 246, 17–18; *Population Schedules of the Twelfth Census of the United States, 1900, Illinois, St. Clair County,* Roll 342, 264–76; *Population Schedules of the Ninth Census of the United States, 1870, Illinois, St. Clair County,* Roll 280, 620–25; *Directory of the City of East St. Louis for 1891–92; Population Schedules of the Thirteenth Census of the United States, 1910, Illinois, St. Clair County,* Roll 323; "McCoy's Brooklyn City Directory, 1897–98," in *East St. Louis City Directory* (East St. Louis: East St. Louis Directory Publishing, 1897–98), 388–89; "C. B. Carroll's Brooklyn Directory, 1898–99," in *East St. Louis City Directory* (East St. Louis: East St. Louis Directory Publishing, 1898–99), 444–45; "C. B. Carroll's Brooklyn City Directory, 1903," 249. See also Boston, *Race, Class, and Conservatism,* 29–31, 46–53.

5. St. Clair County Recorder, *St. Clair County Marriage Licenses, 1878–87, Book 1; Population Schedules of the Tenth Census of the United States, 1880, Illinois, St. Clair County,* Roll 246, 17–18; "McCoy's Brooklyn City Directory, 1897–98," 388–89; "C. B. Carroll's Brooklyn City Directory, 1898–99," 444–45; *Population Schedules of the Thirteenth Census of the United States, 1910, Illinois, St. Clair County,* Roll 323, 151–66.

Eric Anderson's comment on the elusiveness of James O'Hara, a North Carolina African American politician, and Merline Pitre's observation on the fragmentary nature of sources on Richard Allen, a Black politician in Reconstruction Texas, are also applicable to John Evans. See Anderson, "James O'Hara of North Carolina," 101–25; and Merline Pitre, "Richard Allen: The Chequered Career of Houston's First Black State Legislator," in *Black Dixie: Afro-Texan History and Culture in Houston,* ed. Howard Beeth and Cary D. Wintz (College Station: Texas A&M University Press, 1992), 74–102. See also James O. Horton, "The Life and Times of Edward Ambush: An Illustration of Social History Methodology," in *History and Tradition in Afro-American Culture,* ed. Gunter H. Lenz (Frankfurt: Campus, 1984), 3–16.

6. Illinois and Missouri Black newspapers offer rich though incomplete sources for examining Brooklyn in the late nineteenth and early twentieth centuries. The *State Capital,* published in Springfield, Illinois, has excellent information on Brooklyn from 28 March 1891 to 10 December 1892. This period encompasses part of Evans's tenure as mayor. Superb coverage of the period from 8 November 1897 through 23 April 1899 is provided by the *Illinois Record,* also published in Springfield, Illinois. The *Illinois Record* was the official organ of the reinvigorated Illinois Afro-American Protective League. A third paper published in Springfield, Illinois, the *Forum,* covers the period from 3 February 1906 through 1911. In St. Louis, Missouri, the *St. Louis Palladium* occasionally reported on events in Brooklyn between 10 January 1903 and October 1907.

7. I am not using modernization to support the "breakdown thesis" or the idea that the migrants' traditional culture and bonds of community were eroded by the urban environment. On the contrary, I contend that as Afro-Brooklynites expanded existing institutions and organizations and formed new ones, they strengthened their traditional

values, such as mutuality, and a freedom-conscious political culture. Their entrance into politics ultimately led to the empowerment of "race" as an organizing principle. See Bender, *Community and Social Change in America;* and John McClymer, "The Study of Community and the 'New' Social History," *Journal of Urban History* 7 (November 1980): 103–18. See also Borchert, *Alley Life in Washington;* Grossman, *Land of Hope;* and Peter Gottlieb, *Making Their Own Way: Southern Blacks' Migration to Pittsburgh, 1916–30* (Urbana: University of Illinois Press, 1987).

8. Doug McAdam, *Political Process and the Development of Black Insurgency, 1930–1970* (Chicago: University of Chicago Press, 1982), 40. See also Goldberg, *Grassroots Resistance.*

9. Frantz Fanon, *The Wretched of the Earth* (New York: Grove, 1968), 35; Minion K. C. Morrison, *Black Political Mobilization* (New York: State University of New York Press, 1987).

10. "C. B. Carroll's Brooklyn City Directory, 1903," 238–39; *History of St. Clair County,* 308.

11. Described as "a prominent colored man," J. W. Bush defeated a white man in the mayoral race in Mason, Tennessee, in 1897. The *Broadax* claimed Bush was the first African American mayor in the state of Tennessee. Evans and Bush are the only Blacks I am aware of who became mayors of biracial towns prior to the twentieth century. See *Broadax,* 24 April 1897, p. 1, col. 3.; and *East St. Louis Journal,* 29 December 1894, p. 3, col. 3.

12. *Belleville Weekly Advocate,* 8 February 1884, p. 5, col. 2; Bateman and Selby, *Historical Encyclopedia of Illinois,* 707.

13. St. Clair County Recorder of Deeds, *Incorporation Index Book 192,* 273; *East St. Louis Journal,* 10 January 1891, p. 2, col. 2.

14. *East St. Louis Journal,* 24 March 1890, p. 5, col. 2; Teun A. Van Dijk, "Analyzing Racism through Discourse Analysis: Some Methodological Reflections," in *Race and Ethnicity in Research Methods,* ed. John H. Stanfield II and Rutledge M. Dennis (Newbury Park, Calif.: Sage, 1993), 93.

15. Brooklyn's pre-1965 election records were destroyed in a fire. The county board consisted of one representative from each township (21), an additional assistant supervisor from each township with a population of 4,000, and another for every 2,500 residents above 4,000. See St. Clair Recorder of Deeds, *Incorporation Index Book 192,* 273; and *East St. Louis Journal,* 24 March 1890, p. 5, col. 2.

16. *Population Schedules of the Tenth Census of the United States, 1880, Illinois, St. Clair County,* Roll 246, 19–24; Lee Williams, "Concentrated Residences: The Case of Black Toledo, 1890–1930," *Phylon* 63 (June 1992): 167–76; Blauner, *Racial Oppression in America;* Grossman, *Land of Hope.*

17. *East St. Louis Gazette,* 11 July 1891, p. 4, col. 2; Bateman and Selby, *Historical Encyclopedia of Illinois,* 308.

Norman L. Crockett reported that mass meetings were often held in Black towns to get community input before important decisions were made. Nell Irvin Painter elevates the mass community meeting to an element of African American political culture. She claims they were the "normal" decision-making process by which "uneducated Blacks" made decisions "to take public community action." See Crockett, *Black Towns,* 81–82; and Painter, *Exodusters,* 22.

18. Rudwick, *Race Riot at East St. Louis,* 190–96; Rose, "All-Negro Town," 352–67; Walter and Kramer, "Political Autonomy and Economic Dependence in an All-Negro Municipality," 225; Wiese, "Places of Our Own," 30–54.

I believe annexation would not have improved things for Afro-Brooklynites because the corporations colluded with corrupt politicians in such cities as East St. Louis to have their property dramatically underassessed. The system allowed the St. Clair County Board of Review to reevaluate assessments, and they generally reduced corporate assessments. It is uncertain whether the town government would have been able to collect fair revenues from industries even if they had located in Brooklyn.

19. Copy of the original deed of transfer, in author's possession (provided by Kathryn Kueker, secretary-treasurer of the National Stock Yards Company, during an interview on 19 November 1996); Arthur Moore, field notes on Brooklyn, p. 5, Works Progress Administration, Federal Writers' Project, folder for Brooklyn, Illinois, Madison County, District 7, Illinois State Historical Library; Agelika Kruger-Khloula, "On the Wrong Side of the Fence: Racial Segregation in American Cemeteries," in *History and Memory in African-American Culture*, ed. Fabre and O'Mally, 135; *American Eagle* (St. Louis), 17 December 1905, p. 4, col. 3.

20. *East St. Louis Gazette*, 8 August 1891, p. 4, col. 2, and 31 October 1891, p. 2, col. 2; *State Capital*, 5 March 1892, p. 1, col. 4; *Atlas of St. Clair County*, 288.

21. *State Capital*, 9 January 1892, p. 3, col. 2; Wiggins, "'Lift Every Voice,'" 47, 50.

22. *State Capital*, 9 January 1892, p. 3, col. 2; Elsa Barkley Brown and Greg D. Kimball, "Mapping the Terrain of Black Richmond," in *New African American Urban History*, ed. Goings and Mohl, 66–115. See also *History of St. Clair County*, 309; and *Forum*, 23 July 1906, p. 1, col. 3.

23. *State Capital*, 9 January 1892, p. 3, col. 2, 12 December 1891, p. 1, cols. 2–3, 13 February 1892, p. 1, col. 7, 27 February 1892, p. 1, col. 5, and 5 March 1892, p. 1, col. 4; *East St. Louis Journal*, 22 October 1906, p. 2, col. 4; Carlson, "Black Community in the Rural North," 77.

In 1881, the Reverend Burton debated Black Baptists in Pulaski County on the topics "Is the Lord's Prayer a Free Communion of All Christians" and "Was Christ a Missionary Baptist?" William Halliburton, an enterprising laborer who supplemented his income as a combination stringer and distributor for the *State Capital*, wrote a weekly column for the Springfield paper under the headline "Lovejoy, Ill." In January of 1892, Halliburton reported that 110 children attended Sunday school at Antioch Missionary Baptist Church and that another 50 participated in Quinn Chapel's. Halliburton did not provide any figures for Corinthian Baptist, a recently organized church, whose membership consisted of disaffected former Antioch congregants. Halliburton was a very active person; in addition to his full-time job and distributing the *State Capital*, he was the assistant superintendent of Antioch's Sunday School. Cora Garrett, Dr. Garrett's wife, was the superintendent.

24. "Lovejoy, Ill.," *State Capital*, 9 January 1892, p. 3, col. 2, 12 December 1891, p. 1, cols. 2–3, 30 January 1892, p. 1, col. 3, 6 February 1892, p. 1, col. 3, 27 February 1892, p. 1, col. 5; "McCoy's Brooklyn City Directory, 1896," in *Directory of the City of East St. Louis* (East St. Louis: East St. Louis Directory Publishing, 1896), 400; "McCoy's Brooklyn City Directory, 1897–98," 389; *Illinois Record*, 23 April 1898, p. 3, col. 1; "C. B. Carroll's Brooklyn Directory, 1898–99," 444; Molefi Kete Asante, "African Elements in African American English," in *Africanisms in American Culture*, ed. Joseph E. Holloway (Bloomington: Indiana University Press, 1991), 20 (Asante quote); Molefi Kete Asante, *The Afrocentric Idea* (Philadelphia: Temple University Press, 1987).

25. *State Capital*, 9 January 1892, p. 3, col. 2; *East St. Louis Journal*, 29 December 1894, p. 3, col. 3.

26. *State Capital*, 9 January 1892, p. 3, col. 2.

27. Wiggins, "'Lift Every Voice,'" 50–52.

28. Vincent P. Franklin, "'They Rose and Fell Together': African American Educators and Community Leadership, 1795–1954," *Journal of Education* 172, no. 3 (1990): 40.

29. For discussion of the various commemorations, see *State Capital*, 30 January 1892, p. 1, col. 3, 6 February 1892, p. 1, col. 3, 13 February 1892, p. 1, col. 7, 27 February 1892, p. 1, col. 5, and 5 March 1892, p. 1, col. 4; and *American Eagle*, 17 December 1905, p. 1, col. 3.

30. *East St. Louis Gazette*, 8 August 1891, p. 4, col. 2, and 31 October 1891, p. 4, col. 3; *State Capital*, 5 March 1892, p. 1, col. 4; "McCoy's Brooklyn City Directory, 1897–98," 389; "C. B. Carroll's Brooklyn City Directory, 1898–99," 444–47; *Population Schedules of the Tenth Census of the United States, 1880, Illinois, St. Clair County*, Roll 246, 19–24.

31. *Belleville Weekly Advocate*, 20 May 1892, p. 1, col. 1; *East St. Louis Journal*, 20 May 1892, p. 3, col. 6.

32. *Population Schedules of the Tenth Census of the United States, 1880, Illinois, St. Clair County*, Roll 246, 23; "McCoy's Brooklyn City Directory, 1906," in *East St. Louis City Directory* (East St. Louis: East St. Louis Directory Publishing, 1906), 400; "McCoy's Brooklyn City Directory, 1897–98," 388.

33. "C. B. Carroll's Brooklyn City Directory, 1905," 19.

34. *Illinois Record*, 20 August 1898, p. 1, col. 3.

35. Quoted in Bracey, Meier, and Rudwick, *Black Nationalism in America*, 221–22.

36. Ibid.; August Meier, *Negro Thought in America, 1880–1915* (Ann Arbor: University of Michigan Press, 1969), 128–30; Emma Lou Thornbrough, *T. Thomas Fortune, Militant Journalist* (Chicago: University of Chicago Press, 1972); Jean Allman and David Roediger, "The Early Editorial Career of Timothy Thomas Fortune: Class, Nationalism and Consciousness of Africa," *Afro-Americans in New York Life and History* 6 (July 1982): 39–55; Harold Cruse, *Plural but Equal: A Critical Study of Blacks and Minorities and the American Plural Society* (New York: William Morrow, 1987), 7–24; Lerone Bennett, *Before the Mayflower* (Chicago: Johnson Publishing, 1987), 83.

37. *Illinois Record*, 13 November 1897, p. 1, col. 3. See also Anthony M. Landis, "They Refused to Stay in Their Place: Black Resistance during the Springfield Race Riot of 1908" (Paper presented at the "Community Building and Resistance: African Americans in the Land of Lincoln" Conference, 17 April 1997, Southern Illinois University at Edwardsville, in author's possession).

38. Shirley Portwood, "'The Party of Promises': African American Political Activism and the Republican Party in Southern Illinois, 1870–1900" (Unpublished manuscript, in the possession of the author); *Broadax*, 1 May 1897, p. 1, col. 4 (second quote); Victor Hicken, "The Virden and Pana Mine Wars of 1898," *Journal of the Illinois State Historical Society* 52 (Summer 1959): 278 (third quote); Keiser, "Black Strikebreakers and Racism in Illinois," 322; Keiser, *Building for the Centuries*, 111, 251; Bridges, "Equality Deferred," 83–108.

39. Meier and Rudwick, "Early Boycotts of Segregated Schools," 394–402; Cha-Jua, "'Warlike Demonstration'"; Portwood, "Alton School Case and African American Community Consciousness," 2–20.

40. *Illinois Record*, 5 February 1898, p. 3, col. 4 (Evans quote), 12 February 1898, p. 3, col. 2 (Archer quote), 19 February 1898, col. 6, and 2 July 1898, p. 1, col. 3; T. Thomas Fortune, *Black and White: Life and Labor in the South* (New York: Fords, Howard, and Hubert, 1884); Meier and Rudwick, "Early Boycotts of Segregated Schools," 394–402; Meier, *Negro Thought in America*, 171–82; Portwood, "Alton School Case and African American Community Consciousness," 18; Cha-Jua, "'Warlike Demonstration.'"

41. "White vs. Black," *St. Clair Tribune*, 24 August 1876, p. 3, col. 5; McCaul, *Black Struggle for Public Schooling in Nineteenth-Century Illinois*, 22–32, 150–53; Carlson, "Black Community in the Rural North," 99–104; Portwood, "Alton School Case and African American Community Consciousness," 4; Meier and Rudwick, "Early Boycotts of Segregated Schools," 400; McCaul, *Black Struggle for Public Education in Nineteenth-Century Illinois*, 127–42; *Illinois Record*, 5 February 1898, p. 3, col. 4; *Population Schedules of the Ninth Census of the United States, 1870, Illinois, St. Clair County*, Roll 280, 622; "C. B. Carroll's Brooklyn City Directory, 1903," 234, 238.

42. *Illinois Record*, 19 March 1898, p. 1, cols. 1–2.

43. Ibid., 10 September 1898, p. 2, col. 2.

44. Ibid., p. 2, cols. 2–3, 5, and 19 November 1898, p. 2, col. 1. See also Cha-Jua, "'Warlike Demonstration'"; Carlson, "Black Community in the Rural North," 109–34; Portwood, "Black Migration to Pulaski County," 37–46; Shirley J. Portwood, "Political Opposition to the Republican Party in Alexander and Jackson County, Illinois, during 1870–1900" (Paper delivered at the "African Americans in Illinois History" Conference, 2 October 1993, DuSable Museum, Chicago, Illinois); Portwood, "'Party of Promises.'"

45. *Illinois Record,* 2 April 1898, p. 4, col. 2, 23 April 1898, p. 1, col. 5, and 2 July 1898, p. 2, col. 2.

46. Ibid., 2 July 1898, p. 1, col. 3, 3 September 1898, p. 2, col. 1, and 10 September 1898, p. 2, cols. 2–3.

47. *Decatur Review,* 1 September 1898, p. 1, col. 3, 2 September 1898, p. 1, col. 1, 4 September 1898, p. 1, col. 6, 7 September 1898, p. 1, col. 2, and 8 September 1898, p. 1, col. 3. The *Decatur Review* covered the riots nearly every day from 1 September through 19 November. See also Hicken, "Virden and Pana Mine Wars of 1898," 263–78; Keiser, "Black Strikebreakers and Racism in Illinois," 592–625; Keiser, *Building for the Centuries,* 111, 251; and Bridges, "Equality Deferred," 83–108.

48. *Illinois Record,* 1 October 1898, p. 1, cols. 1–2, and p. 2, cols. 3–4. Lawrence A. Newby ran for Cook County commissioner in 1900, challenging the Democratic party in much the same way that Evans and Hall were challenging the Republicans. *Broadax,* 1 May 1900, p. 1, col. 6.

49. Alton officials interpreted the ruling narrowly and only admitted the children of Scott Bibb, the plaintiff. They claimed other Blacks who wanted to attend mixed schools would have to bring their own suits. See *Illinois Record,* 1 October 1898, p. 1, cols. 1–2, and p. 3, cols. 3–4; Meier and Rudwick, "Early Boycotts of Segregated Schools," 398–400; Meier, *Negro Thought in America,* 172–74; and Portwood, "Alton School Case and African American Community Consciousness," 4.

On the Page bill, which proposed a segregated vocational school for Blacks, see *Illinois Record,* 19 February 1899, p. 1, cols. 1–2, and p. 2, col. 4, 8 April 1899, p. 1, cols. 1–2, and p. 2, cols. 5–6; and Carlson, "Blacks in the Rural North," 99–100.

50. *Broadax,* 26 August 1899, p. 1, col. 2, and 23 September 1899, p. 1, col. 1.

51. *East St. Louis Journal,* 20 February 1903, p. 2, col. 3, and 8 June 1903, p. 3, col. 3; *Illinois Record,* 30 September 1896, p. 3, col. 2, and 12 February 1898, p. 2, col. 2; *St. Louis Palladium,* 16 April 1904, p. 1, col. 6; Frederick F. Vanderberg St. Clair County Criminal Case Files, 1903, Criminal Case Files Cross Reference List as of 7-7-82, 1024, microfilm, St. Clair County Circuit Court; Frederick F. Vanderberg Criminal Case Files, St. Clair County, Roll No. 276, Sequence No. 1000158, Case No. 008 (1899), Roll No. 276, Sequence No. 100111, Case No. 121 (1899), Roll No. 302, Sequence No. 100074, Case No. 148 (1899), and Roll No. 74, Sequence No. 100043, Case No. 2332 (1913).

52. *St. Louis Palladium* noted that on 29 March "Mr. and Mrs. Elizabeth Evans lost their baby boy." See *St. Louis Palladium,* 9 April 1904, p. 8, col. 1.

53. *East St. Louis Journal,* 27 March 1906, p. 2, col. 3, and 1 April 1906, p. 2, col. 3. Interestingly, just before the 1917 race riot in East St. Louis, it would be charged that African Americans were being "colonized" to vote for the Republican party.

54. Huey L. Perry, ed., *Race, Politics, and Governance in the United States* (Gainesville: University of Florida Press, 1997), 1; *Forum,* 14 April 1906, p. 2, col. 2. See also Joseph P. McCormick II and Charles E. Jones, "The Conceptualization of Deracialization: Thinking through the Dilemma," in *Dilemmas of Black Politics: Issues of Leadership and Strategy,* ed. Georgia A. Persons (New York: HarperCollins, 1993), 66–84; and Georgia Persons, "Towards a Reconstituted Black Politics?" in *Dilemmas of Black Politics,* ed. Persons, 225–45.

55. *East St. Louis Gazette,* 21 November 1874, p. 3, col. 3; Harold Gosnell, *Negro Politicians* (Chicago: University of Chicago Press, 1935), 83–84. See also Allen Spear, *Black Chicago: The Making of a Negro Ghetto, 1890–1920* (Chicago: University of Chicago Press, 1967), 118–20; and David Katzman, *Before the Ghetto: Black Detroit in the Nineteenth Century* (Urbana: University of Illinois Press, 1973), 203–6. According to Donald G. Nieman, under the caucus and convention system, Blacks in Washington County, Texas, were a powerful force in local and state politics during the 1870s and 1880s. See Donald G. Nieman, "Black Political Power and Criminal Justice: Washington County, Texas, 1868–1884," *Journal of Southern History* 55 (August 1989): 395–96. In Pulaski County, Carlson (Portwood)

found the opposite was true; there the primary system helped African Americans get on the ticket. See Carlson, "Black Community in the Rural North," 126.

56. *Forum*, 14 April 1906, p. 2, col. 2, 19 May 1906, p. 10, col. 2, and 28 July 1906, p. 7, col. 2; *Illinois Record*, 10 September 1898, p. 2, cols. 2–3. Carlson (Portwood) discusses the failure of white Republicans to endorse and support African Americans for elective office in Pulaski County, Illinois, during the period 1870 to 1900. See Carlson, "Black Community in the Rural North," 126–32.

57. The African American notion of manhood is perhaps best expressed by W. E. B. Du Bois on the purpose of education: "And the final product of our training must be neither a psychologist nor a brick mason, but a man. And to make men, we must have ideals, broad, pure, and inspiring ends of living—not sordid money-getting, not apples of gold." While such African American men as Frederick Douglass and W. E. B. Du Bois may have opposed male chauvinism, in general Black males' use of *manhood* embodied male supremacist notions similar to those manifested in white workers' usage of *manliness*. For workers, the term also connoted, according to David Montgomery "respectability, defiant egalitarianism, and patriarchal male supremacy." Nancy Fraser and Linda Gordon in their highly suggestive article on the historical development of the term *dependency* articulate the relationship(s) between independence, whiteness, and masculinity. See W. E. B. Du Bois, *The Souls of Black Folk* (1903; reprint, New York: Bantam Books, 1989), 19; David Montgomery, *Workers' Control in America: Studies in the History of Work, Technology, and Labor Struggles* (Cambridge: Cambridge University Press, 1979), 13–14; and Nancy Fraser and Linda Gordon, "A Genealogy of *Dependency*: Tracing a Keyword of the U.S. Welfare State," *Signs: Journal of Women in Culture and Society* 19 (Winter 1994): 309–36. See also David Roediger, *Towards the Abolition of Whiteness* (London: Verso, 1994), 127–80; and Gail Bederman, "'Civilization,' the Decline of Middle-Class Manliness, and Ida B. Wells's Antilynching Campaign (1892–94), *Radical History Review* 52 (Winter 1992): 5–30.

58. *Illinois Record*, 10 September 1898, p. 2, col. 2.

59. *Forum*, 20 October 1906, p. 2, col. 1.

60. *East St. Louis Journal*, 7 November 1906, p. 2, cols. 1–4 (chart entitled "Unofficial Vote Cast in East St. Louis at Election November 6, 1906"), and 8 November 1906, p. 2, col. 2; Gosnell, *Negro Politicians*, 83–84.

61. At Evans's death, he had $167.66 in the bank, $5.00 in his saving account, $40.00 of interest on a bank fund, and $38.00 of personal effects. His estate also received $2,708.00 from the sale of the "Woodworth" property. He died without leaving a will. After his debts of $2,527.00 were paid, including Elizabeth's widow's award of $938.00, her administratrix's commission of $177.52, and a bill of $7.30 to the Masonic Lodge, approximately $107.91 was given to each of his surviving children, Dennis, Jessie, Evelyn, and John L.

Elizabeth Evans was semi-illiterate (she could read but could not write), though the censuses from 1890 and 1910 list her as literate. As administratrix of John's estate, she signed the papers she filed with the St. Clair County Probate Court with a mark (*X*). See John Evans Probate Record, St. Clair County, Roll No. 269, Sequence No. 100041, Case No. 899 (1910); and *Population Schedules of the Tenth Census of the United States, 1880, Illinois, St. Clair County*, Roll 246, 17–18; and *East St. Louis Gazette*, 21 November 1874, p. 2, col. 3.

Chapter 5: Proletarianization, Dependency, and Underdevelopment, 1886–1910

1. *Population Schedules of the Tenth Census of the United States, 1880, Illinois, St. Clair County*, Roll 246, 19–24; *Population Schedules of the Twelfth Census of the United States, 1900, Illinois, St. Clair County*, Roll 342, 264–76; *Population Schedules of the Thirteenth Census of the United States, 1910, Illinois, St. Clair County*, Roll 323, 152–66. A discrepancy exists between the number of adult Black men and the number of employed Black males

as a result of classification. I have defined an adult male as at least eighteen years old, but industries employed males as young as fourteen.

2. *Population Schedules of the Twelfth Census of the United States, 1900, Illinois, St. Clair County*, Roll 342, 264–76; *Population Schedules of the Thirteenth Census of the United States, 1910, Illinois, St. Clair County*, Roll 323, 151–66; Jack S. Blocker Jr., "Patterns of African-American Migration in Illinois, 1860–1930," 3, 7–14 (Paper presented at the "Community-Building and Resistance: African Americans in the Land of Lincoln," Conference, April 1998, Southern Illinois University at Edwardsville).

3. Carole Marks, "Black Labor Migration: 1910–1920," *Insurgent Sociologist* 12, no. 4 (1985): 5–6; Carole Marks, "Black Workers and the Great Migration North," *Phylon* 46 (June 1985): 148–61; Carole Marks, *Farewell, We're Good and Gone: The Great Black Migration* (Bloomington: Indiana University Press, 1989), 4–18; Carole Marks, "The Bone and Sinew of the Race: Black Women, Domestic Service, and Labor Migration," *Marriage and Family Review* 19, no. 1/2 (1993): 150; Joe W. Trotter Jr., ed., *The Great Migration in Historical Perspective: New Dimensions of Race, Class, and Gender* (Bloomington: Indiana University Press, 1991), 1–21; Joe W. Trotter Jr., "African Americans in the City: The Industrial Era, 1900–1950," in *New African American Urban History*, ed. Goings and Mohl, 299–319; Kenneth Goings and Raymond A. Mohl, "Toward a New African American Urban History," *New African American Urban History*, ed. Goings and Mohl, 1–15. See also Johnson and Campbell, *Black Migration in America*, 65; Lewis, "From Peasant to Proletarian," 77–102; Portwood, "Black Migration to Pulaski County," 37–46; James R. Grossman, "Blowing the Trumpet: The Chicago Defender and the Black Migration to Illinois," *Illinois Historical Journal* 78 (Summer 1985): 82–96; and Lee Williams, "New Comers to the City: A Study of Black Population Growth in Toledo, Ohio, 1910–1930," *Ohio History* 89 (Winter 1980): 5–24

4. I compiled the names and occupations of men and women listed as "col" who resided on streets in Brooklyn. The directory included Black men in the following occupations: common laborers (57), farmers (12), artisans (4), storekeepers (3), saloon owners (2), teamsters (2), teacher (1), and bookkeeper (1). It also listed 11 employed African American women: 7 laundresses and 4 seamstresses. See *Directory of the City of East St. Louis for 1891–92*; and *Population Schedules of the Tenth Census of the United States, 1880, Illinois, St. Clair County*, Roll 246, 19–24. See also Horton, "Life and Times of Edward Ambush," 7; and Curry, *Free Black in Urban America*, appendix B.

5. Trotter, *Black Milwaukee*, 226. Trotter's periodization represents only the era covered in his monograph; he does not include the post–World War II era.

6. Logan, *Negro in American Life and Thought*; Gerald David Jaynes, *Branches without Roots: Genesis of the Black Working Class in the American South, 1862–1882* (New York: Oxford University Press, 1986); Jay Mandle, *The Roots of Black Poverty: The Southern Plantation Economy after the Civil War* (Durham, N.C.: Duke University Press, 1978); Jay Mandle, *Not Slave, Not Free: The African American Economic Experience since the Civil War* (Durham, N.C.: Duke University Press, 1992); Harold D. Woodman, "Class, Race, Politics, and the Modernization of the Postbellum South," *Journal of Southern History* 63 (Winter 1997): 3–22; Harper, *Metro-East*, 308; Theising, "Profitable Boundaries," 83–101; Blocker, "Patterns of African-American Migration in Illinois," 4–5; Arthur Moore, field notes, Federal Writers' Project, folder for Brooklyn, Illinois, Madison County, District 7, Illinois State Historical Library.

7. *Population Schedules of the Twelfth Census of the United States, 1900, Illinois, St. Clair County*, Roll 342, 264–76; *Population Schedules of the Ninth Census of the United States, 1870, Illinois, St. Clair County*, Roll 280, 620–25; *Population Schedules of the Tenth Census of the United States, 1880, Illinois, St. Clair County*, Roll 246, 19–24; *Population Schedules of the Thirteenth Census of the United States, 1910, Illinois, St. Clair County*, Roll 323, 152–66; *The Social and Economic Status of the Black Population in the United States: An Historical View, 1790–1978* (Washington, D.C.: Bureau of the Census, 1978): 72; Carlson, "Black

Community in the Rural North," table 7, 141; Christopher K. Hays, "The African American Struggle for Equality and Justice in Cairo, Illinois, 1865–1900," *Illinois Historical Journal* 90 (Winter 1997): 267–68.

8. *Population Schedules of the Twelfth Census of the United States, 1900, Illinois, St. Clair County,* Roll 342, 264–76; *Population Schedules of the Thirteenth Census of the United States, 1910, Illinois, St. Clair County,* Roll 323, 164, 166; *The Social and Economic Status of the Black Population in the United States: An Historical View, 1790–1978,* 72; Katzman, *Before the Ghetto,* 105.

9. James C. Davis, interviews by author, 1 August, 2 August, and 3 August 1989.

10. Suzanne Model, "The Effects of Ethnicity in the Workplace on Blacks, Italians, and Jews in 1910 New York," *Journal of Urban History* 16 (November 1989): 29–31; Rudwick, *Race Riot at East St. Louis,* 22 (quote on Swift); Monsanto Chemical Works, *Monsanto,* 17 (emphasis added); Ronald Bailey, "Economic Aspects of the Black Internal Colony," in *Structures of Dependency,* ed. Frank Bonilla and Robert Girling (Stanford, Calif.: Institute of Political Studies, Stanford University, 1973), 56; Wright, *Life behind a Veil,* 79; Mandle, *Roots of Black Poverty;* Leon Litwack, *Been in the Storm So Long: The Aftermath of Slavery* (New York: Vintage, 1980); Roger L. Ransom and Richard Sutch, *One Kind of Freedom: The Economic Consequences of Emancipation* (London: Cambridge University Press, 1983); Trotter, *Black Milwaukee,* xii. See also Thomas, *Life for Us Is What We Make It,* 42; Trotter, *Black Milwaukee,* 226–41; Katzman, *Before the Ghetto,* table 13, 219; and Kenneth L. Kusmer, *A Ghetto Takes Shape: Black Cleveland, 1870–1930* (Urbana: University of Illinois Press, 1976), table 9, 74.

11. *Population Schedules of the Tenth Census of the United States, 1880, Illinois, St. Clair County,* Roll 246, 19; Katzman, *Before the Ghetto,* table 11, 218; Kusmer, *Ghetto Takes Shape,* table 7, 71; Blassingame, *Black New Orleans,* table 7, 230 (urban South); W. H. Harris, "Work and Family in Black Atlanta," 319–30.

12. Harry Braverman, *Labor and Monopoly Capital: The Degradation of Work in the Twentieth Century* (New York: Monthly Review, 1974), 444; *Population Schedules of the Twelfth Census of the United States, 1900, Illinois, St. Clair County,* Roll 342, 264–76; *Population Schedules of the Thirteenth Census of the United States, 1910, Illinois, St. Clair County,* Roll 323, 151–66; David Brody, *The Butcher Workmen: A Study of Unionization* (Cambridge, Mass.: Harvard University Press, 1964): 4–5; James R. Barrett, "Unity and Fragmentation: Class, Race, and Ethnicity on Chicago's South Side, 1900–1922," in *"Struggle a Hard Battle": Essays on Working-Class Immigrants,* ed. Dirk Hoerder (De Kalb: Northern Illinois University Press, 1986), 233; David F. Noble, *Forces of Production: A Social History of Industrial Automation* (New York: Oxford University Press, 1986).

13. D. J. Harris, "Black Ghetto as Colony," 11 (quote); Donald J. Harris, "Capitalist Exploitation and Black Labor: Some Conceptual Issues," *Review of Black Political Economy* 8 (Winter 1978): 133–51.

14. R. C. Hill, "Race, Class, and the State," 47 (quote), 48.

15. Whatley, "African-American Strikebreaking from the Civil War to the New Deal," 537–38.

16. *Population Schedules of the Thirteenth Census of the United States, 1910, Illinois, St. Clair County,* Roll 323, 151–66; Sharon Harley, "When Your Work Is Not Who You Are: The Development of a Working-Class Consciousness among Afro-American Women," in *We Specialize in the Wholly Impossible: A Reader in Black Women's History,* ed. Darlene Clark Hine, Wilma King, and Linda Reed (Brooklyn, N.Y.: Carlson, 1995), 26; Ruthie Bennett, interview by author, 30 May 1997; David Katzman, *Seven Days a Week: Women and Domestic Service in Industrializing America* (New York: Oxford University Press, 1978); Katzman, *Before the Ghetto,* 222; Glenn, "From Servitude to Service Work," 8; Monica L. Jackson, "And Still We Rise: African American Women and the U.S. Labor Market," *Feminist Issues* 10 (Fall 1990): 58; Wright, *Life behind a Veil,* 79; Trotter, *Black Milwaukee,* 250.

17. *Population Schedules of the Thirteenth Census of the United States, 1910, Illinois, St. Clair County,* Roll 323, 153–54, 160, 161, 163, 166; Harley, "When Your Work Is Not Who You Are," 27, 26; Earl Lewis, *In Their Own Interests: Race, Class, and Power in Twentieth-Century Norfolk, Virginia* (Berkeley: University of California Press, 1991), 35–36; Earl Lewis, "Expectations, Economic Opportunities, and Life in the Industrial Age: Black Migration to Norfolk, Virginia, 1910–1945," in *Great Migration in Historical Perspective,* ed. Trotter, 27; Shirley J. Portwood, "Black Victoria," *Journal of Negro History* 77 (Spring 1992): 61–73.

Norma J. Burgess and Haywood Derrick Horton cited several factors for Black women's disproportionate labor participation rate, including "economic necessity, societal expectations, structural conditions, and past familial experiences," but they selected gender role socialization for further study, implying that culture in the form of "generational transmissions" was the central factor. Conversely, Sharon Harley offered a materialist explanation. She unequivocally declared poverty rather than Afro-American cultural values explained married Black women's historically high labor participation rates. In support of her argument, Harley presented numerous examples of Black male and middle-class Black women's opposition to women working outside of the home. See Norma J. Burgess and Haywood Derrick Horton, "African American Women and Work: A Socio-Historical Perspective," *Journal of Family History* 18, no. 1 (1993): 55; and Harley, "When Your Work Is Not Who You Are," 27.

18. *Population Schedules of the Thirteenth Census of the United States, 1910, Illinois, St. Clair County,* Roll 323, 153–54, 160, 161, 163, 166.

19. Marks, "Bone and Sinew of the Race," 154; *Population Schedules of the Thirteenth Census of the United States, 1910, Illinois, St. Clair County,* Roll 323, 151–66.

20. Bateman and Selby, *Historical Encyclopedia of Illinois,* 706; Harper, *Metro-East,* 82–84.

21. *Forum,* 26 May 1906, p. 2, cols. 2–3.

22. "C. B. Carroll's Brooklyn City Directory, 1905," 18; "Gould's Brooklyn Business Directory, 1906," in *East St. Louis City Directory* (East St. Louis: East St. Louis Directory Publishing, 1912), 801–2; *Population Schedules of the Thirteenth Census of the United States, 1910, Illinois, St. Clair County,* Roll 323, 156–58, 160, 163; Davis, interviews by author, 1 and 3 August 1989; Bateman and Selby, *Historical Encyclopedia of Illinois,* 706; *Forum,* 26 May 1906, p. 2, cols. 2–3; Hamilton, *Black Towns and Profit,* 16, 34.

23. *Population Schedules of the Thirteenth Census of the United States, 1910, Illinois, St. Clair County,* Roll 323, 156, 158–59. William Terry, Brooklyn's town clerk, was the census enumerator. Terry identified Ms. Purgley as "black." The thirty-three-year-old Purgley boarded with James and Josephine Beasley. Terry listed the entire household as "black." Beasley was a judge who had previously been the postmaster and a schoolteacher. He and Josephine had been recorded as "white" in every census and city directory since 1891. Purgley was most likely white as well.

24. *Cleveland Gazette,* quoted in Katrina Hazzard-Gordon, *Jookin': The Rise of Social Dance Formations in African-American Culture* (Philadelphia: Temple University Press, 1990), 129; "Gould's Brooklyn Business Directory, 1906," 802–3; *Population Schedules of the Tenth United States Census, 1880, Illinois, St. Clair County,* Roll 246, 21; *East St. Louis Gazette,* 1 May 1886, p. 3, col. 3, and 21 November 1874, p. 3, col. 2; *State Capital,* 30 January 1892, p. 1, col. 3, and 13 February 1892, p. 1, col. 7; *Directory of the City of East St. Louis for 1891–92;* "C. B. Carroll's Brooklyn City Directory, 1903," 240–41; *Population Schedules of the Thirteenth Census of the United States, 1910, Illinois, St. Clair County,* Roll 323, 151–66; Davis, interviews by author, 1 and 3 August 1989; Roger Lane, *Roots of Violence in Black Philadelphia, 1860–1900* (Cambridge, Mass.: Harvard University Press, 1986).

25. *Population Schedules of the Thirteenth Census of the United States, 1910, Illinois, St. Clair County,* Roll 323, 151–66.

26. Rudwick, *Race Riot at East St. Louis,* 197; Dillard, "Civil Liberties of Negroes in Illinois since 1865," 608. See also Theising, "Profitable Boundaries," 109–10.

27. *Population Schedules of the Thirteenth Census of the United States, 1910, Illinois, St. Clair County,* Roll 323, 151–66.

28. Lane, *Roots of Violence in Black Philadelphia,* 114; *East St. Louis Journal,* 19 March 1892, p. 2, col. 6; Davis, interview by author, 3 August 1989.

29. Hamilton, *Black Towns and Profit,* 9, 28, 55–56; Crockett, *Black Towns,* 54–55; *St. Louis Palladium,* 23 January 1904, p. 4, col. 2; Kevin K. Gaines, *Uplifting the Race: Black Leadership, Politics, and Culture in the Twentieth Century* (Chapel Hill: University of North Carolina Press, 1996), 128–51; Virginia Boynton, "Contested Terrain: The Struggle over Gender Norms for Black Working-Class Women in Cleveland's Phillis Wheatley Association, 1920–1950," *Ohio History* 103 (Winter/ Spring 1994): 5–22; Brown and Kimball, "Mapping the Terrain of Black Richmond," 66–115, especially 97–105; Portwood, "Black Victoria," 61–73; Cynthia Neverdon-Morton, *Afro-American Women of the South and the Advancement of the Race, 1895–1925* (Knoxville: University of Tennessee Press, 1989).

30. *Population Schedules of the Thirteenth Census of the United States, 1910, Illinois, St. Clair County,* Roll 323, 153, 155–57, 164; Marks, "Bone and Sinew of the Race," 163; Hunter, "Making a Way," 232–34.

31. *Population Schedules of the Thirteenth Census of the United States, 1910, Illinois, St. Clair County,* Roll 323, 153, 155–57; Davis, interview by the author, 3 August 1989. Davis was extremely knowledgeable about the history of vice in the area, perhaps because of his involvement. At his death on 23 September 1996, he was facing federal charges for accepting bribes to protect a prostitution ring operating out of two white-owned massage parlors located in Brooklyn. See *Belleville News Democrat,* 24 September 1996, p. B3, cols. 1–2.

32. *Forum,* 26 May 1906, p. 2, cols. 2–3; *Population Schedules of the Thirteenth Census of the United States, 1910, Illinois, St. Clair County,* Roll 323, 155–57.

33. Davis, interview by the author, August 3, 1989; the Maher-Maher-Claybrooks transactions appear in St. Clair County Recorder of Deeds, *Book 376,* 209, and *Book 334, 437;* "C. B. Carroll's Brooklyn City Directory, 1903," 241–42, 254; St. Clair County Recorder of Deeds, *Book 326,* 140, *Book 332,* 607, *Book 376,* 209, *Book 334,* 201, 437, 463, *Book 276,* 426, *Book 390,* 65, 67, 70, 89, *Book 388,* 151, *Book 354,* 566, *Book 396,* 403, *Book 342,* 396, and *Book 360,* 387.

34. *Population Schedules of the Thirteenth Census of the United States, 1910, Illinois, St. Clair County,* Roll 323, 152–53, 163.

35. Ibid., 151–66.

36. Rose, "All-Negro Town," 360–61. See also S. Philip Morgan, Antonio McDaniel, Andrew T. Miller, and Samuel H. Preston, "Racial Difference in Household and Family Structure at the Turn of the Century," *American Journal of Sociology* 98 (January 1993): 798–828; Hunter, "Making a Way," 233–34; Harriette Pipes McAdoo, "Transgenerational Patterns of Upward Mobility in African-American Families," in *Black Families,* ed. McAdoo, 148–68; and Sudarkasa, "Interpreting the African Heritage in Afro-American Family Organization," 37–53.

37. *Population Schedules of the Tenth Census of the United States, 1880, Illinois, St. Clair County,* Roll 246, 19–24; *Population Schedules of the Twelfth Census of the United States, 1900, Illinois, St. Clair County,* Roll 342, 264–76; *Population Schedules of the Thirteenth Census of the United States, 1910, Illinois, St. Clair County,* Roll 323, 151–66.

38. *Population Schedules of the Twelfth Census of the United States, 1900, Illinois, St. Clair County,* Roll 342, 264–76; *Population Schedules of the Thirteenth Census of the United States, 1910, Illinois, St. Clair County,* Roll 323, 151–66.

39. *Population Schedules of the Tenth Census of the United States, 1880, Illinois, St. Clair County,* Roll 246, 19–24; *Population Schedules of the Twelfth Census of the United States, 1900, Illinois, St. Clair County,* Roll 342, 264–76; *Population Schedules of the Thirteenth Census of the United States, 1910, Illinois, St. Clair County,* Roll 323, 151–66.

40. McDaniel, "Power of Culture," 31, 32; Antonio McAdoo, "Historical Racial Differ-

ences in Living Arrangements of Children," *Journal of Family History* 19, no. 1 (1994): 64, 68; *Population Schedules of the Thirteenth Census of the United States, 1910, Illinois, St. Clair County*, Roll 323, 155, 159; Morgan et al., "Racial Difference in Household and Family Structure at the Turn of the Century," 823; Hunter, "Making a Way," 237–38.

41. *Population Schedules of the Ninth Census of the United States, 1870, Illinois, St. Clair County*, Roll 280, 620–25; *Population Schedules of the Tenth Census of the United States, 1880, Illinois, St. Clair County*, Roll 246, 19–24; *Population Schedules of the Twelfth Census of the United States, 1900, Illinois, St. Clair County*, Roll 342, 264–76; *Population Schedules of the Thirteenth Census of the United States, 1910, Illinois, St. Clair County*, Roll 323, 151–66.

42. Bethel, *Promiseland*, 122–23; Marks, "Bone and Sinew of the Race," 151; Grossman, *Land of Hope*, 105–7; Darlene Clark Hine, "Black Migration to the Urban Midwest: The Gender Dimension, 1915–1945," in *Great Migration in Historical Perspective*, ed. Trotter, 132; *Population Schedules of the Thirteenth Census of the United States, 1910, Illinois, St. Clair County*, Roll 323, 151–66, especially 152, 158. The three neglected but necessary tasks Marks pointed out that women performed included (1) sustaining the family while her husband, father, or sibling sought work elsewhere or finding work for herself in the new area; (2) contributing to the transportation cost from the peripheral to the core area; and (3) supporting themselves or supplementing the family's income once the family arrived in the core area.

43. *Population Schedules of the Twelfth Census of the United States, 1900, Illinois, St. Clair County*, Roll 342, 264–76; *Population Schedules of the Thirteenth Census of the United States, 1910, Illinois, St. Clair County*, Roll 323, 151–66.

44. Morgan et al., "Racial Difference in Household and Family Structure at the Turn of the Century," 807; *Population Schedules of the Thirteenth Census of the United States, 1910, Illinois, St. Clair County*, Roll 323, 151–66. The Public Use Samples are self-weighting samples of households derived from microfilm copies of manuscript census reports.

Chapter 6: The Black Municipality and the White Colonial County, 1898–1915

1. "Gould's Brooklyn Directory, 1906," 796; *East St. Louis Journal,* 22 October 1906, p. 2, col. 4, and 20 February 1903, p. 2, col. 3; *Forum,* 14 April 1906, p. 2, col. 2; "McCoy's Brooklyn City Directory, 1896," 400; "McCoy's Brooklyn City Directory, 1897–98," 388; "C. B. Carroll's Brooklyn City Directory, 1898–99," 444; "C. B. Carroll's Brooklyn City Directory, 1900," *East St. Louis City Directory* (East St. Louis: Republican Print, 1900), 470; "C. B. Carroll's Brooklyn City Directory, 1903," 232–59; "C. B. Carroll's Brooklyn City Directory, 1905," 20.

John Evans is listed in the "Gould's Brooklyn Directory, 1906" on page 796 as a village trustee, but he is not included among the town's officers on page 794. During Evans's 1906 run for the state legislature, the *Forum* claimed he was a current trustee in Brooklyn. The evidence tends to support the view that Evans was a board member in 1906.

2. *East St. Louis Journal,* 20 February 1903, p. 2, col. 3; "C. B. Carroll's Brooklyn City Directory, 1903," 232–59.

3. *East St. Louis Journal,* 20 February 1903, p. 2, col. 3, and 9 May 1915, p. 1, col. 3; "C. B. Carroll's Brooklyn City Directory, 1905," 20.

4. Nore, "African Americans in Edwardsville City History," 6; St. Clair County Recorder, *Marriage License Index,* 66, 191–93.

5. *Population Schedules of the Tenth Census of the United States, 1880, Illinois, St. Clair County,* Roll 246, 621, 623. *East St. Louis Gazette,* 1 May 1903, p. 3, col. 3; *State Capital,* 30 January 1892, p. 1, col. 3, and 13 February 1892, p. 1, col. 7; *Directory of the City of East St. Louis for 1891–92;* "C. B. Carroll's Brooklyn City Directory, 1903," 240–41; "Gould's Brooklyn Business Directory, 1906," 802–3.

Jennings was a worker, and Evans and Barnes had been driven into the proletariat, though Barnes was able to retain his farm. Barnes's class position is complicated because while he worked in the stockyards, he employed a farm laborer to tend his farm.

6. "C. B. Carroll's Brooklyn City Directory, 1897–98," 388; "C. B. Carroll's Brooklyn City Directory, 1898–99," 444; "C. B. Carroll's Brooklyn City Directory, 1900," 470; "C. B. Carroll's Brooklyn City Directory, 1903," 249; "C. B. Carroll's Brooklyn City Directory, 1905," 20; "Gould's Brooklyn Business Directory, 1906," 794–800.

7. *Illinois Record,* 23 March 1898, p. 3, col. 2; "C. B. Carroll's Brooklyn City Directory, 1905," 20 (quote).

8. "McCoy's Brooklyn City Directory, 1897–98," 388–89; "McCoy's Brooklyn City Directory, 1896," 400; *Illinois Record,* 23 April 1898, p. 3, col. 1.

Jesse Hollman appears as a village trustee in the 1897–98 city directory on page 383, but on page 389 his name is spelled with only one *l.* In the 1898–99 directory, it is spelled with one *l.* See "McCoy's Brooklyn City Directory, 1897–98," 383, 389; and "C. B. Carroll's Brooklyn City Directory, 1898–99," 445.

9. "C. B. Carroll's Brooklyn City Directory, 1903," 236, 240–41, 243; "C. B. Carroll's Brooklyn City Directory, 1897–98," 389; "C. B. Carroll's Brooklyn City Directory, 1898–99," 445–47; "C. B. Carroll's Brooklyn City Directory, 1900," 471.

10. "C. B. Carroll's Brooklyn City Directory, 1903," 241–42, 254; Carmichael and Hamilton, *Black Power,* 46; James Beasley's 1898 campaign for the school board against Vanderberg was an exception to the Evans group's general policy.

11. *Broadax,* 1 May 1897, p. 1, col. 4, and 18 November 1899, p. 1, cols. 1–2.

12. Since there are no extant membership lists of either party, I determined that party members elected to the village board of trustees were leaders of their respective party. I then examined the class of the board members affiliated with each party between 1896 and 1903. The 1903 city directory identifies members of the Peoples party on the village board. Admittedly, this method is imprecise, but in the light of the scanty information available, it is the best reconstruction of each party's leadership that I can produce at this time.

13. *East St. Louis Journal,* 27 January 1898, p. 3, col. 4; "C. B. Carroll's Brooklyn City Directory, 1898–99," 445; "C. B. Carroll's Brooklyn City Directory, 1900"; "Brooklyn, Illinois," in *East St. Louis and the East Side City Directory, 1912* (East St. Louis: East St. Louis Directory Publishing, 1912), 303. See also *East St. Louis Journal,* 27 February 1913, p. 3, col. 5.

James H. Thomas, Brooklyn's marshal, most likely issued the riot call. Edward Green was on the board of trustees in 1912 and 1913. He was erroneously identified by the *East St. Louis Journal* as having participated in an embezzlement scheme devised by Mayor Randall Cole.

14. Bail Bond to Sheriff, statements included in Frederick F. Vanderberg Criminal Case Files, St. Clair County, Roll No. 267, Sequence No. 100111, Case No. 121 (1899); *Population Schedules of the Tenth Census of the United States, 1880, Illinois, St. Clair County,* Roll 246, 21; *East St. Louis Journal,* 8 May 1899, p. 3, col. 4, and 10 May 1899, p. 3, col. 6; Frederick F. Vanderberg St. Clair County Criminal Case Files, 1903, Criminal Case Files Cross Reference List as of 7-7-82, 1024, microfilm, St. Clair County Circuit Court; Frederick F. Vanderberg Criminal Case Files, St. Clair County, Roll No. 276, Sequence No. 1000158, Case No. 008 (1899), Roll No. 276, Sequence No. 100111, Case No. 121 (1899), and Roll No. 302, Sequence No. 100074, Case No. 148 (1899); "C. B. Carroll's Brooklyn City Directory, 1903," 236.

15. *East St. Louis Journal,* 14 March 1892, p. 1, col. 1, 1892, and 25 March 1892, p. 2, cols. 3–4.

Nothing suggests that the Flannigan group was a branch of the populist Peoples party. It was probably adopted because its opponents were called the Citizens party.

16. John Evans was temporarily out of elective office. He was now a painting contractor, but the teachers who were allied with him were reasserting their dominance in town and township politics. The school principal and the first and second assistant principals

all held political office. Washington, the mayor, was first assistant principal. Charles Jones was still principal, but he had replaced Evans as the supervisor for Stites Township. Fred A. Jones, the second assistant principal, was a tax collector for the township. In 1902, Evans returned to politics and won the election for tax collector. See "C. B. Carroll's Brooklyn City Directory, 1898–99," 444; "C. B. Carroll's Brooklyn City Directory, 1900," 470; "C. B. Carroll's Brooklyn City Directory, 1903," 238, 241, 244, 249; and "C. B. Carroll's Brooklyn City Directory, 1900," 472.

17. Bateman and Selby, *Historical Encyclopedia of Illinois,* 707; *East St. Louis Journal,* 13 November 1900, p. 3, col. 2; "Republican-inspired plot" quoted in Rudwick, *Race Riot at East St. Louis,* 10.

18. Bateman and Selby, *Historical Encyclopedia of Illinois,* 707; *East St. Louis Journal,* 20 December 1905, p. 2, col. 3. Nevertheless, the realty company's motives may have been questionable. Elliott Rudwick reported that after the 2 July 1917 race riot, the Real Estate Exchange "revived" plans to establish a separate territory for Black East St. Louisians. See Rudwick, *Race Riot at East St. Louis,* 70.

19. *Population Schedules of the Twelfth Census of the United States, 1900, Illinois, St. Clair County,* Roll 342, 158; "C. B. Carroll's Brooklyn City Directory, 1903," 236–44; "C. B. Carroll's Brooklyn City Directory, 1905," 20; Thomas R. Pegram, "The Dry Machine: The Formation of the Anti-Saloon League of Illinois," *Illinois Historical Journal* 83 (Summer 1990): 177, 184; Norman H. Clark, *Deliver Us from Evil: An Interpretation of American Prohibition* (New York: W. W. Norton, 1976).

In 1883, the Illinois legislature passed the Harper High License Act, which established the minimum costs for liquor licenses. A license to sell hard liquor cost $500, and one for only beer and malt liquors cost $150.

20. Frederick F. Vanderberg St. Clair County Criminal Case Files, 1903, Criminal Case Files Cross Reference List as of 7-7-82, 1024, microfilm, St. Clair County Circuit Court; *East St.Louis Journal,* 20 February 1903, p. 2, col. 3.

21. *East St. Louis Journal,* 20 February 1903, p. 2, col. 3.

22. "McCoy's Brooklyn City Directory, 1897–98," 390; "C. B. Carroll's Brooklyn City Directory, 1898–99," 447; "C. B. Carroll's Brooklyn City Directory, 1900," 476; "C. B. Carroll's Brooklyn City Directory, 1903," 259; "Gould's Brooklyn Directory, 1906," 800; *Population Schedules of the Thirteenth Census of the United States, 1910, Illinois, St. Clair County,* Roll 323, 151–66; "Brooklyn, Illinois," 313.

23. "C. B. Carroll's Brooklyn City Directory, 1903," 236–44; *St. Louis Palladium,* 7 July 1906, p. 4, col. 2.

24. *East St. Louis Journal,* 8 June 1903, p. 3, col. 3; *Chicago Tribune,* 10 June 1903, p. 12, col. 2; *Washington (D.C.) Bee,* 27 June 1903, p. 1, col. 4; *State Capital,* 30 January 1892, p. 1, col. 3; "C. B. Carroll's Brooklyn City Directory, 1903," 238. See also Dennis B. Downey, "A 'Many-Headed Monster': The 1903 Lynching of David Wyatt," *Journal of Illinois History* 92 (Spring 1999): 2–16.

25. *State Capital,* 2 January 1892, p. 1, col. 1; *Illinois Record,* 29 January 1898, p. 2, cols. 1–2.

26. *East St. Louis Journal,* 30 September 1896, p. 3, col. 2; *Illinois Record,* 12 February 1898, p. 2, col. 2.

27. *St. Louis Post-Dispatch,* 7 June 1903, p. 1, col. 7; *East St. Louis Journal,* 8 June 1903, p. 3, col. 3 (quote); *Chicago Tribune,* 7 June 1903, p. 1, col. 6; *Belleville Weekly Advocate,* 12 June 1903, p. 2, cols. 1–4.

28. *St. Louis Post-Dispatch,* 7 June 1903, p. 1, col. 3, 8 June 1903, p. 10, cols. 3–4, and 14 June 1903, p. 3, col. 4.

29. Ibid., 8 June 1903, p. 10, cols. 3–4; *East St. Louis Journal,* 8 June 1903, p. 3, col. 3.

30. *East St. Louis Journal,* 8 June 1903, p. 3, col. 3.

31. Ibid. (emphasis added).

32. Ibid., 5 June 1903, p. 1, col. 3; *Belleville Weekly Advocate,* 5 June 1903, p. 6, col. 3.

33. *St. Louis Post-Dispatch,* 5 June 1903, p. 1, col. 1, and 11 June 1903, p. 4, col. 3. For a sanitized account of these events, see Bateman and Shelby, *Historical Encyclopedia of Illinois,* 748–49. Bateman and Shelby portray Mayor Kern in a heroic and tragic light.

34. *Belleville Weekly Advocate,* 26 June 1903, p. 4, cols. 1–4; *St. Louis Post-Dispatch,* 11 June 1903, p. 4, col. 3.

35. *St. Louis Post-Dispatch,* 9 June 1903, p. 1, col. 1, and 10 June 1903, p. 10, col. 1; *East St. Louis Journal,* 12 June 1903, p. 3, col. 1; *St. Louis Palladium,* 13 June 1903, p. 1, col. 4.

36. *St. Louis Palladium,* 13 June 1903, p. 1, col. 4.; *Decatur Daily Review,* 4 June 1893, p. 1, col. 4; *Decatur Republican,* 4 June 1893, p. 3, col. 7; *Broadax,* 12 June 1897, p. 1, col. 3. See also Sundiata K. Cha-Jua, "'Join Hands and Hearts with Law and Order': The 1893 Lynching of Samuel J. Bush and the Response of Decatur's African American Community," *Illinois Historical Journal* 83 (Autumn 1990): 195–96.

37. *East St. Louis Journal,* 12 June 1903, p. 3, col. 2.

38. Cox, *Caste, Class, and Race,* 551–60.
Cox underemphasized the extent of Afro-American resistance, however. Black activists, especially in the North, often blockaded the community against invasion and mobilized residents into defense networks. See Dominic J. Capeci Jr., "The Lynching of Cleo Wright: Federal Protection of Constitutional Rights during World War II," *Journal of American History* 72 (December 1986): 859–87; Cha-Jua, "'Join Hands and Hearts with Law and Order,'" 199–20; and Cha-Jua, "'Warlike Demonstration.'"

39. *St. Louis Palladium,* 23 January 1904, p. 4, col. 2; *Decatur Daily Review,* 17 August 1908, p. 4, cols. 3–4; Cha-Jua, "'Join Hands and Hearts with Law and Order,'" 200. See also Gaines, *Uplifting the Race.*

40. *St. Louis Palladium,* 23 January 1904, p. 4, col. 25 (first and second quotes), and 5 September 1903, p. 1., col. 4 (third quote). For evidence that the BTWIL used both moral suasion and direct action, see ibid., 3 October 1903, p. 1, col. 3.

41. Ibid., 9 January 1904, p. 4, col. 1 ("populated" quote), 29 August 1903, p. 1, cols. 1–2 ("purity" quote), 5 September 1903, p. 1, col. 4, 12 September 1903, p. 1, col. 1 ("thieves" quote), 19 September 1903, p. 1, col. 3 ("quite a number" quote), 26 September 1903, p. 1, cols. 3–4, 10 October 1903, p. 5, col. 3 ("beaten" and "threatened" quotes), and 23 January 1904, p. 4, col. 2 (Essence's fears quotes).

42. Ibid., 12 September 1903, p. 1, cols. 1–2, 26 September 1903, p. 1, cols. 3–4, 3 October 1903, p. 5, col. 3, 10 October 1903, p. 5, col. 3, 7 November 1903, p. 8, col. 2, 5 March 1904, p. 8, col. 2.

43. Ibid., 26 March 1904, p. 8, col. 1 ("anybody" quote), 27 February 1904, p. 8, col. 1 ("dialectical logic" and "erroneous ideas" quotes), col. 4 ("White Wall" and "Sneak" quotes), 23 January 1904, p. 4, col. 2 ("respectable citizens" quote), 12 September 1903, p. 1, col. 1 ("young men and young women" quote), 5 March 1904, p. 8, cols. 2–3, 12 March 1904, p. 8, col. 4.

44. Ibid., 10 October 1903, p. 5, col. 5 (first Essence quotes), 14 November 1903, p. 8, col. 2 ("closing of plants" quote), and 7 November 1903, p. 8, col. 2 ("Charge brave soldiers" quote); Hazzard-Gordon, *Jookin',* 173.

45. *St. Louis Palladium,* 23 January 1904, p. 4, col. 2, and 30 April 1904, p. 1, col. 5; Peter Baldwin, "Antiprostitution Reform and the Use of Public Space in Hartford, Connecticut, 1878–1914," *Journal of Urban History* 23 (September 1997): 709–38.

46. *St. Louis Palladium,* 23 April 1904, p. 1, col. 3, and 2 May 1903, quoted in Lawrence O. Christensen, "The Racial Views of John W. Wheeler," *Missouri Historical Review* 67 (July 1973): 537. Wheeler became a minister in 1903, and on at least two occasions, he served as interim minister at St. Paul's AME Church in St. Louis.

47. *St. Louis Palladium,* 30 April 1904, p. 1, col. 5, 28 May 1904, p. 1, col. 4, and 16 April 1904, p. 1, col. 6 (quote).

48. Quoted in Christensen, "Racial Views of John W. Wheeler," 542.

49. *St. Louis Palladium,* 7 July 1906, p. 4, col. 2.

50. *East St. Louis Journal,* 22 October 1906, p. 2, col. 4.

In 1906, Burton Washington was elected mayor. John Evans and Benjamin Jones were the only members reelected from the previous board of trustees. Charles S. Dorman replaced Anthony Speed as marshal, and William Terry was reelected clerk. George Hicks, the assistant marshal, was a Euro-American. See *East St. Louis Journal,* 22 October 1906, p. 2, col. 4; and *Population Schedules of the Thirteenth Census of the United States, 1910, Illinois, St. Clair County,* Roll 323, 162.

51. Hamilton, *Black Towns and Profit,* 110, 131.

52. Robert Jackson et al. Criminal Case Files, St. Clair County, Roll No. 22, Sequence No. 100078, Case No. 3579 (1913) (quotes); "Brooklyn, Illinois," 303; "C. B. Carroll's Brooklyn City Directory, 1903," 247; "Gould's Brooklyn Directory, 1906," 795–96; "Gould's Brooklyn Business Directory, 1906," 801; *State Capital,* 12 December 1891, p. 1, cols. 2–3; "C. B. Carroll's Brooklyn City Directory, 1898–99," 445; *East St. Louis Journal,* 27 February 1913, p. 3, col. 5.

Bletson's older brother Henry, the town clerk in John Evans's second administration, died in office and was replaced by Burton Washington in 1891. Oscar Bletson, a trustee from 1896 to 1898, lost his seat during the Peoples party's 1898 sweep of board positions. Edward Green was a principal participant in the Brooklyn riot of 1898. See *East St. Louis Journal,* 27 January 1898, p. 3, col. 4.

53. Robert Jackson et al. Criminal Case Files, St. Clair County, Roll No. 22, Sequence No. 100078, Case No. 3579 (1913).

54. Ibid.

55. Ibid.

56. Frederick F. Vanderberg Criminal Case Files, St. Clair County, Roll No. 000072, Sequence No. 100111, Case No. 003894 (1913), Roll No. 000074, Sequence No. 100063, Case No. 002337 (1913), and Roll No. 000220, Sequence No. 100175, Case No. 003850 (1913).

57. W. E. B. Du Bois, *Black Reconstruction in America: An Essay toward the History of the Part Which Black Folk Played in the Attempt to Reconstruct Democracy in America, 1860–1880* (1935; reprint, New York: Harcourt Brace, 1962), 724. See also Rabinowitz, *Southern Black Leaders of the Reconstruction Era;* Holt, *Black over White;* and Anderson, *Race and Politics in North Carolina.*

58. *East St. Louis Journal,* 30 May 1915, p. 3, col. 5.

59. Frederick F. Vanderberg Criminal Case Files, St. Clair County, Roll No. 000072, Sequence No. 100111, Case No. 003894 (1913), Roll No. 000074, Sequence No. 100063, Case No. 002337 (1913), and Roll No. 000220, Sequence No. 100175, Case No. 003850 (1913); Rudwick, *Race Riot at East St. Louis,* 197–200; Dillard, "Civil Liberties of Negroes in Illinois since 1865," 608.

60. Rudwick, *Race Riot at East St. Louis,* 184, 199; Dillard, "Civil Liberties of Negroes in Illinois since 1865," 608.

61. *East St. Louis Journal,* 7 May 1915, p. 3, col. 6, 9 May 1915, p. 1, col. 3, and 30 May 1915, p. 3, col. 5; "Gould's Brooklyn Directory, 1906," 796; "C. B. Carroll's Brooklyn City Directory, 1905," 18; "Brooklyn, Illinois," 304, 309, 313. Both William Wests also signed the petition.

In 1933, a similar event occurred. Henry L. Moore reported in 1933 that two political organizations existed in Brooklyn: the Brooklyn Democratic Club, a local representative of the Progressive Club, and the Republican Club, which embraced the Peoples Improvement party. The police force, led by Chief Tobias Crittendon, killed one man and intimidated voters. The county sheriff's office took control and replaced the police force. See Schoen, *Tales of an All-Night Town,* 81.

62. *East St. Louis Journal,* 7 May 1915, p. 3, col. 6, 9 May 1915, p. 1, col. 3, 30 May 1915, p. 3, col. 5, and 16 February 1913, p. 3, col. 5; "Gould's Brooklyn Directory, 1906," 796.

63. James H. Thomas Sr. et al. Criminal Case Files, St. Clair County, Roll No. 000075,

Sequence No. 100139, Case No. 005927 (1915), and Roll No. 000079, Sequence No. 100063, Case No. 006420 (1917).

64. *East St. Louis Journal,* 7 May 1915, p. 3, col. 6, and 9 May 1915, p. 1, col. 3.

65. The newspaper accounts must be read with caution because on 7 May, the *Journal* reported that John L. Evans's ticket was not permitted on the ballot, but on May 9, it claimed it was James Thomas's slate that was not allowed on the ballot. According to the 7 May article, Evans filed suit, but according to the article on 9 May, Thomas did. By comparing the newspaper reports with the indictments, I have determined that the suit was brought by John L. Evans and the Peoples Improvement party. See *East St. Louis Journal,* 7 May 1915, p. 3, col. 6, and 9 May 1915, p. 1, col.3.

66. Ibid.

67. Ibid., 11 May 1905, p. 3, col. 4; Anthony Speed Criminal Case Files, St. Clair County, Roll No. 295, Sequence No. 100077, Case No. 129 (1905), and Roll No. 295, Sequence No. 100078, Case No. 130 (1905).

68. "Statement of Robert Jackson," in James H. Thomas Sr. et al. Criminal Case Files, St. Clair County, Roll No. 000070, Sequence No. 100140, Case No. 006011 (1915). Jackson's continual reference to Costly as mister must reflect class distinctions because the age difference between them was only two years—Costly was thirty-five and Jackson thirty-three. Costly owned a barbershop, while Jackson was a laborer. Jackson's statement also revealed that he did work elsewhere while employed as a Brooklyn police officer.

69. *East St. Louis Journal,* 7 May 1915, p. 3, col. 6, 9 May 1915, p. 1, col. 3, and 11 May 1905, p. 3, col. 4; James H. Thomas Sr. et al. Criminal Case Files, St. Clair County, Roll No. 000075, Sequence No. 100139, Case No. 005927 (1915), and Roll No. 000079, Sequence No. 100063, Case No. 006420 (1917).

70. *East St. Louis Journal,* 30 May 1915, p. 3, col. 5.

71. James H. Thomas Sr. et al. Criminal Case Files, St. Clair County, Roll No. 000070, Sequence No. 100140, Case No. 006011 (1915).

72. James H. Thomas Sr. et al. Criminal Case Files, St. Clair County, Roll No. 000075, Sequence No. 100139, Case No. 005927 (1915); "C. B. Carroll's Brooklyn City Directory, 1903," 252–53; "Gould's Brooklyn Directory, 1906," 798; *Population Schedules of the United States Census, 1910, Illinois, St. Clair County,* 160; "Brooklyn, Illinois," 309. See also Robert Jackson et al. Criminal Case Files, St. Clair County, Roll No. 22, Sequence No. 100078, Case No. 3579 (1913); and Frederick F. Vanderberg Criminal Case Files, St. Clair County, Roll No. 276, Sequence No. 1000158, Case No. 008 (1899).

In the 1903, 1906, and 1912 city directories, Bedford, spelled Bifford in 1912, is the only person in Brooklyn under the last name of King, so I reason that Nancy must have been his wife. All of the witnesses who appeared before the grand jury except Randall Cole and Julie Kegler had obvious connections to the Peoples Improvement party.

73. James H. Thomas Sr. et al. Criminal Case Files, St. Clair County, Roll No. 000075, Sequence No. 100139, Case No. 005927 (1915), Roll No. 000079, Sequence No. 100063, Case No. 006420 (1917), and Roll No. 000079, Sequence No. 1000029, Case No. 006014 (1918).

74. James H. Thomas Sr. et al. Criminal Case Files, St. Clair County, Roll No. 000070, Sequence No. 100140, Case No. 006011 (1915).

75. Theising, "Profitable Boundaries," 71–74, 104.

76. Rudwick, *Race Riot at East St. Louis,* 184; Theising, "Profitable Boundaries," 103; Dillard, "Civil Liberties of Negroes in Illinois since 1865," 608. Norman L. Crockett found that business success gave candidates an advantage in elections, and as a result most Black town mayors were prosperous businessmen. In Brooklyn, however, Frederick Vanderberg was the only Black entrepreneur elected mayor. Afro-Brooklynites generally elected educators, laborers, and artisans as mayors and as members of the village board of trustees. See Crockett, *Black Towns,* 85.

77. Rudwick, *Race Riot at East St. Louis,* 184.

Conclusion

1. For discussion of urban Black towns during the great migration, see Rose, "All-Negro Town," 356–57; Wiese, "Places of Our Own," 30; and Wiese, "Other Suburbanites," 1496.

2. Walter and Kramer, "Politics in an All-Negro City"; Walter and Kramer, "Political Autonomy and Economic Dependence in an All-Negro Municipality."

Index

Numbers in bold italic refer to pages containing tables.

and the small towns of, 19; golden era of, 11, 12–13, 20, 147, 152, 163; incorporation of African Americans into, 81–85, 151–52; industrialization of, 11–17, 20, 84, 147, 151–52, 225n.20; industrial suburbs in, 11–16; location of, 2; periods of industrialization in, 11; strategic advantages of, 13–14
Metropolitan dominance theory, 19, 25
Midkiff, Harry, 136
Miles, J., 139
Miller, Daniel, 94
Mills, Isaac R., 136
Milwaukee, Wis., 160
Mining, 2, 41, 91–92
Ministers, 58, 69, 70, 71, 79, 102
Mitchell, "Click," 195
Mixed schools, 20, 79, 107–9, 115, 119, 135, 197
Model, Suzanne, 155
Modernization, 118
Monsanto Chemical Company, 16, 156
Monsanto (Sauget), Ill., 12, 22
Montgomery, David, 247n.57
Montgomery, Isaiah T., 143
Moore, Arthur, 31, 152
Moore, Denver, 31
Moore, Emma, 168
Moore, Font, 176
Moore, George, 168
Moore, Hattie, 176
Moore, Henry L., 256n.61
Moore, Thomas, 109, *110*
Morgan, J. P., 13, 18
Morris, Nelson, 13, 18, 82, 84
Moses, Wilson Jeremiah, 7
Mound Bayou, Miss., 2, 5, 8, 84, 89, 153, 167, 169
Mousfield, August, 92
Mulattoes: versus blacks, 48; in Brooklyn, 49; in census data, 52, 67, 232n.14; competing for political power, 181–82; as an elite, 48; female-headed households among, 64; intermarriage with blacks, 56, 68; in leadership positions, 67–71; in the ministry, 70; occupations of, 69; wealth skewed toward, 60

Naming practices, 63
National Afro-American League, 21, 132, 137
National Association of Colored Women, 137
National Black Convention (1835), 44
National Black convention movement, 66, 80

National City, Ill.: Brooklyn contrasted with, 14; consolidation proposal for, 188; and decentralization policy, 12, 13, 22; incorporation of, 19, 20, 83; as industrial suburb, 11, 12; meat-packers in, 12, 83; as unincorporated, 13
Nationalism. *See* Black nationalism; Protonationalism; Territorial nationalism
National Stock Yards, 2, 12, 17, 20, 82–83, 84
Newborn, Emma, 101
Newby, Lawrence A., 137
Newell, Mrs., 228n.2
New Philadelphia, Ill., 34, 35, 42
Newport News (Madison), Ill., 178, 198–201
New York City, 156
Nicholas, America, 86
Nicholas, Nelson, 86, *110*
Nicodemus, Kans.: Brooklyn as predating, 45; business diversity in, 169; failure to obtain a railroad, 42; in Hamilton's *Black Towns and Profit*, 8; as isolated rural community, 2, 84; as known in Black America, 5; literacy rate in, 235n.8; vice controlled in, 167; whites dominating business in, 164
Niedringhaus, Frederick, 13, 18, 152
Niedringhaus, Heyward, 13
Niedringhaus, William, 13, 18, 152
Nore, Ellen, 35
Norfolk, Va., 161
Norton, W. T., 36
Nuclear family: decrease in, 219; in 1850, 49, 61, 62, *62*; in 1870, 95, *96*; in 1880, 98, *98*; in 1900, *173*; in 1910, *174*, 176, 178

Occupations: of African American women, 160–61, *160*; artisans, 58, 72, 90–91, 157; bartenders, 165; boat captains, 54; boatmen (roustabouts), 55, 91, 154; butchers, 90, 157–58; in census data, 52; and color, 47; common laborers, 2, 49, 91, 117, 154, 156, 219; cooks, 160, 165, 168–69; and deskilling of labor, 157–58; disparity in Black and white, 57–58; farming, 58, 87–89, 117, 152–53, 236n.16; farm laborers, 58, 89, 153; of female Afro-Brooklynites, 97, 159–63, 165–66, 168; laundresses, 160, 161; low-paying work for African Americans, 16–17, 156; of male Afro-Brooklynites, 54–55, 57–58, *57*, 71–72, 87–92, *88*, 152–59, *153*; of mulattoes, 69; office work, 162; prostitution, 166, 167, 169, 198, 202–3, 207,

SUNDIATA KEITA CHA-JUA received his B.A. from Tougaloo
College, his M.A. in political science from Sangamon State
University, and his Ph.D. in history from the University of
Illinois at Urbana-Champaign. He is currently an associate
professor of historical studies at Southern Illinois University
at Edwardsville.

Typeset in 10.5/12.5 Adobe Minion
Composed by Jim Proefrock
at the University of Illinois Press
Manufactured by Thomson-Shore, Inc.

University of Illinois Press
1325 South Oak Street
Champaign, IL 61820-6903
www.press.uillinois.edu